# Deadly Decision in Beijing

Three decades after 1989, historical materials are now available for understanding the Tiananmen protests in a new light. In a play-by-play account of the elite politics that led to the military crackdown, Su addresses the repression of the protest in the context of political leadership succession. He challenges conventional views that see the military intervention as a necessary measure against revolutionary mobilization. Beneath the political drama, *Deadly Decision in Beijing* explores the authoritarian regime's perpetual crisis of leadership transition and its impact on popular movements.

YANG SU is Professor of Sociology at the University of California, Irvine and a scholar of social movements, revolution, and political violence. His book *Collective Killings in Rural China during the Cultural Revolution* was a winner of the Barrington Moore Book Award and an Honourable Mention of the Charles Tilly Book Award of the American Sociological Association.

# Deadly Decision in Beijing

*Succession Politics, Protest Repression, and the*
*1989 Tiananmen Massacre*

Yang Su

*University of California, Irvine*

CAMBRIDGE
UNIVERSITY PRESS

Shaftesbury Road, Cambridge CB2 8EA, United Kingdom

One Liberty Plaza, 20th Floor, New York, NY 10006, USA

477 Williamstown Road, Port Melbourne, VIC 3207, Australia

314–321, 3rd Floor, Plot 3, Splendor Forum, Jasola District Centre,
New Delhi – 110025, India

103 Penang Road, #05–06/07, Visioncrest Commercial, Singapore 238467

Cambridge University Press is part of Cambridge University Press & Assessment,
a department of the University of Cambridge.

We share the University's mission to contribute to society through the pursuit of
education, learning and research at the highest international levels of excellence.

www.cambridge.org
Information on this title: www.cambridge.org/9781009100762

DOI: 10.1017/9781009122061

First published 2023

*A catalogue record for this publication is available from the British Library.*

ISBN 978-1-009-10076-2 Hardback
ISBN 978-1-009-11420-2 Paperback

Most dictators are overthrown by higher officials of their own regimes, simply because the higher officials want to promote themselves with at least one of them becoming the new dictator. If the reader has doubts about this, I suggest he consult the New York Times Index for the previous six months or so and check the numbers of cases in which dictators have been overthrown . . . Whatever government or party has the full allegiance of a country's armed forces is to all intents and purposes politically impregnable . . . If it [the success of a popular uprising] is rare in the study of actual overthrows of dictatorship, it is very common in the romantic literature. The Bastille was actually taken by a regiment of regular infantry, but it is still the legend that it was a Paris mob.

Gordon Tullock, Autocracy (Springer Science & Business Media, 2012), 9–10

I, Ishmael, was one of that crew; my shouts had gone up with the rest; my oath had been welded with theirs; and stronger I shouted, and more did I hammer and clinch my oath, because of the dread in my soul. A wild, mystical, sympathetical feeling was in me . . . With greedy ears I learned the history of that murderous monster.

Herman Melville, Moby-Dick, chapter 41

# Contents

**Part IV    The Political Impact**

# Figures

# Tables

# Preface

The tragedy shocked the world. Since then, the military suppression of a peaceful protest has been minutely and thoroughly documented by able historians.[1] Few can summarize the gist of the event better than Timothy Brook:

> On the night of June 3, 1989, tens of thousands of soldiers armed with assault rifles forced their way into the city of Beijing and drove unarmed student protesters from the central square at Tiananmen. When hundreds of thousands of citizens and students blocked their paths, the soldiers opened fire. On the morning of June 4, thousands lay dead and dying in the streets, the hospitals, and the homes of Beijing.[2]

The most extraordinary aspect of the event is a decision to deploy conventional combat troops to pacify a protest. The scale of tragedy was a result of the scale of the operation, one that involved 24 group armies, more than 180,000 men, and untold numbers of tanks and assault rifles. While Brook and his fellow historians focus on the military operation itself, my investigation in this book is about how the state leaders made that extraordinary decision in the first place. A closer look shows that ending protest was more a pretext than it was the real cause.

As my writing came to completion in 2020, the faraway events described in the book found poignant resonance in the news in the United States. In Beijing in 1989, a general secretary of China's Communist Party was in a precarious position and his patron was under pressure to unseat him; then a former general secretary's death triggered a student protest, which met brutal suppression by the military. In Washington, DC in 2020–2021, a defeated president of the United States refused to concede the election and instigated a citizen insurrection, and before his successor took over as the commander in chief of the United States military, he pressured generals to stage a coup.[3]

Both moments featured a disputed political leadership transition, popular unrest, and the actual occurrence or the possibility of military interference. In the case of China, the army was sent in and armed assault by the troops killed thousands, while in the case of the United States, top military generals felt the pressure from the commander in chief but resisted.[4] That the two countries represent two fundamentally different political systems only underscores an important point. That is, military transgression into domestic politics is a peril hung over modern governments of all types, as real for a mature democracy as for an authoritarian regime.

It is a widely acknowledged norm among modern nations that some level of separation between the military and domestic politics is desired.[5] "Because we fear others, we create an institution of violence to protect us, but then we fear the very institution we created for protection," as noted by a scholar.[6] That is, the military as a force is created to deal with external threats, not for domestic politics. The fact that it is powerful makes it all the more important to keep it at arm's length. If it is used at all in the domestic realm, it should be used like an "airbag," only for emergencies.[7]

The decision rests on the political figure at the top, a supreme leader in China, for example, or a president in the United States. Even as the civilian commander of the military, however, he cannot bring the army into the civilian sphere at will. Before he can use the "airbag," so to speak, he needs to first make the case of an "emergency." To a large extent his rule is beholden to the regime's elite factions, the public, and the international community. He would endeavor to proclaim disorder so severe that military restoration is justified.

Social unrest often serves as a perfect pretext. The method of billing a popular protest as a menacing revolution has an automatic appeal. That was exactly how Deng Xiaoping and his supporters made their case in 1989. But under the surface, there was another real "emergency" at work. That is, a crisis in the octogenarian leader's succession plan: his current candidate had been endangered and a new heir must be chosen, but in the meantime he found himself in a position of diminished power. Military action would be a political play to reset the power dynamics. In other words, while the protest appeared to trigger the military decision, in reality both the protest and the military action were advanced by a third underlying factor – the crisis of succession politics.

Such moments of "contention triangle," as this book calls it, are all too familiar in our time. Other examples include the 2011 Tahir Square protest in Egypt, and the 2004 Orange Revolution in Ukraine and its subsequent replays. With those past episodes in mind, one may wonder, what could happen if major world powers such as Russia and China experience new rounds of succession crisis? For that matter, we must also remember that nondemocratic governments account for more than two-thirds of political systems in the world. Therefore, special cycles of social unrest caused by leadership transition, frequently so severe that the military is involved, deserve urgent and serious scholarship.

From that perspective, a calendar of leadership transition is in the central place of analysis. It traces an exogenous source of social unrest in a regime's seasonal changes – its electoral cycle or the life cycle of strongman rulers. While lessons can be drawn from the failures of democratic systems, particularly useful are the lessons learned from authoritarian systems, where succession politics – leadership transitions that follow no democratic rules – becomes the subject matter. How does the ruler designate and raise a successor? Before power changes hands, can the ruler and the chosen successor get along? Will others contest the successorship? At what point can such contests disable the system?

Answering these questions faces two obstacles. The first is mental. We scholars need to move away from a tendency to treat those authoritarian systems as something simply "bad," devoid of the politics that we normally understand. We should overcome such a bias and restore them to terms we normally use to describe a political system – government officials' "re-election" prospects, a top leader's concern for his legacy, elite alliance and partisanship, policy disputes, interaction between the elite and the public, and, finally, institutional boundaries and transgressions.

A second obstacle is informational. We normally lack data about elite politics from those closed systems. During China's Cultural Revolution in the 1960s, for instance, journalists and scholars had to rely on information such as the order of leaders' appearances at a public event to decipher the "power struggles."[8] The secrecy of North Korea's regime in the 2020s is such that a round of international news coverage was aroused when the supreme leader, Kim Jong-un, appeared to have lost a significant amount of wight.[9]

This book benefited from an unusual amount of information that has accumulated since the Tiananmen Square movement. With thousands of innocent lives lost, the gravity of the tragic event inspired intense public interest and gave rise to a small industry of information gathering and publishing. Among the wide range of contributors are a former general secretary of the party, a former premier of the government, former officials privy to government dossiers, and numerous journalists and independent researchers. This richness of materials allowed me to present the "politics" in terms that we normally use and comprehend. The result is a detailed account of elite contentions taking place inside government compounds, and an analysis that looks beyond the assumption that a "bad" government would automatically suppress social protest.

# Acknowledgments

This book is based on source materials already available in the public domain. But its writing has been greatly assisted by my numerous conversations with a particular group of China experts. They are former leaders and activists of the Tiananmen Square movement who live in exile in the United States. Some of them have become scholars themselves. Although they are no more privy to China's elite politics than a researcher such as myself, their deep knowledge of the system affords me penetrating insights. If the thesis I present here sounds familiar to them, that should come as no surprise, for my thinking has been stimulated, transformed, and shaped by listening to their views. I thank them for their support for my research, and for their sacrifices in pursuing an ideal to make China a better place. For reasons that I hope can be appreciated by my readers, I can only acknowledge them collectively without using their names.

At different stages of my research and writing, I enjoyed assistance, advice, and encouragement from four leading authorities on the history of Tiananmen. They are Timothy Brook, who generously shared his research materials, Andrew Nathan, Jeff Wasserstrom, and Perry Link. When this project was presented at various seminars, I also benefited from the comments of students and four pre-eminent sociologists: Michael Mann, Craig Calhoun, Ching Kwan Lee, and Min Zhou.

For intellectual as well as moral support, I would like to acknowledge my wife Junling Ma; my colleagues Wang Feng and Edwin Amenta; and my former mentors Andrew Walder, Doug McAdam, and John McCarthy. They make themselves constantly available to me. Wang Feng's unfailing faith and genuine interest in the project was a constant source of motivation and assurance. Andrew Walder lent his expertise and kindness at a number of critical conjunctures; a teacher with high standards, his praises can do wonders.

For reading part or the whole of various drafts, in addition to those I mentioned above, I was generously assisted by Qindian Chen, Jasun Chen, Lei Guang, Henry Hail, Dana Moss, Cam Owen, David Snow, David Meyer, and Brooke Su. I am indebted to their comments and editing. Cam Owen gave a complete polish of my English for the entire book. Qindian Chen assisted with the index and footnotes. For his expert copyediting in the final stage, my deep appreciation goes to John Gaunt of Cambridge University Press. I thank three anonymous reviewers for their constructive suggestions as well as their recognition of the value of the manuscript. Finally, my debt of gratitude is owed to Lucy Rhymer, Rachel Blaifeder, and Michael Watson, three editors of Cambridge University Press.

If my previous book on China's Cultural Revolution was about human sufferings inflicted by Maoism, this new book, in a sense, is about a cast of characters working hard to move China away from that monstrous system. Those efforts include Deng's reform on the government's side and the pro-democracy movements on society's side. Much has changed in China since then, and in retrospect the work of those people now looks even more valuable. I see many of them as my heroes. I dedicate this book to them.

# Main Characters

**Chen Xitong** (陈希同) ("x" is pronounced as "s" as in the English word "see") Mayor of Beijing and a member of the Politburo of the central government. A conservative ally of Premier Li Peng, he actively promoted a hard line against the student protest.

**Chen Yun** (陈云) Aged eighty-four in 1989. One of the most respected older leaders and the head of the conservative faction. He and Deng Xiaoping formed "Twin Politics" in the reform era. His official title was chairman of the Central Advisory Committee.

**Deng Liqun** (邓力群) ("q" is pronounced as Enlish "ts") (no relation to Deng Xiaoping) A party ideologue with clear conservative views. Instrumental in waging attacks against Hu Yaobang and then, after Hu's dismissal, Zhao Ziyang. Reportedly a conservatives' candidate to replace Zhao Ziyang as general secretary.

**Deng Xiaoping** (邓小平) Aged eighty-four in 1989. The supreme leader. While having nominally retired from the state and the party, he held the title of Central Military Committee (CMC) chair. According to a rule that later came to light, all party leaders were required to defer to him on the most important issues.

**He Dongchang** (何东昌) Chair of the nation's Educational Commission. A conservative ally of Premier Li Peng, he presented the student protest in a negative light to support a hardline policy and to undermine General Secretary Zhao Ziyang.

**Hu Qiaomu** (胡乔木) A party ideologue with clear conservative views. He was instrumental in waging attacks against Hu Yaobang and then, after, Hu's dismissal, Zhao Ziyang.

**Hu Yaobang** (胡耀邦) General secretary between 1980 and 1986. His death on April 15 triggered the 1989 Tiananmen Square movement. A former protégé of Deng Xiaoping, a reformer, hence a target of the conservative faction. He was removed from his post after his sympathetic handling of a wave of student protest in 1986–1987.

**Hu Qili** (胡启立) A reformer leader in charge of ideology and propaganda in the Standing Committee, an ally of General Secretary Zhao Ziayng. Instrumental in formulating the moderate policy in Zhao's "New Take." Dismissed along with Zhao's removal.

**Hua Guofeng** (华国锋) No official position in 1989. Mao's designated successor. In 1976 he led a coalition of leaders to arrest the Gang of Four, including Mao's widow. He was ousted from leadership by Deng by 1980.

**Jiang Zemin** (江泽民) Formerly the mayor and party sectary of Shanghai, tapped by Deng and his conservative rivals as the Zhao Ziyang's replacement as general secretary.

**Li Peng** (李鹏) Premier, second in the Standing Committee after General Secretary Zhao Ziyang. Representative in the first line for the conservative camp led by Chen Yun and Li Xiannian.

**Li Xiannian** (李先念) Aged eighty in 1989. An elderly leader and one of the key allies in the conservative camp with Chen Yun. He advocated a hard line against the protest and was an instrumental in unseating General Secretary Zhao Ziyang. He promoted Jiang Zemin as the new party chief.

**Li Ximing** (李锡铭) Party secretary of Beijing City and a member of the Politburo. A conservative ally of Premier Li Peng, he was one of Beijing City leaders for a negative report on the student movement, which was the basis for the April 26 editorial.

**Qiao Shi** (乔石) Reformer leader in charge of public security. Ally of General Secretary Zhao Ziyang in the Standing Committee.

**Yang Shangkun** (杨尚昆) Aged eighty-two in 1989, de facto chief commander running the CMC for Deng. One of the key leaders in carrying out the June 4 operation, along with Li Peng. Eased out in 1992 to make way for new General Secretary Jiang Zemin's military control.

**Yao Yilin** (姚依林) A conservative leader in charge of the economy, ally of Premier Li Peng in the Standing Committee.

**Wan Li** (万里) A reformer ally of General Secretary Zhao Ziyang. President of the National Congress.

**Wang Ruilin** (王瑞林) Deng Xiaoping's chief aid, a position similar to the chief of staff in other systems.

**Yan Mingfu** (阎明复) Minister of Civil Affairs. A progressive leader and an ally of General Secretary Zhao Ziyang, he worked to facilitate communication between the government and the students in the hope of defusing tension.

**Ye Jianying** (叶剑英) Died in 1986. A marshal and the highest-ranked military officer in 1976 when Mao died. He assisted Hua Guofeng to arrest Hua's rivals, the members of the "Gang of Four," including Mao's widow. He then helped Deng Xiaoping return to power.

**Yuan Mu** (袁木) A spokesman for the State Council. Served as a key figure in the student–government dialogue. An ally of Premier Li Peng, trying to turn a dialogue into an attack on General Secretary Zhao Ziyang.

**Zhao Ziyang** (赵紫阳) ("zh" is pronounced "j" as in the English word "John") General party secretary at the outset of the 1989 student movement and number one in the organizational chart of the "first-line" leadership structure. He is the leader of the reform faction with Qiao Shi and Hu Qili as his allies in the Standing Committee. He took a reconciliatory approach toward the student protest. Removed from his post after he refused to support the martial law decision.

# Chronology

## Before the 1989 Tiananmen Square movement

| | |
|---|---|
| April 1976 | A Tiananmen Square protest for which Deng Xiaoping is framed and dismissed. |
| September–October 1976 | Death of Mao and arrest of the "Gang of Four," including Mao's widow, Jiang Qing. |
| August 1977 | Eleventh CCP Congress. Deng returns to power. |
| December 1978 | Third Plenum of the Eleventh Central Committee criticizes Mao loyalists who advocate the "Two Whatevers" policy. |
| 1978–1979 | Stimulated by a freer political climate, thousands of big-character posters appear on walls west of the Forbidden City in Beijing (the Democracy Wall). |
| September 1980 | Zhao Ziyang replaces Hua Guofeng as China's premier. |
| June 1981 | Hua Guofeng resigns as chairman of the CCP and Hu Yaobang takes the position under the title of CCP general secretary. |
| November–December 1986 | Students in Hefei, Shanghai, Beijing, and some other major cities demonstrate in the streets. |
| January 1987 | Hu Yaobang is dismissed from the post of CCP general secretary. Zhao Ziyang becomes CCP general secretary. |

## During the 1989 Tiananmen Square movement

| | |
|---|---|
| April 15 | Hu Yaobang dies of a heart attack. |
| April 16–17 | Wreaths and elegiac couplets appear in Tiananmen Square and at many Beijing colleges. Around 2,000 university students march to the square. |

April 19–20    Minor skirmishes occur between policemen and students at Xinhua Gate of the government compound at Zhongnanhai. Students in some universities start a class boycott.

April 22    Around 50,000 students march to the square overnight to participate in Hu Yaobang's funeral. Three students kneel on the steps and demand a meeting with Premier Li Peng.

April 23    The Beijing Student Autonomous Union Provisional Committee is founded.

April 23    Zhao Ziyang leaves Beijing for North Korea, leaving Li in charge.

April 25    Outside troops begin to move into Beijing Military District

April 26    A *People's Daily* editorial labels the movement "a planned conspiracy" and "turmoil."

April 27    About 100,000 students march to Tiananmen Square to protest the editorial.

April 29    A State Council spokesman holds a dialogue with students. Students are not satisfied.

April 30    Zhao Ziyang returns from North Korea to Beijing, resuming his post in charge.

May 4    Students hold a march in commemoration of the May 4th movement of 1919. Zhao Ziyang strikes a conciliatory tone and begins to experiment with a moderate policy. However, his attempt to reverse the April 26 editorial fails due to Deng's and Li's objections.

May 5    The Beijing Student Dialogue Delegation is formed. Most students in Beijing return to class.

May 11    Deng Xiaoping–Yang Shangkun Conversation. Jiang is mentioned.

May 13    Three thousand students start a hunger strike in Tiananmen Square. A huge number of students begin to occupy the square.

May 14    A high-level state delegation starts an emergency dialogue with student activists. The meeting goes chaotically because different students have totally different agendas in mind. The hunger strike continues.

May 15    Gorbachev arrives. The state has to hold the welcome ceremony at Beijing Airport.

May 17    Zhao Ziyang pleads for toleration but is overruled by Deng. The meeting at Deng's residence that decides on martial law.

May 18    Zho Ziyang resigns.

May 19    Li Peng declares martial law, but the martial law troops are blocked by Beijing residents and students. More and more students from universities outside Beijing arrive in the city.

| | |
|---|---|
| May 22 | The army orders its soldiers to pull back to the suburbs. |
| May 26 | Troops begin to infiltrate to positions inside the city. |
| June 3 | Military suppression starts. Students and other civilians killed on its paths of advance from the outskirts of Beijing to the square. |
| June 4 | The remaining 4,000 students leave the square after they are completely encircled by troops. |
| June 9 | Deng congratulates his officers on the suppression. |
| September 4 | Deng retires from the CMC, passing the chairmanship to Jiang Zemin. |

**After the 1989 Tiananmen Square movement**

January–February 1992    Deng's Southern Tour.

# Abbreviations

| | |
|---|---|
| 2FM | Two-way factionalism model |
| 3SM | Three-way succession model |
| Beida | Beijing (Peking) University |
| BAAUS | Beijing Autonomous Association of University Students |
| BDDUS | Beijing Dialogue Delegation of University Students |
| BWAF | Beijing Workers' Autonomous Federation |
| CCP | Chinese Communist Party |
| CAC | Central Advisory Committee |
| CMC | Central Military Committee |
| GLD | General Logistics Department |
| GPD | General Political Department |
| GSH | General Staff Headquarters |
| MR | Military region |
| NPC | National People's Congress |
| PAP | People's Armed Police |
| PLA | People's Liberation Army |
| PSB | Public Security Bureau |
| RSM | Revolution suppression model |
| SC | Standing Committee of the Politburo |
| SEZ | Special Economic Zone |

# 1    Introduction
## A Decision to Kill

The fate of the Tiananmen Square movement was sealed on May 17, 1989, two weeks before its tragic end, with the decision to initiate martial law. On that critical day, Deng Xiaoping convened a meeting at his residence attended by his right-hand man in charge of the military and five members of the Politburo's Standing Committee, the highest leadership body in the Party Center. Several participants would in later years offer their recollections and they agreed on this important point: urged by Deng, the Standing Committee passed the decision to declare martial law. Had that been a formal vote, the outcome would have been close: two offered their outright support, two dissented, and the fifth demurred first before joining the yes tally. In any case, the point may be moot, as Deng had de facto veto power.[1]

Deng's elegant home was snuggled deep in a web of Beijing *hutong*. During normal times, quiet reined the surroundings. But that fateful spring was no normal time. The city was inundated by raucous protest crowds. In Tiananmen Square, just a few miles away, student hunger strikers had begun to faint, and ambulances wailed in and out around the clock. Many Beijing residents also took to the street in solidarity. In sizes rarely seen in the country, marches and demonstrations raged on. According to one statistic, that day alone witnessed more than 1.2 million street protesters.[2] Checkpoints by student marshals slowed the traffic. On his way back to the Zhongnanhai compound, an irritated Li Peng, the premier, and his chauffeur took a long detour, taking them more than thirty minutes for an otherwise ten-minute drive.[3]

The martial law decision was momentous. Out of the public eye, General Secretary Zhao Ziyang submitted his resignation on the second day; Deng chose Jiang Zemin, then a member of the Politburo and the party chief of Shanghai, to be the new general secretary. The army was deployed on May 19. Two weeks later, on the night of June 3 and in the early morning of June 4, troops marched from the outskirts into the city center, killing thousands of unarmed civilians and ending the protest movement that had lasted for about a month and a half.[4]

At first glance, this decision to kill seems straightforward: an authoritarian regime suppressed a burgeoning revolution. Protest represents "challenge" or "insurgency" to the regime, and the state's default position is "repression." It seems commonsensical that a government like China's would send in troops to crack down. Indeed, that is exactly how prevailing accounts have depicted the history of Tiananmen in 1989.

Those accounts were initially developed from an "outside-in" angle; that is, from the vantage point of the protest movement, constructed when data on internal deliberations of government leaders were not available, at least during the event or in the first few years thereafter. When such information becomes accessible and an "inside-out" perspective can be adopted, the validity of the interpretation deserves a second scrutiny.

Rich information often accompanies the weight of a great event. Tiananmen in 1989 is increasingly becoming a gold mine for research, joining the ranks of the French Revolution, the American Civil War, the Russian Revolution, the Chinese Cultural Revolution, and other significant historical events. For comparative political scientists, it opens a candid window into the opaque world of authoritarianism. For social-movement scholars, it provides a rare opportunity to examine elite deliberations of repression, a much-needed correction for a literature that is overwhelmingly written from the perspective of mobilization and mobilizers.

Three decades after 1989, a mountain of research materials has been accumulating. If past work had to guess the thinking process of the decision makers, we now hear from them directly – through their diaries, memoirs, and recorded conversations. Time also tested the authenticity of a few documents that claimed to have come from government dossiers, while a number of activist scholars have compiled ambitious and meticulously sourced chronological accounts. A new line of inquiry, with the focus on elite politics, is now possible. The pages that follow in this book are the fruit of such an inquiry.[5]

This book advances a new line of interpretation on the state–protest relationship during the 1989 Tiananmen events. The spotlight is on the state side: what the decision makers did and how and why they came to do it during the event. Immediately clear from the inquiry is that the leaders were busy engaging in factional politics rather than working to end the protest. Instead, they were busy in taking advantage of the protest for gain in the ongoing battle of power succession. At stake, for the younger leaders, was the advancement or termination of their career; for the elderly leaders, it was the direction of the country and the legacy of their lifetime's work.

The two considerations – to avoid a revolution and to win factional advantage – need not contradict each other. For one thing, a protest movement does not always pose an immediate danger. Official pronouncements notwithstanding, state leaders' private assessments can be a different matter. As importantly, even if the elites share a common fear, their differing interests play a role in making specific policies of response. Politicians do not have to ignore the system's survival to engage in politics. Therefore, protest is not merely a threat; it is also a "resource" for the very state leaders whose rule is being challenged.

Indeed, scholars of social movements and collective action are among the first to point out that state elites do not always repress and that they may *facilitate* instead.[6] These researchers have put forward various models of the "political opportunity structure," a theoretical pillar in the field.[7] My findings stay consistent with this insight, but my work extends it to an entirely different empirical problem. My focus is not mobilization itself, but the state's reaction to it. While those social-movement scholars' models are movement-centered, looking at how elite politics can present an "opportunity" for protest, my new theoretical perspective looks at how a protest can become a "resource" for political elites and is thus "politics-centered."[8]

### The Revolution–Counterrevolution Narrative

The Tiananmen Square movement was a series of student-led peaceful demonstrations in Beijing that lasted for a month and a half between April 15 and June 4, 1989. To varying degrees, it spread to other major cities as well. It is named for the occupation of the square by protesters (starting with a hunger strike) and the final violent, bloody actions to clear the square by the government's use of the military.[9] Never before or after under China's communist rule has a truly popular protest reached such a scale, intensity, and depth and ended in a tragedy of such magnitude. It was also a watershed moment. Within China, Deng's economic reform was at the crossroad, and the protest was a reflection of intense political discontent among students and intellectuals. Its tragic end, vividly documented by television crews of the international media, was imprinted in the public consciousness at once as a spectacle, an inspiration, and a historical trauma.

Globally, 1989 witnessed a tidal wave of revolutions that effectively ended the Cold War. While Poland might be seen as the most significant forerunner for its long-standing Solidarity movement, China's Tiananmen protest marked the very first wave of "unarmed insurrections" – as scholars would later call them – in that year.[10] Undoubtedly, it served as an inspiration for people everywhere living under communist rule. Visible methods of harsh repression inspired communist rulers as well. In an extraordinary moment soon after the Tiananmen massacre, Erich Honecker, the general secretary of East Germany, visited Beijing. He shook hands with Deng Xiaoping and praised China's firm action. Not long after his return, when Honecker faced a wave of protest against his own regime that winter, he contemplated using "the Beijing solution." His attempt failed and the regime fell, as did many other communist governments.[11] A common storyline across the communist bloc is that peaceful protest succeeded in bringing down communist rule. As one exception, Tiananmen therefore is seen as a revolution that failed.

Since then, Tiananmen as history has been told in a standard narrative of two acts: an act of revolution by the populace, followed by an act of counterrevolution by the government. The protest was seen as a movement that aimed to bring down a regime, and its scale and its power were seen as capable of such a task. Following that logic, the government's military crackdown was seen as a necessary measure to save the regime.

Before it became scholarly canon, this narrative was first introduced by two unlikely partners: the Chinese government eager to justify its action and an international media eager to amplify a popular movement. In the years since, the government has never ceased to "regard the slaughter as appropriate" and brand such slaughter as "pacification."[12] The government's main defense rested on the claim that force was used only as a last resort. In other words, had it not been for this military endgame, Chinese communist rule would have ended then and there in 1989; the violent crackdown effectively stopped a revolution.

Shortly after the crackdown, the government staged a victory lap on June 9. An energized Deng, aged eighty-four, appeared before a group of military generals and officers to hand out medals and deliver a speech. His energy level was far from the more subdued image of himself. In his remarks, he did not deny the killing. Rather, he laid out a few lines of justification: it was indeed an operation of pacification in response to a violent uprising and a necessary measure to save the regime from an anti-party and anti-socialism conspiracy:

> This storm was bound to come sooner or later. This is determined by the general international climate and China's own small climate. It was bound to happen and is independent of man's will . . . The incident became very clear as soon as it broke out. They have two main slogans: one is to topple the Communist Party, and the other is to overthrow the socialist system. Their goal is to establish a totally Western-dependent bourgeois republic.[13]

Deng pointed out that "some comrades do not understand the fundamental nature of this event and mistake it as purely an issue of how to handle demands from the masses." He asserted that initial turmoil (*dongluan*) developed into a violent uprising (*baoluan*), in which "weapons were stolen" and "many of our soldiers were injured or even killed."[14] This characterization of the events would be the guide for the lengthy official report, delivered by Beijing mayor Chen Xitong later in the month.[15]

Is any of this – the official story of the 1989 events according to Deng and the party – true? One of the central arguments – that there was a violent uprising prior to June 4 – was a blatant lie, and the world knew it.[16] But the public and even scholars are debating his two other major claims – first, that Tiananmen was a revolutionary attempt at toppling the regime, and second, that the only way to stop the movement was to deploy military force.

Existing accounts mostly concur with both claims. Newspaper reporters and researchers alike believe that Tiananmen was a revolutionary attempt, albeit one ending in failure, and that the government had no choice outside the military solution. "In the end," writes an eminent China scholar, "the state leaders were left with only two choices, either to repress the students or to face the prospect of eventually stepping down."[17] In other words, we find ourselves by and large in agreement with Deng Xiaoping even when we all mourn the dead and condemn the act on moral grounds. Indeed, for three decades since 1989, writings on Tiananmen have been dominated by this revolution–surpression narrative, particularly in analyzing the decision of the government and the outcome of the protest.

In the academic literature, McAdam, Tarrow, and Tilly spell Tiananmen as a revolutionary situation, an endorsement of the revolution–counterrevolution narrative published in their influential treatise *Dynamics of Contention*. They dub Tiananmen a "revolutionary situation" – a popular uprising that aimed at overthrowing the government despite being short of achieving a "revolutionary outcome."[18] A more elaborate explanation for the martial law decision can be found in Dingxin Zhao's book *Power of Tiananmen*, one of the most important works on Tiananmen:

> During the 1989 Movement, the state dealt with the movement in the following ways. First, it tolerated the movement. When tolerance did not work and the movement escalated, the government verbally threatened the students with a *People's Daily* editorial. However, when the editorial did not work, the government adopted limited concessions in order to contain the movement. Unfortunately, limited concessions could not co-opt the students; therefore, the state implemented martial law and deployed a huge number of troops to Beijing. Martial law and the soldiers were initially aimed primarily at intimidating the students and the Beijing residents. It was only when a show of force was unable to end the Tiananmen Square occupation that the government ordered the repression.[19]

Zhao's characterization suggests the following points. First, the regime is perceived as working collectively as a whole. He notes the internal debate and conflict, but he insists that conflict did not significantly determine the final outcome. Second, the regime did not want the protest and did everything it could to end it. Third, the regime at times made concessions as a tactical move, with stopping the protest as the ultimate goal. Fourth, the use of military force was a logical end after other, softer, methods did not work. The common thread behind Zhao's reasoning is a united group of elites who shared the same ideological belief and the same fear of a regime collapse. Therefore, he writes, "since most top leaders in China during the 1980s had joined the revolution long before the communists took power, it was almost impossible for them, 'reformers' and 'hardliners' alike, to give up the power for which millions of their revolutionary comrades died. Thus, military repression became their only choice."[20]

If Dingxin Zhao's analysis portrays a regime that came together for *ideological* reasons, then Ezra Vogel's account in his majestic book *Deng Xiaoping and the Transformation of China* may be called *managerial*. In his telling, Deng and other key players differed in their assessment of the situation and their proposed solutions. They all seemed to be doing their best to manage the task at hand – to resolve the crisis presented by the protest. Li Peng, the premier, advocated a hardline approach, while Zhao Ziyang, the general secretary, proposed accommodation. Yet both are portrayed more like managers in a boardroom than political enemies. So was Deng, depicted like a patriarch adjudicating the debate and giving a final say in good faith. Vogel does not endorse Deng's crackdown and calls it a "tragedy of such enormous proportions," yet he appears equally sympathetic with Deng's decision when he writes, "As much as we scholars, like others concerned about human life and the pursuit of liberty, want to find clear answers that explain the causes of that tragedy, the truth is that none of us can be certain what would have happened had different courses of action been taken."[21] In other words, the result seemed to be inevitable, with Deng's hands forced by the circumstances.

Prevailing as it is, this revolution–counterrevolution narrative does not exist without challengers.[22] The most forceful response came from dissidents-turned-scholars. For instance, in a series of essays, Wu Guoguang – a former Zhao Ziyang aide and a professor currently teaching in Canada – asserted that Deng's decision for military action was tantamount to a "coup," whose real purpose was to remove Zhao Ziyang.[23] Dai Qing, another prominent dissident journalist, in her book *Deng Xiaoping in 1989* also provides an account of the supreme leader using the protest as a pretext for political gain.[24] This view was shared by another high-profile dissident, Bao Tong, who was Zhao's top aide.[25] Academic scholars also questioned the revolutionary capacity of the movement. As will be reviewed in a later chapter, the research by Walder and Gong is an example. They started their study to document workers' participation but concluded that the workers' involvement was limited only to some activists close to students.[26] Neither was there any report of support coming from the vast population of peasants.[27] In other words, the student movement was narrowly based. Writing as early as 1989, the editors of *Annual Register*, a famous publication on world events, offered this exceedingly insightful observation:

The cheering demonstrators in Beijing's Tiananmen Square, superficially very much like those in Wenceslas Square in Prague, neither had coherent objectives nor were they the brave youthful front of a nation-wide mass emotion. They proclaimed general aspirations rather than demanding particular means of realizing them, save a boneless plea for "democracy." It was a courageous adventure which will have its reward one day; but, without a mass will behind it, it succumbed to the military power of the state.[28]

In his deeply researched account of the June 4 massacre, Jeremy Brown deems the military decision and operation a "profound failure of governance." After a meticulous narrative of what happened, his book devotes an entire chapter to question whether calling in troops was necessary and whether the scale of bloodshed was inevitable:

But what if the government had been more patient? Was letting the movement "die out on its own" a realistic way to avoid violence? ... If Deng Xiaoping, Yang Shangkun, Chen Yun, Li Xiannian, Wang Zhen, and Li Peng had been brave enough to wait, it might have been possible for them to meet their goals of clearing Tiananmen Square and disbanding the autonomous student and worker organizations. They could have averted the massacre.[29]

Brown also believes that the depth of the tragedy was avoidable. "Just as the killing was not inevitable, the scale and scope of the massacre was not set in stone. It did not have to be as bad as it was." Further, "Emphasizing the victims of the atrocity, however, shows how inaccurate and inhumane it is to think of the crackdown as a success. The massacre was a profound failure of governance."[30]

Nonetheless, the revolution–counterrevolution rendering of history has remained canon, suffering little wear and tear as it has aged. Writing in 2015, Minxin Pei, another prominent China scholar, declares,

In 1989, the regime had its closest brush with death when millions of protestors demonstrated in major cities throughout the country, calling for democracy and venting their anger at official corruption. The party was saved only with the help of the People's Liberation Army (PLA), whose tanks crushed the peaceful protestors around Tiananmen and in Beijing on June 4.[31]

## Shifting the Focus of Repression Research

The counterrevolution model is intellectually rooted in a long-standing academic tradition. Theoretical contributions on state responses in social-movement literature are predominantly written through the lens of "repression," with the state seemingly caring exclusively about dispelling protest. Such a lens focuses on the "protest–repression" interface and pays scant attention to policy debates within a regime. In a sense, it is a perspective that is politics-free.[32]

This perspective is increasingly untenable, though, as empirical findings tend to show a mismatch between state action and protest: the effects of repression may be an inverted U shape, and strong repression may "backfire."[33] Scholars also find that many modern countries adopt methods to "manage protest" rather than "disperse crowds."[34] Among them, even authoritarian regimes adopt policing methods learned from Western countries to contain or channel, rather than crush, protests.[35] Some state elites may even help protesters and become allies.[36] A leading scholar observes that state actions normally include "mobilization," "facilitation," and "rewards";[37] another uncovers four types of state response: no response, accommodation, nonviolent repression, and repression.[38] How does one account for the variety of *responses*, as opposed to the presumed usage of *repression*?

Appearing in recent years, new research has shifted the focus of state repression onto government insiders. Nelson Picardo presents California during the 1930s as a case in which authority figures actively pursued countermovements as a tactic to deal with farmers' mobilization. Similarly, Jenny Iron makes an argument about Mississippi during the early civil rights movement in the late 1950s.[39] These studies set out to examine state response to protest by looking not at the protest but at state elites. Picardo starts his paper by observing,

> The involvement of the power elite in social movements has been a neglected area of research. The investigation of elites has generally been limited to that of local elites, political parties, and philanthropic foundations, and their involvement in social movements is believed limited to resource support (either to further or deter the progress of an insurgent social movement) or the institutional obstruction or facilitation of the movement. I contend that under specific conditions, the power elite may become *active mobilizers, leaders, and supporters*.[40]

David Cunningham collected data from FBI counterintelligence memos and demonstrated the inner working of the state's covert repression and its impact on the ebb and flow of the New Left movement. His elegant analysis lends great weight to his call that "our focus needs to shift to study the repressors themselves" for some movements. Training the investigative eye on state actors and state operations, his study is a promising example for future research to go beyond the concept of "political opportunities" in treating the state's impact.[41]

Joseph Luders argued that different responses to the civil rights countermovement across the southern states can be accounted for by "the behavior of public authorities" – the governors, the police, and others. For instance, in North Carolina, active state-led suppression of white supremacist mobilization severely limited the prospects for white countermobilization during the 1954–1965 period. Governors Hodges and Sanford warned the Klan against violence and called for law and order. Similarly, in South Carolina, Governor Hollings took a few effective steps to suppress anti-rights harassment and violence. As a result, both movement and countermovement were less extensive in the Carolinas than in other southern states such as Louisiana, Mississippi, and Alabama. A memorable quote by Hollings illuminates the relations between the state, the countermovement, and the movement:

> When Martin Luther King marched in . . . we had black policemen policing the streets and the incidents, and when one of them stepped out of line there was a black policeman leading him into the paddy wagon and they threw away their cameras. They said this isn't what we want. And they went on down to Montgomery where Bull Connor, the sheriff, had his hoses and police dogs.[42]

Elsewhere, the state response to popular mobilizations has been richly featured in historical accounts, demonstrating the imprint of elite politics. In high-profile cases that ended in revolutionary change, the authorities often refrain from using utmost force for other political considerations. Gorbachev forwent past methods of military intervention during the 1989 East European revolutions,[43] and later during the 1991 disintegration of the USSR itself.[44] In some cases, an initial harsh repression backfires, tying the hands of the elite in later parts of the unrest, as in the case of the shah in the Iranian Revolution of 1978–1979.[45] There are cases in which high-profile politicians step up to become champions of popular insurgencies, as in Hungary in 1956 and the Philippines in 1984.[46] Most germane to the subject of this book are cases in which divisions within state elites produce results that are far from the typical counterrevolution approach – which happened in Romania in 1989, where the security force defected to the revolution, and in Egypt in 2011, where competition between the military and state security ended in the military's adoption of the protest.[47] This book joins with this line of scholarship on repression by probing the elite chambers of decision making and competition.

### New Materials on Tiananmen

No doubt state response to a large degree depends on the level of threat. Yet, since such level is often contested and constructed by politicians, looking at protest alone is insufficient to explain why a specific reaction is adopted. Examining how major players inside the polity behave, if information is available, becomes important. Past research fails to do so partly due to the lack of data. However, it is also strongly influenced by movement-centered traditions,[48] which are deeply entrenched in a repression narrative for a case like Tiananmen in 1989, even after research materials on elite politics have now become abundant.

The first wave of such information came from government dossiers smuggled out by Chinese dissidents, for example, the *Tiananmen Papers* (and its

Chinese version, *June Fourth: The True Story*), which is rich with data on insiders, such as behind-the-scenes conversations and meeting minutes of the Politburo. It was initially reported that the materials were smuggled directly from the government's classified dossier. Upon closer examination, a more accurate characterization of these materials is they are write-ups of those files. Direct quotations are still extensive. These sources and their credibility were questioned when they first came out in 2001, but the content has been corroborated by other sources since then.[49] Among the high-quality confirmations of key events is a collection of party leaders' speeches published under the title *The Last Secrets* in 2019. Addressing two post-Tiananmen meetings in June 1989, the leaders, including Deng, Li Peng, Jiang Zemin, and some twenty others, reflected on the events of Tiananmen around the theme of justifying the dismissal of Zhao Ziyang.[50]

A considerable amount of information has also come out in the form of personal recollections by key protagonists, including Li Peng (then premier), Zhao Ziyang (then general secretary), Chen Xitong (mayor of Beijing, member of the Politburo, and the author of the official report on June 4), Deng Liqun (member of the Politburo, rumored to harbor ambition to succeed Zhao Ziyang as general secretary), Bao Tong (Zhao's chief of staff), and Xu Jiatun (Zhao's ally, the head of Xinhua News Agency in Hong Kong). In one way or another, each wrote a book that was published outside China.[51]

Added to this genre of records are accounts by dissidents who had worked inside the system before and during 1989, including Chen Yizi (head of a think tank under Zhao Ziyang), Bao Tong (Zhao's chief of staff), Dai Qing (a renowned journalist and adopted daughter of the late defense minister), Wu Guoguang (a high-ranking researcher and speech writer working for Zhao Ziyang), and Wu Wei (another staff member of Zhao Ziyang's inner circle).[52]

Similar accounts by insiders are also made available through three prominent journalists, Zhang Wanshu, Lu Chaoqi, and Yang Jisheng, who worked for the highest organs of the Party propaganda – Xinhua and the *People's Daily* respectively.[53]

In China, after the death of an elderly leader, a major party press traditionally publishes a multivolume "life chronology" (*nianpu*) in his or her honor. By now, such published chronologies include those for former leader Deng and three of his top-tier comrades-in-arms – Chen Yun, Li Xiannian, and Wang Zhen. A conspicuous exception is the absence of a relevant volume for a fourth elder, Yang Shangkun, for the period covering 1989 to 1992.[54]

To help me evaluate the vast information from the aforementioned materials, I consulted a group of individuals who participated the 1989 movement directly and in a high-profile fashion. I have no access to any top state leaders. Nor am I able to conduct interviews in China. Yet, for better or worse, many public figures in connection with the Tiananmen affair are, or were at one time or another, residing overseas, so I was able to interview many of them.

These published materials not only provide incredibly valuable information on insiders' policy deliberations and contentions; surprisingly they also contain hard-to-get information on the movements and operations of the martial law troops. This information first came from an unlikely source: an official publication entitled *One Day on Martial Law Duty* (戒严一日) by a military press. This ensemble of recollections on the military mission was presumably intended to glorify the military and was contributed by more than 200 officers and soldiers, including lieutenant generals, major generals, and colonels, all the way down to corporals and privates.[55] Using the two volumes as a lead, Canadian historian Timothy Brook was able to construct a fairly complete picture of the June 3–4 military action in his book *Quelling the People*, while Chinese historian Wu Renhua further identified the troops down to unit level in his book *The Martial Law Troops in the June 4th Affair* (六四事件中的戒严部队), published in Hong Kong.[56]

I have extensively used research published in Chinese by four scholars. I relied on Yang Jisheng's *The Political Struggle during the Reform Era*, for his insight on and chronicle of pre-1989 elite politics. Next, I rely heavily on Wu Renhua, who has published three books in Hong Kong on military operations during Tiananmen. Also helpful is Chen Xiaoya's monumental contribution, *The History of the Pro-democracy Movement in 1989*, which comes in three volumes totalling 1,725 pages with more than 4,400 footnotes. This publication appears to contain the most comprehensive sources, which is further enriched by her own research as a journalist, including interviews with a group of experts and witnesses who offered assistance with the sources and their own testimony. Important to my study are the writings of Dai Qing, a fourth author who was herself deeply involved in the Tiananmen movement in 1989 as a public intellectual and the daughter of a high official of the party. I am greatly indebted to her two earlier collections of essays and the development of the overall thesis of the book has greatly benefited from her ideas. She further articulated a framework that centered on the supreme leader as the driving force in her most recent book, *Deng Xiaoping in 1989*. Although I gained access to the book late in the process of my research and writing of this book, I am comforted to find that my thesis dovetails neatly with the tenets of hers.[57]

Drawing on these and other materials, my book unpacks the workings of a political regime during a period of major protest. Instead of treating state elites as a unified whole, I present players and factions who were in competition and conflict. I trace earlier steps of elite deliberation and infighting and focus on how these steps led to policies that became consequential to the protest.[58] Out of this effort is a politics-centered model that features what I call "protest–

politics–response." Here, "politics" turns into the focus of inquiry, and state reaction is understood as "response" instead of "repression." Such a shift in perspective yields critical insights which have been lacking in past analytical interpretations.

### The Issue of Source Reliability

The rich array of sources is a researcher's fortune. My method of treating them is based on two differing considerations. On the one hand, it would be professional negligence not to do our best to fully use all the possible information, especially considering how difficult it is to obtain information about the inner working of a communist regime. The goldmine of information becoming available on Tiananmen is a rare opportunity.

On the other hand, we should use the sources judiciously. It would be a fool's errand to use any information at face value. Nor should we place equal confidence in them without distinction. Take the memoirs and recorded reflections as an example. Are they truthful to the facts? Do the authors, often former state leaders, have an ax to grind? Some other materials, such as the *Tiananmen Papers*, for another example, come into the public domain in a mysterious way, and they may or may not be the source they are first declared to be. Are they still useful?

One way to establish confidence is to compare information from multiple sources and different origins, or to verify by checking writings that were penned by former political opponents. Take one of the most consequential events as an example. As recounted in the opening paragraph of this book, Deng and a host of other top leaders met on May 17 and decided on the military crackdown. Under the heading "Standing Committee Meeting Held in Deng Residence," the *Tiananmen Papers* starts its account this way:

> In the morning of May 17, a meeting of the Politburo Standing Committee of the CCP Central Committee was held at Deng Xiaoping's residence. Participants included Deng Xiaoping, Yang Shangkun, Bo Yibo, Zhao Ziyang, Li Peng, Qiao Shi, Hu Qili, Yao Yilin. The following is a summary the meeting's minute.[59]

If I have only this one source, whose origins are less than clear, I will not be in a strong position to establish the fact that the meeting took place, let alone a detailed account of it including who, when, where, and what.

Thankfully we have writings by two key participants. Premier Li Peng starts the day's diary entry: "May 17. At 4:00 p.m., Comrade Xiaoping convened a meeting to discuss the current situation. Participants included Zhao, Li, Hu, Yao, and Shangkun. Wang Ruilin was also present. That was a meeting that decided China's fate."[60]

Another participant, General Secretary Zhao Ziyang, also offered an independent account which starts, "On [May] 17, I made a request by phone to see Deng. Later Deng's office notified me to go to Deng's residence for a meeting, one that was attended by the members of Standing Committee and Shangkun."[61]

Finally, very solid confirmation of the event came in the form of a post-Tiananmen speech by Li Peng in a collection of party documents published in 2019.[62]

This level of cross-support is not always possible, however, so confidence levels vary from one detail to another. Therefore, when the preferred method of triangulation is not possible, I will indicate the lack of confidence and let readers judge for themselves. For example, while the *Tiananmen Papers* proves to be very accurate in its outline of major events given the existence of other supporting documents, its recording of detailed conversations between leaders lacks independent sources for verification.[63]

Smuggled to the United States by an anonymous dissident (pseudonym Zhang Liang), the *Tiananmen Papers* is a compilation of materials about the events, official meeting minutes, leaders' remarks, and analysis of the 1989 Tiananmen Square movement and the government's response to it. It was first published in English and initially characterized as authentic documents from the government's dossier. Soon scholars found that this was not the case. Instead, it is a *compilation* of original materials, consisting of excerpts, summaries, and editorializing. This twist dampened its credibility for a time and inspired scholarly debate.[64]

The credibility of the *Tiananmen Papers* has experienced a resurgence in recent years, as it has become increasingly verifiable by the emergence of plentiful source materials from other channels. These include superb reporting by prominent journalists such as Yang Jisheng (Xinhua), Zhang Wanshu (Xinhua) and Lu Chaoqi (*People's Daily*).[65] Most important of all, two of the highest leaders during Tiananmen, former premier Li Peng and former general secretary Zhao Ziyang, both published their "diaries" or "recorded conversations," and their reflections have confirmed many details recorded by the *Tiananmen Papers*.

What about skepticism about the word-for-word transcripts of "private conversations"? Some scholars may question whether "private" conversations can even be recorded in the first place, but I contest the notion of "privacy." Indeed, such "private" conversations were routinely recorded, as is evident in many similar daily entries in the life chronology of a top leader published after his death.[66] A key to understanding this phenomenon lies in the absence of boundaries between "private" and "public" life in the communist regime, a far cry from Western systems. The leaders could keep such conversations confidential if they chose to. But, by the same token, they could decide at a later time to publish them with great fanfare. In any event, what a leader said would not go wasted without dutiful recording.

To be sure, no definitive history of elite politics of communist China is possible until the regime opens its archives for research. Until then we still have to work with what is possible to come by to advance scholarship, by definition a work in progress.

## Protest as Elite Resource

Zooming in on the details of what happened behind the scenes, it becomes clear that top leaders of the party-state never saw the Tiananmen student movement as the kind of threat that could topple their regime. Instead, they could afford to be busy using the protest to leverage their own political interests. They did so by engaging in activities such as "contentious labeling," channeling the protest to a certain direction, and making a spectacular show of military might. In contrast to their public declarations, private deliberations lacked evidence of intentions to end the protest. Deng Xiaoping appeared to have already decided that student protests "would not end up with much." At the height of the 1989 crisis, Deng privately reassured his listener, "A good economy sets a foundation . . . Now [with this foundation], there is no unrest among the peasants across the nation; nor among the workers, by and large."[67]

So what was the deadly decision based on? If the leaders did not make such a decision out of a sense of threat, what was on their minds? The course of my research was therefore directed away from a narrow focus on the student movement and perceptions of it. In doing so, I examined the broader context of politics, especially the thought processes and motivations of elite players. Among them the most prominent player is Deng Xiaoping, a supreme leader. As such, elite conflict regarding succession issues came into focus.

The signs had been there all along. The movement was triggered by the death of a secretary general of the Chinese Communist Party who had been groomed by Deng but later dismissed; it was thrust upon the secretary general who was in a precarious position; Deng's reform agenda was at a crossroad, and this protest further presented an opportunity for Deng's rivals to discredit his reform policies and possibly install a new leader; and, finally, it represented a defining crisis for an eighty-four-year-old supreme leader whose policies and legacy were hanging in the balance.

### Worries about Rivals versus Worries about Revolutionaries

In the nondemocratic system, a communist leader's concern is to respond to those at the top or within the top, with little regard for the public. This idea is in line with the concept of "state autonomy," an analysis developed by Skocpol and others to explain democratic systems.[68] In communist regimes, state autonomy might actually be more salient. This insight has not been appreciated enough by existing scholarship, which tends to exaggerate revolutionary potentials of popular unrest in communist countries. To elaborate on this point, Tullock observes that the most likely cause of a dictator being overthrown comes from high officials in his own regime while the chances of his being deposed by popular forces is rare:

> Most dictators are overthrown by higher officials of their own regimes, simply because the higher officials want to promote themselves with at least one of them becoming the new dictator. If the reader has doubts about this, I suggest he consult the New York Times Index for the previous six months or so and check the numbers of cases in which dictators have been overthrown.[69]

Tullock goes on to write,

> The last, and in many ways least likely, way in which a dictator may be overthrown is by a genuine popular uprising. This is rare, not only in my own opinion but that of most people who have seriously looked into the matter ... History shows that, in the last resort, success or failure hinges on the attitude which those armed forces of the status quo government will take toward an insurrection ... Whatever government or party has the full allegiance of a country's armed forces is to all intents and purposes politically impregnable ... If it [success of a popular uprising] is rare in the study of actual overthrows of dictatorship, *it is very common in the romantic literature.*[70]

In other words, even in a time of major unrest, politicians are as much concerned with their rivals as they are with the protesters, if not more so. And ongoing protest enters the political equation as a new factor.

### Protest as a Differing Value

The theoretical premise behind the revolution–counterrevolution narrative (or the revolution suppression model, to be discussed below) treats popular protest as a threat, particularly when the scale of protest is significantly large. A corollary of this conception is that the state elites form a united front in their response. But in real-life cases, threat level varies. So does the degree of coherence of state actors.

The perception of threat not only varies from one protest to another, but also within the course of a protest. Elite players assess the situation differently, either in good faith or to their political advantage; they do not automatically rush to "repress." Instead, they constantly frame and reframe the nature and the scale of the protest, doing so with a focus on their rivals.

One politician's curse can be another's blessing, and vice versa. In a communist regime, when a popular protest occurs, the usual first order of business is disassociation. One faction may turn the situation into a political weapon by pinning the responsibility on opponents. The other side, under whose watch "things have gone wrong," may not be able to avoid the blame; they may then try to salvage the situation by painting the protest in a less ominous light. On extremely rare occasions, they may even attempt to legitimize it as a rightful expression of "the will of the people." As such, in one way or another, protest can often be a resource for elite conflict.

How do we measure the amount of political advantage, or the usefulness, of such a resource? A clue to this question lies in a comparison between a politician's re-election prospect in an electoral democracy and a leader's political standing in a communist system. The target audience in the former is the voters, and advantage is measured by "vote counting."[71] The target audience in the latter consists of the supreme leader and a limited number of oligarchs. In this sense, political standing can also be measured by "vote counting," albeit with a much smaller target audience and an unequal distribution of power (e.g., individuals such as the supreme leader having more, or more weighted, "votes" than others).[72] As will be shown in the following pages, in 1989 the student protest would be a major issue that affected the "votes" of confidence cast on the frontline leaders by the supreme leader and the important oligarchs.

### Forms of Elite Contribution to Producing and Ending Protest

During a major protest, top leaders are often at the forefront of state responses. They act with the purpose of "scoring points" for themselves or undercutting their opponents, or even using the opportunity to reset the entire political landscape. The forms discussed below are ideal types in the conceptual sense, as real-life action usually varies and may take the form of a combination of two or more of them.

*Sponsorship* is used by a leader, most likely the supreme leader, who launches a mass campaign and uses the party-state apparatus to lead, to finance, and to organize.[73] Examples include political campaigns in the Mao and Stalin years. At first glance, one may assume that this form of state response may not be available for those protests such as Tiananmen that were initiated from below. But, as will be seen, for a political actor on the ground, the distinction between state-sponsored movement and popular protest is academic: a state-sponsored campaign always involves popular initiatives, and a popular event, if it is to go on, always has at least some level of state support or acquiescence.

That leads to the second kind of elite contribution: *Co-optation*. A friendly faction of leading officials frames the protest in a positive way, e.g., it is "patriotic in its intention," "orderly and peaceful"; it "correctly identify problems the party is also working on," and so on. If the faction prevails over their adversaries, they may even adopt the movement as their own.

Third, officials under the supreme leader normally cannot start a new movement of their own. Rather, they can only pledge support for one that has already been launched, by forces from either above or below, an elite option we may call *alliance*. Indeed, they often feel compelled to jump on the bandwagon and embrace or oppose, a perilous undertaking that could make or break a political career. Like buying stocks or betting on a horse, it is hard to predict whether one will end up on the winning or losing side. Therefore, *evasion* becomes the fourth, and important, option.

Most common is *public framing*. As mentioned above, in the absence of independent media outlets, state leaders have great discretion on how a protest is presented. Different facts are picked to fit a narrative, and "facts" can also be manufactured if needed. Is it patriotic or "anti-party and anti-socialism"? Is it orderly or chaotic? And so on and so forth. As I show below in this book, the overarching concern of the conflicting factions in 1989 was not so much ending the protest as winning debates of public framing.

To be sure, measures of *repression* can always be deployed from early on, but they are not chosen exclusively for the purpose of *suppression*. Rather, the selective use of these measures is often intended to *channel* or even *facilitate* the protest.

Finally, the ultimate means of repression, a *military operation*, may or may not target just the protest. It could also act as a form of *coup d'état*, in the sense that the introduction of military power transforms the political landscape. In the case of Tiananmen, it was a soft kind of *coup d'état*: the military is deployed to target elite players as deterrence only, because no arrest of elite players was ever needed.

### Three Models of Political Division and Their Differing Predictions

It would be too simplistic to assume that all an elite actor cares about is defending the system. So also would it be to assume that all he cares about is pushing a policy according to his ideological orientation. Priorities and alliances shift according to political moments.

Political leaders may have three layers of identity. The first concerns their official capacities. As members of the polity, they are first and foremost defenders of this system. They also have role-specific identities based on the division of labor and the power hierarchy, such as the general secretary, the vice chair of the Military Committee, and the premier.

The second concerns factional affiliations. In democratic systems, such alliances often come in the form of alignments with political parties, while in communist systems divisions operate through labels like reformers and conservatives.

Third, one might adopt identities through the important political fight of the time. Unlike the first and second sets of identities, these are more situational and fluid. The main focus of top leaders (including Deng himself) in Beijing leading up to the 1989 conflict was on the emerging post-Deng political landscape. On top of factional affiliations that already exist, one might follow one of the three camps within succession politics, as described further below.

These three layers of identity are not mutually exclusive: "Politicians routinely promote their understanding of the general welfare, while, in the back of their minds, considering how those actions will affect their popularity. Often, the two concepts overlap."[74]

A first perspective, the *revolution suppression model*, exclusively focuses on one-dimensional identities to explain the behaviors of state elites. That is, they are understood solely as defenders of the communist system against collapse. While such an identity is correctly recognized, and it applies to almost everyone in the top echelon, the model errs in assuming that this identity is the most important all of the time.

A second model, the *two-way factionalism model*, oversubscribes pre-existing factional affiliations with the division between "reformers" and "conservatives." For long, observers of communist regimes have followed a tradition of divining the opaque politics through the lens of "factionalism." Key moments – such as Budapest in 1956, Prague in 1968, and the tidal waves of 1989–1990 – are understood as conflicts between the "reformers" and the "conservatives." They are stories of reform heroes, such as Nagy of Hungary, Dubček of Czechoslovakia, and Yeltsin of the USSR, who fought the hardliners.[75] The tradition is particularly well heeded among scholars of China's elite politics,[76] and many accounts of Tiananmen have been written in this vein.[77]

### Three-Way Contention in Communist Succession

Supreme leadership is a fact in the history of communist states, although it is given no official title. Just as real is the politics of transferring its authority. The system forsakes hereditary rules and rejects democratic election; hence it relies heavily on the incumbent ruler to choose and then groom a successor. Fatal failures visited major figures such as Lenin, Stalin, Mao, and Tito. It is an exacerbated version of the "crown prince problem" known to autocrats.[78] Committing too early and growing a powerful heir as a result, the ruler's own authority might be threatened; choosing too late, the heir might not be strong enough to head off rivalry.

In a communist system, such as the USSR and China, the supreme leader might designate a candidate but put him under the check of one or multiple "counter-heirs." In his old age, a ruling "triad" – as experts of Soviet communism such as Myron Rush and Robert Conquest call it – is formed, which includes the ruler, the heir, and the counter-heir.[79] This arrangement is still precarious, as the ruler can still lose confidence and dispose of the heir. Mao sequentially disposed a Liu, a Lin, and a Deng, then on his deathbed appointed a Hua. Hua indeed succeeded Mao, who died, but he could not survive his rivals' challenge.

Deng was someone who vowed to break the cycle. By the eve of Tiananmen, however, the system under him had followed the same script. It was a three-way contention for the top, a "triad" of collective parties that featured Deng himself, his reform protégés as "heirs," and a conservative faction operating as "counter-heirs." Also reminiscent of the past, the crown prince problem confronted Deng as well. He had just disposed of a general party secretary and was about to remove another during the 1989 Tiananmen events. In doing so, he often enlisted help from the conservative "counter-heirs."

My three-way depiction of the polity is, to a large degree, an extension of previous factionalism models. I will continue using labels such as "conservatives" and "reformers," but I will take into account factors outside ideological commitment. Most importantly, I stress the fluidity of identities, alliances, and divisions.

*Three Models Compared*

Three theoretical models can be summarized from the discussion so far. The revolution suppression model draws inspiration from classical events such as the French Revolution, in which the rebellious nature of the revolt was unambiguous to political elites. It is essentially a "society-versus-the-state" narrative, with political elites being more or less united. Its explanation of Tiananmen's military crackdown treats such crackdown as the default solution of a repressive political machine.

Another model, the two-way factionalism model, on the other hand, splits political elites into two factions, viewing one of them as possible allies of the social movement. It is a modified version of the previously mentioned "society-versus-the-state" narrative, with the society having a sympathizer from within. It is also one of the most common frameworks used to understand elite politics in authoritarian systems. Its explanation for Tiananmen's military crackdown considers such a crackdown as a result of the protest's reformist allies losing to its hardline adversaries.

The third model I propose in this book, called the three-way succession model, incorporates another significant element, rather than relying on the protest itself, to explain the decision. This alternative model places the supreme leader at the center of elite politics due to his unmatched power and the important role that succession concerns played in the contentious episode. The protest certainly was not separated from these succession concerns, but it also did not replace them as the top priority for political elites. Instead, the protest changed the political landscape, transforming the means through which political elites can fight for control and in effect becoming a resource. To allude to what will be covered in the following chapters, among the other key players under Deng, the incumbent heir used it to maintain "good graces" with Deng, while his rivals used it to undermine such trust. Deng eventually used the protest as a justification to demonstrate his military power. This is the three-way succession model's explanation for Tiananmen's military crackdown.

The three models are built on differing assumptions, as summarized in Table 1.1. The revolution suppression model starts with the assumption that a revolutionary situation has arisen, and that the regime is in danger of collapse. As such, the defining issue of elite politics at that time is to fight this possibility – that is, to suppress the protest. Since they are confronted by a common threat, the elites react to the situation more or less as a united front – see the first column of the table under the revolution suppression model.

By comparison, the two-way factionalism model does not assume that the government is already in an unstable situation. The two-faction framework applies to both normal times and periods of great upheaval. Even during large protests, the top priority is still less clear-cut. However, what is rigid about this model is that it presumes a two-faction divide and uses this divide as the key to understanding individual behavior (see the second column of Table 1.1).

The three-way succession model questions whether a revolutionary situation has occurred. This model identifies political succession as the defining issue. It

Table 1.1 *Comparing the assumptions of three models*

|  | Revolution suppression | Two-way factionalism | Three-way succession |
| --- | --- | --- | --- |
| A revolutionary situation? | Yes | Not assumed | Not assumed |
| Defining political issue | Protest suppression | Protest suppression and succession | Succession |
| Elite alignment | United front | Two factions | Evolving alliances |

is based on historical conditions and theoretically draws inspiration from studies of elite politics where "re-election" is considered central.[80] Compared to the two-way factionalism model, this new model also rejects the static view of factionalism. It depicts a process of factional alliance in a three-way contention, in which groupings are fluid (see the third column of Table 1.1).

As formulated, the three models offer contrasting sets of empirical predictions about elite politics during the historical 1989 Tiananmen incident.

The differing predictions of the revolution-suppression model versus the three-way succession model are as follows:

- The revolution-suppression model presumes a large-scale protest to be revolutionary in a communist regime, while the three-way succession model treats this issue as an empirical question and calls for investigation.

- For the revolution-suppression model, state leaders are mainly concerned with how to end the protest, while the three-way succession model predicts a wide variety of choices over time and across groups, whose goal is mainly to frame and channel the protest to their advantage.

- For the revolution-suppression model, the martial law troops were employed to restore order, while the three-way succession model suggests that the troops were called in to serve a greater purpose and for a long game, but foremost to strengthen Deng's position. His use of military power was to carry out his removal of Zhao and to enhance his bargaining power in his contest with his conservative rivals over the direction of the country, including the choice for a new leadership.

- For the revolution-suppression model, the scale and manner of using the military are a response to the protest, while the three-way succession model suggests that the military operation was disproportionate in its scale, and that its purpose was to showcase symbolic power.

The differing predictions of the two-way factionalism model versus the three-way succession model are as follows:

- The two-way factionalism model presents an elite alignment of two factions, while the three-way succession model suggests that Deng the supreme leader forms a faction of his own, hovering over the two factions.

- The two-way factionalism model implies a static lineup of two camps throughout the course of Tiananmen, while the three-way succession model suggests the fluid nature of the elite alignment, as players could always change sides to take advantage of an opportunity or retain power, often at the expense of a prior allegiance or ideological preference.

- The two-way factionalism model suggests an alliance between a reformer and the protesters, while the three-way succession model predicts that the protest could be poorly connected to potential elite allies.

- The two-way factionalism model reasons that suppression is a result of the elite allies losing out to the hardliners, while the three-way succession model suggests that the driving force behind the policy was the supreme leader.

- The two-way factionalism model casts Deng, for his military suppression, as a conservative politician, while the three-way succession model posits that he remained a reformer despite all, which was made clear by his trajectory in post-crackdown events.

## The Organization of the Book and Summary of Chapters

After this introductory chapter, I will divide the historical narrative into four parts to offer evidence for evaluating the above three models.

*Part I, Party-State Leadership in the Deng Era (Chapters 2 and 3): The Limitations of Deng's Power as Supreme Leader and the Crown Prince Problem*

In Chapters 2 and 3, I describe the party-state leadership under Deng, the communist supreme leader. He enjoyed exceptional power and authority, but just as important, his power had limits, which is the key to understanding why he needed to "play politics" as others did. Chapter 2 narrates his ascendance to power and, on his way up, how he was helped by his future rivals. Chapter 3 explores the crown prince problem, another limit on Deng's power that came with old age. Already in his eighties, Deng's succession plan was constantly endangered by factional infighting and the elusiveness of his own trust in the potential heirs. The background presented in these two chapters is important because succession politics would take center stage in the 1989 saga.

*Part II, Elite Politics and the Making of the Tiananmen Protest (Chapters 4, 5, and 6): How Elites Coproduced the Tiananmen Protest with Students*

In Chapters 4, 5, and 6, I show how the party leaders ended up coproducing the Tiananmen protest movement. Chapter 4 chronicles the fight between General Secretary Zhao and Premier Li over how to label the unfolding events, while no action was taken to stop the protest. Chapter 5 turns to Deng to explain the meaning of his two long spells of silence and his private reassurance to Zhao, and his later alliance with former rivals to condemn the protest. Days before his final decision, his conversation with his military man shed light on his true intentions. Chapter 6 returns to the two rivals, General Secretary Zhao and Premier Li. While briefly in charge, Li did not order any real action against the protest but encouraged "dialogue," which in effect lent legitimacy to student organizations. Zhao experimented with a conciliatory approach, but his plan was snarled by elite infighting and student radicalism. In sum, in one way or another, the leaders' actions inflamed the movement to new heights.

*Part III, The Decision for Military Intervention (Chapters 7, 8, and 9): Martial Law Was Overkill, but Mainly Not Aimed at Protesters*

In Chapters 7, 8, and 9, I address the martial law decision itself. Was the protest serious enough for the extraordinary measure? Chapter 7 presents evidence that it was not. China in 1989 was fiscally sound and internationally independent. The student movement was reformist in nature and lacked broad support, and, if not prompted further, would have declined and died. Chapter 8 explores Deng's decision in its political context, including dismissing General Secretary Zhao and appointing a new leadership. Chapter 9 narrates the military operation on June 3–4. The spectacular display of military might was an overkill, and the clearing the of square could have been done by a small fraction of the troops.

*Part IV, The Political Impact (Chapter 10): Deng's Succession Plan Prevails in Post-Tiananmen Events*

Chapter 10 uses post-Tiananmen events further illustrate the meaning of the Tiananmen decisions. Deng chose Jiang Zemin as the new leader, but he was a compromise candidate who was also backed by the conservatives. Deng pushed for his reform agenda and through a spectacular Southern Tour in 1992, triumphed over the conservative offensive and won over Jiang. In hindsight Deng played a political long game in 1989, and his Tiananmen decision figured prominently in his favor.

*Conclusion (Chapter 11): Tiananmen and China's Communist Authoritarianism*

The last chapter juxtaposes the empirical patterns of Tiananmen with the three alternative models of China's elite poltics. I conclude that the three-way succession model aligns with the historical facts better than the other two models. I end the book by exploring three institutional features of China's communist authoritarianism. By placing succession politics front and center, this book glimpses the future through the lens of the past.

*Part I*

# Party-State Leadership in the Deng Era

The book as a whole presents evidence to evaluate three models of elite decision making during the 1989 Tiananmen Square movement. Part I, however, will pave the way. It addresses historical events surrounding Deng's ascent to the supreme leadership after Mao's death in 1976, covering a period leading up to 1989. My goal is to first draw up a portrait of the power hierarchy and relations. These two chapters are to set the stage.

Little guidance on power relationship can be found in the regime's official blueprints, such as its written constitution or an organizational chart. Power in such a system is often declared, yet hidden, and it is at once institutional and fluid. The nature of the power relationship, therefore, is better explored through its latest history. We gain insight by examining the regularity, or the lack thereof, of its past actions. Hence, the analytical approach is to chart action-structure iterations, in the vein articulated by sociologist Anthony Giddens.[1] In other words, for the purpose of setting the stage, I will recount a great many preludes.

In three ways, Part I serves as preparation for forthcoming chapters' narratives.

First, it introduces the major characters of the party-state leadership, those who would play important roles in the 1989 political drama. They include:

- Deng Xiaoping, the new supreme leader. His ascent was a dialectical process of self-empowering and self-limiting: the way he accumulated power required him to share it. In addition, as an elderly man in his eighties, he had to delegate much while exercising his power. Such sharing and delegation became the major sources of elite alliance and division.

- Chen Yun, Deng's ideological rival and a colleague of his generation. He was among those who helped Deng to ascend to the top. He became Deng's equal in policy disputes, forming the "twin-summit politics."

- Zhao Ziyang, general secretary, Deng's close reform ally prior to 1989. He reached the top of the organizational chart after the downfall of his predecessor, Hu Yaobang. He could have been Deng's successor if all had gone well.

- Li Peng, premier, a conservative loyal to Chen Yun, serving as counterpoint to Zhao in the first-line leadership in charge of the day-to-day operation of governance. Li and Zhao represented gravitational pull from the two ideological camps.

Second, the stories are organized around the recurrent patterns that would re-emerge again during the 1989 conflict:

- *The centrality of the supreme leadership.* The communist state never lives without a supreme leader, the final arbiter of its personnel and policies. It was true in the USSR under Lenin, Stalin, or Khrushchev; so was it the case in China under Mao, Deng, and beyond. It was so even when the official line proclaimed "collective leadership." In the late 1980s, Deng remained the supreme leader even in his supposed "retirement."

- *The deciding effect of the military power.* This pattern is evident in the ascent of Deng. Upon Mao's death, his friends in the military staged a coup and later assisted him to unseat Mao's chosen successor. It also foreboded Deng's decision to retain chairmanship of the Central Military Commission after he "retired." It would have profound consequences in 1989.

- *Constraints on the supreme leadership.* Deng built his legitimacy partly by condemning Mao's personality cult and vowing a "collective leadership." He kept his word – to some extent. No sooner had he consolidated power, than he began to unload much of it. Not only did he need to respect his rivals of his own generation, as an aged ruler in his eighties; he also had to negotiate with his potential successors who were doing the governing.

- *The crowned prince problem and the issue of trust.* The problem bewitched Mao as the elderly ruler, prompting an episode in which he snared Deng as a potential successor. For his part, Deng elevated and then discarded Hu Yaobang. The same fate would befall to Zhao Ziyang in 1989.

- *Large social protest as a liability for the incumbent.* History recycled several times: first, the downfall of Liu Shaoqi, Mao's designated successor, during the Cultural Revolution in the 1960s; then, in an earlier episode of Tiananmen protest in 1976, Deng was framed and disgraced. Again, in the years of 1986 and 1987, Hu Yaobang, then the general secretary, was doomed. It escaped no one in the spring of 1989 that the upcoming storm could undo the then general secretary, Zhao Ziyang.

Lastly, I provide an analysis of Zhao Ziyang's precarious position on the eve of the Tiananmen Square movement. He would have been removed, the argument goes, with or without a student movement. His economic policy met setbacks, he could not make headway in the military, and he was constantly attacked by the conservatives. On the other hand, Deng constantly reassured him, which gave him a high degree of confidence. What is indisputable, though, is that Zhao's position had indeed become the number one political issue. The proverbial last straw could tip the fine balance. It is within this context that elite reactions to the Tiananmen Square movement must be understood.

# 2    The Coming of the Deng Era
1976–1987

On his deathbed in 1976, Mao disposed Deng Xiaoping, then an heir apparent, from a top leadership position and elevated someone else as the new flag bearer. But Deng made a comeback in the following years, as he not only unseated Mao's designated successor but also pushed the country in a direction away from Mao's line. By 1980, he had appointed himself the military chief (chair of the Central Military Committee), and two younger men, Hu Yaobang and Zhao Ziyang, to head the party and the government respectively. He became the new supreme leader. The era of Deng hence commenced.

The communist state cannot live without a supreme leadership, although it never openly acknowledges it. It is at once an irony and a commonplace for a political system known for its tortured relationship with truth and reality. Unlike systems with a king, an emperor, a president, or a prime minister, there is no official designation for such a form of the highest authority. Founding dictators such as Lenin and Mao would enjoy an extreme concentration of power and recommend no one to occupy that status after them. "Collective leadership" was something they envisioned for the system after their death.[1]

Supreme leadership hence is present within any communist state at any particular moment in time. The aforementioned founding dictators obtained it through claims of building the party and the country. Later comers – such as Stalin, Khrushchev, and Deng, did so by expanding control over the party, the state, and the military simultaneously. This is true even for post-Khrushchev and post-Deng political regimes that prominently touted "collective leadership," producing supreme leaders such as Brezhnev and Jiang Zemin.[2]

In the post-Mao era leading up to 1989, Deng was a transitional figure, at once a personal ruler and an agent of change. On the one hand, regardless of his official titles (or lack thereof), he was de facto supreme leader given his undisputable authority over the party, the state, and the military. On the other hand, he assigned himself the task of moving the system toward one of "collective leadership." It seemed as though he was no sooner acquiring power than unloading it.

The limits of his power were partly imposed by himself. Unlike Stalin or Mao before him, in his ascent Deng did not purge factional rivals. Indeed, he intentionally allowed factions to exist, as well as situating himself in their midst. He tolerated, endangered, mingled, bargained, and managed. On the whole, he had thrived by the spring of 1989.

This comparatively democratic side of Deng undeniably has its origin in his personal character, but, as will be further elaborated below, it was also a result of political necessity – a consequence of how he acquired power in the first place. Replacing Mao's chosen man, Deng's rule was not built on a claim as the heir. So he turned the tables to build a new type of legitimacy. Following the USSR's Khrushchev two decades earlier, he turned against the deceased leader's legacy by liberating Mao's victims and forming an anti-Mao coalition.

This political rallying cry of rejecting the "cult of personality," however, planted the seed of a contradiction in his newly acquired supreme leadership obtaining supreme power on the promise of undoing it. Deng delivered his promise of undoing earnestly, which consisted of two efforts. First, he shared power with other major elderly leaders, permitted policy and personnel disputes, and allowed de facto factions to exist. Second, Deng focused on the transfer of power to young leaders. Other communist autocrats before him, such as Stalin and Mao, accumulated power without giving much thought to who would succeed them.[3] In contrast, Deng was already aged seventy-six in 1980 and would be eighty-five in 1989. He needed to be different; he wanted to pass his authority to young leaders as soon as he obtained it.

In this chapter, I recount the historical events that led to what some scholars have labeled "twin-summit politics," a factional landscape that represented the first set of limitations to Deng's rule. Upon Mao's death, he returned from political exile, forged a new coalition to unseat Mao's successor, and shared this newfound power. In the next chapter, I address Deng's relationship with the specific candidates he chose for political succession. Together, these chapters provide background for the three-way contention that animated the top party leadership on the eve of Tiananmen: Deng versus his conservative rivals, Deng versus his potential successors, and Deng's potential successors (reformers) versus the conservatives.

### Succession Crisis, Popular Protest, and Elite Conflict in the Year of Mao's Death in 1976

Deng's own path to the pinnacle of power can serve as a study in chaotic leadership succession itself.

Deng was groomed by Mao at one point, but his hopes were quickly dashed in the mid-1970s, when Mao's wife, Jiang Qing, and her allies worked to undermine his candidacy. Deng's rivals successfully framed a popular protest in 1976 as a counterrevolutionary conspiracy and Deng as its mastermind. Deng was dismissed from leadership positions and sent back to political exile.[4]

Earlier, during the ten-year long Cultural Revolution (1966–1976), Mao had already destroyed two of his potential successors. Liu Shaoqi fell from the position of "first-line" leader and state president to the "number one capitalist roader in the party."[5] He was subsequently expelled from Beijing and died in 1969 anonymously in a prison cell in Kaifeng, Henan.[6] Later came Lin Biao, whose heir-apparent status was even written into the party constitution. Accused of a *coup d'état* in 1971, Lin fled the country on a hastily arranged flight and died when the plane crashed in Mongolia.[7]

By 1973, aged eighty with drastically deteriorating health, Mao started to groom two individuals simultaneously: Wang Hongwen, thirty-eight, later a member of Jiang Qing's clique known as the Gang of Four, and Deng Xiaoping, sixty-nine.[8]

### Deng as Mao's Potential Heir

Deng had been Mao's protégé throughout his career. Their shared history dated back to their shared suffering from ultra-left persecution in the 1920s at the Jiangxi guerrilla base. As summarized by David Shambaugh, Mao was responsible for many key junctures of Deng's meteoric rise in the party, including his ascent at the base when Mao himself was rehabilitated, and his important military commands during both the Anti-Japanese War and the Civil War. After 1949, Mao put Deng in charge of the Southwest Administrative Region, and in 1950 he summoned him to Beijing. Once in the Party Center, Deng occupied a diverse set of important positions in civilian government – vice premier, vice chairman of the Finance and Economic Commission, minister of finance, general secretary of the Central Committee Secretariat of the party, and director of the CCP Organization Department. He belonged to a small number of leaders who accumulated the highest credentials in civilian affairs on top of their illustrious military record.[9]

Deng was on the rise until his fall along with Liu Shaoqi in 1966, during the very first year of the Cultural Revolution, when he was dubbed "the number two capitalist roader inside the party." He was exiled from Beijing, his life spared only because of his personal tie to Mao. Then, on March 2, 1973, Deng was recalled to Beijing as a potential heir, in competition with another candidate, a member of the Gang of Four.[10]

In grooming possible successors, Mao divided power between Deng Xiaoping and the much younger Wang Hongwen, with Deng in charge of the government and the military and Wang the party and ideology. Deng was appointed vice premier, taking over the duties of the premier, as Zhou Enlai had been diagnosed with cancer by then. On the military side, he was made the new director of the General Staff.[11] Given his wartime credentials, it was no accident that Deng was given more military power than Wang Hongwen, an advantage that proved to be profoundly significant as events further unfolded.

For the next two years and until Premier Zhou's death in January 1976, the Gang of Four had relentlessly attacked Premier Zhou Enlai and Deng Xiaoping. A national mass campaign to repudiate Lin Biao, the latest disgraced heir apparent, was recast as "Repudiate Lin and Repudiate Confucius," a thinly veiled campaign against the premier. Soon after, Deng became the direct target. His effort to end mass campaigns and to resume economic activities was repudiated as "rightist restoration." Mao wavered between the two sides, siding with Zhou and Deng at one moment then with the Gang of Four the next.[12]

### The 1976 Tiananmen Protest: Its Cause and Its Ending

In January of 1976, Premier Zhou Enlai passed away. Unsatisfied with the funeral Zhou received, Zhou's supporters began laying wreaths in Tiananmen Square in late March – in anticipation of April 5, or Qingming, the Chinese Festival of the Dead. According to one account, the number of mourners and protesters had reached more than a million by April 4. At this critical juncture, Mao was on his deathbed and ruled by having his nephew relay commands to the Politburo. This nephew, however, was a close ally of the Gang of Four. Deng Xiaoping was hence in a precarious position.[13]

The mass discontent targeted the Gang of Four and, by extension, Mao. In a system where unsanctioned protest was normally treated as a counterrevolutionary crime and thus almost nonexistent, Zhou Enlai's death provided a window of opportunity. Using mourning the dead as cover, popular protest first appeared in the cities of Nanjing and Shanghai, then found a new ground in Tiananmen Square in Beijing. Quickly, blessed by Mao, the Gang of Four labeled the protest a counterrevolutionary conspiracy, and Tiananmen Square was cleared. Deng was framed as the protest's mastermind and formally expelled from the party leadership one last time.[14]

Here, for lessons that would echo thirteen years later in the events of 1989, it is worth pausing to reflect on why a popular protest could emerge and grow to the magnitude that it did, a rare feat in communist China. To be sure, much of it was due to the public's intense emotions exploding from losing Zhou Enlai, a beloved and celebrated leader known for his devotion to the country and his sympathy with victims of the Cultural Revolution. However, the protest would not have reached such a scale without some level of support from within the government. The Gang of Four stood to reap the benefits of the outbreak by shifting blame onto their rival, Deng Xiaoping.[15]

While there are many similarities between 1976 Tiananmen and 1989 Tiananmen, their endings could not have been more different. The process of clearing the square on the night of April 5, 1976, involved no martial law troops. Five battalions of Beijing Garrison troops remained in the background, hidden in adjacent buildings. The government waited until quiet moments past midnight, when the crowds had dwindled to less than 1,000 participants, before it sent in 3,000 militia and 3,000 plainclothes policemen. They carried only clubs. No guns. After the crowds were cleared, the troops quickly showed up to help cordon off and secure the square. The operation was conducted gingerly and quietly, involving a minimum of violence. There were few injuries, no deaths, and a low number of arrests.[16]

Military action was not the solution in 1976. At the time, the Gang of Four did not have control over the military, while the allies of their opponents did. It would be to their *disadvantage* to bring more troops into the capital or to dramatize the power of the military. Although Jiang Qing suggested a military solution in a Politburo meeting on April 1, 1976, her more sensible allies quickly shut her down.[17] One account recorded a heated exchange between Jiang Qing and Wang Hongwen. Upon Jiang's suggestion of sending militiamen and soldiers with firearms, Wang sarcastically remarked, "If you want to carry weapons you can! If you want to open fire you can too! But by no means will I be responsible for this crime."[18]

## Mao's Successor Facing Challenges from the Gang of Four

Although the Gang of Four successfully used the April 1976 protest to topple Deng Xiaoping, Mao did not elevate Wang Hongwen or anyone else from the Gang. Instead, he designated a new person, Hua Guofeng, as the official successor.

Hua's rise to power, however, would be on shaky ground. In imperial times, an emperor would crown a prince at a young age so he was given enough time to grow his own power base.[19] Unfortunately Hua was hastily installed and Mao died soon after, in a matter of months. His challenge was twofold.

First, he faced opposition from the Gang of Four, a majority of the top seven leaders listed in party announcements of Mao's death. With Marshall Ye Jianying's supposed leave of absence, Hua all but stood alone facing the Gang in the Politburo's standing committee.[20] It was small wonder that members of the Gang openly demanded meetings to discuss "leadership issues in the era after Chairman Mao" or "Comrade Jiang Qing's job problem." Rumor had it that their plan was to install Jiang Qing as party chairman, Zhang Chunqiao premier, and Wang Hongwen as president of the People's Congress.[21]

A second challenge was that Hua did not have any roots in the military, a prerequisite to become a top leader who truly counted. Thankfully, neither did any member of the Gang of Four. So Hua's strategy was to mitigate this weakness by establishing an alliance with the army generals. He decided to hold only "extended SC meetings" as a way to bring in a few allies, among them Ye Jianying and Li Xiannian, two revolutionary veterans of Deng's generation.[22]

### Using the Military to Arrest the Gang of Four

Jiang Qing and her Gang were no friends to the generals. If anything, as zealous leaders of the Cultural Revolution persecutions, they already had many enemies within the military. Three out of the country's ten marshals, He Long, Chen Yi, and Peng Dehuai, had died their victims. The Gang of Four seemed to be somewhat cognizant of this problem, but their perception of its gravity was flawed and their solution foolish. In their power base, Shanghai, they mobilized and trained a large number of worker militia. It was reported that 30 million yuan in renminbi (RMB) had been appropriated from the municipal revenue over the years, and many weapons were manufactured. On September 21, 1976, a Shanghai leader was summoned by the Gang to Beijing to be quizzed on "the preparedness of the Shanghai militia."[23]

To army generals, these efforts by the Gang of Four were pitiful. General Xu Shiyou, the commander of the Nanjing Military Region close to Shanghai, showed his contempt when he said,

> Never mind that Wang Hongwen is a vice chair of the CMC and Zhang Chunqiao director of the Political Department [of the CMC]. Nobody in the military listens to them. All guns are in our hands. The best they can do is to deploy a few divisions of workers' militia. It won't make a dent ... [I] need just one group army to exterminate the entire militia of Shanghai. The 60th Group Army is garrisoned in Wuxi, precisely for that.[24]

The generals had to wait for an opportune time to move against this faction. It was reported that Marshal Ye Jianying often used the following phrase to convey his predicament when Mao was still alive: "Worrying about the vase when you aimed at the mouse." For him, the mouse was Jiang Qing and the vase was Mao. Only after Mao's death did the idea of using force against the Gang of Four seem to be feasible. On the day Zhang Chunqiao and Wang Hongwen met with a militia leader from Shanghai, two other marshals conferred and then sent this message to Marshall Ye Jianying: "The Gang of Four are counterrevolutionaries capable of doing anything. We must be vigilant, not to allow them to make a move first." They warned that the Gang could conspire to assassinate Deng Xiaoping and detain Marshal Ye himself, and conclude that "we must take action before they do."[25]

A flurry of secretive discussions was underway, in which Marshal Ye was the central figure. Yang Jisheng documented a long list of illustrious names in the military and the party-state, who visited Ye's residence in the western suburbs of Beijing during this period. Critically, Ye secured the blessing of Chen Xilian, the military man in charge of the CMC, whose allegiance was murky at first.[26] He also talked to Li Xiannian and Chen Yun, two of the highest-ranking civilian leaders. General Wang Zhen brought Chen Yun over to Ye's residence.[27]

At the same time, with his power threatened by the Gang of Four, Hua Guofeng was working on the same idea. His deliberation took on a sense of urgency when he received intelligence on the Gang's possible conspiracy in preparation. According to one such report, Jiang Qing and Zhang Chunqiao secretly made detailed inquiries on the Central Guard Regiment – its forces, weapon, barracks, shifts, and so on. They also asked an officer to regularly report back on any development. Alarmed, Hua Guofeng went to see Wang Dongxing, who oversaw the regiment. An alliance with the military generals ensued, followed by a successful operation to arrest the Gang of Four.

In the afternoon of October 6, 1976, a Politburo meeting was convened in Zhongnanhai ostensibly for reviewing the galley of the fifth volume of Mao's *Selected Works* and the plan for Mao's memorial mausoleum. Hua Guofeng and Ye Jianying had arrived early, sitting before the screen and facing the entrance. Hidden behind this screen, however, was a squad of soldiers, led by Wang Dongxing, a leader overseeing the Central Guard Regiment and the longtime chief of Mao Zedong's bodyguard unit. It is speculated that Wang Dongxing's willing participation was due to fear of Jiang Qing's rise and possible revenge. For years as Mao's closest personal aide, his duties had included keeping the wife, Jiang, from seeing the husband, Mao, an unenviable task resented by Jiang. Elsewhere in Beijing at the same hour, army units under General Geng Biao followed orders from Hua and Ye and took over three key media headquarters: the Central Broadcast Station, Beijing Broadcast Station, and the Xinhua News Agency.[28]

At 7:55 p.m., Zhang Chunqiao was the first of the Gang of Four members to arrive. He was immediately approached by multiple guards and escorted forward to the main hall. There he could not find his usual seat, only to see two sofas occupied by the solemn-looking Hua Guofeng and Ye Jianying. Hua recited from a prepared statement, stating that Zhang had committed "unpardonable anti-party and anti-socialism crimes, in collusion with Jiang Qing, Wang Hongwen, and others." Zhang did not resist at all as he was taken away. In contrast, Wang Hongwen, the youngest of the Gang, vehemently resisted arrest. Apparently, as Hua read, Wang broke away from the guards and attempted to choke Ye Jianying. He was quickly subdued and taken away in handcuffs. Yao Wenyuan came last and was arrested quietly.

At 8:20 p.m., another squad of soldiers arrived at Jiang Qing's residence. Zhang Yaoci, commander of the Central Guard Regiment, recited from another prepared statement before taking Jiang away. He cited an "order from Premier Hua Guofeng" to detain her, for her "crime of dividing the Party Center."[29]

Less than two hours after the military operation, the Politburo held an emergency meeting at 10:00 p.m. Hua Guofeng chaired the meeting, while Marshall Ye Jianying played the central role. Ye informed the Politburo of what had happened earlier in the evening and proposed that Hua Guofeng be promoted to chairman of the Party and chairman of the Central Military Committee. The vote was unanimous.[30]

Deng Xiaoping received the news at his house. Although the Party Center did not announce the momentous news to the public until a week later, residents in Beijing, particularly those with high connections, quickly learned of it. He Ping, Deng's son-in-law, rushed home on his bike to report the news, according to the memoir of Deng's daughter:

> No sooner than he [He Ping] entered the house had he cried: Hurry up! Come on over! Seeing his excitement on his sweaty face, we in the family sensed that something big must have happened. In those years, we suspected that our house was bugged, so whenever there was important discussion, we adopted a method to beat the bugging. That day, all of us – father, Deng Lin, Deng Nan and me – walked into the bathroom, and then we turned on the shower. In the noise of the shower, we surrounded He Ping, who detailed how the Party Center smashed the Gang of Four.[31]

### Deng's Comeback

When Mao died on September 9, 1976, Hua Guofeng had been installed as the top leader for less than five months. A new "crown prince" in a shaky position, his grip on power would not last long. He did not fall victim to Jiang Qing and her Gang of Four colleagues thanks to his alliance with Deng's military allies, but he would eventually be unseated by this latter group of power holders.

#### *Debate on Mao's Legacy*

Hua Guofeng started with a mandate as the successor personally appointed by Mao. "When you are in charge, I am at ease," the late chairman reportedly had said in one of two handwritten notes. The trust was further conveyed by another alleged to exist: "Carry on according to the previous line." The value of this mandate cannot be exaggerated in a nation that had worshiped Mao for decades and, at the time, ten years into the Cultural Revolution, was ruled by loyalists to Mao's ultra-leftist side at every level. Unsurprisingly, Hua's guiding principle as the new leader was vowing to carry on Mao's legacy. He even articulated this ideology or strategy into a succinct expression of "Two Whatevers": "Whatever decisions made by Chairman Mao we will uphold; whatever instructions given by Chairman Mao we will follow."[32]

At the same time, however, his power base was thin – in the party, in the state, and more seriously so in the army. He was a novice – he did not join the Politburo until 1973 – and so pitiful compared with veterans such as Deng Xiaoping and Chen Yun who had entered the core of the party leadership many years before 1949. He owed his fortune to Mao's personal attention: in 1971 Mao had made a visit to his home province where Hua was the party chief.[33] Unlike Deng, who enjoyed deep personal as well as professional connections with many in the Party Center, Hua cut a lonely figure amid political titans.

Hua's policy of Two Whatevers was a thinly veiled attempt to prevent Deng's comeback. Abiding by whatever Mao had said would include Deng's dismissal following the April Tiananmen protest. Mindful of such a connection, Deng's allies pushed for a re-evaluation of the protest. The opening salvo was launched by none other than Chen Yun, who started his post-Mao career as one of the most effective advocates for Deng (although he became an archrival in later years). In a two-week work meeting of the Party Center in March 1977, Chen made a high-profile speech that directly challenged Hua. "My view on the Tiananmen incident is that most of the people were there to mourn Premier Zhou and to show their concern with who would succeed Premier Zhou. The bad elements mingled in the crowd were extremely few," said Chen, refuting the label "counterrevolutionary incident." In rejecting another Maoist assertion that Deng was the mastermind, Chen went on,

> Comrade Deng Xiaoping had nothing to do with the Tiananmen incident. For the sake of the revolution and the party, some comrades have suggested that Comrade Deng Xiaoping return to a leadership position in the Party Center. That is absolutely correct and thoroughly necessary. I support this idea wholeheartedly.[34]

Deng's allies also worked to bring the country out of its enchantment with Mao. One of Deng's key lieutenants, Hu Yaobang – whose death would trigger the student movement in 1989 – was the driving force behind this campaign. Having just returned to politics as a Cultural Revolution victim, he was in charge of one of the party's important ideological organs, the Central Party School. Directed by Hu, a flagship party newspaper started an ideological debate on the "standards of truth." If "truth" is to be evaluated by "practice," then what Mao had said might not be that sacred; it could be re-evaluated. No wonder Maoist leaders in Hua's camp openly criticized the article, and Hua himself counseled "keeping a distance from the Truth Standard Debate."[35] Also noteworthy was support from top military leaders such as marshals Ye Jianying, Nie Rongzhen, and Xu Xiangqian; all gave speeches to promote the article.[36]

*The Weight of Military Credentials*

That Deng would become a towering figure among his peers was no accident. Up to that point, Deng was the only leader in the CCP's history besides Mao to enjoy "access to factional networks in both the military and civilian systems."[37] He was an accomplished strategist of the revolutionary war with a superb battle record. Compared with Chen Yun, who was considered the party's number one authority on economic issues, Deng possessed more credentials in military affairs. On the other hand, compared with Marshal Ye Jianying, his kingmaker who led the mission to arrest the Gang of Four, Deng possessed more credentials in civilian affairs. During the revolution, Deng was the coleader of the Second Field Army and a key figure in the crucial Huai–Hai campaign of 1948.[38] Teiwes reports that, when military ranks were granted in 1955, Deng was not among the named marshals only because no "civilian" leader would hold the title.[39] Even Ye Jianying, the highest-ranking soldier at Mao's death, was reverential of Deng's military accomplishments. During a private meeting in around 1977, Deng respectfully addressed Ye as "Old Marshal," and Ye quickly replied, "you too are an old marshal, and you are the *leader* of the old marshals."[40]

When Deng was called back to Beijing from his political exile in 1974, the military were allocated to his portfolio, with titles including vice chair of the CMC and joint chief of the staff of the PLA. He wasted no time in waging a rectification campaign (*zhengdun*) within the military, appointing a new troupe of high-ranking officers. Deng's 1976 downfall disrupted his reorganization effort, but he picked it up again soon after he resumed the same military posts a year later.[41] His subsequent return to power, indeed his unseating of Hua Guofeng and ascent to the position of supreme leader, was marked by two paralleled lines of effort – to consolidate his grip over the military and to use this power as a way of influencing party politics. These two steps worked hand in hand perfectly.

Deng's deep roots in the military also helped him win over the "kingmaker" after Mao's death. Following the arrest of the Gang of Four, Marshall Ye Jianying reportedly sent his children for Deng "immediately." He personally debriefed Deng about the arrest.[42] As close as Ye was to Deng, however, then being the highest party leader among the military, Ye split his allegiance between Deng and Hua Guofeng. A loyalist of Mao throughout his life, it was not easy for him to go against Mao's will and unseat Hua. At least not right away. In a dramatic account, Ye had a private gathering celebrating his eightieth birthday on May 14, 1977, and invited most military leaders in Beijing but not Deng. When the party started, however, Deng made an unexpected entrance and sat next to Ye. He then proceeded to make himself the center of attention, and even took over as the master of ceremonies. Caught by surprise, Ye and his men had no choice but to play along with collegiality and mirth. Significantly, others in the party were impressed by Deng's self-assertiveness and believed that Deng and Ye "were in the same boat."[43]

There were other occasions in which Deng wrestled to control the military from the Ye–Hua alliance. For example, in the fall of 1977, Deng and Ye engaged in a dispute over the nomination of the PLA's chief of staff. Ye wanted Yang Chengwu, acting chief of staff at that time, and had support from important generals. But since this candidate did not belong to Deng's networks and had been active in repudiating Deng after Deng's 1976 downfall, Deng pushed for Yang Yong, the commander of the Xinjiang Regional Military Command. At the end both sides agreed on a third general nominated by an important Deng ally, Li Xiannian. Yang Dezhi, the eventual appointee, had been an officer under Deng's command during the Anti-Japanese War.[44] A few other key posts also went Deng's way. He nominated Luo Ruiqing as the CMC's secretary general in charge of daily military affairs, and appointed Wei Guoqing as director of the Political Department, Hong Xuezhi as director of the Logistic Department, and Zhang Zhen as the head of training of high-ranking officers. As a result, Ye Jianying became virtually a figurehead in the CMC.[45]

Once Deng had secured control over the PLA's headquarters in late 1977, he resumed his disrupted 1976 rectification campaign. In a speech given during a CMC conference, he pointed out that the goal was to "solve leadership problems" at each level of the PLA. He demanded that every officer be evaluated for their behavior during the Cultural Revolution. He further accused many of "engaging in factional activities" and subjected them to expulsion from the military. Conveniently, though, as Jing Huang has pointed out, most of them did not belong to Deng's own "mountaintop."[46] Those newly appointed – such as Yang Yong, Luo Ruiqing, and Wei Guoqing – became Deng's point men; they rearranged all the positions of commanders and commissars at the army level and above. In some key regional military commands (RMCs), such rearrangements occurred even down at the division level.[47]

### Unseating Hua Guofeng

Nominally, Hua Guofeng, chairman of the party and premier of the state, was still the CMC chair. But this institutional title would give him little authority over the military, as he quickly learned. Sensing his diminishing power within this branch of government, he planned a ceremony in hopes of strengthening his image as the commander in chief. On April 12, 1978, he instructed the navy to prepare an inspection that he would conduct himself after a scheduled visit to North Korea in May. For this, he would make a stop in Dalian, home base of the North Sea Fleet. Initially, Hua's request appeared to have been followed by Su Zhenghua, the Navy commissar. However, the navy commander and chief of staff suggested that such a plan had to be formally approved by the CMC. So when word reached the CMC, Luo Ruiqing, one of Deng's newly appointed point men, ordered an immediate suspension of all activities and notified Deng, who in turn gave instruction to cancel the inspection ceremony. Perhaps more noteworthy, Deng did so without consulting Hua Guofeng or Ye Jianying, who – at this point in time – stood organizationally *above* him both in the party's Central Committee and in the CMC. Understandably upset, Hua Guofeng refused to answer the phone when Luo Ruiqing called to inform him of Deng's decision and its result.[48]

As this humiliating snub was unfolding, Hu Yaobang, Deng's point man in charge of propaganda and ideology, organized the publication of what would soon be a well-known article in the *Guangming Daily* entitled "Practice Is the Only Standard of Truth," within the same week. The party's propaganda department under Hua then started a campaign to push back. Here, Hua specifically ordered other official media outlets not to "engage in the debate,"[49] but Deng went against Hua and mobilized supporters to push forward, with the aim of dismantling Maoist restrictions on his end.[50]

Here again, the military advantage came into play. Deng called up Luo Ruiqing, the CMC's chief of the staff, and scheduled a speech at the All-Amy Conference on Political Work. In the speech, Deng argued that the essence Mao Zedong thought was the principle of "seeking truth from facts," which means that even remarks by Mao could be refuted by facts. While the party's propaganda department continued to refuse to print such articles, Yang Yong, another of Deng's point men in the military, instructed Chi Haotian, the director of PLA headquarters' political department, to organize an all-army campaign to further examine the *Guangming Daily* article. Subsequently, Luo Ruiqing personally instructed the *Liberation Amy News* to publish a new article, "A Most Basic Principle of Marxism," in support of the truth standard thesis. Finally, Deng summoned the party's propaganda boss, a Hua supporter, and bluntly told him to stop suppressing the debate.[51]

Deng's gain in party-state politics was cemented by the Third Plenum of the 11th Party Congress in December 1978 and a subsequent Politburo meeting. As a result, among the SC members, only Wang Dongxing was an ally of Hua Guofeng. The other four members were Deng Xiaoping and those who followed him, comprising Chen Yun, Ye Jianying, and Li Xiannian. Deng's advantage over Hua was also staggering in the Politburo: twenty out of twenty-six. The situation for Hua Guofeng worsened around the New Year of 1979. In a "meeting of democratic life," Chen Yun, a new SC member, led a frontal assault on Wang Dongxing, Wu De, Ji Dengkui, and Chen Xilian – the four remaining Politburo members who supported Hua Guofeng. The four submitted their resignation after the meeting and Hua turned in his own after a year.[52]

After Hua stepped down, Deng did not follow Mao or Hua to become the head of all three major institutions. He started what was known as the "Deng–Hu–Zhao system," with Hu Yaobang as the party head (general secretary), Zhao Ziyang as the premier, and Deng as the CMC chair. It was 1980, and Deng was already seventy-eight years old. Clearly, Hu Yaobang, or possibly Zhao Ziyang, would become the core leader to succeed him. The following year, Deng proposed the "termination of life tenure" and asked anyone who was older than seventy years to step down. The Central Advisory Committee (CAC) was created to house the seniors, chaired by Chen Yun, a central figure whose prestige was second only to Deng's.

## Twin-Summit Politics

Deng's way of exercising power was deliberately different from that of Mao. Mao placed himself above others, tolerated no dissent, and sent his dissenters – real or imagined – to exile, jail, or death. In contrast, Deng surrounded himself with his revolutionary peers, even when they became his detractors later on. Situated at the top of post-Mao politics, he was hardly alone. Yang Jisheng, a journalist, historian, and leading expert on the subject, used the label "twin summits" to explain this phenomenon:

> Deng Xiaoping and Chen Yun were inseparable and equally strong. They checked each other's power, with neither having the upper hand. No major decision could be made without the consent of both. Therefore, the political landscape in the reform era took the shape of twin summits, although the summit of Deng was slighter higher, as he was the de facto first chair.[53]

### Deng's Chief Policy Rival, Chen Yun

Born in 1905, and only a year younger than Deng, Chen was one of the most senior revolutionary leaders of the party. He was elected into the Politburo as early as 1931, at the age of twenty-six. During the Long March, he was sent to the Soviet Union to relay information about the Chinese revolution to Stalin. Upon his return, he was selected to be in charge of the party's organizational department, a crucial position that identified and appointed party officials. He was credited, along with other leaders such as Liu Shaoqi and Deng Xiaoping, with having been instrumental in elevating Mao to the status of a semi-god-like leader in the Yanan political campaigns of 1942. By 1949, the new republic's leadership ranking placed him as the fifth, two positions higher than Deng.[54]

For his supporters, Chen was a humane, urbane, and kind intellectual. He was known to resent the harsh methods of internal struggle favored by Mao.

This is perhaps partly because he himself was repeatedly sidelined and persecuted.[55] Chen also did not harbor any ambition to become a supreme leader himself. Unlike Mao and Deng, who served as commanders during wartime, his portfolio included duties that were mainly civilian in nature. After 1949, he was considered the country's economic tsar by Mao and the party. Mao repeatedly relied on him to rescue the country from financial ruin caused by Mao's own disastrous policies. Mao was quoted as praising Chen's essential role in these matters: "A superb general is missed when the country is in danger; a wise wife is needed when the family finance is dire."[56] During the Deng years, Chen positioned himself not as a rival who wanted the position of leadership, but as a colleague who could debate with him on equal grounds.

Chen was known to be the champion and theorist of two economic ideas – flexible rural ownership and certain elements of the market. This made Chen a de facto dissident of Mao's more hardline socialist economic policies. In his speech at the 1956 party congress, Chen refrained from praising the so-called socialist transformation championed by Mao, as he believed that agricultural collectivization had undermined small-scale "household manufacturing" and the marketing of subsidiary products, thus hurting peasant income.[57] In a report on village production of 1961, which was completed in the wake of the disastrous Great Leap Forward and the three-year famine, Chen praised private plots and encouraged the raising of pigs by individual families.[58] It is a testimonial to the validity of these ideas and to his political skills that Mao did not purge him outright in their long-standing debates.

Chen's experience made him a natural ally of Deng in the initial few years following 1976. The two extended their political alliance to full co-operation during the first economic reform. This reform, known as the household responsibility system, was experimented with in Sichuan and Anhui by Zhao Ziyang, the future general secretary, and Wan Li, the future head of the National Congress. It was subsequently made a national policy by the Party Center in the early 1980s. The main components of the new policy included liberating farmers from the rigid collective type of ownership and injecting mechanisms of the market into China's socialist economy.

Unlike Deng, however, Chen was an orthodox believer in socialism despite his dissent from Mao's radical policies. For him, there was no contradiction. He saw public ownership, the command economy, and central planning as defining features and unmovable principles. In contrast, flexible ownership and market commodities were merely supplementary, not the main, features of a socialist economy. It was this "conservative" side of Chen Yun that would become an ideological juxtaposition to Deng's daring embrace of market elements. Should they be expanded or eliminated? The two "summits" emerged out of this core philosophical difference, from which a host of political issues were to arise: for example, whether the special economic zones – with an economy consisting mainly of foreign investment firms – were outside the permissible scope of socialism. In the end, the polity became divided into two discernible opposing camps, often colloquially referred to as "reformers" – the Deng group, and "conservatives" – the Chen group.[59]

### Deng's Heirs and Counter-Heirs

As the new supreme leader, Deng practiced a leadership style that emphasized consultation and consensus building.[60] The buzzword of this time period was "collective leadership." While it hardly changed the fact that Deng was the final arbiter of all decisions, the effort had its significance. Some specific measures were taken to increase the level of institutionalization of governing. Couching the so-called "second line" of leadership, the old leaders of Deng's generation were asked to retire into the Central Advisory Committee (CAC), headed by Chen Yun. At the "first line," daily operation was driven by people in their late fifties or early sixties. Among them were the top leaders: in 1986, the general party secretary was Hu Yaobang, the premier was Zhao Ziyang, and the permanent secretary and vice chair of the CMC was Yang Shangkun (who was much older than other first-line leaders). The highest decision-making organ was the Standing Committee (SC) of the Politburo, consisted of five or so first-line leaders.

The political forces of the reformers versus the conservatives were evenly balanced. At the second-line level, Deng was the lone reformer among his peers. The other seven of the "eight elders" were ideologically aligned with Chen Yun, in their insistence on keeping socialist features as the core character of the national economy. This was a strong coalition, and they were ready to block Deng on personnel appointments or new initiatives. In comparison, the first-line leadership in the Standing Committee was equalized by individuals appointed by Deng, including Hu Yaobang and Zhao Ziyang and people belonging to Chen Yun's camp, including Li Peng and Yao Yilin.

Premier Li Peng, son of a martyr, was raised by late Premier Zhou Enlai and his wife Deng Yingchao, two of the most respected leaders of the older generation within the party. Li was reportedly a mediocre bureaucrat but rose to the top thanks to wide support among the old revolutionaries. He was promoted to premier after Zhao Ziyang vacated the position to become general secretary. Yao Yilin was a longtime protégé of Chen Yun and another firm believer in the command economy. In the state council, he would work with Li Peng to undermine Zhao Ziyang on economic issues. Later on, he voted with Li to impose martial law in Beijing in May 1989.

The conservatives' power was also reinforced by three other members of the Politburo. First, Deng Liqun, an essayist and ideologue, who earlier played an instrumental role in helping Deng defeat the Gang of Four and Hua Guofeng.

Considered by the Chen Yun camp as a candidate who could compete against Hu Yaobang for the position of general secretary, Deng Liqun would ferociously attack Hu and Zhao Ziyang (and obliquely Deng Xiaoping). The other two are Chen Xitong and Li Ximing, the mayor and the party secretary of Beijing City respectively. As the capital's executives, they would prove to be enormously serviceable to the conservative camp once the 1989 Tiananmen protest began.

Yet, as powerful as he was, Chen Yun never seemed to harbor an ambition to replace Deng. Nor did it seem possible given Deng's full grip over the army. So, with his upper hand, Deng played along magnanimously. He governed, maneuvering in the face of resistance and criticism, and leveraged his advantages. First among his effective tools was his command of the military. Deng still kept the CMC chair for himself, having replaced and reappointed many generals, and enjoyed the impeccable loyalty of Yang Shangkun, his chief executive in the CMC. This foundation of command was rock solid and deceptively inconspicuous. It did not need any public display or reinforcement, and everyone with a basic understanding of power dynamics recognized its existence and weight – Chen Yun being no fool. Second, Deng put his men to handle ideological debates and propaganda (similar to mass media outlets in Western democracies). As I will elaborate further below, Deng's hold on this front did seem at times to be less stable, partly because his own reformer allies would sometimes deviate from his doctrine. Nevertheless, Deng largely had effective control, and he always won the publicity fight over his proposed policies. With military and ideological fronts paving the way, Deng's reformist agenda had its run and yielded captivating results.

Alas, while Deng enjoyed many great successes in governing, his plan for the seemingly imminent power transition loomed as a great question mark. While there were multifaceted factors, the root of the problem was, in large part, the twin-summit politics. Both sides had a high stake in the game, and the conservatives were working fiercely to undermine potential successors favored by Deng. But this is a story to be told in the next chapter.

## Discussion and Conclusion

In this chapter and the following one, we explore what institutional and historical factors elevated Deng and how the same factors limited his capacity to operate. The discussion will pave the way for a better understanding of his options and the decisions he made later in 1989. I argue that the manner in which Deng acquired his power made it necessary for him to share power with others. To his credit, he was very willing to share. One of these groups was his former comrades-in-arms, led by Chen Yun, who in turn became his policy critics. Leading up to the 1989 upheaval, this "twin-summit politics" setup functioned as one of the two pillars of the regime's factional configuration. This state of affairs was rooted in the communist state as a political institution and was shaped by the historical events that propelled Deng to the top.

### Deng's Claim to Rule and Its Constraining Consequences

Deng's commitment to collective leadership was an outcome of the history of his rise. He stood out among his peers because of his extraordinary qualities and a unique set of credentials: he was tenacious; he had been in charge of the party, the state, and the military; he had a revolutionary war record second to few and enjoyed a strong following in the military; he was once cultivated by Mao as a successor; and so on. Among all these factors, his intimate connections with military leaders played a critical role. At critical junctures during Deng's last rise to the top, it was his friends in the military who arrested the Gang of Four after Mao's death, and later supported him to topple Mao's successor Hua Guofeng.

Yet it is one thing to capture power, another to justify its legitimacy in the long run. To emphasize his credentials or showcase military control was not sufficient to settle his claim as the new leader. Adding to his vulnerability was that he was a usurper who unseated Mao's designated successor. So Deng set to work on amassing additional political assets, in alliance and in legitimacy.

First, he masterfully turned his departure from Mao into a political asset. Echoing Khrushchev's secret speech against Stalin to start his new era, Deng put his foot down and fortified it by starting campaigns against Mao's violent legacy. He repudiated Mao's past political campaigns, rehabilitated victims, and reinstated them into leadership positions. What went wrong under Mao? Deng pointed to Mao's "mistake in his old age" and a system of personal dictatorship. He vowed to "restore" "collective leadership," and end leaders' lifetime tenure. In doing so, he made alliance with the old revolutionaries, including Chen Yun, and the next generation leaders like Hu Yaobang and Zhao Ziyang, who would serve as his point men of reform.

In short, Deng built his rule not on the notion that he was Mao's heir, but on the notion that he was undoing the Maoist system of personal rule and lifetime tenure. As the supreme leader, Deng governed, to a large extent, to deliver these promises.

### Deng the Personal Ruler versus Deng the Promoter of Collective Leadership

"Collective leadership" is supposedly an antidote to the personal monopoly of power or "cult of personality." As a political weapon, it serves as a critique against diseased dictators such as Stalin and Mao. As an ideal, it gives living authoritarian leaders a blueprint for what the system should become after their death. It made its imprint in the politics in post-dictator eras such as those under Khrushchev and Deng. Within this framework, a would-be supreme leader is willing to improve institutional arrangements and to share power with others. Most decisions are made by a voting committee of oligarchs, such as a Politburo, Presidium, or Standing Committee.

Myron Rush suggested that the political system of the USSR existed as a mix of dictatorship and "collective leadership," or, in his terms, between personal rule and oligarchy. The system swung between these two extremes, forming a cyclic pattern. Before 1953, under Lenin and Stalin, personal rule dominated. The portion of oligarchy increased after Stalin, along with the campaign against the "personality cult" launched by Khrushchev and continued later by Brezhnev.[61] This history was mirrored by the leadership transition from Mao to Deng and then from Deng to his successors.

In the meantime, Deng was unquestionably a supreme leader. He enjoyed outsized power at the top, and was the final arbitrator of all political disputes. His power base unprecedentedly reached deep into all three major institutions – the military, the party, and the state.

### Twin-Summit Politics and Three-Way Contention

Deng enjoyed strong backing from many leaders of his own generation who acted as "king-makers" would, especially in the fight against their common rivals in the Maoist camp. But starting in the mid-1980s, many such allies turned into his policy critics. Struggling to keep pace with the boldness of Deng's economic reform, they considered that many new measures deviated from socialist principles. Unlike Stalin or Mao before him, however, Deng did not use political purges to respond; on the contrary, he practiced "collective leadership." He and Chen formed "twin summits" at the top, leading two factions of younger leaders in the "first line." A vertical divide cut through.

True to his commitment to end lifetime tenure, Deng joined other elderly leaders and retreated into semiretirement, holding only advisory positions. Conceivably, one of the younger leaders would succeed Deng as the future supreme leader. Yet, in an age-old dilemma known as crown prince problem, Deng's relationship with his heirs would encounter trouble again and again. Herein lay another division, between Deng the supreme leader and his would-be successors. That will be the topic of next chapter.

Together, the vertical and horizontal divisions produced a three-way contention between Deng, his reformer heirs, and his conservative rivals, or counter-heirs.

# 3    The Fate of Two Successors
## 1980–April 15, 1989

In January 1987, two years before his death would trigger the 1989 Tiananmen protest, General Secretary Hu Yaobang was dismissed from his post. At Deng Xiaoping's behest, a so-called "party life meeting" was convened and it lasted five days. A slate of speakers was prearranged to accuse Hu of political mistakes, including Deng Liqun, an ideologue from the conservative faction. The meeting ended with Hu's self-criticism.[1] When the meeting concluded on January 15, Hu was seen sitting on the steps of Huairentang Hall, crying.[2]

In Chapter 2, I described how Deng worked with policy rivals and in essence formed a leadership structure known as "twin-summit politics." In this chapter, I move on to describe another key dimension of the party-state leadership – his relationship with his frontline lieutenants. As noted previously, the Deng era started in 1980 in the form of a "Deng–Hu–Zhao" administration, with Hu Yaobang heading the party and Zhao Ziyang heading the government. Hu and Zhao were the point men for Deng's reform efforts and arguably his potential successors.[3] Alas, neither of them lasted: Deng disposed of Hu Yaobang abruptly in 1987 and removed Zhao Ziyang during the 1989 movement.

Conventional explanations for the breakups often point to the seeming ideological divergence between Deng and his heirs. It is commonly believed that Deng was more conservative than his potential successors, and indeed much evidence exists for this point.

However, there is no solid empirical evidence for this commonly held view. It is hard to imagine that a politician would choose political conviction over the imperative to maintain power. In other words, Deng's disciples, like Hu and Zhao, are more likely to have striven to align with Deng ideologically. The appearance of their ideological divergence may at times reflect disconnect or a lack of co-ordination. As frontline operators of Deng's reform, Hu and Zhao often had to initiate bold measures and chart new territories. In fact, they did not rise to the top by following; rather, they often pioneered new policies that Deng would later adopt as his own.

So what doomed Deng's successors? It is the "crown prince problem," a well-documented dilemma that has plagued autocrats everywhere in human history. If a ruler commits early and raises a strong heir, his own power might be threatened; if a ruler chooses too late, the heir might not be strong enough to fend off challengers. According to theorists, this inherent element of any ruler–heir relationship makes trust difficult to maintain.[4]

The problem becomes more serious within the communist system, as it does not officially admit the existence of any autocrat, let alone set up any rules for power succession. Past communist dictators, such as Stalin and Mao, often chose a candidate but at the same time put him in check by installing one or more "counter-heirs." The ruling body hence often took the shape of a "triad."[5] Under those dictators, none of the heirs survived the ensuing power struggles; many of them even lost their lives.[6] Deng himself once suffered the fate of such a potential heir under Mao, as recounted earlier in this book. And now the table was turned. His subsequent relationship with Hu Yaobang and Zhao Ziyang would follow a similar script.

This brings us back to twin-summit politics. That is, Deng was concurrently managing two fronts: in the fight with his conservative rivals led by Chen Yun he relied on his reformist lieutenants (Hu Yaobang and Zhao Ziyang), but in clashes with his own reformist lieutenants he used the very same conservative rivals led by Chen Yun. Within this picture of three-way contention, Deng's trust took on a new perspective. His trust in Hu Yaobang or Zhao Ziyang no longer rested purely on his personal assessment but became a function of the political pressure mounted by his conservative rivals. By extension, it was also a function of the heirs' ability or inability to fight back against antireform challenges.

Taken together, in this chapter and the previous one I present a political landscape marked by two major divisions – the reformer–conservative split and the ruler–heir conflict. This picture will prove useful for understanding the 1989 events to be presented in later chapters.

### Deng's Retirement in Progress

*A Prelude under Mao*

Moving to the "second line" was the first step of the retirement for Deng and other elders, leaving the party-state's daily operation to the "first line" of younger leaders. Such an arrangement, according to Wilson and Ji, originated as early as the 1950s, in part due to Mao's concern over the succession issue. The idea was brought into practice in 1962 after a party meeting that questioned Mao's leadership throughout the Great Leap Forward (which resulted in a large-scale three-year man-made famine). Mao, voluntarily or otherwise, yielded the power of daily governing to others, with the top leadership divided into the first-line leaders in charge of day-to-day operations of the party-state and the second-line, older leaders supposedly involved in broader issues of strategy and policy. Mao was a second-line leader, and Liu Shaoqi was a first-line one joined by Deng Xiaoping as his second in command. Five years younger than Mao, Liu was at the time also considered Mao's chosen successor.[7]

That experiment did not end well. Four years later, in 1966, Mao launched the Cultural Revolution and banished Liu and Deng. Initially during that spring, Liu and Deng actively promoted Mao's campaign as they understood it and attempted to manage the situation. For a while Mao deliberately stayed away from Beijing. When he was ready to attack, he abruptly returned to the capital from Wuhan. In his "My First Big-Character Poster: Bombard the Headquarters," he declared that the first-line leaders had done it all wrong. He proceeded to purge Liu and Deng as the number one and number two "capitalist roaders inside the party." Both were stripped of their job and expelled from Beijing. Liu died a solitary death in Kaifeng, Henan in 1969. Deng was sent to Jiangxi to perform physical labor.[8]

A snub by Mao of Liu Shaoqi was a detail worth recording here for its future resonance in 1989. On the evening of July 18, 1966, Mao had just returned to Beijing and settled in his residence in the Diaoyutai compound. Liu Shaoqi nervously hurried over from Zhongnanhai and requested an interview. He waited in vain in the anteroom for hours, only to be told by a secretary that Mao "needed rest" after the journey. Liu left without seeing Mao. "It was an act of extraordinarily contemptuous discourtesy to his most senior colleague," observed McFarquhar and Schoenhals. Earlier in the day, Mao had chosen to be briefed by Kang Sheng and Chen Boda, both Liu's detractors.[9] A similar moment would play out on May 17, 1989, as Zhao Ziyang asked for a one-on-one meeting with Deng and was similarly denied, and Zhao lost his job as the party's general secretary that evening.[10]

What is the nature of the relationship between an elder leader and his possible successor, or between a second-line leader and his first-line point man? Liu Shaoqi's rise and his eventual fall illustrate a pattern with a few key features. First, the first-line point man serves at the pleasure of the second-line supreme leader. The former might have great success in cultivating his own power base, but his claims to legitimacy continue to rest on the approval of the latter. Second, as the first-line point man's influence and power base grow, the supreme leader begins to feel uneasy and such uneasiness in turn sows a host of doubts. Making matters worse, in the eye of the supreme leader, inevitably the first-line point man increasingly deviates from the supreme leader's "correct" political ideology. Third, the first-line point man is pitted against political opponents who not only still occupy prominent positions, but also are at times emboldened by the supreme leader. Ultimately, the first-line point man will be double-crossed. Fourth, the potential heir has the tendency to overestimate the trust granted him by the supreme leader. Often, he has good reasons to believe in that trust since he is implicitly or explicitly declared and viewed as the chosen successor, accompanied by the supreme leader's frequent generous private assurances before the supreme leader decides to change his mind.

### Anointing Hu Yaobang

Throughout the history of communist China, Deng was perhaps the only person who lived on both sides of such a relationship. As part of a first-line leadership along with Liu Shaoqi (who was Mao's potential successor), he was purged in the early days of the Cultural Revolution. Next, Deng was recalled by Mao and groomed to be a successor himself, only to be disgraced again.

After Mao's death, Deng moved to the other side of the relationship, when he became the elderly supreme leader himself. He seemed to be deeply aware of this history and took many measures to avoid repeating it. He did his best to reject the personality cult, consulted his peers, retained no formal position in the party or the government (but for the CMC chairmanship), allowed the "twin-summit" politics, moved to end life tenure, instituted term limits, and so on.[11] His intention and his efforts produced many positive changes in China's politics.[12] Nevertheless, in the end, under his leadership, China failed to escape the same succession trap that had bewitched Mao and many other supreme leaders.

After his decisive political victories over Hua Guofeng, in February of 1981 he introduced a brand new team of leaders. Hu Yaobang's elevation was perhaps meant to be about anointing a potential successor. Vogel's narrative of this period emphasizes the meaning of "chief executive," as he calls the new leadership a "Deng administration" and its inception an "inauguration."[13] Also included in the new team were Zhao Ziyang and Wan Li, two capable reformers from Deng's point of view. They had been battle-tested in pushing forward Deng's reform agenda. Zhao would soon become the new premier in charge of economic matters, and Wan a vice premier in charge of the ongoing rural reform. They could hence potentially become candidates too. But it was lost on no one that the party boss was the default choice. This implication would increasingly bear on the mind of political players during Hu Yaobang's tenure. It would come to a head in the year of 1986, leading to Hu's dismissal in January 1987.

That Deng chose Hu Yaobang in 1981 was no surprise; there was much in the younger man for the supreme leader to like. They even shared some superficial similarities. Both were bright men of short stature; both were from China's southern region; both belonged to the Hakka sub-ethnic group, known for its distinct dialect, its emphasis on education, and its rebellious spirit; and both joined the revolution at a very young age.[14] Perhaps the most substantive similarity that would bond the two was that both were victims of Maoist purges or purges by Mao himself. Joining the Red Army as a fourteen-year-old country boy, Hu was renowned for his ability to conduct propaganda work among his Hakka people, using his native dialect, in the CCP's early guerrilla base in southern China. Once, due to factional infighting, at age sixteen, he was accused of being a member of an "anti-party" group known as the AB Clique and almost executed. He was spared only by a last-minute reprieve.[15] He would become a victim again in later campaigns, especially during the Cultural Revolution.[16] Also, Hu bonded with Deng as early as 1937 in Yanan. In 1949, he was appointed the commissar of the 18th Regiment, which would later become part of the 2nd Field Army, the unit led by Deng. After the Liberation War, Hu was assigned to become a civilian official in Sichuan, Deng's home province, under the Southwestern Region Administration, which was then headed by Deng. In 1952, at Deng's suggestion, Hu was called to Beijing to become the first secretary of the Communist Youth League.[17]

As early as 1974, Deng wasted no time calling Hu Yaobang back from political exile. But they would both fall again in 1976, only to re-emerge after Mao's death in the same year. Upon hearing the news of the Gang of Four's arrest, Hu sought out the son of Marshal Ye Jianying and passed the marshal a note that read, "Stop repudiating Deng – Rejoice! Reinstate the wrongful cases – Rejoice! Focus on economic development – Rejoice!"[18] These words suggest that Deng and Hu's ideological commitments were all but identical in the early post-Mao years.

After the Cultural Revolution, Hu built his image as a capable hand and a reformer. He was first appointed the executive vice president of the Central Party School. In that capacity, he was put in charge of waging major theoretical debates, including the historical op-ed "Practice Is the Only Standard of Truth" (for its significance, see the last chapter). This propaganda campaign brought the end of Mao's personality cult and paved the way for the nation to open up. He was then appointed the Central Committee's director of the Organizational Department, responsible for reinstating wrongfully accused cadres.

According to Yang Jisheng, in Tianjin City alone, during the Cultural Revolution, 38,000 individuals were dismissed from their job and sent to the countryside. Among those liberated were Chen Yun, Peng Zhen, and many other top-rank officials. In a speech in 1977, Hu characterized the situation nationwide: "wrongful cases pile up like mountains."

This campaign of reinstatement reached a high note on November 15, 1978, with the issuance of a new verdict on the "Tiananmen incident" of 1976. The Party Center announced that the popular protest was "a revolutionary act, whose purpose was to mourn Premier Zhou and to denounce the Gang of Four." Consequently, nationwide all of the individuals previously charged were ultimately exonerated and vindicated. Indeed, many were even hailed as heroes.[19] In an extraordinary historical twist, the newly proclaimed heroes included Wang Juntao and Chen Ziming, two young men who were arrested in the square in April 1976. They would later become prominent leaders of the 1989 movement whom we shall encounter again in Chapter 7.[20]

A decent soul who often spoke passionately and vehemently, Hu Yaobang was a high official beloved by past political victims, progressive intellectuals, and energetic students. In repudiating past injustices, many of these intellectuals went as far as criticizing the party itself. While this might have been tolerated or even accepted by Hu as the party general secretary, old guards like Chen Yun and Wang Zhen would be extremely furious. His politics often alarmed the old revolutionaries, including Deng at the end. And political rivals within his own generation, such as the ideologue Deng Liqun, were waiting for an opportunity to attack and unseat him.[21]

**The Problem of Trust: The Deng–Hu Edition**

Resistance and opposition were expected. In fact, politicians like Hu Yaobang relished challenges and even thrived in a combative environment. Victories must be particularly satisfying, when battles were waged on behalf of Deng, a fellow reformer and the superior. Among his relished victories were his effort to reinstate the previously victimized officials, defeating the Two Whatevers, and pushing forward the rural reform that instituted the household responsibility system.

*Possible Divergence of Political Views*

Over time, however, some discernible divergence emerged between Hu and Deng. A thorny issue was how much freedom could be allowed intellectuals, artists, and writers. By then, the party had openly admitted mistakes of the past, but Deng seemed reluctant to embrace unlimited criticism of all sorts. Could the venting amount to an attack on the system? Where would one draw the line?[22]

Another case in point was how to handle popular protest. In the past, any popular protest would automatically be treated as an anti-party crime. Following the reversal of the verdict on the 1976 Tiananmen incident, however, a public forum known as Democracy Wall in Beijing was permitted to exist for a year. Tolerance seemed to be in the air in the new political climate. Emboldened, activists added democracy and human rights to the list of demands. An electrician named Wei Jingsheng hailed democracy as the "fifth modernization." Here again, on this issue, Hu's stewardship was on the liberal side.[23]

Deng's stance, taken as whole and especially understood in hindsight, however, was conservative in nature. Often he would not intervene until a debate had gone on for a while, but when he did join the conversation, he would normally be on the opposite side from Hu. Looking at their interactions retroactively, one wonders: did Hu deliberately disobey his boss? And if yes, how could he have kept his job for so long?

It is easy to simply attribute the Deng–Hu divergence (later the Deng–Zhao divergence) to ideological disagreements. That is, Hu's beliefs gradually evolved into a liberal-democratic kind, while Deng remained a steadfast Leninist.[24] Yet this analysis fails to explain why Hu, as a politician, would risk "job security" for the sake of ideology. Do politicians normally hide or bend their opinions in order to survive political challenges? Perhaps more importantly, underlying this ideology-centered analysis is a problematic assumption that Deng's position was clear and consistent.

### Sometimes Deng's View Was Difficult to Discern

"In every even year, liberalism runs amok," the party ideologue Deng Liqun once memorably remarked, "then in the odd year, the left counterattacks."[25] Historian Yang Jisheng echoed this observation and documented a cyclical pattern between 1976 and 1989. Actual data fit the commentary remarkably well. For example, a liberal wind blew in the even year of 1978, as the country witnessed the debate of truth standards, the defeat of the Two Whatevers, the reversed verdict on the 1976 Tiananmen incident, and the appearance of the Democracy Wall. Then, in the odd year of 1979, the political climate was tightened, as Deng articulated the so-called "Four Cardinal Principles," the Democracy Wall was shut down, and activist Wei Jingsheng was arrested. The years from 1986 to 1987 provide a similar outlook. In 1986, Deng gave a series of speeches that officially promoted "political reform." Liberal intellectuals were consequentially encouraged and staged echoing forums. In December, university students took to the street and called for democratic changes. Then, in 1987, Hu Yaobang was dismissed, followed by many liberal intellectuals punished and stripped of their party membership.[26]

This cyclical pattern explains how evenly matched the two sides were. But it also shows how difficult it was to read Deng's mind, even for an insider like Hu. Deng's stance at times as a Leninist conservative became clear only in retrospect. To be sure, he stated his conservative philosophy as early as 1979 in his famous "Upholding Four Cardinal Principles" speech. He seemed unequivocal on the mantra "Socialism, the dictatorship by the proletariat class, the leadership of the Communist Party, and Marxism, Leninism and Mao Zedong Thought."[27] Yet didn't he also argue for "reform and opening up" as an equally important pillar? He himself would put the Four Cardinal Principles and "reform and opening up" together and call them "Two Fundamental Points."[28]

Moreover, the Two Fundamental Points presented no more than abstract labels. They offered little guidance to judge whether something specific, such as an event, a piece of art, a movie script, or an individual, was "anti-party," or "anti-socialism." This is a well-known process called *dingxing* – making a politically charged label. Which also means there was always room to contest the *dingxing* for a particular event, a particular movie script, or a particular person.

Take an early 1979 forum as an example. Aiming to push forward new ideas and a new agenda, Hu Yaobang and his allies convened a multiday conference entitled the Meeting without Concrete Agenda on Theoretical Work. In the party's parlance, "theoretical" means ideological. Hu encouraged the participants to "do away with any taboo, smash any mental shackle, and fully extend democracy in the theoretical debate."[29] They did. In fact, their speeches heeded Hu's encouragement so well that two conservative ideologues, Deng Liqun and Hu Qiaomu, made reports to Deng Xiaoping to complain. Deng Xiaoping swung toward the conservatives and asked Hu Qiaomu to write the famous "Upholding Four Cardinal Principles" speech for him. Two days after Deng's speech, the conference was aptly adjourned.[30] Here, it is not clear whether Hu crossed Deng by initiating such a meeting in the first place, or by allowing the meeting to go too far.

Deng Xiaoping's Four Cardinal Principles speech also effectively resolved another controversy. Shortly afterwards, the Democracy Wall was shut down and activists were arrested. But here again, Deng's attitude was difficult to anticipate. A reasonable argument can be made that some public forum could exist without violating the Four Principles. After all, the wall emerged in the wake of rehabilitating the 1976 Tiananmen protest. And Deng permitted its existence for more than a year.[31]

Notably, in the same speech Deng Xiaoping further articulated his objection to popular protest in general. He cited a wave of social protests as a phenomenon of "stirring up turmoil." "Raising demands of one type or another that are unreasonable or unresolvable, [the bad elements] instigated or misled some in the masses. They raided government agencies, occupied offices, conducted sit-ins, and blocked traffic," he recounted. "[T]here was this so-called Chinese Human Rights group. It even put up a big-character poster calling for the American president to 'care for' China's human rights."[32]

It was within such an institutional dynamic that Hu Yaobang operated as a politician. On the one hand, he had great success in pushing forward his liberal agenda, and his boldness helped him become a political star and reach the top. On many issues, he was able to bring Deng onto his side.

On the other hand, there was a delicate balance to strike. The deciding factor was the trust and confidence in him that Deng could afford and was willing to give. More often than not, Hu's clashes with Deng on critical issues such as popular protest were likely to work in favor of his rivals.

## The Fall of Hu Yaobang

*In the Wolf's Den*

From day one of his tenure, General Secretary Hu was in the thick of the "twin-summit politics." Waiting and watching were Chen Yun and his older peers in the second line and his point men in the first line. These detractors included Deng Liqun and Hu Qiaomu, who were members of the secretariat in charge of ideological and propaganda matters. They were often tasked with writing speeches for Chen Yun and Deng Xiaoping, so they enjoyed direct access to the older men's ear. As such, they were among the most formidable critics and able to command a network of opposition backed by Chen Yun and commonly known as the conservative faction. They sometimes sent critical reports to the second-line leaders; if the criticism secured the elders' support, they would then draft memoranda for wide circulation. Hu Yaobang's power was limited and his position precarious.[33]

Less than a year into his job, an "editorial controversy" threatened to tarnish his reputation. On March 10, 1981, the *People's Daily* published an editorial ordered by Hu Yaobang. It criticized a political tendency of "mainly guarding against the right." Here the "left" referred to the Maoist past or the new rigid orthodoxy of socialism, while the "right" referred to the dangers of capitalist systems (such as private ownership and the market). In the eyes of Hu Yaobang and his reform colleagues, the so-called anti-right rhetoric had become an obstacle to further carrying out the reform.[34]

The editorial alarmed Hu Qiaomu. In a report to Deng Xiaoping, he charged that it "made reference to 'guarding against the left' more than 20 times, while none about 'guarding against the right.'" Deng's reaction seemed noncommittal, saying that the correct way should be guarding against both, or "whichever shows up." Hu Qiaomu was nonetheless encouraged, as he further pressured the *People's Daily* to issue a retraction. The leader of the newspaper resisted Hu Qiaomu's directive, for he believed that a retraction would damage Hu Yaobang's prestige. "People may infer that Hu Yaobang has run into some political trouble with larger consequences." The controversy died, perhaps thanks to Deng's equivocal attitude. At the time, Deng deemed the problem of the editorial not as serious as "some comrades see it."[35]

A more serious showdown took place two years later. On January 20, 1983, around the time Chen Yun was celebrated for the publication of a volume of his works on economic development, Hu Yaobang made a speech that was considered an affront to the old guru.

Chen's doctrine included three key ideas: a command economy with supplementary market mechanisms, balanced development, and central planning.[36] Such "balanced development" was hailed as one of the most original and independent-minded ideas. If the idea of "balance" was a counterpoint to the radical excess of the Maoist past, in the reform era, however, it was used as a check on new reform initiatives. Deng and his men – such as Hu Yaobang and Zhao Ziyang – advocated boldness, while Chen Yun and his men – such as Deng Liqun and Yao Yilin (later Li Peng as well) – called for "balance." The policy pendulum swung back and forth between reform and "adjustment."[37]

Hu Yaobang's January speech was pushing the envelope in its rhetoric. "We must thoroughly and systematically reform, and resolutely and orderly reform," he told an audience. "What is a thorough and systematic reform, then? Thoroughness means encompassing all the sectors, all the regions, all the agencies, and all the work units." The tone was seen as an obvious challenge to Chen Yun's idea of "balance." No wonder Hu Qiaomu tried to block the speech's circulation to the entire party. Once again, Deng was called upon to intervene, but circulation went ahead.[38]

### Conservatives Attacked Hu Yaobang

But the speech controversy did not end with Deng's words. On March 17, Hu Yaobang presided over a party Standing Committee meeting on financial and economic issues. The stated agenda was for Yao Yilin and Song Ping, who were in charge of the State's Planning Commission, to give reports. Attendants included Deng Xiaoping and Chen Yun. Unexpectedly, out of the meeting's order, Chen Yun pulled out a stack of papers and gave a long speech. Chen devoted his entire speech to repudiating Hu Yaobang's mistakes on economic issues, including his January speech. In his memoir, Deng Liqun counted ten items altogether.[39] Chen used harsh language, even suggesting that Hu start studying from the beginning, as a "intern at the grassroots level in the Ministry of Finance or the Planning Commission." Hu Yaobang, being junior to Chen, had to concede and admit to all the charges. Deng Xiaoping, however, was not pleased by Chen's speech at all. He expressed his displeasure: "The purpose of today's meeting is for us to hear reports." Nevertheless, Hu Qiaomu wasted no time before making Chen's speech a party document circulated to provincial and municipal leaders.[40]

Many in the party leadership saw Chen's speech as part of a *coup d'état* to unseat Hu Yaobang. Bypassing the routine channel of communication within the party, Hu Qiaomu and Yao Yilin announced an "Extended Work Meeting of the Central Committee." Xi Zhongxun and Wan Li, reform leaders on Hu's side, were alarmed and went to see Deng Xiaoping. Deng assured them that the announced meeting would not be held, and "The Hu [Yaobang]–Zhao [Ziyang] leadership framework will not change."[41]

From Hu Yaobang's perspective, it was indeed a close call over which he could have lost his job. He told Li Rui, a close ally, an episode that was quite telling. One day, Hu Qiaomu came to see Hu Yaobang and told him, unsolicited, "After you leave your work as the general secretary, you can do something else. But let us keep our friendship forever." "I was shocked by his remark," Hu Yaobang confided to his friend on his deathbed. "The meeting under plan was about 'changing the horse,' but Deng [Xiaoping] protected me."[42]

In each of these early engagements, Deng remained firmly on Hu's side. Hu survived as general secretary despite the headwind. Deng's continued confidence in him was the decisive factor. That would eventually change, however. The turning point, as is often the case, would be popular protest. The misgivings of the supreme leader would reach their limits. A protest may add the final straw, or, just provide the pretext for a change of heart. Either way, when it happened, the first-line chief executive would fall. It was the case in 1966 for Liu Shaoqi and in 1976 for Deng Xiaoping. The same would play out between 1986 and 1987 for Hu Yaobang. So would it for Zhao in 1989.

### Pitfalls in Managing Student Protest

Street protest was something to which Deng and the allies of his generation had been unequivocally hostile. As communist organizers, they themselves had successfully mobilized many demonstrations against the Guomindang regime before 1949. They were acutely schooled in the conspiratorial aspect of popular protest and knew its power. After 1949, Mao launched repeated mass campaigns, which victimized many of them. In the early 1980s, their aversion was coupled with fear of the so-called "Polish disease." Both Chen Yun and Deng Xiaoping reportedly closely followed the Solidarity movement and addressed similar dangers in China on multiple occasions.[43]

To society at large, especially among students and intellectuals, however, the illegitimacy of protest was not a foregone conclusion. The very issue seemed to be appropriate for political contention. First, protest was a right clearly written in the Constitution. Second, didn't the party just reframe the 1976 Tiananmen protest and hail it as a "patriotic and democratic movement"? Didn't leaders, including Deng Xiaoping and Hu Yaobang, repeatedly call for "liberating minds" and for "extending socialist democracy"? Third, often protest participants would declare that they intended to do nothing more than improve upon the existing system. Each new protest, therefore, could conceivably gain a positive *dingxing* (labeling), they believed, only if the leaders got the facts straight.

Since the shutdown of the Democracy Wall in 1979, street demonstrations had been rare. For a time, any students gathering, even celebratory parades, could be frowned upon. Yet they continue to occur, and some events even made high-profile news and were hailed by the authorities. One famous mass event took place around midnight of March 20–21, 1981, following the victory of the men's national volleyball team in an important game. Four thousand Beijing University students marched around the campus. The main spirit was celebration, completed with red flags and bright torches. The slogan "Unite in Solidarity; Revive the Chinese Nation" was supposedly coined by the crowds, and the event was embraced by the media, which was featured in the *People's Daily* two days later.[44] Another event jolted the October 1, 1984, National Day Celebration with added excitement. The parade on Tiananmen Square, which was habitually rigidly scripted, was suddenly disrupted by a spontaneous act by a group of Beijing University students. When their contingent arrived in front of the inspecting platform, they suddenly unfurled a giant banner that read: "Hello, Xiaoping!" The students not only were not punished, but also became overnight celebrities, with their photographs captured by major newspapers across the nation.[45]

Then came a wave of demonstrations in 1985, but these were getting contentious. The year marked the fortieth anniversary of victory in the Anti-Japanese War. Partly in response to the news that Japan's prime minister had paid respect to a shrine that housed war criminals in August, Beijing University students went beyond the previously scripted celebration activities on September 18. They put up posters and organized marches to the square and called for the boycotting of Japanese goods. In response, the government sent school leaders to conduct "dialogues" with the students and invited trade experts to explain why trade the relationship with Japan was mutually beneficial. Zhu Houze, the Party Center's propaganda chief at the time, told Yang Jisheng that the protest was effectively ended by the "dialogues." "In ending this student protest," Yang Jisheng observed, the government "did not use the army, nor political intimidation. Instead, leaders and cadres engaged students in equal-footing dialogues ... That is Hu Yaobang's preferred model of handling student protests."[46]

In the following year, another stormy wave of student protests would cost Hu Yaobang his job. This wave was inspired, ironically, by a series of speeches by Deng Xiaoping calling for political reform as a prerequisite to carrying his economic reform further. On June 10, 1986, Deng told a group of leaders after the release of some government reports on economic issues, "By this time, it is clear that it will not do if we do not start the political reform. Reform should include political reform ... It should be slated in our agenda now." On June 28, Deng told a meeting of the Standing Committee, "if we do not take up political reform, the economic reform will fail." On September 3, he told a Japanese visitor, "If we do not reform the political system, we will not be able to consolidate the achievements of the economic reform." On November 9, he remarked in an interview with the Japanese prime minister Yasuhiro Nakasone,

"We have increasingly felt the necessity and urgency to reform the political system."[47]

### Deng's Initial Stance Was Often Ambiguous

It was unprecedented for Deng Xiaoping to put so much emphasis on political reform. These speeches, taken as a whole, seemed to signal the beginning of a new era. Other leaders in the reformers' camp, including Zhu Houze, Wan Li, and Wang Zhaoguo, echoed the message with their own speeches. The party's propaganda machine was moved into high gear. An op-ed was published in the *People's Daily* on August 30, 1986, under the title "Political Issues Can Be Discussed." A similar op-ed seven years earlier had been considered so poisonous that it was reported to Deng Xiaoping, who ordered the author expelled from Beijing. Times seemed to have changed. On September 5, the *People's Daily* carried a report that the entire secretariat convened to study Deng's article "The Reform of the Institutions of the Party and the Government."[48]

There were other welcoming signs. Starting in July, many academic conferences were held. Some lively discussions even obliquely questioned "Four Cardinal Principles." On August 7, Liu Binyan, a famous writer whose work had previously been attacked by the conservatives, was invited for an interview by Wan Li in his own house. On September 8, the *People's Daily* published a long essay by Liu Zaifu, another controversial liberal intellectual. In it, Liu Zaifu exhorted "socialist humanism" in literature. Physicist Fang Lizhi, Liu Binyan, and journalist Wang Ruowang – three of the most prominent victims of the 1957–1958 anti-rightist campaign – toured the country and gave rousing lectures, often attended by thousands.[49]

The student protest first erupted on December 1, 1986, at China University of Science and Technology (CUST) in Hefei City, Anhui. At issue was the election of representatives to a local-level people's congress. Students put out posters complaining about the "unfair" and "undemocratic" procedures, including the slate of candidates imposed from above. The protest met a friendly reception from the university's leaders. Taking a cue from the previous year's approach advocated by the party, the school leaders engaged students in "dialogues." On the evening of December 4, a public meeting was held where the slated candidates met with voters. Eight students approached the podium to give speeches, calling for building CUST as a "special zone for democracy." Physicist Fang Lizhi, as vice president of the university, also gave a speech, echoing Deng Xiaoping's call for political reform. "The discussion about political reform has long been made, but many did not know where to start," he told the students. "I think this current debate is a good place to start."[50]

The protest quickly spread to other university campuses. In the following days, four other major universities joined the protest. On one occasion, 2,000 students rushed into the city government building. Then, in the two weeks that followed, the protest wave reached Shanghai, the second-largest center of higher education after Beijing. Students from major campuses, including Fudan University, Tongji University, and Shanghai Jiaotong University, poured into the streets. What followed in Shanghai included a dialogue between Mayor Jiang Zemin, who would become the general secretary during the 1989 Tiananmen protest, and student protesters at Shanghai Jiaotong University, as well as a sit-in outside the city government's main building. The city dispatched 2,000 police to disperse the crowds in the early morning. In the meantime, the student movement further diffused to Hangzhou, Nanjing, Chengdu, Xi'an, Tianjin, and Wuhan. By December 23, Beijing's leading universities, Tsinghua University and Beijing University, had followed suit.[51]

Although some arrests were made (student leaders were quickly released without charge), under Hu Yaobang's leadership the overall government response was one of "dialogue." It is not clear whether this soft approach made a difference. In any event, the wave of protest was quickly contained. In the New Year of 1987, the atmosphere calmed down. One of the "winners" from the student movement was Jiang Zemin, then Shanghai mayor. He was willing to engage with student protesters and make concessions. His flexibility and charm had real effects. During one of his "dialogues," he recited Lincoln's Gettysburg speech in English before proceeding to lecture the students. "About democracy, you only know its surface, not the substance." Jiang admonished his listeners, "You are too young." Reportedly the video recording of this exchange found its way into Zhongnanhai, where the old leaders were delighted to witness a local executive who was both firm and able.[52] In a later historical twist, Zhao Ziyang's "dialogue" approach in 1989 would fail to diffuse student protest and make room for Jiang to become the party's general secretary.[53]

### The General Secretary Blamed and Dismissed

In the wake of the 1986 wave of student protest, Hu Yaobang was not so much faulted for his handling of the student movement as for somehow igniting the movement in first place. He was accused of being soft in implementing the "Campaign against Bourgeois Liberalization," including his failure to discipline a few key intellectuals. On December 30, Deng gave a very stern speech, with Hu and other leaders in attendance:

> Wherever the leadership was not firm, there was turmoil and agitation. This is not a matter only for one or two places, nor for one year or two years. It is due to the

failure of the last few years in upholding the banner of anti-bourgeois liberalization. It is a result of a wavering attitude.

With this analysis, the student movement was unequivocally labeled a serious political problem, and Hu Yaobang was placed squarely at the center of blame. In the same speech, Deng specifically singled out Fang Lizhi, Wang Ruowang, and Liu Binyan as the individuals behind the unrest. He suggested their expulsion from the party. "Wang Ruowang from Shanghai has been madly active, and we have been saying to expel him." At this point he turned to Hu Yaobang: "Why haven't you done that?"[54]

Two days later, on January 2, 1987, Hu Yaobang submitted his resignation to Deng Xiaoping.[55] On January 4, Deng Xiaoping summoned the top leaders (Zhao Ziyang, Chen Yun, Yang Shangkun, Bo Yibo, Wang Zhen, Wan Li, and Peng Zhen) to his residence for a meeting. During the meeting, Deng produced the letter by Hu Yaobang and passed it along for each to read. Deng said they should agree to his resignation, to which all in attendance agreed. A "party life meeting" then took place on January 10, lasting until January 15. Bo Yibo was charged with presiding over the meeting, but Deng was conspicuously absent the entire time. The speeches included Deng Liqun's five-hour marathon and Hu's own self-criticism. He accepted the charges about his being soft on "guarding against the right," and concluded, "I have committed a serious mistake in political principles." After the meeting ended, he sat on the stairs of Huairentang Hall and cried. His friends came over to console him. That night, Wan Li sent over a pot of his favorite meat stew.[56]

His dismissal was made official by an extended Politburo meeting on January 16. "Extended" because it was also attended by older leaders such as Deng Xiaoping and Chen Yun who were no longer official members. At the start, Deng announced that he, not General Secretary Hu Yaobang, would preside. Chen Yun gave the only speech. "The meeting unanimously agrees to the resignation of Comrade Hu Yaobang . . . and unanimously proposes that Zhao Ziyang be the acting general secretary of the Central Committee," according to the official record. As though he was not confident enough, Chen Yun ended his speech with an interesting line: "Beware: this meeting of ours is legitimate."[57]

Zhao Ziyang was recorded as one of Hu's critics in the "party life meeting," and he was tapped for Hu's job. Understandably, some faulted him for not supporting his partner and fellow reformer. In his recorded remarks years later, Zhao vehemently denied pursuing advancement at Hu's expense.[58] His claim is believable. He had been enjoying his job as the premier, and his sympathy and support would not have saved Hu's job anyway. In that system, one knows when to fall into line.

As for Deng, the reshuffling was on his own initiative but also a concession to Chen Yun's side. He did not seem to take much pleasure in it. "It was my first time being able to see Deng Xiaoping at such a close range," recalled a participant in the extended Politburo meeting on January 16:

> When Chen Yun was speaking [to criticize Hu], Deng held himself still without any movement; his two eyes stared forward blankly, paying no regard to anyone. When Chen finished, Bo Yibo waved his hand in front of Deng's face to signal. Deng had no reaction the first time. Bo then waved again, and Deng seemed to wake up. He said, "Oh, I did not notice [that Chen had finished] . . . I have no objection. Why don't we raise our hands as a vote of endorsement [for Chen's speech]."[59]

After Zhao was promoted, the position of premiership went to Li Peng, a clear nod to the conservatives' pressure. Moreover, Zhao would be discharging his new job precariously, facing the same opposition that had brought down Hu Yaobang. By the eve of 1989, he had angered the Chen Yun camp, and he was mired deeply in a recrimination campaign arising from a price reform setback. Deng's elderly rivals had restarted the talk of "changing the horse." The student protest in the wake of Hu Yaobang's death was seen as the last straw. Earlier, when deliberating Hu's replacement, Chen Yun had proposed Deng Liqun, as rumor had it. Deng Xiaoping appointed Zhao instead, but Chen's intention nonetheless underscored the peril Zhao was facing.

### Zhao Ziyang Elevated

*Another Capable Reformer*

Premier Zhao Ziyang, aged sixty-seven in 1987, had been the other half of Deng's team in the first line. The "Deng–Hu–Zhao" system had been victorious since 1980, with a modus operandi of "two controls, one result": Deng held grip on the military, Hu was in charge of propaganda, and Zhao Ziyang brought in the economic fruits of reform. Deng's team was therefore winning the argument over their rivals by the threat of military power, by public opinion campaigns, and by the results of reform – the GDP numbers and improved living standards.

Despite early results, Deng's reform was only in its infancy. Deng stood his ground by promoting Zhao, another ardent champion of his reform program.

If Hu Yaobang was a party operative who had made a career mostly in Beijing, Zhao Ziyang had been a chief executive of local governments. During the revolution, he was a young officer in the 129th Division of the 8th Route Army. In 1939, he attended a lecture by Deng Xiaoping, the division's political commissar. In 1945, Zhao made a speech on land reform that drew Deng's personal praise. After 1949, he moved up step by step as a local leader until he became the first party secretary of a weighty province, Guangdong, in 1974. Later, it was Deng who personally chose Zhao to head his home province when he was reinstated in 1976. "When you get to Sichuan," Deng reportedly offered these parting words to Zhao, "don't tie your hands. Never mind that some may accuse you of belonging to the 'Restoration Squad'," using a term coined by the Gang of Four at the time. A year later, when Deng was once again disgraced, Zhao refused to divulge Deng's remarks in order to protect Deng from the Gang of Four. Deng was impressed.[60]

Zhao's tenures as the number one chief executive in Guangdong and Sichuan established him as a forward-looking, pragmatic, and effective leader. He was known for his stewardship in the area of economic development, earning a popular saying in China of the time: *Yao chiliang, Zhao ziyang* ("Want enough food? Go find Zhao Ziyang"). His success was partly due to his courage to allow flexible farming, the so-called responsibility system, when it was still a taboo. Under this approach collective land was parceled out and the household became the farming unit. While the land was still collectively owned, harvest varied depending on a household's work. Incentives grew. That was politically dangerous, as it had been advocated by Liu Shaoqi, Deng Xiaoping, and Chen Yun in the 1950s and early 1960s and repudiated by Mao during the Cultural Revolution. In the very first wave of economic reform, this approach was "rediscovered" by Zhao and Wan Li, another provincial chief of Anhui, and systematically implemented across the nation with spectacular results. When he became premier, Zhao implemented a similar reform in the industry sector.[61]

By all accounts, Zhao was a liberal thinker compared to most of his peers in the Party Center. He would prove to be as liberal as Hu Yaobang, but, because of the economic, hence less political, nature of his work, the fact was not conspicuously apparent before his appointment as the new party secretary in 1987. While not a favored choice for the conservative camp, his appointment was accepted by Chen Yun and his cohorts as a concession for removing Hu Yaobang. Their hope might have lain not in resisting Zhao's appointment but in finding an opportunity to unseat him quickly enough. "If the arrangement was part of a deal stitched up between Deng and Chen Yun as Deng's price for removing Hu Yaobang," wrote Wilson and Ji, "Chen would have been aware that Zhao's prospects were poor, given Zhao's commitment to political reform, his record on economic policy, and his unresponsiveness to PLA demands while he was in charge of the state sector. Zhao was clearly vulnerable."[62]

To what extent then, did Deng make a misjudgment, as he would later claim?[63] It was disingenuous for Deng to say, in the wake of Tiananmen, that "neither Hu nor Zhao was the choice right" for the party secretary job, and that he made "mistakes" in choosing them. That claim was more a rationalization of his decision to fire them.

Similar to the case of Hu Yaobang discussed above, the divergence between Deng and Zhao was not as significant as Deng later wanted people to believe. Before his downfall as party leader, Zhao never challenged party rule nor advocated anything remotely like the Western-style electoral system. In his recorded conversations with journalists, he candidly discussed the evolution of his political thinking over the years. "The political reform I imagined, up until 1989, was not a multiparty system, nor a Western-style parliamentary democracy," he said. "What needed to be changed was not the fact that the party rules, but the way it rules."[64] The changes he advocated included enhancing transparency in decision making, facilitating "dialog," improving the existing election system of the People's Congress, separating party affairs from state executive affairs, and so on. None of these measures is intrinsically antithetical to Leninist one-party rule.[65]

Zhao's progressive views on reform concerning both economy and political system were initially his credentials, not liabilities. For these credentials, Deng trusted him and appointed him premier. Also, because of these credentials, Deng promoted him as the new general secretary.

### Pushing for Reform Despite Peril

The year Zhao became general secretary, he and his colleagues staged the 13th Party Congress with a resounding reformist program. The slogan "socialist market economy" was officially written into party documents. That was no small feat, considering it was a strident departure from Chen Yun's doctrine. In other words, Deng was able to keep his reform agenda alive and well even after conceding to Chen Yun by dismissing Hu Yaobang. "The 13th Party Congress was a huge success. The situation looked really good afterwards," recalled Zhao Ziyang, "The plan for 1988 was to make big strides in both reform and opening up." Among the new reform measures, Hainan Province was slated as a new special economic zone after Shenzhen and Zhuhai; a new "Enterprise Law" would stipulate a separation between property rights and management rights, and there was talk about making laws to protect private enterprise. Even the idea of shareholding ownership was broached.[66]

In the meantime, the old ideological debates showed no sign of subsiding. After the propaganda chief, Zhu Houze, a Hu Yaobang protégé, was dismissed and replaced by a conservative figure, a new campaign against "bourgeois liberalization" was launched in the name of a response to Deng Xiaoping's December speech on Four Principles. A number of liberal intellectuals – Fang Lizhi, Wang Ruowang, and Liu Binyan – were accused of being the masterminds behind the 1986 student protest and expelled from the party.[67]

A new boogeyman for conservative attacks, Zhao Ziyang, however, seemed to refuse to learn a lesson from Hu's downfall. Perhaps he was buoyed by

Deng's ostensible support. From day one, he downplayed the so-called "anti-bourgeois-liberalization" campaign. In a speech in January, he reminded his audience that Deng's policy had "two fundamental points": upholding the Four Cardinal Principles as well as reform and opening up. The tenet of his remarks was to emphasize the latter and warn against "overextending" the campaign.[68] On another occasion in the same month, at a Spring Festival gala, he spoke about the campaign but again tried to push back the conservatives by admonishing them against repeating the "leftist mistakes" of the past.[69] On a third occasion, he stressed the second of the Two Fundamental Points again and mentioned Deng Xiaoping's name to support it: "Reform, open up, and be flexible. Who articulates this point the earliest, the most often, and the most profoundly? Comrade Deng Xiaoping!"[70]

Zhao's resistance is extraordinary, and amounts to swimming in dangerous waters if we remember how Hu Yaobang was dismissed. Was he openly defying Deng? He did not think so and he was also confident that Deng would not take it that way. "As the campaign against 'bourgeois liberalization' started, many worried that our basic line decided since the 3rd Plenum [of the 11th Party Congress in 1978] would change accordingly. I gave the Spring Festival Gala speech to dispel such notions, reiterating the Two Fundamental Points."[71] Indeed, his reading of Deng was correct. On February 25, Deng summoned five top leaders, including Zhao, and offered his endorsement of Zhao's Spring Festival Gala speech. "This speech is great. You all should support Ziyang's work ... Reform and opening up at this time are by no means too fast. They are moving steadily."[72]

### Deng Was Weakened after Hu Yaobang's Dismissal

If Deng succeeded in steadying his ship by having Zhao Ziyang at the helm, the overall makeup of the post-Hu administration signified reduced strength on Deng's side. Instead of having both the number one and number two positions, Deng agreed to appoint Li Peng as the new premier in charge of economic work. Li owed his rise to the other elder leaders and was firmly rooted in the Chen Yun camp. Also promoted to the Standing Committee was Yao Yilin, a vice premier as well as a longtime friend and protégé of Chen Yun's. On the reformers' side, in addition to Zhao, were Hu Qili in charge of propaganda and Qiao Shi in charge of public security. Deng had proposed two other reformers, Wan Li and Tian Jiyun, to join the Standing Committee, but the nominations were thwarted by the conservatives.[73]

With Deng's tacit support, Zhao Ziyang as the new general secretary scored some victories, albeit ones that would come back to bite him. In the lead-up to the 13th Party Congress, Zhao ordered the disbanding of the Central Secretariat Policy Research Institute, which was led by Deng Liqun, the conservative ideologue. This effectively removed Deng Liqun and Hu Qiaomu as key arbiters on the ideological front. In their place, Zhao's ally Hu Qili was installed to oversee propaganda and media affairs.[74] During the party congress, Zhao engineered to completely remove Deng Liqun from all of his leadership posts.[75] Ostensibly, the fall of Deng Liqun, whom Chun Yun had once groomed to become the general party secretary, was the result of a series of votes. Deng Liqun lost his position not only in the Politburo, but also in the 230-member Central Committee. According to his memoir, Deng Liqun suspected that Zhao had undermined him by disbanding his policy institute and changing the election rules.[76] Yang Jisheng reported that Chen Yun was beyond furious at this, saying, "This is all because of the trickery of Bao Tong and Li Rui," two foot solders of the reformer's camp supporting Zhao. Chen here was referring to a letter Li Rui had written that attacked Deng Liqun's antireform history and personal flaws. The letter ultimately reached Deng Xiaoping via Bao Tong and Zhao Ziyang.[77]

## The Problem of Trust: The Deng-Zhao Edition

### Zhao Ziyang as a Possible Heir

In appointing Zhao Ziyang to the position of the new general secretary, how much did Deng Xiaoping also mean to designate him as his heir apparent? We might never know for sure. Examining Hu Yaobang's six-year tenure in its entirety, we can see that he was used mainly as a chief executive. Deng made no effort to expand Hu's influence beyond the domain of party ideology and organization and into the realms of economic policies, or above all into the military.[78] This is understandable partly because of Hu's age. He was already seventy-two in 1987. Yet this analysis does not preclude Hu's chances. Deng's thinking must have been evolving. Ever a pragmatic leader, he applied the approach of "feeling the pebbles to cross the river" on this matter as well. Hu's sudden and undignified fall attests to this latter view.

In Zhao Ziyang's case, by comparison, Deng seemed to mean more. Again, age must have been a factor. Zhao was four years younger than Hu, not yet seventy in 1987, and Deng himself was really old, then eighty-four. Deng's investment in Zhao was multifaceted, all pointing to the goal of giving Zhao interlocking power over three domains: the government, the party, and the military. After he had been premier for six years, the government had become his "home base." The new job as party chief would grow his power in the party. For military power, Deng installed him as the first vice chair of the CMC. At least on paper, Zhao was made second in command of the military, behind only Deng and ahead of Yang Shangkun, Deng's first-line leader in charge of the armed forces.

For the next two years until his fall in 1989, Zhao had been making little progress in all three areas, however. He was a diminished chief executive and his prospect of becoming Deng's successor was very much in doubt. In the government and in the economic domain, he found his previous power base eroded. His hold on the economy was weakened when he relinquished his premiership in late 1987 and dissolved the Central Finance and Economics Leadership Group (CFELG) in mid-1988.[79] The economy was in fact officially in the hands of two conservatives, Premier Li Peng and Vice Premier Yao Yilin.

### A Headwind against Reformers

The headwind of factional politics was particularly strong at the crossroad of Deng's reform program. "As market forces cut through command economic channels, more decentralization became the logic of development and encroached upon the very core of the old system: state ownership and the set of vertical control mechanisms," wrote two observers of the period. "In the process, controversial reforms permitting joint ventures, private enterprises and share companies have produced changes in the social structure of interests. As a result, the traditional Marxist and Maoist principles could no longer offer clear-cut theoretical guidelines for the Party in promoting China's socio-economic development."[80]

On the side of Deng and Zhao, the problems created by the initial reform could only be solved by further reform. In this process, they were willing to challenge socialist orthodoxy. Later, Deng would answer the "theoretical" challenge and supposed market institutions could be named "socialist."[81] For Chen Yun and Li Peng, however, the problems were seen as the result of too much reform in too short a time. Hence, Chen Yun's old dictum of "balanced development" was put to frequent use, and "readjustment" was a euphemism for slowing down reform.

"If the goal was to provide an improved version of Chen Yun's Soviet model with Chinese characteristics, it seemed already to have gone far enough," an expert writes, "but if one were to follow the logic of Zhao's approach, then it had hardly penetrated the periphery of the command system. The struggle between Zhao Ziyang and the central planners gradually accelerated and was reflected in a faster pace of policy oscillations between further decentralization and readjustment."[82]

The history of later decades was very kind to Deng and Zhao's approach. For example, two of Zhao's bold ideas – the coastal strategy and the price reform proposal – proved to be essential for China's economic takeoff. But Zhao would not stay in the leadership position to claim the credit. The year of 1988 was seen as his Waterloo. The coastal strategy was still an experiment, and price reform exacerbated huge inflation. Even scholars neutral to political debates consider his decision to move ahead on price reform at that moment to have been misjudged. On the eve of the 1989 student movement, a fear factor was afoot with news of bank runs and soaring prices.[83]

At that juncture, Zhao was squarely blamed, and his power was further curtailed in the economic debates. Two major battles were fought in 1988, and Zhao lost both. The first took place at Beidaihe in August 1988 over the timing and duration of price reform, which the leadership had previously decided to carry out at the Politburo's working session two months earlier. Zhao proposed immediate implementation and a three-year timetable in order to establish a mature market as soon as possible. Li Peng and Yao Yilin countered with a proposal that would take eight years and would entail reimposition of central control and partial rollback of Zhao's reforms.

A month later at the 3rd Plenum of the 12th Central Committee, even the compromise solution was negated; price reforms were postponed indefinitely, and a two-year readjustment of the economy was ordered. These moves, both deplored by Zhao, once again placed the authority to deal with dislocations in the economy in the hands of the central planners, hence benefiting Li Peng in the power struggle. For the moment, reform was in abeyance.

### Zhao Makes Few Inroads in the Military

Deng's promotion of Zhao within the military also encountered resistance from three sources. The first was from Yang Shangkun. Yang had a mandate from Deng to oversee military reform, which entailed demobilizing a million men and appointing younger officers. He moved many of his men into the upper echelons. He did so by exploiting CMC rules to bypass Zhao, who was nominally the first vice chair. Those so promoted were known as "generals of the Yang family" and included Yang Baibing, Yang's half-brother.[84] Once, Deng arranged a military inspection for Zhao to raise his profile. But when the news leaked to Yang Shangkun, he phoned Zhao that he would like to go along. A war veteran and high-ranking general, Yang's appearance would have overshadowed Zhao, and defeat Deng's initial purpose. In the end, Zhao called Deng to cancel it.[85]

Another kind of resistance came from Deng's opponents in the CAC. In arranging personnel for the 13th Congress, Deng appeared to have tried to elevate Zhao's power in the military by nudging aside two military men. He moved Yang Shangkun to the largely ceremonial national presidency and Chief of Staff Chi Haotian to defense minister, in the hope of raising Zhao as the first vice chair of the CMC. Alas, none of these changes was put into effect. As late as mid-1988, Yang continued to handle day-to-day matters of the military, presumably with Deng's approval – a sign that Deng's confidence in Zhao as the right person to lead the army was already waning.[86]

Third, Zhao's appointment was resisted by rank-and-file officers and soldiers. As a sign of the army's resistance to an outsider, the PLA media openly criticized Zhao's call to reform the party's ideological work within the military. Articles also began to appear that denounced Zhao's championing of "self-support" plans for the PLA. A lieutenant general even openly denounced Zhao's proposal as pushing the military in a dangerous direction. In late 1988, Zhao had to make what in effect amounted to a self-criticism following his advocacy of a "self-subsidy and self-development" policy for the PLA.[87]

### Caught between Twin Summits

In the party, within his domain proper, the general secretary operated under the gaze of elder leaders. "The two elders were not in agreement; it is very difficult to be the general secretary." Zhao recalled,

> When Chen Yun asked me to convene a meeting, Xiaoping tended to say no. Chen Yun wanted meetings so he had an occasion to air his views. But Xiaoping tried to avoid meetings so that he could give us instructions directly. "Why don't we have a meeting?" Chen Yun would demand. To that I replied: "Well, first you and Comrade Xiaoping had better agree to one. I am only the co-ordinator in chief, am I not?" Then you have Li Xiannian complaining that "Zhao Ziyang only listened to Deng. Not me."[88]

Nor did Zhao have the power to form his own "cabinet." Earlier in 1987, a "Six-Person Group" was formed to prepare the slate of leadership personnel, including who would be on the Standing Committee of the Politburo (SC) to be approved in the upcoming 13th Party Congress. It was led by Bo Yibo, another elder from the conservative camp. This was the process that successfully blocked Wan Li and Tian Jiyun, two reformers favored by Zhao and Deng, from joining the Standing Committee. Also through this process, Zhao's victory of removing Deng Liqun rang hallow, as the propaganda post went to another conservative ideologue, Wang Renzhi. Zhao had to accept it with a sigh:

> The important personnel decisions were not made at my level . . . Sometimes I did not even have any input. The Six-Person Group did not have the last say either. They had to go the elderly. A decision was made if Xiaoping and Chen Yun saw eye to eye . . . I was the general secretary, but can I change the director of the Organizational Department? No. I was not happy with propaganda head Wang Renzhi. I even scolded him once. Yet I could only scold him; I was not able to fire him. He got someone behind him.[89]

The conservative elders openly criticized Zhao from day one. Deng Liqun recorded at least three instances in which Chen Yun gave Zhao an earful. The first time, the disapproval was relayed through Bo Yibo. The second time, Chen paid a personal visit. It was even recorded that Chen looked directly at Zhao's eyes, both hands holding Zhao's shoulder: "Your responsibility cannot be greater! How many people died before we achieved the victory of revolution? Hu Yaobang did not live up to this responsibility. Now you should."[90] According to Deng Liqun, a year later Chen was clearly unhappy with Zhao's performance. In a speech in 1988, Chen made eight points of criticism of Zhao's work. Deng Liqun's assessment is that Zhao failed to address any of these points.[91]

Behind closed doors, Chen Yun, Li Xiannian, and other elders soon started to urge Deng to "change the horse" again. "A torrent of removing Zhao was afoot in Beijing," as one of Zhao's close aides put it.[92] Reports abounded and their veracity varied. It is unclear to what degree the "torrent" was real, but what remains undisputable is the subjective perception of its ferocity. "At that time the wind was indeed blowing both within the country and abroad," Zhao later recalled. "Many began to worry for me, saying that I could be another Yangbao [someone removed from the post of general secretary]."[93] Yan Jiaqi, a renowned political scientist and a Zhao supporter, began to pen a serious essay warning against "personnel changes by extra-institutional procedures."[94]

*Zhao Was Aware of the Efforts to Unseat Him; Deng Offered Reassurance*

Zhao Ziyang was aware of the torrent. The fact that at this time the economic situation was not looking good also gave older leaders opportunities to question his leadership. At a Politburo meeting, elder leader Wang Renzhong demanded that SC members, particularly Zhao, accept responsibility and voice self-criticism.[95] At the end of 1988, a Hong Kong newspaper reported that Li Xiannian had explicitly suggested that Deng dismiss Zhao in a meeting in Shanghai where both vacationed. The report reached Zhao, and he wrote a note to Wang Ruilin (Deng's aid in chief) asking for clarification.[96] A few days before the 1989 New Year, Li Peng and Yao Yilin openly criticized Zhao at a "party life meeting" of SC members. They focused on price reform, with a larger point that Zhao should step aside on economic issues. "Yao Yilin was not someone who was straightforward. Nor did he like to take the lead," recalled Zhao, "But this time he was very direct and very aggressive. They must have been emboldened by the support behind them."[97]

If Zhao's position seemed untenable, he was still getting mixed signals. Against the "torrent," Deng seemed unfazed, at least as far as Zhao could tell. Deng had given him many private assurances over the same period. "Deng repeatedly conveyed his 'bottom line' to me. That is, the general framework of leadership personnel would not change, and I would serve for two terms," recalled Zhao.[98] After Li Peng and Yao Yilin attacked Zhao at the party life meeting, Deng summoned Li and reiterated his support for Zhao. He even instructed Li to officially bring his message back to the Standing Committee. Zhao learned about the conversation from Li.[99]

During the Chinese New Year of 1989, about two months before the outbreak of the Tiananmen Square movement, Zhao had a long conversation with Deng in Deng's Shanghai vacation home. It is unclear whether, by that time, Deng had made up his mind to crown Zhao as his successor or just wanted to test Zhao's loyalty. He said he had deliberated for a long time and decided to resign from his position as CMC chair and pass it to Zhao. Deng made it clear that this way Zhao would be made stronger so that he could pre-empt "the interference from the older comrades." That would not be possible "if [I] do not step down entirely but retained the position as CMC chair [without passing it to you]." Zhao, taking a page from historical lessons of past would-be successors, wisely rejected the proposal. "Politics in the East is different from politics in the West," he even went philosophically in his reply. "If you do not intervene, while they [the conservative elders] do, the situation for us [the first-line leaders] will be worse." After Zhao's remarks, Deng took a moment to ponder, and said, "Very well, then. Let us do as you suggest. Let us wait for another year to talk about this again."[100]

## Discussion and Conclusion

On the eve of the 1989 Tiananmen Square movement, political gravity revolved around the general secretary as a leadership position. The country, to borrow an analogy from a very different setting, was approaching an election year. The possibility of fundamental change was in the air. Would Zhao have to go? Who could succeed him? Moreover, the matter went beyond whether Zhao Ziyang could keep his job. At stake was the direction of Deng's reform program: speeding up or slowing down?

As will be shown in later chapters, the Deng–Zhao relationship was the key to understanding Tiananmen's inception, development, and end. For example, the limits of the supreme leader's own power, imposed by either his policy rivals or his heirs, help explain why Deng seemed hesitant at times, which in turn provided the political opportunity for protest. Zhao's perception of Deng's confidence helped to explain his early actions, and his realization of the loss of such trust explains why he waged a campaign of "bureaucratic insurgency." The need to wrestle power away from Zhao explains Deng's alliance with his conservative rivals.

There are two schools of thoughts on the depth of Zhao's trouble. Some suggest that his situation was already so precarious that he would have been replaced with or without Tiananmen. The list of cited evidence is long, including his setbacks in economic policy, his failure to advance in the military, the old leaders' attempts to oust him, the attacks by ideologues such as Deng Liqun, and the signs of displeasure from Deng himself.[101] Others point to opposite evidence. More than once, Deng told Zhao that he would appoint him CMC chair soon.[102] Earlier, Deng had reportedly instructed Standing Committee members that Zhao was set to serve two terms. In the meantime, Deng gave multiple private assurances to Zhao.[103]

What is indisputable, though, is that Zhao's position had indeed become the number one political issue. It was clearly on Deng's mind, and he was facing intense pressure from his political rivals. The proverbial last straw could tip the balance. It is within this context that elite reactions to the Tiananmen Square movement must be understood.

The story of Zhao Ziyang's fortune will play out in the pages to come. His downfall would follow a similar script to the case of his predecessor, Hu Yaobang. Popular protest would prove to be a liability for the chief executive, seen as either a political lapse in previous work or an ongoing mismanagement of events. The support of the supreme leader would be critically important, yet elusive to discern. Both Hu and Zhao erred by banking on it too much. In truth, such trust could take drastic turns especially when the supreme leader himself was under pressure.

On a rainy night in 1988, about a year before Zhao's downfall, the tomb of his mother, located in Henan Province, was raided. The act was daring and treacherously outrageous, as the perpetrators also stole the corpse, which had been buried for more than twelve years. It was no small blow to Zhao Ziyang's spirit, but he was able to instruct local officials to "handle it in a low-profile way."[104] If the transgression was meant to bring ill fortune to the descendants of the dead, it did.

# Part II

# Elite Politics and the Making of the Tiananmen Protest

A conventional conception treats popular protest as an anthesis to the state. In this conception, the producers of a movement belong to the society, whereas government officials will counter that effort; in other words, they repress. In a second conception of the state–protest relationship, some leaders within the government could be sympathetic to the protest and may even help advance the protest's cause. The protest then ebbs or flows depending on the fortune of the supporting faction among the elite. Lastly, in a third conception, state leaders use the protest to their political advantage with little regard to ending it. They do so partly because they are preoccupied by other political issues of the day or otherwise do not consider the protest a major threat. In this last conception, state leaders may be less interested in ending the protest than in using it.

Which of the above perspectives best describes the state's interaction with the Tiananmen protest in 1989? We peruse an answer in the next three chapters, covering a period from the outbreak of the protest and during its spectacular progress.

- Chapter 4 focuses on the first-line leaders in charge of day-to-day governance, especially General Secretary Zhao Ziyang and Premier Li Peng. We examine their actions – and, as importantly, inactions – in the period starting April 15, the day of Hu Yaobang's death, to April 26, the day of the publication of the government's first official response in the form of an editorial.

- Chapter 5 focuses on Deng Xiaoping during the period from April 15 to 26, and to May 17 when he convened the meeting that decided on martial law.

- Chapter 6 returns the focus to Zhao Ziyang and Li Peng, covering the time from the April 26 editorial until the outbreak of the hunger strike on May 13 and the martial law decision on May 17.

Until they resorted to military intervention, did state leaders do all they could to stop the protest? The prevailing line of existing scholarship suggests that they did. The facts documented here in these chapters will question this characterization. From the outset, every time the government issued a major response, protest participation shot up. What, then, was the leaders' intent? Did they mean to end the protest, only to fail? As I will show, their intentions to end the protest were elusive at best. Their actions in effect co-produced the Tiananmen protest.

# 4 Early Response and the Growth of the Protest
## April 15–April 26, 1989

The standard narrative of social protest in an authoritarian regime is one of the people fighting against the state. The protest is a challenge, and the state's response is to end it. The driving force behind the production of a protest, therefore, comes from the society; to the extent the state is concerned, it is a force of resistance, also known as "repression." This perspective expects government reactions that impede mobilization, including verbal condemnation, police deployment, and so on. If the government reacts in other forms that are hardly repressive, – for example, silence, inaction, tolerance, indulgence, and even facilitation – then these are seen as part of a strategy of elite actors who aim at the ultimate goal of repression.[1]

Empirical tests for such a characterization have been thin, partly for the lack of data on individual decision makers. How elite actors in the government think or act – to confront, to comprise, or to strategize – is inferred in hindsight from observations of overall policies. An organizational goal of repression is presumed as the starting point.

My investigation of the Chinese government's response in the initial stage of the Tiananmen protest follows a different track. I was able to chronicle and examine what leaders did or did not do at an individual level. Consequently, a different picture emerged. Analyses of the key leaders' motivations and considerations led to an inevitable conclusion that there was no such a thing as an organizational goal to end the protest, at least not during this first period of a historical event that would last six more weeks. To put it succinctly, elite action in fact coproduced a large-scale protest that would not have been possible without their contribution.

In the beginning, as previously unseen throughout the history of communist China, initially demonstrations encountered scant reaction from government channels. The protesters found themselves in a surreal, unprecedented political environment. Columns of students "pushed through the only slightly resisting ranks of police officers and into Tiananmen Square," wrote one observer. "The police barriers were spaced every few hundred yards, and each successive breakthrough drew greater cheers than the last, building the momentum of protest."[2]

To help deciphering this state of inaction, there was a midnight phone call between Li Peng and Zhao Ziyang. "At 11:30 p.m.," wrote Li Peng in his diary in a frustrated tone about student sit-in on April 19, "I urged him [Zhao Ziyang] to deliberate (*yanjiu*) and [take action] immediately. But he said he would not do so until the next morning. As far as Xinhua Gate [a gate of the central government compound and the site of the sit-in] was concerned, he said he did not know the details, and said, so long as the students did not beat, smash, or torch things, we should not do anything."[3] For his part, Zhao corroborated this account in remarks made during his house arrest after Tiananmen: "In the night of April 19, Li Peng called me all unexpectedly. 'Students are at the Xinhua Gate; why have there been no measures taken [against them]?' He asked. I answered: 'Qiao Shi [Zhao's ally in the Standing Committee in charge of security] is in charge on the site. He has a few plans he will use when necessary.'"[4]

## Summary of What Happened

At the outbreak of the 1989 Tiananmen student protest, the five-member Standing Committee (SC) of the Politburo was represented quite evenly by the two "summits." Deng's side included Zhao Ziyang, the general secretary, and two allies in charge of propaganda and security, Hu Qili and Qiao Shi. Comparably, Chen Yun's side included Li Peng, the premier, and Yao Yilin, the vice premier in charge of the economy. Together they formed a "collective leadership" in the first line, holding regular meetings and making decisions by vote. If they could not resolve an issue by themselves, Deng, often in consultation with Chen Yun and others, would intervene. If we think of the SC as the highest body of executives, Deng and other "second-line" leaders functioned like a board of directors or a parliament. Politically, Zhao Ziyang represented the reformist camp, and Li Peng the conservative.

The timing of the then emerging student movement meant it could not be immediately squashed, as it coincided with, and functioned as, public mourning for the passing of Hu Yaobang, a beloved national leader. During such periods of societal grief, the party's political norms counseled restraint and compassion. Protesting space was further extended thanks to a dispute between the two top leaders. Zhao Ziyang insisted on one approach, and Li Peng on the other. Both sides were strong: Li Peng's hardball advocacy had the party's tradition on its side, while Zhao Ziyang held the number one position in the organizational chart. Institutionally, their strengths were compatible as well. Li Peng had allies in the Beijing city government and the country's education system. Zhao Ziyang had people in charge of both propaganda and security as well as connections with liberal intellectuals. Hence, an impasse ensued.

The turning point came in the form of a curious act by Zhao Ziyang. In the middle of it all, Zhao left Beijing to visit North Korea. In his absence, Li Peng quickly moved Beijing's damning report of the student movement up to the Party Center and even garnered an endorsement from Deng Xiaoping. As a result, Li won the framing battle to label the protest an anti-party crime. By this time, however, the protest had grown into an enormous force. Students believed in their right to protest, and they felt righteous in their action; as important, they now had established a citywide independent student union. The *People's Daily* published an infamous and scathing editorial, but it failed to intimidate students into submission. Instead, it further unleashed the demonstration like an avalanche. More than a million subsequently flooded the city's streets and the square.

Thus went the starting phase of the 1989 Tiananmen Square movement. Contrary to the notion that state elites would automatically do their best to "repress" the protest, the above account suggests the opposite. They were busy doing everything else and, in effect, acting almost like coproducers of this large-scale movement. Certainly, state elites never admitted this fact in any of the public pronouncements they issued during or after 1989, which is understandable because those who had done so would have been accused of being coconspirators. Instead, they normally justified their action or inaction as good-faith efforts for the purpose of ending the contentious episode. They portrayed themselves as "honest" bureaucrats – people who wanted to get things done – more than politicians – people who had their own interests and might stand at odds with others.

### Initial Inaction Due to the Institutional Norm of Respecting the Dead

Hu Yaobang's death, on April 15, 1989, was considered untimely and the news sent shockwaves through Beijing and elsewhere. In the public imagination, the former general secretary had been a symbol of youth and rigor, partly because for many years he was the head of the Communist Youth League before his rise to the party's top. In his seventies, he was seen as a generation younger than Deng and other leaders in their eighties. Since his dismissal two years earlier, the nation had not heard much from him; nor had there been any news about his health. Relitigating the perceived injustice of his dismissal, student protesters displayed banners that at once mourned the dead and attacked his alleged tormentors: "Those who should live, die; those who should die, live."[5]

A beloved figure among intellectuals and young people, Hu himself once expressed a sense of astonishment at the affection he encountered everywhere after his fall.[6] According to Wu Renhua, many intellectuals felt a strong sense of guilt for not having been able to support him in 1987. Hopes of alleviating this guilt had been simmering, and Hu's death provided the moment for release.[7] In death, Hu seemed destined to become another Zhou Enlai, the late premier whose death led to an avalanche of public mourning that triggered an earlier Tiananmen protest in 1976 (as described in Chapter 2 above).

Two uncanny details drew further comparisons between Hu and Zhou Enlai. According to Hu's daughter, he fell ill on April 8 when attending a Politburo meeting. After he left for Zhongnanhai that morning, a book was left open on his desk in his bedroom, which frugally doubled as a study. The title? *The Biography of Zhou Enlai*. After his collapse with a stroke, he was transferred to Beijing Hospital, a special hospital for higher-ups. Then, another coincidence: Hu was treated and subsequently passed away in the very room where Zhou Enlai drew his last breath.[8]

### *Li Peng Was Rumored to Have Caused Hu Yaobang's Heart Attack*

During the first days of the student protest, rumors abounded as to how Hu had died. One version depicted a heated quarrel between Hu and Li Peng, which reportedly drove Hu to a heart attack. The state media went to great lengths to refute this narrative, with many leaders giving detailed testimonials and recollections. Based on the available materials, a brief account can be constructed, which would demonstrate the extraordinary closeness and respect the comrades showed each other in public. This norm – in the time of life and death – was so strong that it applied even to mortal political enemies.

In the morning of the Politburo meeting, which revolved around educational matters, Hu sat between Vice Premier Tian Jiyun and Defense Secretary Qin Jiwei. During a lengthy speech by Li Tieying, the head of the State Educational Committee, Hu experienced chest pain and breathing difficulties. He then asked Zhao Ziyang, the chair of the meeting, if he might leave. Hu Qili (an SC member) told him not to move. Jiang Zemin brought nitroglycerin tablets out of his pocket. Yan Mingfu urged others to hurry, and someone else helped apply the medicine. Later, Wen Jiabao (the party chief of staff) supervised Hu's transfer to the hospital and reported back to the meeting. Once settled, every top leader visited, including Zhao Ziyang, Li Peng, Yang Shangkun, Peng Zhen, and Song Renqiong. Deng Xiaoping and Wang Zhen sent representatives on their behalf, as they were too frail to come themselves.[9]

In his memoir, Premier Li Peng, who was rumored to have clashed with Hu Yaobang, recounted how much he cared about Hu's health and what he did exactly:

> On the morning of April 9, I went to Beijing Hospital to visit Comrade Hu Yaobang. The chief physician told me that Yaobang's health had been stabilized . . . he was not yet out of the danger zone. With the permission of the doctors, I entered the patient's room and saw Comrade Yaobang, who looked in pretty good spirits. We talked for more than ten minutes. He gave me the following comments with sincerity: "I heard

good reviews about you in the new position as premier. You handled matters with an even keel."[10]

Li Peng advised him to take care and to follow the doctors' orders. "There will be no real danger," Li assured Hu. During the visit, Hu's wife Li Zhao even solicited Li Peng's help to persuade Hu to change his behavior as a patient:

> His wife Li Zhao asked me to talk to Comrade Yaobang about a doctor's order. As a patient who had suffered a stroke, he was required to pass water and solids on the bed. But Yaobang was not used to this and insisted on coming down. This being in the dangerous period, particularly the first seven days, that should not be allowed. I did convey these to Yaobang and he orally accepted my advice.[11]

It is difficult to know how sincere these gestures were because one needed to show public displays of affection in moments of this sort, even if the recipient of such displays was one's political opponent. Such is the skill required in a system that denied the existence of political factions. Comradeship was seen as a character trait everyone should have. It is within this context that, in the immediate aftermath of Hu Yaobang's death, the same leaders were understandably hesitant to fashion a hostile response to the public outpouring of grief. Their hands were tied even if they saw that mourning as layered with political attacks.

The Hu family set up a temporary memorial hall in their residence in a *hutong* by Changan Avenue. Many came to show their respect, including dignitaries who were close friends of Hu's. Significantly, they included not only supporters of reform policies, but also many on the other side of the political debate. Throughout his long and illustrious career, Hu befriended many powerful figures who might or might not have agreed with his reform agenda. Among them was Zhang Aiping, a revolutionary general who shared not only the difficult days of the Long March during the revolutionary war, but also a fate as a victim of the Cultural Revolution. "Sudden sorrow fails my throat for speech / Past memories flood the gate of my heart," ran the poem he recited for the occasion.[12] Li Xiannian, one of the most prominent critics of Hu Yaobang and Zhao Ziyang, was reportedly shocked by the news. "How can this be possible? How can this be possible?" he said. "I just had a phone call with him a few days ago. From the sound of his voice, he seemed to be doing really well." The author of this account even speculated that Li seemed to show a sense of remorse for his active role in Hu's dismissal.[13]

According to the *People's Daily*, Beijing was plunged in an outpouring of sorrow, regret, sympathy, and condolence. When Wang Guangmei, the wife of the late president Liu Shaoqi, bought a bucket of flowers for the occasion, the florist refused to accept her payment. "This flower bucket should be used as the token of our heart from our humble store," they told Wang.[14] The affections of the people in the street were so deeply felt that at one point Hu's wife formally asked for permission from the Party Center to open their residence to the public for two days.[15]

### Condemning Hu Yaobang's Dismissal as Unjust

In the meantime, the political meaning of Hu's death was not lost. He was lauded as "the Soul of China," proclaimed as a giant banner hung on the Monument of the People's Martyrs in the center of Tiananmen Square. It highlighted the integrity of the man and suggested that China's future lay in the reformist agenda, of which Hu was a visible embodiment. To praise him as a great man was, explicitly or implicitly, to condemn his mistreatment.

The message was articulated by a group of intellectuals at a hastily convened conference on April 19. In the meeting, political scientist Yan Jiaqi criticized the dismissal of Hu Yaobang as "personnel change by undue process." About the ongoing public events in Beijing, he said, "Nowadays when I have visited Tiananmen Square, I have found many speaking of two points: first, mourn Hu Yaobang, and second, China is short of democracy." Yan's sentiment was shared by other high-profile speakers.[16]

These ideas seemed to animate the nascent protest in the street. The "Seven Demands" put forward to student leaders included:

No. 1: The Party Center should re-evaluate Hu Yaobang's achievements and mistakes.
. . .
No. 4: Negate the campaigns of "Clearing up Spiritual Pollution" and "Anti-liberalization"; reinstate the citizens who were wrongfully accused.[17]

These demands unambiguously argued that the 1987 dismissal of Hu was unjust and that the conservative campaign was wrongly reactionary.

The discourse celebrating a hero's life was also keen on identifying "villains." Premier Li Peng was particularly singled out from the start. As mentioned earlier, he suffered from tales of his quarrel with Hu Yaobang at the Politburo meeting that caused Hu's heart attack. "Li Peng, come out! Li Peng, come out," cried the student protesters at an overnight sit-in at the gate of Zhongnanhai, the party leadership's compound. On the day of Hu Yaobang's funeral on April 22, hundreds of thousands of students lingered outside the Great Meeting Hall of the People after the ceremony had ended. It was rumored, which may or may not be true, that Li Peng promised to come out to receive student representatives.[18]

### Deng Was Also Targeted

The dissent was not limited to an attempt to discredit the conservative figures and to appeal to the supreme leader, Deng Xiaoping; it was aimed at Deng himself as well. After all, truth be told, Deng was the central decision maker in Hu Yaobang's dismissal.

Most explicit attacks included such banners as "Those who should live, die; those who should die, live!" Or this: "Yaobang died at 73; Xiaoping lives at 84; Look at the political realm, what gives?"[19] Before one of the first marches, Wu Renhua, a junior professor at the China University of Politics and Law, worked with a few others to make a giant memorial wreath on the afternoon of April 17. When done, he hung a small bottle of Maotai wine on it, which was carried all the way to Tiananmen Square that afternoon. Wu later wrote that his true intention was to show respect to those who had passed away, in line with the Chinese tradition of giving drink and food to the dead. It was later revealed that government security agents deemed the hanging of the bottle to be a serious political offense and set up an investigation. The reason was not difficult for a Chinese speaker: "small bottle" is pronounced *xiao ping* in Chinese.[20]

## Indecision as Two Leaders Clash

### The Legality and Politics of Student Protest

Protest activities are seen as illegal in communist China, notwithstanding its constitutional provisions on freedom of speech and association. In his report after the crackdown, Beijing mayor Chen Xitong reasoned that student protest during the 1989 Tiananmen events was illegal because (1) the constitution had specifically banned the so-called "Four Bigs," including "big public posters" (*dazibao*), in a ten-article legislation about marches, rallies, and demonstrations; (2) the Beijing city government required a permit for any protest (the law is in bad faith since city government granted zero permits for any protest); (3) the occupation of Tiananmen Square would be against the administrative rules of the square; and (4) there also existed rules against attempts to form "illegal organizations."[21]

Yet, like all other laws in China, these laws may or may not be enforced, depending on the politics of the moment.[22] Translated into steps taken on the ground, the public security apparatus would forbid certain acts of social protest on college campuses while allowing others. At the top of all taboos was forming an independent organization. Usually, arrests would be immediately carried out for that violation. Different degrees of tolerance were occasionally granted to other forms of protest, such as posting essays, gatherings, or marches.[23]

Attempts at protest by college students never stopped, so neither did the party-state's efforts to nip them in the bud. According to Shen Tong's memoir *Almost Revolution*, beneath the tranquility of Beida's campus life there were constant cat-and-mouse games between would-be protest mobilizers and security agents. Big-character posters would be put up in the Triangle Spot (*sanjiaodi*, a traditional spot for public speeches and informal gathering), and they would be torn down overnight. Since both sides needed the protection of invisibility that nighttime provided, some of these posters would never see the light of day.[24]

If any posters did survive, they could in turn give rise to gatherings in the Triangle Spot. Students claimed constitutional legitimacy and went on holding peaceful protests and attacking Beijing City's prohibitive regulations. At least once every year leading up to 1989, the gatherings developed into marches beyond the campus gate, alarming the university administration and the city police. The campus gates would often be locked down, and city police arrive at nearby traffic intersections to block students. Leaders of two official student organizations – the Communist Youth League and the Students' Association – were dispatched to the grass roots to counsel against participation.[25]

In the spring of 1989, the protest seemed to sail unopposed for the first ten days or so. "This time may be different," students thought, taking notes of the Tiananmen protest in 1976 and its re-evaluation under Deng. The public mourning of Premier Zhou Enlai was first labeled a counterrevolutionary event but later deemed a patriotic movement in the post-Mao era. Former leaders of official student organizations report that for some reason the steps used in previous years to stop protest were not taken in 1989; they received no instructions to stop students during the first days of protest after Hu Yaobang's death.[26]

For more than a week, the student movement in Beijing started and grew without meeting any significant discouragement, harassment, or warning. That was unprecedented. While it might be partly explained by the "grace period" for mourning, as discussed above, this is only part of the story. Three confrontations between the two highest leaders in the Party Center, as Li Peng recorded in his diary, provide additional insight.[27]

### Clashes between Zhao and Li

At 9:00 a.m. on April 20, three days after Hu Yaobang's death, members of the Standing Committee gathered in Zhao Ziyang's office and discussed issues regarding the student demonstrations and Hu's memorial activities. "I suggested that the Center should have a clear-cut stand," Li Peng wrote, "to direct and then to stop the spontaneous memorial activities of the students." But Zhao Ziyang disagreed: "In order not to provoke them further, we should not intervene so long as students are not engaged in beating, smashing, or looting [*da za qiang*]."[28]

Frustrated, Li Peng sought advice from Yang Shangkun, an act that seemed to suggest political savvy. Yang, although not a member of the Standing Committee, was in fact an extraordinary figure in the regime as the executive vice chair of the CMC; that is, Deng's number one man in the military. Indeed, as this saga unfolded in later months, Li and Yang, as the head of the government and the head of the army respectively, were designated by Deng to be in charge of the martial law troops on the night of June 3–4. For the moment, however, Yang did not seem too eager to get on Li's side. Echoing Zhao Ziyang, he advised that students should be "allowed to engage in legal activities in order to calm the situation."[29]

A second confrontation between Li and Zhao took place at 11:30 p.m. on April 19, the following day. At issue was the standoff at the Zhongnanhai gate. "I urged him to deliberate [*yanjiu*] and [take action] immediately. But he said he would do so the next morning. As far as Xinhua Gate was concerned, he said, he did not know the details, and said, so long as the students did not beat, smash, or torch, we should not do anything."[30] Zhao's own account confirmed the gist of their clash: "On the night of April 19, Li Peng called me unexpectedly. 'Students are at the Xinhua Gate; why haven't there been any measure taken [against them]?' He asked. I answered, 'Qin Shi is in charge at the site. He has a few plans and he will use them when necessary.'"[31]

Li Peng recorded a third confrontation at another SC meeting on April 20. Zhao reiterated his position: "We should not intervene so long there is no beating, smashing, or looting behavior." In response, "I [Li] pointedly objected to his view. I said that the situation has been changing. Many students are on the fence but can be manipulated by a handful of people with ulterior motives. The Party Center should have a clear-up stand [against the protest activities]. But my view was not adopted."[32]

Zhao's view apparently prevailed thanks to his position as general secretary and number one in the first-line leadership, coupled with support from figures like Yang Shangkun and his allies within the SC. After Hu Yaobang's funeral on April 22, the policy for dealing with the ongoing student protest was stated in three talking points by Zhao Ziyang: (1) persuade students to resume class, (2) conduct dialog with students and intellectuals, and (3) avoid bloodshed by all means.

Li Peng seemed to have no other choice than to go along until, that is, he was temporarily in charge in the absence of Zhao Ziyang, who embarked a trip abroad on April 23. Zhao made these comments right after the funeral when he took the elevator down with key SC members. On the second day, when Li Peng saw Zhao off at the airport, Zhao reiterated these three points when Li again asked for instructions on how to handle the situation.[33] These views were echoed by Qiao Shi, who said on the same occasion, "These three points are a good method to calm down students and contain the student protest."[34]

*The Student Movement Ballooned*

The time between Hu Yaobang's death on April 15 and his state funeral on April 22 witnessed a government that was mostly quiet, tolerant, and at times accommodating. A key to understanding this situation is Deng's long spell of silence on the matter. On the front line of governing, Zhao Ziyang, as the party chief, was able to prevail over Li Peng. For more than a week, Beijing's university students appeared to have opened an unprecedented door, freely airing their grievances against the state in the form of wall posters, public speeches, marches, and rallies. The messages started with mourning the death of Hu Yaobang, but they gradually covered more and more systemic political problems.

During this initial stage, police and security forces normally made their presence more perfunctory than aggressive in responding to protesting students. Typically, unarmed men in uniform first formed blockade lines at traffic intersections, but these men quickly dispersed when student marchers pushed forward. No arrests were made.[35] The most significant confrontation between students and the police took place during an event known as the Xinhua Gate Sit-In on the nights of April 19 and 20, about which Li Peng and Zhao Ziyang had a contentious phone call. Although the student movement later framed the incident as one of "police violence," a claim that was largely unfounded,[36] the incident was more an emblem of the soft side of the government response than an example of repressive action.

On the night of April 19, according to Li Peng, the number of students sitting in reached more than 2,000 at one point. Even after the Beijing city government had issued a warning against trespass, students repeatedly tried to pass by the security lines.[37] Under the direct supervision of Qiao Shi (a Zhao Ziyang ally and SC member), the government sent a large number of troops to reinforce the gate. Students were later forcefully transported to their respective campuses in the early hours of April 20. In the process, there were minor injuries on both sides, although the exact causes are disputed.[38] While "police violence" became a rallying cry in the subsequent mobilization that led up to the great showdown on April 22 (the day of Hu Yaobang's funeral), the Xinhua Gate confrontation between the two sides again represented government restraint, rather than a forceful crackdown.

The student mobilization reached its first climax on the day of the funeral on April 22. The night before, students – in the tens of thousands – marched from the college district in the western suburbs to Tiananmen Square and waited there overnight. In the afternoon following the funeral ceremony, most protesters refused to leave the square. In one of the iconic moments of the student movement, three student representatives knelt on the steps of the Great Hall of the People and held up a petition letter on a scroll, which asked for an audience with state leaders.[39] When their request was snubbed, students announced a citywide boycott of university classes.

By this time, the movement had reached another milestone rarely seen in the country: the founding of independent student organizations. As mentioned previously, such a development represented a line that cannot be crossed for the party. The first independent organization was established on the evening of April 19 on Beida campus, which in turn proposed forming a citywide alliance, the "Preliminary Organizing Committee for Establishing Solidarity Student Associations." Two days later, a report by the Public Security Bureau on these "illegal organizations" reached Li Peng's desk. He immediately issued his instructions to Li Tieying (head of the State Educational Committee): "This matter requires utmost attention. [We should] immediately notify the universities and disband it, according to law." The State Educational Committee issued its third "notice" to all higher-education sections, reiterating the illegality of independent student associations.[40] That notice seemed to have little effect.

### Zhao Ziyang Leaves Town

The political balance in Beijing was immediately shattered when Zhao Ziyang left Beijing on April 23. Two voices quickly evolved into one. In leaving, Zhao abdicated his duties in Beijing at this critical time, which was an extraordinary bet. The decision at the time might have seemed brilliant in some way, but it would prove to be a miscalculation. He would pay dearly for it.

On the morning of April 20, Vice Premier Tian Jiyun made a special request for Zhao's audience. Formerly a subordinate of Zhao's for many years, Tian was one of his closest friends and allies among the top leadership. In 1987, he was nominated by Zhao to join the SC as a sixth member (the motion failed).[41] Tian made a point to meet Zhao in order to advise him not to take the pending trip to North Korea. "Comrade Ziyang, for the last few days, the situation has been less than peaceful in Beijing and a few other cities in the country; so would you please change the plan of the North Korea visit?" "I also have the same thought," replied Zhao, "but if we arbitrarily change the schedule of a state visit, the outside world [waijie] would read instability into our political situation. Therefore I will stick to the original plan."[42]

Zhao made the trip on April 23, the day after Hu Yaobang's funeral. The extraordinary significance of his departure was not lost on Li Peng, who extended an unusual gesture of goodwill. He came to the Beijing train station to see Zhao off. Li Peng wrote in his diary,

> At 4:30 in the afternoon, I went to the station to see off Ziyang. But he did not seem to welcome my presence. "Are we supposed to simplify the protocols and etiquettes?"

said Zhao, "Your coming has gone beyond what protocol requires you to do." I replied, "It is worth it to go beyond for once. Nowadays there are so many rumors flying around, and we are said to be unfriendly to each other. A send-off can demonstrate solidarity in the Party Center." He did not say anything more.[43]

## Li Peng, Now in Charge, Pushes His Policy Agenda

On that spring afternoon, there must have been many things on Li Peng's mind, but solidarity certainly was not one of them. He wasted little time, pushing his agenda with great speed.

On the same evening, Li Peng visited Yang Shangkun to "analyze the situation." They concluded with a plan to go and see Deng Xiaoping together. The following day (April 24), he convened the first official SC meeting after Zhao's departure. For the first time since the protest had broken, he occupied the number one position among his peers and got to preside over the meeting. The formality and gravity of the meeting were clearly demonstrated by the roster of attendants. They included not only the rest of the Standing Committee members – Yao Yilin, Hu Qili, and Qiao Shi – but also key Politburo members in charge of those important power bases of the central government, including Yang Shangkun (the military), Wan Li (the People's Congress), Rui Xingwen (propaganda), Yan Mingfu (the United Front), Wen Jiabao (chief of staff), Tian Jiyun, Li Ximing (party secretary of Beijing), Song Ping, and Ding Guangen. The meeting set a clear tone, one advocated by Li Peng all along. The idea of an editorial in the *People's Daily* was proposed.[44]

Yang Shangkun and Li Peng went to Deng Xiaoping's residence at 10 a.m. on April 25. After listening to their reports, Deng endorsed Li Peng's views. Li lost no time publicizing Deng's remarks before nighttime arrived. The April 26 editorial was published the next day.[45]

## The Puzzling Decision by Zhao Ziyang to Leave the Country

Why would Zhao leave on the eve of a looming maelstrom? It remains one of the mysteries of the 1989 Tiananmen story. That he should not have done so seems obvious in hindsight. To leave is to concede control of the narrative. The damage was not repairable. What was he thinking? Ostensibly, he cited diplomatic protocols that needed to be followed. But with a firm ally like North Korea, delaying an arranged visit should obviously not be any problem at all. He seemed to have realized this possible objection, so he added another reason: that changing the schedule would make the Chinese government appear to be in trouble.

Yet the real considerations must lie elsewhere. Possibly he wanted to use this to shift the responsibility to Li Peng. Along this line, he might have calculated that Li's harsh approach would not be effective in pacifying students but could backfire. By leaving the scene for a period of time, not only would he escape the blame for the possible escalation, but he might also return as a rescuer.

In the late morning of April 22, after the funeral, the Standing Committee members shared an elevator, along with a few other Politburo members, Li Ximing (party secretary of Beijing), Jiang Zemin (mayor of Shanghai) and Li Ruihuan (mayor of Tianjin). Li Peng made a suggestion: "Comrade Zhao, since you will take leave tomorrow, shall we hold a Politburo meeting this afternoon?" This was echoed by Li Ximing, who added, "I hope the Center issue a clear line, so we can quickly put a halt to the student protest." To that Zhao Ziyang replied, "Time is too pressing, so we need not hold a Politburo meeting especially for that. In the last few days, everyone has put in a lot of work; ultimately the task is up to every one of the people." He added as he looked at Li Peng, "When I am away, you are in charge of the daily operation of the Party Center."[46]

Zhao Ziyang's calculation was clearly recognized by Li Peng. In his diary, Li recorded another episode. On the morning of April 23, the day before Zhao's departure, Li Tieying (head of State Education Committee), a Li Peng ally, made a call to Zhao. Li Tieying again appealed for holding a Standing Committee meeting, presided over by Zhao himself. To back up his argument, he reported to Zhao that "the student protest is escalating and that the target is Comrade Deng Xiaoping." He suggested that he give a report to the Standing Committee in the meeting. But Zhao told him, "I am leaving this afternoon. There is no longer time. You can just report to Li Peng." Interestingly, another Li Peng ally, Li Ximing, made yet another call to Zhao Ziyang, making a similar plea and asking him to postpone his trip. One has to suspect that there was some co-ordination.[47]

"Obviously, Zhao Ziyang has decided to leave this mess for me to clean. What unkind motives!" concluded Li in his diary. He backed his suspicion with what he saw as a peculiar feature of the student movement – he was repeatedly singled out as a target. "Why was I the person to whom the students demanded to submit the petition scroll [on April 22]? Why not Zhao Ziyang?" The content of the petition was mainly about the re-evaluation of Hu Yaobang as the former general party secretary, a matter that belonged to the party system, not the State Council. Should the general party secretary (Zhao) be the more appropriate person to appeal to than the premier (Li)?[48]

Suspicion of Zhao's intention notwithstanding, Li Peng must have been ecstatic for the opportunity created by Zhao's absence. In the heat of the contention between the two voices, Zhao's absence spelled doom for his sunny approach. Worse, many of his allies had to go along with the new party line once that side's argument had won the day.

### The Role of the Deng–Zhao Relationship in Zhao's Miscalculation

Should Zhao Ziyang, one of the most brilliant politicians in the communist system, have known better? His decision would be more understandable than it first appeared if we place this decision-making process in the context of another extremely crucial factor: Deng Xiaoping, the supreme leader of the time and the ultimate judge of any political dispute.

From Zhao Ziyang's perspective, Deng Xiaoping had placed unwavering trust in him, with Deng's most recent assurance explicitly conveyed in one-on-one conversations that occurred on the eve of his North Korea trip. Such assurance had repeatedly been given many times before. When a Hong Kong newspaper reported an attempt by Li Xiannian to dismiss Zhao in late 1988, Zhao passed a note through Deng's chief of staff, Wang Ruilin: "There are many rumors in the country and abroad; are you aware of them?" Deng replied with a statement that the personnel structure in the Party Center should not be changed.[49] Again, in December of that year, after Li Peng and Yao Yilin had taken the lead to criticize Zhao Ziyang in a meeting, Deng gave a long speech to reiterate his support for reform, implicitly for Zhao. "China would go nowhere without reform," he said. The speech in turn prompted Li Peng to see Deng, hoping to clarify his earlier remarks. Deng used the occasion to give Li an earful and concluded with a resounding endorsement of Zhao's tenure as the party head. He stated that Zhao would be a general secretary for two full terms (ten years), and that Li should share this message with his colleagues, including Zhao.[50]

Earlier in 1989, Deng had personally summoned Zhao to his residence:

> I have given it long deliberation, although I have not talked to anyone else about my conclusion. Now you are the first person to hear this: I would like to resign as the Central Military Committee chair and pass the position to you. If I do not retire entirely as the CMC chair, it is difficult to prevent other old comrades from interfering with your job. This state of affairs must change.

Zhao declined this offer, and the two of them agreed to revisit the issue in one year.[51] In the communist system, the position of CMC chair carried with it a sort of power of the highest order. The transfer of this power would have made the succession complete.[52]

Deng's trust did not seem to waver up to the eve of Zhao's North Korea trip in April of 1989. Before his departure Zhao stopped by Deng's residence. Deng suggested that, when Zhao came back from North Korea, he would convene a meeting to officially announce that Zhao would serve two terms as the general party secretary. He also added that this plan had obtained endorsement from both Chen Yun and Li Xiannian.[53]

The extraordinary level of trust is unmistakably shown in this long list of confidential conversations. It served as a secret handshake between a supreme leader and his would-be successor. Zhao might have met many setbacks, the political situation might have seemed murky, and potential rivals might have at times been emboldened. But beneath all this – hidden from the public view – Zhao seems to have had a trump card. It is, then, no wonder he was reported to be very upbeat in the morning after Hu Yaobang's funeral in the Great Hall, unfazed by hundreds of thousands of students outside. He was in such a good mood that he climbed up to the roof of the building, inspecting the crowd. A cameraman even caught his smiling face.[54]

Later events proved that Zhao was being naive, but when he decided to go ahead with the trip he did not appear to be burdened by any doubt.

How did Zhao factor in Deng's trust in his approach to handling the ongoing student demonstration? Zhao wanted not only to weather the storm, but also to transport the enthusiasm of youth toward supporting reform, even possibly in the realm of politics. As a result, he was keen to highlight the positive side of the student protest and worked to frame it as a popular referendum in his favor. He instructed Hu Qili and Rui Xingwen, two top leaders in charge of the media and propaganda, "News media should publish the positive side more and recognize the patriotic passions of the students."[55] In a meeting with a group of officials and academics, Zhao reminded everyone that "this wave of the student movement in fact can be an opportunity for solving a couple of important problems of great social significance."[56]

Zhao might have had good reason to believe that Deng's trust in him meant more. Even though Deng's past intolerance of student-led protests and intellectualism was clearly on the record, it was still possible that Zhao saw a Deng Xiaoping less familiar to public view. As one of the closest subordinates of Deng's, Zhao witnessed long years of Deng relishing out-of-the-box reform ideas. Was it not Deng who had advocated political reform in 1985–1986? At one point, Deng reportedly confided to Hu Yaobang and Zhao Ziyang, "you people are too impatient, you don't fully recognizing that many old comrades are still alive." That is a stunning message, implying that Deng himself might welcome political opening had it not been for other "old comrades."[57] Above all, don't many reiterations of trust mean something profoundly promising?

In short, as Zhao was weighing his decision, the highest consideration must be Deng's trust. That frame of mind explains his extraordinary decision to leave. Deserving or not, he felt very reassured. When he departed, if Deng was firmly on his side, it did not matter whether he made the trip or not; if anything, it could be a good idea to shift the leadership duties to Li Peng for a time.

**A Harsh Verdict: The April 26 Editorial**

*Li Peng's Allies in the Beijing City Government Prepared a Report*

The Beijing city government was led by two of Li Peng's allies, Li Ximing as the party secretary and Chen Xitong as the mayor. On April 24, the city's standing committee of the party met and concluded that the student movement in Beijing had now evolved into a dire situation. The protest was seen as "a product of various enemy forces from within and without the party, and within and without the country." In its essence, the student movement was "spearheaded at the Party Center" and "aiming at the overthrow of the communist party."[58] Such labeling was as clear-cut as it could be; the action it implied the government should take was therefore unmistakable.

Then, Li Ximing and Chen Xitong lost no time making arrangements for their perspective to be adopted by the Party Center. Later that morning, they appeared in the office of Wan Li, the president of the People's Congress. Wan Li was a reformer with strong credentials as well as being a friend and ally of Zhao Ziyang, but as a former party secretary and mayor of Beijing, he was also well connected to the capital city's government. When Chen and Li first sat down in his office inside the Great Meeting Hall of the People, they addressed Wan Li as "our old leader." They presented a report compiled by the city government.[59]

Chen Xitong summarized the main thrust of the report as follows:

> The student movement in Beijing has been getting more and more serious. Reactionary organizations have come out to operate publicly: they mobilized students into a class strike, and teachers into a teaching strike. As of today, the class strike has affected 39 universities in Beijing city, with more than 30,000 students involved.

To that, Li Ximing added,

> The students did not have this level of capacity [of mobilizing]; there are black hands behind them. For example, Beida students were the most active, and behind them is Fang Lizhi's wife Li Shuxian. Fang Lizhi may seem to refrain from having a direct hand in the movement, but he is the connection between the students and the media from foreign countries.[60]

*Li Peng Rallies More Support*

Wan Li seemed to show serious concern, deeming their report "very important." Li and Chen nudged Wan to make a motion for the Party Center to adopt the report. To that Wan's reply was that Li and Chen should talk to Li Peng directly.[61] Perhaps the true purpose of their visit was to enlist critical support before the official meeting. That Wan Li was an ally of Zhao Ziyang made this task all the more meaningful – it could neutralize potential opposition.

The same morning Li Peng also made a point to talk to Wan Li and two other people, Yao Yilin and Song Ping. Yao and Song had been in the same camp as Li Peng in past debates. Only Wan Li needed persuasion. According to Li Peng, Wan relayed the messages from Li Ximing and Chen Xitong and suggested a meeting at Party Center level. "I agreed with Wan Li's suggestion ... and decided on a Standing Committee meeting at 8:00 p.m., to be attended also by other related comrades," wrote Li.[62]

The so-called "bumping-heads meeting of the Standing Committee" endorsed the Beijing report. Li Peng proposed three possible actions to be taken next:

> First, the *People's Daily* was to publish an editorial "with gravity," which would convey the conclusions of the bumping-heads meeting. Second, the Party Center and the State Council were to issue a joint notice to the country's provinces and cities. Third, in Beijing a mobilizing meeting was to be held, attended by a large number of cadres from the party, the military, and the government.[63]

### Deng Comes to Li Peng's Side

On the morning of April 25, at ten o'clock, Deng Xiaoping received a visit from Li Peng and Yang Shangkun at his residence. After their report, Deng gave a long speech, recorded verbatim by Li Peng. The speech was almost perfectly in line with Li Peng's view on the issue of the protest. In fact, it went further, with a rich supply of philosophizing and historicizing of the student movement. Deng's speech served as the basis for the April 26 editorial published the next day. Indeed, much loaded terminology used in the editorial was directly adopted from there: "a clear-cut stand," "turmoil," "a result of the large climate within and without the country," and so on.[64] Li Peng himself immediately ordered that the speech be disseminated to all party members.[65]

The editorial was published on April 26 with great fanfare – it was not only printed prominently in the *People's Daily*, the *PLA Daily*, and the *Red Flag* magazine, but also broadcast via loudspeakers on every university campus in Beijing.[66] While the loudspeakers were blaring, the mobilizing meeting of Beijing cadres also took place, attended by more than 10,000.[67]

### The Editorial Backfired

However, the editorial did the opposite of ending the student movement. Its broadcast on university campuses caused immense disappointment and fury, according to a would-be student leader: After the broadcast, according to a would-be student leader,

For a time the campus turned dead quiet, as though every living creature had stopped breathing and the earth stopped moving. Then all the sudden, came the sound of an explosion as a glass bottle was thrown from the window of a dormitory building to the ground . . . When the students threw out all the glass bottles they had, they began to throw cooking pots, plates and plastic containers, along with their screams of protest.[68]

In the past when the government had harshly labeled a fledgling movement in the making, the activists would not be organized enough to give a collective response. But this time was different. The negative verdict came down at a time when a citywide alliance of independent student organizations had been set up. On the very morning of April 26, an international news conference was in session under a banner that read "The Constitution stipulates that citizens enjoy freedom of speech and demonstration." The newly elected president of the Beijing Autonomous Association of University Students (BAAUS) held the conference and addressed close to 100 reporters from all over the world.[69] The next day, a student demonstration was launched. With more than a million participating, it took an hour and a half for the marching crowds to pass east along the Tiananmen Square section of Changan Avenue.[70]

That was exactly what Zhao Ziyang might have anticipated: a harsh approach could not stem the tide of the movement. If he was somehow vindicated, however, he also lost the battle to label the movement. That would be a steep price to pay. "Between April 24 and the morning of April 30, I was not in Beijing. Hence, I did not know what was going on," Zhao ruefully wrote later, "In North Korea I received the telegraph on the early morning of April 26, carrying Comrade Xiaoping's speech and the Standing Committee's meeting minutes. I immediately telegraphed back: 'I fully support Comrade Xiaoping's correct decision on the current turmoil.'" When Deng had spoken, Zhao himself had to adopt the label "turmoil."[71]

### Discussion and Conclusion

Earlier in this chapter, I already noted a few reasons why Li Peng held a hardline stance and advocated harsh measures. For example, he belonged to the conservative faction that had helped fire Hu Yaobang as general secretary two years earlier. Triggered by Hu's death, the student protest targeted Li by name. Can we count him as a leader who was doing everything he could to end the protest? On the one hand, there is strong support for such a characterization. For example, he pushed Zhao Ziyang to convene SC meetings and to make the Party Center's objection known early. He urged strong measures to stop a midnight sit-in. Finally, he produced, in Zhao Ziyang's absence and through working with Deng, the April 26 editorial, which set the tone for the repression to come.

On the other hand, there is also counterevidence. First, Li Peng joined other leaders in staying silent about the student activities during the first few days in adherence to showing respect for the dead. Second, his objection to the protest remained verbal rather than substantive with an obsession to labeling it negatively. Third, he knew a strong label could backfire as the premier who was on top of the state machine that closely monitored the protest. His engineering background would also have helped him realize that a confrontational approach, especially in the wake of the large turnout by the students at Hu Yaobang's funeral, could only inflame the situation.

Therefore, Li Peng was hardly in favor of repression: from the first stage of Tiananmen to the famous editorial, he seemed to be concerned more with how the protest was labeled than with whether it could be ended, and he seemed willing to risk further incensing the protest.

The reason is not hard to understand. As discussed in Chapter 3, popular protest in the communist state, as long as it is framed unsympathetically, could be blamed on the party's chief, who, at the time of Tiananmen, was Zhao Ziyang.

Nor did Zhao Ziyang seem to rush to end the protest. He refused to label it negatively, he persistently counseled patience and restraint, he objected to government intervention even in serious situations such as the Xinhua Gate standoff, and finally he left the country altogether for a significant period of time. The question remains why.

The first factor to consider is whether his job as the general secretary was already in jeopardy. As I discussed in Chapter 3, there are good reasons to suspect that was the case, and, importantly, he was aware of "a movement of sacking Zhao afoot in the capital city." Therefore, an unexpected event could be a welcome change, not to mention that the protest was being waged in defense of the last general secretary. Second, the protest was already taking place. He could not contest this fact, and his only hope was to frame it as something benign. Third, if addressing the protest carried some risk, then disowning it provided him with a strategic exit, which might explain why Zhao chose to leave at the height of the student protest.

For these actions to work in his favor, Zhao Ziyang relied on what would be the fourth and most decisive factor: Deng's trust in him. That would prove to be his biggest miscalculation. But as late as the night before Zhao's departure for North Korea, Deng repeated his pledge of passing the CMC chairmanship to Zhao. Maybe Deng was deceptively Machiavellian, or maybe his thinking was evolving. We will never know.

What about Deng Xiaoping? Was he the ultimate leader in favor of repression then? Yes, if we consider the tone he set for the editorial and his later decisions. At the same time, government inaction during the early disputes between Li Peng and Zhao Ziyang was only possible because of his long spell of silence.

Many, particularly Zhao Ziyang's supporters, believed that Deng made the decision on the editorial because he was "duped" by Li Peng, Chen Xitong, and Li Ximing.[72] This line of thinking portrays a Deng Xiaoping as an old man who had passed his time of shrewd political judgment and initiative. That is far from the truth. Deng was still very much of his own man.[73] His verdict on the protest was part of his long game. In the next chapter I will turn to Deng's role.

In sum, none of the key leaders fits the conventional mode of a repressor. To the contrary, their actions and inaction in the earlier stages of the events of 1989 contributed to the making of the Tiananmen protest as we know it.

# 5 Where Was Deng Xiaoping?
## April 15–May 11, 1989

Historical accounts show no trace of Deng participating in public life between April 25 and May 11, 1989. Sources that recorded the gap include *Deng Xiaoping: Life Chronology*, an official publication by the Central Archive Press. According to the chronology, on April 25 Deng spoke to Yang Shangkun and Li Peng, and what he said became the guide for the April 26 editorial published that evening. The chronology then curiously reports no activities for more than two weeks. Then it picks up on May 11, recording one item of Deng's daily schedule – receiving a diplomatic delegation led by the president of Iran. The chronology then resumes as normal, documenting his official activities on May 13, May 16, May 17, and so on.[1]

In the previous chapter, we examined the behavior of the three highest leaders in the first ten days of Tiananmen. There, I included Deng, but I mainly focused on Zhao Ziyang, the general party secretary, and Li Peng, the premier. I noted Deng's long spell of silence before making known his hardline verdict. The meaning of his silence and the thinking behind the verdict, however, remain unexamined. Was he too old to be cognizant of what was happening, or was he waiting for the right moment to speak up? Did he act out of his institutional instinct, or was he paving the way for something bigger?

These questions will be explored further in this chapter, which covers a period beyond the first ten days. Interestingly, he disappeared from the public eye, after giving the speech that served as the basis for the April 26 editorial, for more than two weeks. Then, on May 11, he had a long conversation with Yang Shangkun, who was in charge of the military and served as his right-hand man. In this chat, he appears to have made up his mind on the major issues. The meeting was omitted from the chronology but is reported by other sources.[2]

Deng's deliberation process is theoretically meaningful, and the timing could be crucial. For example, the revolution suppression model suggests that Beijing's military solution was adopted only when the student protest escalated and social order was out of control. To support that argument, the government, as well as many academic writers, cite the intensified wave of student mobilizations (in the form of a hunger strike) and the turmoil it caused. But one important fact contradicts the escalation claim. The hunger strike did not start until May 13, while Deng's remarks hinting at a military endgame were made on May 11. Just as critical, what was he doing during this second period of silence?

Where was he? There were rumors during the protest that Deng Xiaoping was flying out to Wuhan to meet military generals.[3] Years after 1989, political scientist Wu Guoguang, a former official in Zhao's inner circle, penned a provocative essay titled "The Mystery of Deng Xiaoping's Disappearance." He suggested that Deng might have been out of town and busy making military arrangements. Zhao Ziyang's recorded recollections attested that he tried but failed to obtain an audience with Deng. After he came back from North Korea on April 30, Zhao was eager to see Deng. But his request was rebuffed by Deng's office. "Comrade Xiaoping has not felt too well lately," Zhao was told.[4] However, years later, under house arrest, pressed by a journalist, Zhao still believed that Deng did not leave town.[5] Whether in Beijing or not, according to some scholars, Deng was most likely focusing on military preparation.[6]

Deng's whereabouts during this period – and more to the point, whether he was preparing the military – are important. This bears directly on how we might come to explain the Chinese government's decision to use martial law as their response to the 1989 Tiananmen Square movement. If he had indeed made up his mind much earlier, it would undermine the conclusion that state elites resorted to the military only after all else had failed, a claim put forward by scholars like Dingxin Zhao.[7] It will also challenge claims that the protest was so dangerous that anything less than a military intervention would fail to save the regime.[8] Both these claims cited the student hunger strike as evidence that softer government methods had failed. However, the hunger strike did not start until May 13. So if Deng had already decided to use the military before May 11, his decision would have had little, if anything, to do with the hunger strike.

Moreover, if Deng had indeed made up his mind early on, how early? Relatedly, did he make the decision on his own or was he persuaded by misinformation? Zhao Ziyang and his supporters portrayed Deng as an ill-informed old man who was easily misled by others.[9] According to Zhao, Deng initially raised no red flag about the demonstrations or about Zhao's handling of them, and had been reassuring him in conversations.[10] Prior to Zhao's departure for North Korea, Deng even reiterated the offer of making Zhao the CMC chair and reportedly instructed Li Peng to "do what Zhao Ziyang said" with regard the ongoing protest. Zhao believed that Deng gave the April 25 speech due to a change of heart.[11]

I extend the question "Where Was Deng Xiaoping" to include the earlier period of silence that led to the editorial and his "disappearance" after that. The April 26 editorial and the May 11 meeting were equally important. If the former was a diagnosis, the latter was a prescription; if the former was a verdict, the latter was a sentence.

In both cases, existing scholarship remains unequivocal about the importance of Deng's role. Less clear, though, is the question of when and how Deng reached these decisions. For example, was he misled by others? Did he settle on the use of martial law only after the protest escalated? Below, as I revisit the history and dissect the elite interaction, I conclude that Deng was well informed and clear-headed, and chose military intervention based on his own internal deliberations. On the metaphorical train that led to June 4, 1989, he was steadfastly in the driving seat.

## Early Reactions to the Student Protest

### *Deng Was in the Know*

Zhao Ziyang and his supporters took the position that Deng assessed the protest with insufficient information. He got the "true nature" wrong, according to this view, because Li Peng and Beijing city leaders fed him only a distorted picture by cherry-picking two aspects of the movement: offensive personal attacks on Deng and anti-party slogans. This analysis depicts a passive Deng and implies his frailty and narrow-mindedness.[12]

In the afternoon of April 15, hours after the death of Hu Yaobang, Zhao Ziyang made a special trip to Deng's residence in Miliang Hutong at Dianmen to personally report the sad news. But the news had preceded his arrival. When Zhao entered the compound, Deng had already recovered a bit from the shock and had instructed his wife Zhuo Lin to make a call to Hu's wife. "Upon hearing the news about Comrade Yaobang," related Wang Ruilin, his chief aide,

> Comrade Xiaoping hastily crushed a cigarette he was smoking. Then for a long moment in silence, he folded ten fingers helplessly in front of his chest. Then all of a sudden, he picked up the cigarette again to take quick and deep puffs. When Ziyang came in, he had already settled down somewhat.[13]

To someone at age eighty-four, news of Hu's death obviously did not come lightly. Like his other colleagues, Deng was eager to show sympathy and respect. He personally attended all of the memorial ceremonies. He also read and commented on the official obituary. As far as the street mourning was concerned, he gave tacit permission through his silence. Yet he was acutely aware of what was going on in the student movement, including personal attacks in the mix. He might have not come out of his residence much, but from day one he routinely sent his three children out to gather information, and his children were keen to report back to him without cherry-picking to please the old man.

Deng was famously close to his children. Of the five children who were in their forties and late thirties, three were very active politically. Deng Nan, forty-two, the second daughter, was a bureau chief of the state's Science Commission and a member of the Central Party Committee of the 17th Party Congress of 1988. She was supposedly the "chief guardian of the Deng clan," jealously guarding her father's reputation and the family interest. Deng Pufang, forty-five, the elder son, was tortured by the Red Guards during the Cultural Revolution and became a paraplegic. In 1989, his official title was president of China's official federation of disabled people, but his influence went far beyond that particular area. At one point in 1988, when Li Xiannian and other elder leaders clamored to dismiss Zhao Ziyang, Pufang urged his father to reject the idea.[14] Apparently, Pufang was well connected with progressive intellectual networks. As documented in *Black Hands of Beijing*, Pufang's friends before 1989 included Wang Juntao and Chen Ziming, two prominent dissidents.[15] Deng Rong, thirty-nine, the youngest child, was the third important adviser to Deng within the family. She had a stint in China's embassy in Washington, DC when the countries resumed the formal diplomatic relationship in 1979. Her official title in 1989 was director of a policy institute in the People's Congress. She was her father's ear in a very literal sense: in public appearances, she could be found at his side, repeating words into his ear and at times also "translating" his strong Sichuan accent.[16]

It is well documented that Deng's children served as his ears, counselors, and enforcers. For example, Zhao reported that "Deng and his family members were not too happy" after Li Peng made the official decision to publicize Deng's April 25 speech. "Deng's family members said that Li hid behind [the editorial] as a good guy, but threw Deng into the first line."[17] On May 3, Yang Shangkun brought Zhao messages from Wang Ruilin and "Deng's children."[18] On the eve of May 4, when Zhao was preparing a speech, Deng Rong asked to add remarks that Deng had been a champion of young people.[19] On May 16, Deng Nan and her siblings were reportedly "angry" at Zhao, who in his talk with Gorbachev revealed that Deng remained the decision maker.[20]

To illustrate how much Deng was in the know, let's see how he was implicated in at least two controversies following Hu Yaobang's death. One was the cancelation of a farewell ceremony. In the afternoon of April 17, two SC committee members – Qiao Shi and Hu Qili – convened a meeting to decide on key items for the memorial services. Among them was a large farewell ceremony for Hu's body on April 21, to be held in the Great Meeting Hall of the People and attended by 10,000 public mourners. But in the same evening, news came down from the Xinhua News Agency that that it was canceled. While officials in the agency did not know who ordered it, they were confident that it was Deng. "Who else dares to overwrite a decision by the Standing Committee?" reasoned an official.[21]

The other was about Hu's obituary. Deng reportedly insisted on deleting the epithet "a great Marxist." According to Yu Guangyuan (a renowned economist and a friend of Hu's), in 1976 when Premier Zhou Enlai died, Mao made a point of withholding such an epithet. That slight was publicized in the earlier Tiananmen protest that year. "I did not want to see Hu Yaobang get the same treatment as Zhou Enlai, so I propose calling Hu Yaobang a 'great Marxist.'" Yu later heard that a "certain leader" was not pleased with his suggestion.[22] An impasse ensued. The family insisted on adding the epithet, while Deng refused to give in. The dispute delayed Xinhua from issuing the obituary for six hours.[23] The veracity of this controversy was partially confirmed by Deng himself. In his speech, which occurred days later, on April 25, he said, "Comrade Yaobang is not qualified. Nor am I. Do not call me a great Marxist after I die."[24]

### Informal Utterance: "It Is Not That Simple"

On the matter of the student protest itself, Deng's first public comments were made on the floor of Hu's funeral on April 22. The location was the Grand Meeting Hall of the People on the west side of the square. Tens of thousands of students had camped on the square overnight. They had come the night before, defying a curfew. At about a quarter to ten in the morning, when Deng arrived at the hall, other leaders came forward to greet him. Among them was General Wang Zhen, clearly irritated by the student protest outside: "Comrade Xiaoping, many of us found the traffic troublesome on the way to this cere-mony. The students are out of line! How dare they camp at a sacred place like Tiananmen Square?" Then he made a startling suggestion to Deng: "Can we just send the police to chase them away?" To that Deng calmly replied, "It is not that simple. Let us talk about that no more today."[25]

It was indeed "not that simple." To begin with, by then, neither Deng nor others in the government had set an overall tone as to how they should talk about the demonstrations. Previously I discussed the significance of *dingxing*, tone setting and labeling in China's party parlance. In this well-known phrase, the second Chinese character, *xing* means "nature," "character," or "essence." The first character, *ding*, can mean both "to discern" and "to decide." It is more a political act than an intellectual exercise, however. To *dingxing*, to set a tone even before engaging in fact finding, is a standard practice in party politics. Therefore, "essence" is not an objective matter, but something that exists in the eye of the beholder. A report's tone reflects its reporter's predisposition, rather than how the events present themselves. Facts can be used to support two opposite conclusions.[26]

So it was not surprising that the Beijing government would submit a report that highlighted all things negative and grave. This was not because officials had to fabricate facts (that is, "facts" were there to glean), but because the Beijing leaders – Li Ximing and Chen Xitong – were ultimately Li Peng's political allies. They only needed to cherry-pick. Deng was equally aware of the facts presented by the Beijing report, as we noted earlier. If anything, since many of the attacks were made directly at him, Deng might have felt it more personally and acutely than the Beijing leaders. In other words, he did not need the Beijing report to decide his position. His position was predisposed by other considerations rather than by the presentation of facts.

### A Hardliner on the Issue of Protest

We may never know how Deng Xiaoping took a long strategic view in his *dingxing*, or tone setting, of the protest. We do know, however, that he was consistent in treating popular protest as unacceptable. As we may recall, he dismissed Hu Yaobang partly for Hu's soft stand on the issue. Deng's intense objection and his reasoning are recorded in a long speech in 1986. He blamed leaders like Hu for lapses in the government's ability to hold political control:

> Student disturbance may not cause any catastrophe, but if you look at the essence of it, it is a serious matter ... Disturbances are likely in places where the leaders are not resolute in taking a clear-cut stand. That is a problem that goes beyond one place or two, nor is it a result of one year or two. It is a result of the wavering attitudes in the campaign against the bourgeois liberal currents.[27]

How to deal with dissent and protest? He suggested coercive instruments of the state. He was unequivocal about jailing activists, and he seemed to signal a willingness to shed blood. Again in 1986:

> Did we arrest Wei Jingsheng [an activist in the Democracy Wall movement]? Did that ruin China's reputation? We not only arrested him but also jailed him. China's reputation did not get worse for that; to the contrary, our image is getting better and better by the day ... China will have no future without the leading position of the CCP or the guiding line of socialism ... As far as the means of dictatorship is concerned, we should not only talk about it, we should also use it.[28] To be sure, we must be prudent when using it – make as few arrests as possible and manage not to have bloodshed. But what can you do if they cause events that involve blood?[29]

It is also worth noting that Deng's harsh stand was not because he thought students were capable of overthrowing the government. To the contrary, at the very outset, he pointed out that student unrests "cannot cause any catastrophe." To him, the capacity of protest was quite weak (if annoying) rather than strong. He was against them out of his stern belief in social and political order.

In the April 25, 1989, speech he gave to Li Peng and Yang Shangkun at his residence, Deng repeated many elements from his 1986 speech. For example, he reminded his listeners, "we should not be afraid of what foreigners might say."[30] His *dingxing* and his solution were also similar: "The student unrest this time is no ordinary student movement; it is political turmoil. In suppressing this turmoil, we should strive to avoid bloodshed. But it may not be possible to entirely avoid it. It looks like we will have to arrest a bunch of people at the end.[31]

## Who Was in the Driving Seat?

### How Deng Reached His Verdict

Deng was the person who set the tone. Indeed, the published editorial closely tracked his April 25 speech – including the tenet, key points, and even a number of quotable phrases. Deng said that the movement was no ordinary student protest, but turmoil, and he urged the party to "take a clear stand"; the editorial was entitled "We Must Take a Clear Stand to Oppose the Turmoil." Deng named a few intellectuals as the masterminds behind the "planed conspiracy"; the editorial coined the phrase "a handful of people with ulterior motives." Deng framed the protest organizations as "illegal"; the editorial declared, "we will never permit any illegal organization."[32]

What is debatable, however, is how Deng reached this point of explicit hostility. From Zhao Ziyang's account of what happened, Deng appears to have had a change of heart. Deng was perceived as being on Zhao's side at the beginning. "On April 19, I visited him in his residence," wrote Zhao. "We discussed my upcoming North Korea trip and the student protest. I shared my view of how we should handle it. He seemed to agree with me."[33] On another occasion, Zhao offered a similar assessment: "About the student protest, we did not have any major disagreement."[34] "The general idea, which Deng supported, was not to exacerbate the conflict."[35] According to Zhao, when Li Peng relayed Zhao's parting instructions in "three points," Deng reportedly replied, "Do what Ziyang said then."[36] So it is not surprising that, to Zhao, Deng changed his mind only because Li Peng, Chen Xitong, and Li Ximing had "tricked" him. Zhao believed that the Beijing party committee provided "false intelligence," which in turn misled both the Standing Committee and Deng. "Upon Li Peng's words, Deng saw a dire state of affairs, hence he issued the assertion [naming the movement a turmoil]," Zhao concluded.[37]

Zhao's post-1989 assessment has been widely shared by supporters both inside and outside the government.[38] No one can doubt Zhao's sincerity in presenting this version of history, given what he heard from Deng directly and how much he believed in Deng's trust. It is also possible, however, that Zhao himself did not buy this image of a passive Deng, so he was trying to spare Deng the responsibility for the Tiananmen tragedy and to shift the blame onto the conservatives.

At first glance, though, Zhao's reading fits the timeline of events. That is, Deng uttered no harsh words on the protest until the last minute. Deng's speech itself offered supporting evidence on this point, when he said, "The handling of the memorial activities and the funeral has been good. But the nature [of the situation] has changed now."[39] Obviously the "handling" covered the student protest in connection with "memorial activities."

Even the account offered by Li Peng's published diary can do little to refute Zhao's version. As we recounted in last chapter, two lines of government reaction emerged in the first days of the student protest, represented by Zhao and Li. On at least three occasions the two top leaders had an argument, according to Li.

There is evidence that Li made efforts to resolve this dispute by lobbying Deng. In the evening after Zhao's departure from Beijing on April 23, at 8:30 p.m., Li met Yang Shangkun to discuss the protest. "He encouraged me to make a visit to Deng and to ask for instructions," writes Li. "I asked him to go along. And he agreed."[40]

There is no official record and there are no personal reflections to ascertain whether or not this meeting took place. Maybe it did, because as the analysis below will suggest, that would be the only reasonable explanation why all the people who attended the April 24 "bumping-heads meeting," including Zhao's allies, unanimously supported Li's hard line, an about-face from Zhao's soft approach when he was in town. We will come back to discuss this point more below.[41]

### Prodded by Li Peng and Allies

At 8:00 p.m. the next day, April 24, Li Peng convened a "bumping-heads meeting" of the Standing Committee.[42] In Zhao's absence, Li became the number one first-line leader and he was in charge. Li Peng reported that the meeting was in fact suggested by Wan Li, another first-line leader close to Deng and an ally of Zhao's. Li stressed this information apparently to indicate that the idea for the meeting was not his own alone. Invited to attend were Wan Li and seven or so others, including Li Ximing, the party secretary of Beijing City, who gave a report.[43]

In Li Peng's telling, in contrast to the impasse that had snarled decision-making up to this point, the bumping-heads meeting unanimously adopted his analysis and proposal. No one, including Zhao's allies such as Hu Qili, Qiao Shi, and Wan Li, was reported as showing any dissent. Indeed, in Li Peng's words, "*All unanimously agreed* that the situation at the present was serious, and that the student protest ... was instigated by some people behind the scenes; in effect, a planned and organized political project that aimed at overthrowing the Communist Party."[44] It is not difficult to see how remarkably similar these words were to those in Deng's remarks to be made on April 25.

Li Ximing spoke on behalf of the Beijing City government. He pleaded that "the Party Center should *take a clear stand* and employ effective measures to stop it."[45] In response, Li Peng proposed three important actions, including a *People's Daily* editorial, a debriefing at the provincial level and below, and a rally of cadres from the central government and Beijing. The meeting ended at around 11:30 p.m. At this time, a phone call came from Deng's office, informing them that Li Peng and Yang Shangkun would be received by Deng in his residence at 10:00 a.m. the next day, April 25.[46]

When Li Peng published his diary in 2004, he must be more than aware of the charge that he had misled Deng. So he took pains to dispel that notion.[47] He went to great lengths to show that his way of operating in Zhao's absence was strictly in accordance with party norms: finding out the "facts" before making a decision (i.e., the Beijing government reports), collective leadership (i.e., the bumping-heads meeting), and consultation with second-line leaders (i.e., Deng's interview and speech). As far as Deng's role is concerned, Li made an effort to strike a very delicate balance. On the one hand, he wants readers to conclude for themselves that Deng was fully in control, hence no one "misled" him. On the other hand, he was supposed to maintain the facade of the first-line leaders' "independence" and show that Deng offered no more than "consultation."[48]

However, something seems amiss in Li Peng's version of the story. First, on the surface, the decisions and language from the April 24 meeting are almost identical to what Deng had to say on April 25. Second, all of a sudden, the government decided to issue a clear response to the protest. How did that happen? Was it only because Zhao had left Beijing and Li stepped up? Third, how could the vote be unanimous? How was it that Qiao Shi, Hu Qili, and Wan Li – three Zhao allies – signaled no dissent? It could only have been possible if the position was set by some higher authority than Li Peng himself.

### Deng Was in Fact in Charge

The most plausible answer to these questions is that Deng had set the tone for the April 24 Standing Committee bumping-heads meeting, either by seeing Li (and Yang Shangkun) personally beforehand – that is, Li and Yang did succeed in their quest for a Deng interview on April 23, the day before the bumping-heads meeting – or by relaying his instruction in other ways. That is, Li did not need to wait until the morning of April 25 to know what Deng had to say. This view was first offered by Wu Guoguang, one of the prominent leading authorities on the inner workings of China's elite politics. "We have reasons to suspect that Li Peng (and the other official narratives) had hidden an important fact," writes Wu, "That is, on the evening of April 23, 1989, Deng issued a secret order to Li Peng, directly or indirectly. It was that secret order that deemed the student protest 'counterrevolutionary turmoil that aims at overthrowing the communist party.'"[49] Wu's speculation has been supported by another writer,

Dai Qing, in her recently published *Deng Xiaoping in 1989*, where she cites a historian and a party politics insider to support her view.[50]

Wu supports his claim by compiling Li Peng's timeline. He cites Zhang Wanshu, a former news chief at Xinhua News Agency. According to the memoir of this journalist, on the morning of April 25, at 10:00 a.m., when Deng's conversation with Li Peng and Yang Shangkun had not yet taken place, Xinhua's department chiefs were convened and debriefed on key points, which were identical to Deng's speech. The meeting was said to have been ordered by Hu Qili earlier in the morning, at 8:00 a.m., two hours before Deng's speech. According to Lu Chaoqi, another news chief with the *People's Daily*, the writing of the April 26 editorial started early in the morning of April 25. Hu Qili personally instructed the newspaper's team on the content of the editorial.[51]

Wu lays out a few other pieces of circumstantial evidence. First, he does not believe that, absent other factors, Li Peng would have been able to get the other participants at the April 24 meeting to go along with him. In addition to Qiao Shi, Hu Qili, and Wan Li, attending the meeting were a few other allies of Zhao, including Rui Xingwen, Tian Jiyun, and Wen Jiabao. Second, Li Peng reported that he had had conversations with Yao Yilin, Wan Li, and Song Ping on the morning of April 24, but Wu suggests that his rank would not have allowed him to do so with Wan Li and Song Ping unless he had a mandate. According to Wu, Li Peng was at best equal in rank with Wan Li, who was the president of People's Congress, and with Song Ping, who was in the Party Center's Organization Department.[52]

In sum, Deng Xiaoping took charge in creating the editorial. Not only was his mind not "misled" by others, but also Li Peng's flurry of action in those two days was more likely directed by a signal from Deng. How the signal was passed remains unknown – a "wink," a note, a phone call, or a midnight interview. Maybe Li Peng and Yang Shangkun did get to see Deng on April 23. Equally possible was a simple phone call from Wang Ruilin, Deng's aide in chief, to relay "instructions from Xiaoping." Such a phone call seems not to have been unusual, according to Li's diary. For example, on the morning of May 11, the day Deng reappeared after the second long spell of silence, Wang Ruilin called Li Peng and gave him an extensive set of instructions from Deng.[53]

### Deng's "Disappearance" after the Editorial

*Zhao Ziyang Needs Clarification and Support*

On April 26, editorial Zhao had reservations but was not able to express dissent from afar. In fact he could do nothing but telegraph his support for Deng's speech. On April 30, 1989, when he came back from Pyongyang, he was anxious to see Deng. Understandably, after the week-long absence from Beijing, he badly needed to catch up, especially on the general direction moving forward. The editorial's backlash effect on the protest seemed to support his reservations. He requested an interview for May 1, and he was declined:

> I was eager to see Deng, face to face, so I could share my views. I would have liked to obtain a nod from him. So I phoned Wang Ruilin to make an appointment. Wang said that Deng had not felt too well lately. "It would be too bad and serious if he were unable to [recover on time] to receive Gorbachev's visit. Therefore, nowadays no business should be reported to him, so as not to disturb him."[54]

The following day, some words were passed all the way over to Zhao Ziyang's residence by a high-ranking official. They were not from Deng Xiaoping himself, but from those close to him – Wang Ruilin and Deng's children, according to Yan Mingfu, who came to visit Zhao. Zhao Ziyang was told,

> As far as the student protest is concerned, the [first-line] leaders of the Party Center should handle it for now. It may not be a good idea to go to Deng. It would be even more difficult if you go to him and he rejects your ideas. In the next few days, it should be acceptable to just defuse the situation [caused by the April 26 editorial] and seek a possible adjustment.[55]

The tenor of these instructions seems to support Zhao's thinking, which reflected a desire to revisit the editorial. There is little ambiguity there. What is ambiguous, however, is the source of such instructions. It came from people close to Deng, rather than Deng himself. Were they in fact what Deng meant? In normal times, a shrewd politician like Zhao Ziyang would be prudent enough not to act on them until they had been confirmed. But those days in China were not a normal time. Further, Zhao did make an effort to seek clarity, yet Deng refused to see him. As we will see from later developments, there is reason to believe that ambiguity was exactly what Deng intended.

It would be twelve days later, on May 13, that Zhao Ziyang finally got the chance to see Deng. By this time, Zhao had implemented a new policy of reconciliation for about two weeks. He did so with no explicit blessing from Deng. The merit of his policy, as far as pacification was concerned, was debatable. But such a debate was ended abruptly in his opponents' favor by a new wave of demonstrations. Many suggest that that outcome, a failure defined by the commencement of a hunger strike and a new height of escalation, was the catalyst for Deng Xiaoping to grade Zhao's performance, and to decide to abandon him. Yet closer inspection of the sequence suggests otherwise – Deng had made up his mind long before.

On that morning, May 13, Zhao Ziyang did not get a one-to-one interview. Also in attendance was Yang Shangkun. Even by that time, as far as Zhao Ziyang was concerned, Deng seemed still to be on his side. Deng did not say much. If he said anything at all, in Zhao's ear it rang like an endorsement. Zhao noted "approval" at at least two points during their conversation, one about anticorruption issues and the other about the protest itself. In any case, Deng did not give any hint that his mind had been made up by this time and that Zhao Ziyang would be removed.[56]

### Deng Ignored Zhao's Request for an Interview

Not only did Deng make himself unavailable to Zhao, but also he committed a total blackout that lasted eighteen days between April 25 and May 11, 1989. While it is common to have a gap here and there, a gap of more than ten days is unusual.[57] Gaps could be a genuine reflection of absence of official activities, due to reasons such as illness. They could be a result of censorship if such information was deemed sensitive.[58]

Little evidence supports the speculation that Deng actually left Beijing. Considering his age and position, a trip like that could not have been so totally discreet as to escape the view of other elite leaders. Zhao Ziyang believed that Deng was in town all the time.[59] Timothy Brook has supported this view from a different angle. If making military arrangements was the goal, Brook argued, then Deng did not need to leave the capital. "Deng's alleged trips to Wuhan probably never happened," Brook observes in his *Quelling the People*:

> Such a visit could have been plausible a decade earlier, when that city was the main military headquarters in central China, but the city's status was downgraded in the military reorganization in the mid-1980s. Furthermore, the men Deng appointed as commanders in the seven military regions in that reorganization were all longtime loyal supporters whose ties to Deng went back to his civil war days as political commissar of the 129th Division and the Second Field Army. Nothing required him to leave the crisis in the capital short of substantial internal opposition within the military.[60]

Nor is illness a believable cause for his absence. He appeared to be in good health and energetic when he decided to appear again. He discharged a diplomatic obligation on May 11, carried out a long conversation the same day, held a meeting with Zhao and Yang on May 13, held the summit with Gorbachev on May 16, and finally presided over the Standing Committee meeting of May 17. His meeting with Gorbachev on May 16 lasted for two and half hours. "Deng was in good spirit, even exuberant, as he healed the breach with the Soviet Union on his terms," according to Foreign Minister Qian Qichen.[61] The television audience might have noticed some signs of old age, difficulty in hearing, and a less than steady hold of chopsticks, but if his health earlier was similar to that on later occasions, it is hard to believe he could not have granted Zhao Ziyang a visit.

So what were the reasons behind his "disappearance"? He removed himself from the public eye to deliberate and prepare his move.

First, disappearance from the public eye was a habit of Deng's when he needed to handle a major policy debate. He would normally keep quiet for a significant period of time before reappearing and giving what were surprising judgments. For example, as described in an earlier chapter, he gave his "Four Cardinal Principles" speech in 1979 only after a freewheeling discussion had gone on for days at a controversial conference convened by Hu Yaobang.[62] In the first days of the 1989 student protest, he gave no public utterance until his April 25 speech, and after this "disappearance" he would disappear from public view again until June 9.

Second, the "disappearing" act was a form of policy statement. As will be presented in more detail next chapter, for more than two weeks after the April 26 editorial, the government's response was marked by Zhao's "new policy." Zhao believed that a conciliatory approach would be most effective in convincing the students to return to the classroom. For this direction to work, though, a softening, or even a reversal, of the editorial's approach would be needed. In this situation, Zhao was trying desperately to meet in person with Deng. Deng's silence was therefore a loud response.

Third, it was a strategic move. Deng was waiting for Zhao and the students to stumble; he would then act decisively in public. Scholars of the repression models suggest that the softer approach, which Zhao was given some space to implement, was an act of good faith. That is, the "government" tried this new tactic in the hope of resolving the protest problem.[63] That was not true. The "government" represented by Deng did not seem to have any "faith" in this softer approach. Rather, as the next section will show, during his absence, he deliberated and finalized his plan to remove Zhao and relatedly to move against the protest.

Fourth, Deng's total blackout, using health as a pretext, was intended to establish an excuse not to see Zhao Ziyang. At the core of the matter was the trust existing between them – that is, the trust the supreme leader had in his chosen successor. Such trust had to be reconfirmed constantly. Zhao's need to be reassured of Deng's trust was insatiable. He sought an audience with Deng whenever possible. And Deng knew this need well, hence the repeated praise, assurances, and promises in the past. In the days between April 25 and May 11, 1989, however, Deng would be extremely duplicitous if he continued to see Zhao and offer his assurances. By leaving his earlier assurances in place, he was already deceiving Zhao.

Deng's "disappearance" was uncannily similar to a previous episode, as recounted in an earlier chapter (Chapter 3). On July 18, 1966, Mao came back to Beijing after a long tour in south China. In his absence, Liu Shaoqi had been entrusted to lead the "first-line" operation, including the Cultural Revolution campaigns. Liu launched the mass movement with rigor and enthusiasm. He took an approach that he deemed appropriate, including dispatching "work teams" to direct student activities. He thought he had Mao's blessing. Earlier, on June 30, Mao sent a telegraph from Hongzhou, stating, "I agree to do it this way."[64] Liu was nonetheless restless and anxious. As soon as Mao arrived in Beijing, he went all the way to Mao's residence. After hours of waiting, someone came out to tell him that Mao would not be available to see him. Days later, Liu's approach was thoroughly repudiated by Mao in his polemic entitled "My First Wall Poster: Bombast the Headquarters." Soon after, Liu, the Chinese president and number two man in the party, was purged.[65]

## The Deng–Yang Conversation on May 11

### Deng Makes Up His Mind

Zhao Ziyang's request for an audience was rebuffed until May 13. When he was finally received by Deng, however, he was not interviewed alone. Also present at the meeting was Yang Shangkun.[66] In other words, his special relationship with Deng as a potential successor had effectively ended. The three-person meeting on May 13 had a very official tone. Deng reiterated his stand, Yang Shangkun seemed eager to endorse it, and Zhao laid out the reasoning behind his soft approach to the protest. Notably, Deng conveyed a sense of urgency but betrayed none of his pending intentions when he said, "The student movement this time has lasted for too long, almost a month now. We – Chen Yun, Peng Zhen, Xiannian, Wang Zhen and Big Sister Deng [Yingchao] – are all anxious. There should be decisive measures."[67] Deng ended the talk with a statement that was in retrospect disingenuous. He seemed yet again to reassure Zhao that he was safe in his leadership position, and that he encouraged a nonviolent way out. "When confronting major political issues, the Standing Committee should be decisive and uphold principles. Having said that, however, as far as this student protest is concerned, we should strive to find a peaceful solution."[68]

By this time, however, Deng had already decided to withdraw his support for Zhao and deploy the military. How can we know? The smoking gun, so to speak, was a lengthy conversation between Deng and Yang Shangkun two days earlier, on May 11, 1989. The content of the conversation is recorded in minute detail by Zhang Liang.[69] Before we get to the conversation, let us highlight four significant points.

The first is the audience of Deng's interview. A private one-to-one meeting was what Zhao had repeatedly requested but could not receive. Now it was given to Yang, Deng's front man in charge of the military. Recall that although Deng had nominally retired from all his posts in the party and the government, he kept the chairmanship of the CMC. Among the three powerbases, the foundation of Deng's power remained rooted within the military. Unlike other domains, his control over the military was not shared by his rivals, nor did it need to function through a Zhao Ziyang or a Hu Yaobang. There, Yang Shangkun, permanent secretary and a vice chair of the CMC, was his man. As discussed in Chapter 3, although Zhao was made the first vice chair of the CMC, his influence remained negligible in the army.

The second significant point centers around timing. The protest had precipitously declined since after the large demonstrations on May 4. Either the new government policy worked or simple fatigue set in. Many students went back to their classrooms. A week after May 4 – on May 11 and 12 – the overall turnout at demonstrations in Beijing reached its lowest point, as I will show in Figure 7.1 in Chapter 7.[70] The Deng–Yang conversation took place while the protest was weak.

The third notable point is Jiang Zemin. His name was mentioned after Deng gauged Yang's opinion on Zhao Ziyang, Chen Xitong (leader of Beijing), and Li Ruihuan (leader of Tianjin). Deng gave Jiang his highest marks and, most importantly, emphasized how well both Li Xiannian and Chen Yun spoke of him. Knowing that a major personnel decision had to be agreed upon by both Deng and Chen Yun (and to some extent by Li Xiannian as well), Deng in effect gave Yang an unmistakable signal that Jiang was his choice as the next general secretary. By inference, Zhao had lost his job.

Finally, the fourth significant point is that Deng asked Yang about the military. In not so many words, Deng touched upon the subject seemingly lightly and quickly wrapped up the talk. While not exactly explicit to an untrained ear, the signal should have been loud and clear to Yang Shangkun. As will be argued below in Chapter 8, the decisions to remove Zhao, elevate Jiang, and use the troops were all inseparable from each other.[71]

## The Deng–Yang Conversation

The conversation took place at Deng's residence, with the two older comrades meeting alone. At first, Yang Shangkun did not appear to know what to expect. He had been Zhao's ally on most issues in the past and, up to this point, a supporter of Zhao's approach regarding the current protest.[72] It took a few minutes before he could sense which way Deng was leaning. They first shared their puzzlement about broad support for the student movement and rehashed a key talking point in the editorial – that a handful of individuals with ulterior motives were playing a role behind the scenes. Then Yang took the initiative to bring up Zhao Ziyang. His tone sounded neutral and potentially on the positive side. He had promised earlier Zhao that he would pass Zhao's desire to revisit the editorial to Deng. "On the handling of the protest, the Standing Committee has held numerous meetings," reported Yang. "Zhao Ziyang's view is to seek a resolution in accordance with the law and democracy. The Politburo has already issued an advisory for the Standing Committee of the People's Congress to convene a meeting in June to study a few popular issues raised by the students."

"How do you see Zhao Ziyang's speech at the Asian Bank?" pressed Deng. Yang was not ready to take a side. So Deng's question prompted Yang to a long analysis. He addressed both the positive side of the new policy – "it was positively received in many locales, and the students in Beijing also began to resume classes" – and the negative side – many local cadres questioned the inconsistency between his speech and the editorial.

From there, Deng launched into a battery of comments and inquiries that gradually and unequivocally showed Yang Shangkun the direction toward which he was leading. It could have been just a figure of speech when Deng said that he too had been contemplating "which would be the better way to resolve this." But his negative assessment of Zhao Ziyang was very obvious.

Deng started by relaying complaints from Li Xiannian and Chen Yun, the other two major old guards. He spoke of his conservative colleagues with no sarcasm or disdain. In fact, his tone was approving. Then, after Yang relayed Zhao's request to recalibrate the April 26 editorial, Deng inquired how the division was drawn among the Standing Committee members. Yang told him that Zhao's idea would be supported by Qiao Shi and Hu Qili and it would be objected to by Li Peng and Yao Yilin. At this point, Deng singled out Yao Yilin for very generous praise: "As far as I am concerned, Yao Yilin was able to hold the banner the highest. He is resolute, and he is consistent." He could have been imagining a vote being taken among the five Standing Committee members when he added, "On a political issue of great significance, the Standing Committee members must be resolute, and must have the courage to stick to principles."

As though these remarks could betray his true intention, he quickly added, "To be sure, we should work to our best in seeking a peaceful way to resolve this student movement." The allusion to a military solution in this statement would not be lost to the number two military man (besides Deng himself) in the country. Between the lines, by this time, it should have been easy for Yang Shangkun to conclude not only how Deng was judging Zhao, but also what the ultimate response to the protest would be.

Deng Xiaoping, however, was not done. His next few queries and related comments reveal that he had already moved on to considering Zhao Ziyang's replacement. "How do you see the handling of student protests in Beijing, Tianjin, and Shanghai?" asked a seemingly curious Deng, moving the topic on to two possible successors of Zhao – Li Ruihuan and Jiang Zemin. By this time, Yang was fully on board and happily played along. He must have known well that Deng was very fond of Li Ruihuan, the Tianjin leader. Certainly he was also aware of the rumors the previous year that Li Xiannian had sat Deng Xiaoping down in a vacation spot in Shanghai and asked Deng to replace Zhao with Jiang Zemin. Hence, the back-and-forth ensued.

Yang praised Li Ruihuan effusively:

> Tianjin's situation is the most under control. Li Ruihuan has not been unequivocal. "If you want dialog, you must follow the rules," Li Ruihuan said. "I do not stop your protest, but you cannot disrupt social order." Li Ruihuan sticks to this basic point: solve the problem as it appears, following the principle of finding truth from reality. Therefore social order in Tianjin is good. I think Li Ruihuan is a thoughtful man.

To which Deng agreed: "Li Ruihuan understands philosophy. He can see things dialectically."

"Shanghai's banner is held high." Yang went on to recount the deeds of Mayor Jiang Zemin, centering on his handling of a newspaper (the *World Economic Herald*) controversy. He offered a bit of reservation at the end, packaged as other people's view. To this, Deng again relayed Chen Yun and Li Xiannian's views, both speaking highly of Jiang Zemin:

> After Jiang Zemin rectified the *Herald*, Comrade Chen Yun said to me, "We should follow Jiang Zemin's unwavering approach in dealing with student protest." And Xiannian said, "Jiang Zemin upholds both the Four Fundamental Principles and Reform and Opening Up. He is acute politically, upholds party principles, and is able to see things from the standpoint of the entire cause."

To that, Yang added more of his own praise of Jiang.

The conversation ended on the essential topic that both men knew was the reason they had met in the first place: Deng was a supreme leader who commanded the highest authority in the military, and Yang, the permanent secretary and vice chair of CMC, was the man "who presided over the daily operation of the CMC on behalf of Deng Xiaoping," as one source puts it.[73] "How is the military?" asked Deng. Yang replied with a few platitudes, such as "the military is in good condition." They did not go into detail.[74] They both knew that they did not need to. According to Brook, Deng and the CMC had already put the military on alert as early as April 25.[75]

Up to this point, Yang Shangkun had a dual role as Deng's military point man and, at the same time, Zhao Ziyang's reform ally. For the past few years, the two functions had coexisted without conflict. In any case, Deng, Zhao, and Yang all belonged to the same reform camp. Earlier that year, even after Deng had given his harsh verdict on the protest, Yang and Zhao still worked closely together.

For example, Yang played go-between for Zhao to seek communication with Deng or his children.[76] Zhao Ziyang also reported that Yang had been taking a moderate stand toward the student protest. Yang was explicitly and vehemently against the idea of using troops when the idea was raised on an earlier occasion. Yang was quoted by Zhao saying in a Standing Committee meeting in April, "Putting the nation's capital under martial law? How do we explain it to the world?"[77]

The May 11 conversation changed all that for Yang. The talk signaled a complete end to the Deng–Zhao relationship, so Yang without hesitation rid himself of his role as Zhao's ally and fully embraced the other half. That shift explains why, two days later, on May 13 and during the three-person meeting, Yang changed his tune. He no longer seemed sympathetic to Zhao's justification for his approach; instead, he solely endorsed whatever Deng was saying. At the meeting at Deng's residence in the evening of May 17, Zhao was surprised to see that Yang quickly seconded the idea of martial law troops. "Shangkun was against martial law ... He apparently changed his mind," lamented Zhao.[78]

## Discussion and Conclusion

Deng's leading role was clear both in the publication of the April 26 editorial and in the May 17 decision to use martial law. Less clear has been how and when he made up his mind. Questions about the timing of events become theoretically meaningful. Repression models of how authoritarian governments respond would suggest that Deng came to realize the need for the military only after the protest had escalated. But what if Deng's planned endgame had already been formulated at the lowest point of the protest?

As discussed in detail in this chapter, there have been speculations that, after the April 26 editorial, Deng might have left Beijing to interview his military generals. Wuhan is a site that was mentioned frequently.[79] While I do not have enough direct evidence to adjudicate that question, a rich body of circumstantial evidence can be used to study his thinking in those few weeks, and it shows the following. First, his mental capacity was good, and he appears to have been fully aware of current events. While he had "retired" on paper and did not receive a formal briefing, his staff and children kept him up to date. That he was fully in touch with reality and had access to full information are important points, because they mean that he would not have overstated the danger of the protest; nor would he have been unaware of the backlash that his hard-line method might cause.

Second, he was the initiator of the process that resulted in the April 26 editorial. It was not true, as the official account suggested, that the front line "correctly" started the action, which happened to be in agreement with Deng's thinking. Nor was it correct that Deng changed his mind after being misled.

Third, during the eighteen days of his "disappearance," Deng likely remained in Beijing to deliberate and decide on two major plans – to dismiss Zhao Ziyang and to activate the troops. His conversation on May 11 with Yang Shangkun unmistakably attests to this point. Most importantly, the conversation took place at the lowest point of the student protest, days before the hunger strike. Therefore, Deng's decision to use the military had only a tenuous relationship with the student protest. He did not base his deliberation on the ongoing protest.

The above conclusions were drawn from my own research. I have also benefited from two essays by Wu Guoguang.[80] As I was completing an early draft of this chapter, another former government insider independently drew very similar conclusions. In May 2018, a four-part interview with Bao Tong was published in the Chinese edition of the *New York Times*. Bao was an important figure in the Tiananmen affair in 1989, as he was a combination of chief of staff and chief speech writer for Zhao Ziyang. After Zhao's fall, he was quickly arrested and imprisoned on the charge of leaking state secrets. He was released and lived under surveillance in Beijing from 1996. Li Nanyang, the daughter of Li Rui, a former secretary of Mao's, managed to interview him at length three times.[81]

Bao traced Deng's plan to remove Zhao as early as April 18, 1989 – three days after the death of Hu Yaobang and the outbreak of the protest. He insisted that, in producing the April editorial, Deng not only instructed Li Peng beforehand, but also commissioned the Beijing government report that was later interpreted as something that "misled" Deng's analysis of the event. Why did Deng wait for so long? Bao believed that the most important factor was Gorbachev's visit in mid-May. "If Deng had dismissed Zhao Ziyang as early as April 24 [after the Hu's funeral], it was certain that Gorbachev would not come. Deng was determined to re-normalize the Sino-Soviet relation in his own hands. He valued this historical legacy."[82]

"Therefore, although he had made up his mind to remove Zhao as early as April, he had to wait until after Gorbachev had left town on May 16," Bao went on to his interviewer. "Then Deng convened a meeting, a Standing Committee meeting, and decided on martial law. Knowing Ziyang would not agree to do so [to declare martial law], Deng then in effect created a situation in which Zhao had to resign. It is not that I force you out, but that you quit yourself."[83]

Bao used the term *coup d'état* to sum up Deng's action. The term captures the extra-institutional nature, the military connection, and the Machiavellian intent, but it is not exactly apt because the term often means an act by lower-level officers in the system, not the top man.[84] Nonetheless, what was unmistakable was the role of Deng, the driver of the train.

# 6    How a Moderate Approach Failed

April 26–May 17, 1989

This chapter presents policy deliberation and elite conflict in the second stage of the student protest – that is, the two weeks following the April 26 editorial, a period of moderate experiments that nonetheless escalated the unrest into a new phase. Students staged the largest demonstration on April 27, repeated the feat again on the anniversary of the historical May 4th movement, and started to occupy the square on May 13 with a hunger strike. These developments unfolded as the government response took a moderate turn upon Zhao Ziyang's return to Beijing.

Given the institutional controls in place at the time, popular forces were never going to be enough to generate large movements like Tiananmen without the assistance of state leaders. As demonstrated in Chapter 4 above, it was the combination of popular force outside the regime and the behavior of state leaders inside that jointly produce the scale of the Tiananmen protest in the first stage. In this chapter, I further extend that argument to the second phase of the student movement. My analysis does not have to assume that the leaders secretly wished or intended the protest to go on. Instead, I argue that regardless of intentions, their protest policies produced the result of sustaining the movement. I will focus on Li Peng and Zhao Ziyang.

The moderation of this second period is manifested in three ways. The first was the continuation of government inaction regarding protest activities. In Zhao Ziyang's absence, the government under Li Peng took no action either prior to or during the day of the large demonstration on April 27. The same happened on May 4 under Zhao. The second component was the start of a series of dialogues, first started by Li Peng and then continued and expanded by Zhao Ziyang. It changed the government–protest relationship, in effect signaling a certain recognition of the protest organizations as legitimate. The third was the lifting of control over the media in covering the ongoing protest, which resulted in a "bureaucratic insurgency" led by Zhao Ziyang to litigate his case in the public domain.

All of the three major decision makers – Deng Xiaoping, Li Peng, and Zhao Ziyang – would claim that ending the protest was their priority. But their politics stood between their methods and any real effect. Deng, as discussed in last chapter, allowed only a short period of time for Zhao to manage, and shut down that window quickly. Li Peng was only concerned with negative labeling, and did nothing to stop the large demonstration. Zhao Ziyang not only refrained from repression, but also led a campaign within the government that echoed the student protest from the outside.[1]

## Li Peng – an Unlikely Enabler

Among the central casting of Tiananmen players, Premier Li Peng is known to have been dead set against the protest.[2] Accordingly, his policies and actions are seen as aimed at nothing less than ending the protest. Yet, despite his rhetoric, he did not impose any physical constraints on the protest, even during the window of time when he was first in command among the party leadership. Neither did he send police to lock down any campus, nor did he send troops to disperse any crowd. On the contrary, some of his policies encouraged the movement's growth greatly.

### Focusing More on Labeling than on Ending

In his diary, Li recorded confrontations with Zhao, in which he repeatedly urged Zhao to take "resolute and decisive action." For example, on the night of April 18–19, he made an angry phone call to Zhao to urge action against the Xinhua Gate sit-in, as narrated earlier.[3] His supposed hard-line image is bolstered by the facts that he was instrumental in producing the editorial and that he supported the martial law decision.

That image, however, was not enough to conclude that he worked *to end the protest*. When you exam his policies, each appears to have inflamed the protest further. A reasonable reading is that he stood to benefit politically from a protest that was Zhao Ziyang's liability. He could have been happy that the protest in fact went on, up until Zhao Ziyang lost power. This analysis is consistent with his behavior during the period between the publication of the editorial on April 26 and Zhao's return on April 30. In the absence of Zhao, he was in charge.

The editorial not only pronounced the movement's overall character as conspiratorial, but also listed specific acts not to be tolerated. For example, independent student organizations were deemed "illegal" and considered an "encroachment" on existing party-sponsored ones; "illegal demonstrations" were to be forbidden. It also warned against "rumormongering and libel," a reference to criticism of the state leaders, and stressed "protecting students' right to study," a reference to the ongoing class strike. In its intimidating tone, the editorial reads in part:

No illegal organization is allowed; stop behaviors that infringe on the righteous status of legal student organizations; criminal charges will be brought to intentional rumor-mongering and libel making; forbid illegal demonstrations; forbid mobilization activities in factories, in the countryside and in schools; punish by law those who commit beating, looting, and burning; protect students' right to study.[4]

Since these policies carried the highest legal authority in the land, one may ask, would the decision makers, such as Li Peng and Deng Xiaoping, mean to enforce them? If students defied those orders, then what would happen?

Perhaps they hoped to end the protest by "verbally threatening the students with the *People's Daily* editorial," as one scholar wrote.[5] But such a reading underestimates Li Peng's and Deng's political skills and is not persuasive. Having been minutely involved with ongoing events, Li and Deng should have foreseen the possibility of backlash.[6] An alternative explanation is that they simply did not care. Deng, as described in the last chapter, had a long-term vision. To label the protest a conspiracy was the first step in paving the way for his other political plays to come. If the student protest ended up even more ferocious, so be it. As a historian has noted, on April 25, the day of his speech, he put the entire military on alert. By the beginning of May, all military leave had been canceled.[7] What about Li Peng?

### Doing Nothing with the Great Demonstration of April 27

Now that Li was the first in command, would he be prepared to implement those "resolute and decisive measures" that he had urged on Zhao Ziyang? During this period, he learned about a student plan to launch a large demonstration,[8] and some of his colleagues in the conservative camp, such as Li Xiannian and Wang Zhen, advocated a large wave of arrests, "in the tens of thousands."[9] What did he do?

In hindsight, it is difficult to speculate what measures the government could have taken to minimize the April 27 demonstration. I invited my interviewees, particularly those who lived through multiple waves of student demonstrations, to speculate. They agreed that outright violent suppression on April 27 would not have been useful, or politically feasible. But many of them suggested two moderate measures that, if taken, could have undermined the effort to launch a demonstration.

The first measure would have been arresting a limited number of student leaders. As documented extensively by Chen Xiaoya, the debate and the planning of the May 27 demonstration went on for days, and a few key student leaders played a critical role.[10] They operated very publicly, including holding news conferences. Reports from the Public Security Bureau, which were excerpted by Zhang Liang, recorded almost everything these student leaders did.[11] At university level, student leaders were targeted. For example,

Zhou Yongjun, the chairman of the all-city alliance, was talked to gently by his university administration; he then issued a cancelation of the upcoming demonstration (it was vetoed by other leaders later in the process).[12] It is conceivable that a few key arrests would have disrupted the planning process. Also, there was a precedent for such arrests. On New Year's Day of 1987, a student demonstration was planned to take place in Tiananmen Square. The government arrested fifty four student leaders, including six from Beida. The protest ended before it grew big, with only a few hundred in the square during the day. And a march of Beida students that evening turned back before reaching the square, partly because of news that the student leaders had been released.[13]

The second measure would have been to lock the campus gates on the day of protest. In those days, the major universities were cloistered communities with walls on four sides, with one gate in each side. One had to show identification to get in and out if the school so preferred. According to my interviewees from Beida, there were instances in the past in which the university locked and secured the gates, effectively preventing students from going out to march.[14] In fact, in their planning sections, some student leaders anticipated such a government measure. Student leader Wang Chaohua was recorded as saying: "Yes, we shall march. If the blocking is not very vigorous, we will break through and leave the campus; if the blocking is too strong, we will march inside the campus; if the campus is also under control, we will start a hunger strike in our respective campuses."[15]

As premier and acting chief of the party, Li Peng had the entire security apparatus at his disposal. But he took none of these measures. Indeed, he took no action at all beyond paying lip service. That may be exactly the point. His main goal was to paint the protest in a negative light.

### Consolidating Gains on Negative Labeling

Nonetheless, Li was by no means idle. After the April 24 bumping-heads meeting and his April 25 morning interview with Deng, Li was still busy working to consolidate his gain in the Party Center's verbal project. His diary informs us that he convened another Standing Committee meeting in the afternoon of April 25. The agenda? It was decided that Deng's speech was to be immediately disseminated among the three big systems (party, government and military). In the evening, he instructed Wen Jiabao, the chief of the Party Central Office, to edit out sensitive information from Deng's speech and send a copy to Zhao Ziyang in North Korea.[16]

This flow of Li Peng's work on the verbal project was undisrupted even after the students announced on April 25 their plan to demonstrate. What was Li busy with on April 26, one day before the protest? "I dispatched the transcript of Comrade Xiaoping's speech prepared by the Party Central Office," Li wrote in his diary. He also reported that he received a returned telegraph from Zhao Ziyang in support of Deng's speech. But he convened no meeting to discuss the reports on the demonstration that was to take place the next day.[17] In other words, Li Peng, along with Deng, after enacting the hardline policy, seemed content with its form and not worried about its effect. The acting chief executive made no plan to act differently from his predecessor Zhao Ziyang, whom he had vehemently criticized.

### The Protesters Encountered No Physical Resistance

The April 27 demonstration in Beijing was the largest to date, joined by hundreds of thousands of students. It took an hour and a half for the main contingent of student marchers to continuously pass the square. Many more citizen onlookers cheered them, offering food and drinks. The large scale demonstration was a huge success.[18]

To be sure, in large part the success was due to the strength of student organizations. Former student leaders' reflections attest to the depth and extensiveness of co-ordination, deliberation, and execution.[19] The mobilization also greatly benefited from ecological factors. In his masterful studies of the event, Dingxin Zhao shows how all the elements were at work, including students' bedding arrangement in the dormitory, communal life on campus, and the concentration of universities in a particular city district.[20]

But the government's indulgence also played a critical role. For example, the same ecological factors discussed by Dingxin Zhao could have been used by the authorities to counter and stop mobilization. The hypothetical measures discussed above – limited arrests and campus lockdowns – would also have worked.

Nevertheless, students and student organizers encountered virtually no physical force. Activists among independent student associations openly and freely formulated the plan, announced the event, and executed it. Rank-and-file students milled around their campuses, first with some apprehension, but quickly growing in confidence in large crowds, and marched out of the campus gates. They did not see any government agents until they reached a major traffic intersection. There, there were soldiers who first formed human walls in a blocking gesture, but they dissolved without using force and gave way to the students. Remarkably, playing out like a script, this scenario repeated itself more than twenty times on the route of the march from Haidian district to Tiananmen Square:[21]

At first, the policemen strenuously blocked the human flow ... but [the protesters] pushed forward strongly and persistently, one wave after another, like ocean tides ... Finally, the dam cracked: the linked arms of the policemen in the first row were broken, followed by a roar of joyful celebration, reaching high to the sky ...[22]

As that was going on, Li Peng followed the day's events from a television screen in Zhongnanhai. He mused aloud, "How can the police stop the flood of demonstrators when they are empty-handed, with no lethal weapons?" sounding as though he were a bystander of history, not a commander of a powerful violent machine. On his way home, the path of his entourage was briefly blocked by a student crowd, which delayed his return home to Wanshoulu Avenue, some twenty kilometers west of Zhongnanhai, until 9:00 p.m. He then had a phone conversation with Wang Ruilin, who relayed some comments from Deng. "Comrade Xiaoping thinks that the handling of today was good – the Party Center did not waiver on its stand, and at the same time bloodshed was avoided."[23]

To be clear, by no means do I suggest that Li Peng, when he was in charge, *should* have used coercive measures against the student protest in 1989. The above analysis is to show the contrast between what he said should have been done under Zhao Ziyang and what really happened under him. This contrast highlights the political nature of the editorial; that is, it was meant more to paint the protest in a negative light than to stop it.

It is also worth noting here that, although nominally in charge, Li Peng operated under the shadow of the supreme leader, as shown in his musing about the feebleness of the police without lethal weapons and the late-night phone call from Deng's chief aide, giving him assurance about how he had handled the day's demonstration on April 27. The disingenuousness in the repression posture did not belong to Li alone.

### *Li Peng Approved Student–Government Dialogue*

Besides the editorial and the April 27 demonstration, Li's third major "achievement" in his brief stint as acting party chief was "dialogue." Through dialogue, the government for the first time elevated the students to the position of a negotiation partner. Contrary to the spirit of the editorial, which declared the student organizations illegal, activists now operated in a space where they were seemingly permitted. Earlier dialogue had been advocated by Zhao but vehemently objected to by Li himself. The renewed permission under Li's own watch would have a profound impact on the continuation of the protest.

The next day, April 28, in a meeting convened by the Beijing City government, university administrators urged the idea of dialogue. In the same afternoon, in an extended Politburo meeting held by Li Peng, Qiao Shi proposed the same idea: "under the current circumstances, we should move quickly to open dialogue with students at various levels." Yang Shangkun seemed to concur, noting that the international media "pleaded with the government to have dialogue with the students."[24] The meeting resolved to form a group of four officials led by Yuan Mu, a spokesperson in the State Council and a loyal foot soldier of Premier Li Peng, to start dialogue on April 29 with "representatives of Beijing students."[25] Li Peng not only endorsed the plan; hours before the dialogue he personally met the group of four to hash out the preparations.[26]

The dialogue started in the afternoon of April 29. It was a sensational event. Never had any past protest been able to elicit a government response like this, much less one that was broadcast live. Students of Beijing's universities were breathlessly glued to the television screen. Untold numbers of people across the nation tuned in as well. The dialogue lasted two hours. While predictably the proceedings were heavily stage-managed beforehand, there were in the meantime plenty of unexpected moments. It started with a student named Xiang Xiaoji protesting the credentials of the forty-five student representatives, most of whom turned out to have been handpicked by the government-run National Higher Education Student Association. The dialogue nonetheless moved along contentiously, covering topics including Hu Yaobang's dismissal, official corruption, news censorship, the April 26 editorial, and the nature of the ongoing protest. Led by Yuan Mu, the government officials evaded challenging questions, and mostly repeated the official talking points.[27] In one of the most memorable exchanges, a student criticized high officials for extravagant hobbies. He held up a magazine cover showing Zhao Ziyang playing golf in a Beijing suburb. Yuan Mu gave no clarification or defense on behalf of Zhao.[28]

That was the first of numerous dialogues to come in the next two weeks. If these dialogues were meant to appease students, they instead became a new source of anger. The list of grievances was long, including issues such as who could rightfully represent the students, whether the dialogue would be broadcast live and in full, what topics could be included, and so on. Additionally, there were arrogance, evasion, and blatant lies on display on the government side. "The government does not have good faith!" became a new slogan of the day. While Li Peng, Li Xiannian, and other like-minded leaders called to congratulate Yuan Mu for his "tai-chi-like dexterity," reviews from students were universally negative. The strongest reaction came from a place more than a thousand kilometers away from Beijing. After watching the television broadcast, 3,000 students gathered at Wuhan University in Hubei. The protesters condemned Yuan Mu's "evasion" on key issues and demanded that "the Center's major leaders should come forward" in future dialogues.[29]

There was another major impact. The dialogue not only tacitly recognized the independent student organizations, but in effect upgraded the organizational strength of the protest. Initially, the government side had tried to dialogue only with the "legitimate student representatives." But that insistence did not last. In the very first dialogue, on April 29, the student side was already mixed with a few protest representatives. A new hierarchy of student organizations emerged, collectively called the Capital Student Delegation for Dialogue. The delegation had grassroots chapters in every university in Beijing. It became a major student union from then on, in addition to the Beijing Autonomous Association of University Students (BAAUS).[30]

In his classic work *The Strategy of Social Protest*, William Gamson conceptualizes the success of a popular movement in two dimensions: new advantage and new recognition. The former refers to policy changes as demanded by the protest, while the latter refers to acknowledgment of the existence of protest leaders as the counterpart in a negotiation.[31] Following this scheme of analysis, the student movement had made a great headway by virtue of being recognized as a counterpart in the "dialogue." Such a partial success carried enormous symbolic value for the activists and ordinary protesters. It worked as great encouragement to the student movement, something Li Peng had vowed he would never do.

We will never know whether Li Peng was naive (unaware of the true effect) or cunning (wanting a sustained protest to bring down Zhao Ziyang). Seeking an answer is not my task here. Instead, I outline Li Peng's three acts to suggest something more concrete: in rolling out his policies supposedly to stop the protest, there is no evidence to show that he cared about the real consequences of his actions. His target lay elsewhere. Recall the student holding up a picture of Zhao Ziyang playing golf. That should explain the willingness and maybe unspoken intentions of Li Peng to start the dialogue, a new policy that was every bit contrary to the April 26 editorial.

### Zhao Ziyang in "Two Weeks with a New Take"

*Returning to Beijing and Facing the Fallout of the Editorial*

Zhao Ziyang returned from North Korea in the morning of April 30, 1989. Li Peng and a few others went to Beijing train station to welcome him. No sooner did Zhao begin to inquire about the protest than Li Peng highlighted something that upset his composure. Li Peng said that protesters had accused Zhao's son of illegal commercial dealings, an allusion to Zhao's own abuse of power.[32]

Li Peng did not make this stuff up. Corruption being a major issue, the demonstrators often flaunted lively slogans such as "Deng Xiaoping's son peddles color [lottery] tickets; Zhao Ziyang's son sells color TVs."[33] A former aide of Zhao's inner circle believes that Li's choice of information was a deliberate and clever political play, meant to keep Zhao off balance from day one upon his return.[34]

The accusation, however, was not Zhao's biggest political trouble. A week earlier, he had left an ongoing political upheaval against his advisers' counsel. It was a calculated move, as Li grudgingly noted in his diary, to leave the mess first and then come back to reap the political benefits. His calculation turned out to be correct in one key respect: under Li's charge, the government took a hard line and it backfired, as the editorial caused the largest demonstration to date. However, as I discussed in Chapter 4, one of the main components in Zhao's reasoning was Deng's unwavering trust in him. Zhao lost this bet, and he was many times worse off.

Zhao's equation was upset first by a severely negative labeling of the protest and Deng's co-ownership of that labeling. If, by this time, Zhao still harbored the notion of Deng's trust in him, the editorial should have served as a wake-up call. There are three ways to see Zhao's loss. First, according to party norm, the chief executive had the ultimate responsibility despite his brief absence from the scene, because a protest was often attributed to the failure of political work prior to its outbreak. Second, unbeknownst to Zhao, Deng came out from the second line in his absence and publicly co-owned the negative labeling. If Zhao wished to reverse what Li Peng had done, it now became impossible. Third, and most important of all, upon Zhao's return the Deng–Zhao relationship had changed. Deng would not even grant him an audience.

The saving grace was that Zhao seemed to have been given time and authority to do it over. Li Peng was still under him; Deng was silent again. Or so he thought. The days after his return are called "two weeks with a new take."[35] Zhao's new efforts constituted "a turning point of the movement," according to scholars such as Chen Xiaoya.[36] Zhao began to give speeches that deviated from the April 26 editorial. Since he did so in the position of general secretary, his view was in effect more than just dissent, but suggested a new policy line.

A conventional view sees Zhao in action here not as a politician, but as a mere manager. He is seen in this role as a representative of the entire government overseeing a new and softer policy and working in attempts to calm down the situation.[37] Supporters of Zhao still held this view firmly many years after 1989. In my interviews with them, they cited the decline in protest following Zhao's May 3 and May 4 speeches, as evidence of the new approach's effectiveness. Only if the students had been more mature and more co-operative, they contend, Zhao would have proved that his approach was correct all along.[38] This view is also somewhat echoed by the government's official history of 1989, in which Zhao is seen as having been given the time to try his method but as having failed in the end.[39]

This managerial view of history misses the political stories. Li and Deng refused to reverse the editorial, which in effect doomed any hope of Zhao succeeding.

Moreover, Zhao was much more than a manager. He would not survive the post-protest reckoning if the protest was labeled negatively. That is, it would not be enough to end the protest if its negative label stayed. By now, he should have realized the erosion of Deng's trust. And he should have known that, without Deng's support, he would be disposed of no matter how the protest ended.

Facing this quandary, something creative seemed to be needed to save his job. Indeed, he would make a leap few Chinese politicians before him – save supreme leaders such as Mao and Deng – have ever ventured to make. The campaign he waged, particularly the party media he unleashed, in those days was more akin to a *protest from within*.

### Formulating a Moderate Policy

On April 30, no sooner had Zhao settled down in his residence than Bao Tong, his chief of staff and speechwriter, came to visit. "A significant portion of students are against the editorial," Bao reported. "It was written coldly, short of sound analysis and persuasion. It misfired at the masses in the middle." Zhao concurred that "it looks like the editorial is flawed."[40] The next day, Zhao convened a Standing Committee meeting, where the editorial quickly became a focal point. "There was heated debate about the *People's Daily* editorial of April 26," noted Li Peng in his diary.[41] As part of his argument for its validity and authority, Li Peng noted that Zhao had wired back his agreement, and he cited Zhao's praise of his work.[42]

On the morning of May 3, Zhao Ziyang paid a visit to Wan Li, a reform ally, a Politburo member, and the president of the People's Congress. Wan was one of the top three reformers promoted by Deng in 1980, along with Hu Yaobang and Zhao Ziyang. At one point, Deng tried to promote him to the Standing Committee, only to be blocked by the Chen Yun camp. At the visit, Zhao shared his views on the issue of "students" with Wan: "We should not accuse them of overthrowing us only because they criticize us. [If we do that], it would be the thinking of bygone days when the class struggle mantra was paramount . . . Things can cool down if we use dialogue and persuasion."[43] To this analysis, Wan Li wholeheartedly agreed. Wan added a few anecdotes in which he tried to bring other leaders such as Li Ruihuan of Tianjin on board.[44] A bodyguard overheard Zhao say at the end, "Hearing your remarks today clears up much uncertainty in my mind."[45]

In the afternoon of the same day, in his own residence in Zhongnanhai, Zhao received another ally, Xu Jiatun, former party chief of Jiangsu Province, and now the party secretary sent by the Center to Hong Kong. They had an extensive conversation about the protest and particularly about the editorial: "I have a share of the responsibility for the *People's Daily* editorial of April 26. The Party Center sent the draft to me in Pyongyang for my opinion. I sent back my approval. So I am happy to take the blame [if it is to be reversed]."[46] Since Xu was also close to Yang Shangkun, he promised Zhao that he would pass his comments to Yang. But Yang did not think it was the right time to lobby Deng. Yang suggested that Zhao can just "go ahead and do it" (i.e., do something about the editorial), and was willing to share the blame.[47] As reported in the last chapter, Zhao also received similar messages passed over by Wang Ruilin and Deng's children that day.[48]

These activities took place in the few days leading up to Zhao's two major speeches. They offer us a glimpse of Zhao's political resources at that time, or, more precisely, his lack of political resources. As he was losing Deng, his position as the general secretary amounted to little. His opponents Li Peng and Yao Yilin undermined him in the Standing Committee, and his take on the issue of the editorial could not obtain an official stamp.[49] Among his allies that he spoke to, Wan Li had a weak power base – the National People's Congress – and Yang Shangkun, as was made clear in the last chapter, would later promptly abandon him, as soon as a split between him and Deng became apparent.[50]

### Zhao Tried but Failed to Reverse the Editorial

Zhao nonetheless marched forward. He outlined his new ideas in two major speeches, one on May 3, addressing the country's youth in marking the seventieth anniversary of a historical student movement, and the other on May 4, to an international economic forum. He presented a few messages that were drastically contradictory to the editorial. While the editorial described the student protesters as duped by conspirators, he praised "patriotic actions by a great many students." While the editorial warned against "turmoil," he advised that "there is no danger of China descending into chaos." While the editorial laid out harsh methods, he pledged to resolve the crisis "through the channels of law and democracy."[51]

The speeches were warmly received by the students, and many provincial governments also sent their concurring reports. But they alarmed conservative heavyweights including Chen Yun, Li Xiannian, and Bo Yibo. Bo is recorded to have quipped, "To tell the young that they are patriotic at this very juncture is equivalent to encouraging their turmoil."[52]

In between the two speeches, Zhao and Li had a one-to-one meeting. Li first politely praised Zhao's first speech, but they quickly engaged in a lengthy and heated debate on the editorial. In effect, Li warned Zhao not to touch it. As expected, Li reminded Zhao of the institutional process that produced the piece and, as important, the support from Deng:

> Comrade Ziyang, as you know, the April 26 editorial was not only written according to the April 24 Standing Committee decisions, but also based on Comrade Xiaoping's

speech. There are perhaps imprecise wordings here and there, but to change its overall tenor is impossible.[53]

Zhao was equally persistent in his reasoning and suggestions:

> I am not against the term "turmoil" in the editorial. But I think [the term] only means the [protest's] scale and its impact on social order, rather than its character. I think we should have another document that distinguishes the great many students and their sympathizers on the one hand, from those radical few who attempt to take advantage of the student protest . . . on the other.[54]

To this, Li Peng coldly replied, "Comrade Ziyang, on this matter I disagree with you."[55] Zhao's new policy line hence enjoyed neither the blessing of Deng, the highest authority, nor an official stamp from the "collective leadership." Therefore, it was akin to well-publicized dissent, despite coming from the party's highest official. Its authority and legitimacy would be contested further in the days ahead.

### Zhao Ziyang's Bureaucratic Insurgency

Zhao Ziyang was at an intersection in his personal career and the nation's history. He might have been deeply convinced that more openness to dissent was both good for China in the long run and an effective antidote to the problem at hand. He must have also been keenly aware that his own job was on the line. Having tried to appeal to Deng, it was now apparent he was losing Deng's support. Having tried to convert his idea into policy through official channels, his political opponents stood in the way. In short, although he was the highest official in the land, he neither commanded the highest authority nor had an organizational system at his disposal.

#### Insurgency from Within

It is not clear how confident he was, by those late hours, in his ability to maintain his own power and to steer China out of a possible tragedy. He nonetheless put up a final fight. His method following his speeches, however, was unusual for the highest leader. He began to depart from the accepted norms and rules of the very organization he presided over. His campaign, if successful, would potentially change the very organization in a fundamental way. In doing so, he became an agent of change, not merely a manager.

Normally we refer to the work of the chief executive of a bureaucracy as *governing*. If she or he decides to change the ways to govern, we call it *reform*. Rarely do we call any of their actions "insurgency" since the term refers to an act that is against a higher authority and performed in a way that is outside the organizational rules. Following the terminology coined by two sociologists,

I suggest that Zhao's work in the two weeks before the hunger strike should be seen as his leading a "bureaucratic insurgency."

In their seminal paper published in 1978, Mayer Zald and Michael Berger observe that there are three extra-institutional ways to make a big change within an organization: organizational *coup d'état*, bureaucratic insurgency, and mass movement.[56] In Zhao's case in 1989, he had neither the desire nor the capacity to arrest Deng and Li Peng in order to force them to go along. Hence, *coup d'état* as a strategy was out of the question. Nor was mass movement feasible. He might have echoed the claims of the student movement, but it would have been an absolute dead end for him or his men to become part of the movement. This was so for two reasons. First, with popular protest seen as a challenge to the state, it would be suicidal for any politician to collude or even have the appearance of collusion. Second, he did not have organizational linkage, covert or public, to the students' protest leadership – a point that will be revisited later in this chapter – despite the fact that as the party head he oversaw a large secret police system and that the majority of protesters were his supporters.

The choice open to him was bureaucratic insurgency, which he adopted. "Bureaucratic insurgency differs from a coup in its target: its aim is not to replace the chief executive but to change some aspect of organizational function. It differs from a mass movement in extent of support and number of adherents." According to Zald and Berger, the goals revolve around making a change to specific aspects of the organization. This typically involves a limited mobilization of personnel; it is an attempt by members to implement goals, programs, or policy choices which have been explicitly denied by the legitimate authority; and lastly its activities therefore take place outside the conventional channels of the politics of the organization.[57]

There were two goals for Zhao Ziyang's protest from within. In the short term, it was about changing the labeling of the protest. In the long run, it was about changing the party-state's relationship with dissent – social and political protests would become a fact of life, rather than extraordinary events. The two goals were interconnected: since Zhao was not able to change the labeling in a way acceptable to the current system, he clamored for a change of the system itself. In the meantime, if he could achieve these goals, he could salvage his own career as well. If he could succeed, he might regain Deng's confidence. Or, more dramatically, he would find a new political asset, rare for a politician in that system: popular support. Either way he had to be able to send students back to the classroom in order to prove the merit of his argument.

*Renewing Student–Government Dialogue*

One of the fronts of his campaign was a renewed wave of government–student dialogues. Zhao advanced what Li Peng generated. Dialogues now proliferated, not only in Beijing, but across the country. Local leaders engaged with the university students in their jurisdictions. Perhaps unintended, dialogues in a way served as bureaucratic channels with which to spread the protest, as no dialogue could or would end to the satisfaction of the students. Protesting about the dialogue itself became commonplace. Chen Xiaoya reports that although the student demonstration in Beijing on May 4 was significantly smaller than the one on April 27, among the demonstrators came many from universities outside Beijing, including colleges from Jilin, Hubei, Liaoning, Jiangsu, Tianjin, Shanghai, Guangdong, Sichuan, Hunan, Shanxi, and Shandong.[58]

Zhao Ziyang offered his candid assessment of the dialogues under Li Peng before his return:

> As far as dialogues with students are concerned, they [Li Peng, Yao Yilin, and Li Ximing] mostly resisted or delayed. The dialogue should have been with the students from the protest, but they do not allow organizations newly established in the student movement to participate, nor the representatives elected by students. Instead, they only let the students from the [original] student unions do the dialogue. Is that not equivalent to a rejection of dialogue? Moreover, during the dialogue they did not take a sincere attitude of listening, but instead equivocated in all manner of ways to the students.[59]

So now, under Zhao, student representatives were no longer selected solely through official channels. On May 3, the Preliminary Committee on Dialogue Delegation of Beijing Higher Education Students was founded. It had no relationship with government-sponsored student associations. Rather, it was a result of democratic elections organized by an alliance of independent student unions, an organization which the editorial had pronounced illegal. The members of the committee later formed the backbone of the dialogue delegation. The committee sent their representatives to present a petition to the administration, the State Council, the Party Central Office, and the People's Congress. "As elected representatives, we propose the following conditions for dialogue," the petition stated:

> No. 1, dialogue should be based on equal standing and a sincere attitude of problem-solving;
> No. 2, student representatives in the dialogue must be elected by the majority of the university students, particularly those who participated in the patriotic pro-democracy movement this April;
>
> . . .
>
> No. 11, we must ensure the personal and political safety of the dialogue representatives from both sides . . .

Unsurprisingly, demands in the preparation and exchanges during the actual debate quickly zoomed in on the issue of labeling. Was it a patriotic movement or an antigovernment conspiracy? Would there be a "post-harvest accounting" that would charge student leaders with crimes? This way, the student protest outside the government echoed the major dissent of the general secretary inside it. Zhao's bureaucratic insurgency worked with the protest for a similar short-term goal: to change the official verdict.

### Letting Official Media Cover the Protest

On another front of his campaign, Zhao changed the long-standing party norm of media control. Implementing gag orders and censorship had been a time-honored tradition for dealing with protests. None of the protest events in the past, including the 1976 Tiananmen protest and the student protests in 1986–1987, were reported as news until after they had ended. Since the beginning of the 1989 protest, however, the *People's Daily*, *Science and Technology Daily*, China Central TV (CCTV), and a few major news outlets occasionally tested the taboo, in the guise of reporting on mourning for Hu Yaobang. The most defiant challenge came from the *World Economic Herald* in Shanghai, but the then party boss of the city, Jiang Zemin, quickly cracked down on it.[60] Overall, by the time Zhao gave his two speeches on May 3 and May 4, the party's media control was still in place and intact. Therefore, reports were exceptions rather than the norm.

That would be changed by Zhao's campaign of bureaucratic insurgency. The earliest instructions that encouraged "openness" and "transparency" came from Hu Qili, a Zhao ally and a Standing Committee member, on April 27, on the same day as the "Great Demonstration." On that morning, he held a meeting with chiefs from major newspapers including the *People's Daily* and the *Guangming Daily*. Some chiefs asked for guidance. "If we do not report [the protest], foreign reporters will," one of the journalists observed. To that, Hu Qili replied, "I think, on this matter, the editor in chief of each newspaper should have the power to decide. No need to get clearance on every matter."[61] Another leader in attendance and also an ally of Zhao, Rui Xingwen, con-curred: "There are many aspects in our journalism work that need to be reformed. Stagnation for many decades has been no good ... News reporting should tell the truth."[62]

Further articulation came from Zhao himself. According to Li Peng, on the morning of May 7, the "propaganda sector" of the party held a meeting attended by leaders of its flagship organizations, including the Xinhua News Agency, the *People's Daily*, CCTV, the Central People's Broadcast, and the highest govern-ment ministries, including the Department of Propaganda and the Ministry of Television and Broadcasting. Hu Qili, flanked by Rui Xingwen and Yan Mingfu (a Zhao ally, in charge of the United Front), conveyed the following message credited to General Secretary Zhao himself:

The main tenet of the student movement has been to advance reform. The issue of anticorruption is only the surface. Deep down, students are concerned with the stagnation of reform, or even regression. Reform not only includes the economy, but also politics and democratization. To move reform forward, we need to have transparency and public assessment … Democracy, freedom, and human rights are the norms of the modern world. Freedom of journalism is its focal point. We should ensure freedom of journalism; we should not betray the will of the people.[63]

This statement was made to the highest officers of the party's media channels, but little of it matched existing party policy at the time. It defied the long-standing tradition of censorship and control. Zhao reversed the official verdict on the student protest, and removed the gag order. His exhortation of freedom, democracy, and human rights ran counter to the usual party denunciation of such subjects. In making the speech, it appears that, having been unable bring the entire government along, he activated his power base as general secretary. At one level, he was giving an executive order, yet at another level, since it was out of the official line, his statement could be merely a call for rebellion from those in the official news and propaganda organizations.

Reception was explosive and favorable, especially among journalists. For long, they had been stuck in a struggle between telling the truth and keeping their jobs. One of the most iconic banners, written in outsized Chinese characters, was simply, "News Must Tell the Truth!"[64] It struck a chord, for it asked for so little yet even that was in short supply. Party newspapers began to report the protest openly and positively. For example, as early as May 5, the first headline of the *People's Daily* read, "University Students and Faculty Welcome Zhao Ziyang Speeches." A large picture showed the protest crowds of the May 4 demonstration. This trend accelerated after the hunger strike started. Between May 13 and May 17, the major news outlets reported the protest on their front pages every day. For example, on May 15, the *Guangming Daily* published photos of students on the square under the headline "Some Students of the Capital in Sit-In and Hunger Strike, Requesting Dialogue." The same day, CCTV broadcast news about twelve intellectuals' efforts to persuade students to end the hunger strike. On May 16, Xinhua reported that some students had begun to faint from the hunger strike. The same day, the *People's Daily* not only reported in a positive tone, but also covered the supporting demonstrations of Beijing residents.[65]

Dialogues also started in the media sector. By May 10, representatives from the top newspapers, including the *People's Daily, China Daily, Economic Daily, Science and Technology Daily, Guangming Daily, China Youth Daily*, and *Beijing Daily*, submitted a petition for dialogue.[66] Between May 11 and May 13, Hu Qili, Rui Xingwen, and Wang Renzhi (a conservative, the head of the party's propaganda department) visited the *China Youth Daily*, the *People's Daily*, the *Guangming Daily,* and Xinhua, where they held town hall meetings.

In the meantime, journalists themselves took to the street in support of students' demand for freedom of speech.[67]

Li Peng wrote in his May 8 diary entry, "The news coverage is already favoring the troublemakers who are causing the turmoil. Yet that is not enough for Zhao Ziyang, who is stirring up the news sector itself."[68] In another entry, he complained that Zhao "takes every possible opportunity to achieve the goals that he cannot achieve in the Politburo meetings."[69] Li Xiannian shared Li Peng's anger at Zhao, as he is recorded to have said,

> The severe degree of trouble is directly attributable to the news and propaganda sector. Instead of offering correct guidance, newspaper, TV, and broadcasts these days put forward endless encouragement and provocation [of the protest], pumping up the waves and tides. It is as though the demonstrators in the street were all patriots while those who stay behind were unpatriotic. Zhao's one single speech seems to have caused much more passion than the April 26 editorial. That is incredible.[70]

## Protest Escalated to Hunger Strike

Notwithstanding the initial splashes he made in the public sphere, Zhao Ziyang's moderate approach faced steep odds to succeed. For one thing, Deng granted a very small window of time – he would dismiss Zhao regardless of whatever effect moderation produced. As we saw in the last chapter, Deng in fact might have made already up his mind to remove Zhao and call in the troops even as the student protest began to subside. Moreover, reconciliation between the government and the students was a half measure at best. As there was never a chance to reverse the editorial, students saw the administration's new measures as ultimately devoid of good faith.

### Student Protest Declines for a Time

By one measure, however, the approach seemed to enjoy resounding success. The student turnout was sizable in the May 4 march in Beijing, but after that it started a precipitous decline. It coincided with Zhao's May 4th speech and the commencement of a new round of dialogue. After the march, the BAAUS announced an end to the class strike. According to the statistics that reached the Public Security Bureau, for the following three days most students heeded the call. For example, 80 percent of students in Tsinghua University resumed class; another 59 percent in Renmin University of China returned to classrooms. At Beijing University and Beijing Normal University, the numbers were less impressive, but still indicate a solid improvement. They reported attendance of more than half.[71] This trend continued unabated for more than a week. As shown in Figure 7.1 in next chapter, by the eve of the May 13 hunger strike, street demonstrations in Beijing had reached a negligible level.[72] There were dissenting students who insisted on continuing the class strike, but they were a small minority. For example, on the evening of Monday, May 8, a group of Beijing University students held a rally on campus and made plea for attendance, but garnered only around 200. On the same evening another gathering was held on the campus of Beijing Normal University. Its attendance did not fare much better, with 300 or so students.[73]

But the quiet did not last long. Nor did the appearance of Zhao's success. The hunger strike that came next was a historical turning point. It started a student occupation of the square that would not end until the tragic night of June 3–4. The political theater found a physical location. The drama featured heroism, sacrifice, and headlong determination on the part of students, as well as sympathy from all walks of life. It was showcased before the world by the around-the-clock reporting of international media, who came to Beijing to cover a historical summit between China and the Soviet Union. As far as ending the protest was concerned, the government's approach in the previous two weeks seems to have become a complete failure.

In this section, I explore the factors contributing to the escalation coming from the protest itself. Zhao's supposed allies, the students, contributed to the making of his misfortune. Popular protest, once unleashed, has its own logic. Any attempt to direct its development rarely meets success. By this time, the movement had entered its fourth week. Never had a protest, genuinely popular, achieved such length and scale. To understand where it might have gone wrong from here, let's examine a few major features.

First, the unresolved stickler is the issue of *dingxing*. The protest's goals converged into one about labeling. There had been a variety of claims in the beginning, including "mourning a leader," "reform," "anticorruption," "political reform," "objective journalism," and so on. Now they centered on the legitimacy of the protest itself. If activism was deemed a crime, activists would not be safe. If the protest started being about democracy and change, now it was about safety, a survival cry to protect the students themselves.

Second, interests began to diverge between student leaders and the rank-and-file protesters. Core leaders were facing a different concern from ordinary participants. They could face decades in prison on the charge of "counterrevolutionary crime" should there be a crackdown. It served their best interest to keep the protest going until it erased such danger. Most students, on the other hand, were tired and fatigued after a long period of excitement and agitation. They feared post-protest punishment to a lesser degree, given that tens of thousands participated in the movement.

Third, the movement was in a "lull." Imagine a chart depicting the protest's turnout: the week and a half following May 4 may be called a "temporal valley." Theoretically, a sociologist attributes such low points to the government's "tactical adaptation," the fact that campaign tactics up to that point had been neutralized.[74] To some degree that analysis is apt in describing the Beijing case. The government's hands-off approach had taken the excitement away. Any plan for one more march would be one too many.

Another scholar suggests that, despite lofty talk, respite from boredom is a driving force behind a youth movement. "Boredom is perhaps the best thread to guide us through the labyrinth," he writes. "Youth are unusually sensitive to its prevalence in a particular age; they share this flair with others who are especially attuned to sensibility, chroniclers and artists. Together they constitute the intolerant vanguard which may trigger off the mechanisms that transform the world into an attractive place."[75] A new phase of "moments of madness" was hence called for.[76]

### Hunger Strike as Tactical Innovation

Therein lies the reason why "tactical innovation" would have a tremendous impact. According to McAdam, excitement ebbs when a protest tactic is no longer fresh and participation declines. Then the movement is regenerated to a new height when the organizers successfully innovate.[77] The advent of the student hunger strike on May 13 was such a tactical innovation. It was a stroke of genius in many ways. It was political theater par excellence.

The protest started to have a physical headquarters, located in the Tiananmen Square, which is the nerve center of the government. It was theater for Beijing citizens, just a bike trip away from everyone who cared to come; it was theater for the nation, as featured in newspapers and on television screens around the clock; and it was theater for the global audience, with the media stationed to cover the Sino-Soviet summit. The plot was simple enough: students wanted nothing more than a fair dialogue with the government, a request they claimed the government had coldly rejected, and they decried the ongoing attempts at such dialogues as disingenuous. That students were willing to die for their cause was moving to many. The new tactic hence broadened the protest's support base. It seemed that whoever was capable of sympathy should be concerned with the students who were quickly beginning to faint. Beijing streets were flooded with supportive residents, coming out to urge the government to "do something." At the peak on May 16, 617 striking students were transported away to the emergency rooms of hospitals, and more than 300,000 citizens marched to the square to support the students.[78]

The new wave of protest directly and seriously interrupted government business. Mikhail Gorbachev, the general secretary and president of the Soviet Union, arrived in Beijing on May 15, the third day of the hunger strike. The original welcome ceremony scheduled on the square had to be canceled. A simpler one was performed in the airport instead. The Soviet leader was rerouted to enter the Great People's Meeting Hall, which faces the square, from the back door. It was unprecedented that Chinese state leaders had to countenance an ocean of protesters amassed outside while they were conducting the solemn business of world diplomacy inside. Opposition was only meters away. On the morning of May 16, a student protester, reportedly looking for a water fountain, ran into the wrong door and broke the glass by accident. The noise startled Deng Xiaoping, who was in the middle of his conversation with Gorbachev.[79]

Tactical innovation not only revives the movement's scale. It often also alters aspects of the nature of the movement itself, for example its leadership. Taking the American civil rights movement as an example, earlier boycotts drew leaders from clergy and lawyers, while later sit-ins would shift the leadership to college students.[80] Similarly, a tactical transformation from marching to hunger strike in Beijing also caused a shift in leadership. In the first stages of the Tiananmen protest, student leaders were often those who had deep connections to public intellectuals, who are a base constituency for reform leaders like Zhao Ziyang. As the hunger strikes were taking place, more radical students emerged to occupy center stage in the newest wave of protest.[81] With dialogue and hunger strike emerging as new protest tactics, two central commands were formed in addition to the BAAUS. Already in previous weeks, the Beijing Dialogue Delegation of University Students (BDDUS) had ascended to a more prominent position than the BAAUS. Now a new group, the Beijing Hunger Strike Command of University Students (BHSCUS), was founded and was poised to take over.

### Escalation Doomed Zhao's New Take

The hunger strike was a blow to Zhao Ziyang. Without it, he might not have kept his job; with it, any hope was gone. It entirely undermined his soft approach and spelled an end to his experiment. And it provided a resounding justification for Deng to carry on with his plan, which perhaps had already been formulated before the hunger strike. Not only was the hunger strike extreme in its tactics and explosive in its power; it also raised the level of confrontation exponentially and drove away supporters and sympathizers within the party. It not only interfered with the Sino-Soviet summit proceedings; it also made the highest Chinese leaders lose face in front of the world, which was totally unacceptable and unpatriotic to them. No longer could those sympathetic from inside the government continue to speak out on behalf of the protest. Nor was it still possible for Zhao's allies, such as Qiao Shi and Yang Shangkun, to stand with him.

Given the hunger strike's decisive nature, could Zhao Ziyang have anticipated its coming and prevented it? If not, could he have done something to mitigate its effect, for example, persuading the hunger strikers to make way for Gorbachev's visit?

A poster calling for a hunger strike appeared on May 11 at Beijing University, as noticed by the Public Security Bureau. The all-city federation of students, the BAAUS, officially announced the plan on May 12 in the afternoon, to be carried out the next day.[82] Zhao did not seem to have any separate channel to learn about the news, hence before May 12 he was unaware of the impending storm. "Upon learning the news," Zhao recalled, "I hastened to make a speech by way of dialogue with workers on May 13." In the speech, Zhao made a desperate plea to the students:

> Even if your requests are not yet satisfied, it is unreasonable to interfere with an international event and do damage to the Sino-Soviet summit. The great majority of Chinese people will not support or sympathize with that. I plead [with you to] set your eyes on the big picture, and do not do something that gives pleasure to the hateful and pain to your loved ones.

Unfortunately, Zhao's plea fell on deaf ears. "But the students just totally ignored my plea," he sighed, "and from that day on, the students began to occupy the square until the June 4 event of bloodshed."[83]

After the hunger strike started, Zhao's officials made strenuous efforts to negotiate with the students. On May 13 and 14, Yan Mingfu was dispatched to engage with the hunger strikers' representatives. Yan was a Zhao ally, a Politburo member, and one of the secretaries of the party's Central Secretariat, a leading body directly under Zhao. His most relevant capacity was minister of the United Front. Like many other leaders in this period, he was a victim of Mao's Cultural Revolution. He was imprisoned for eight years in the infamous Qincheng Prison, and his father, also a party official, died there. At work also was Tao Siliang, another child of Mao's victims, a bureau chief under him in the United Front in charge of intellectuals.[84] She was deeply connected with the intellectuals, who in turn enjoyed close relationships with student leaders. She was able to bring the necessary parties together, including Yan Mingfu, the intellectual go-betweens, and the student leaders.[85]

The BAAUS leaders, represented by Wang Dan and Wang Chaohua, had become leaders partly for their pre-protest association with intellectuals, and were more attuned to elite politics. Recall that the protest started with the grievances around elite politics, specifically Hu Yaobang's dismissal. They were aware of Zhao's position and the importance of saving his job for the reform cause. Hence, they were willing to compromise even though the hunger strike had been planned and announced by their very group. By contrast, the leaders of the other two groups gained their credentials and notoriety during the protest thanks to their valor or rhetorical skills. They excelled in idealistically envisioning freedom and democracy but had little experience in pragmatically considering real politics. They relished the movement itself, and they feared post-protest persecution. In a sense, keeping the movement going became an end in itself. Therefore, they adamantly insisted on the reversal of the editorial as a precondition to winding down the protest, even though it was not something possibly delivered by Yan Mingfu or even Zhao Ziyang. They stood firm at the negotiation tables, as Yan Mingfu fruitlessly pleaded with heart-to-heart speeches and tears.[86]

On the afternoon of May 14, about twenty-four hours after the start of the hunger strike, the air in Beijing was tense. Many had begun to faint, and ambulances began to drive in and out. In the editorial building of the *Guangming Daily* a few miles away, the nation's most prominent liberal intellectuals were assembled for a meeting. The force behind it was apparently Yan Mingfu and Tao Siliang. Dai Qing, herself a renowned journalist and a close friend of Tao's, was instrumental in putting together the list of names of the attendees. Wang Chaohua, the student leader of the BAAUS, addressed them as "teachers": "I am here to ask for help, my teachers. The mood of the students on the square is [blank here, inaudible] ... Now the BAAUS is no longer able to command them. The situation in the square is out of control." Then she proceeded to recount the failed negotiation at the United Front Ministry earlier in the morning, and said, "Knowing you are holding a meeting here, the United Front asked me to come here. They gave me a list of your names and asked me to invite you to go to the square to persuade and plead with them to leave the square."[87]

The same evening, the "Twelve Sages" were transported to the square. Led by Dai Qing, they gave speeches one by one. They praised the student movement as a "patriotic movement for democracy" but pleaded with the students to end the hunger strike and make way for the Sino-Soviet summit. The students were all excited to see their luminaries at close range, but they refused to leave. I was a student sitting among them.

### Deng Xiaoping and Zhao Ziyang Split

*Zhao and His Allies Knew They Had Failed, and a Startling Revelation*

In the afternoon of May 15, on the third day of the hunger strike, Yan Mingfu and Hu Qili visited Li Peng in his office. They pleaded with him, saying that in order to resolve the ongoing crisis, the Party Center had to acknowledge the April 26 editorial as a mistake and the student protest as a patriotic action. "But I disagreed," Li Peng wrote in his diary. "I said, isn't the current situation exactly a turmoil? So how can we say the editorial is wrong?" He also told his two guests to pass his reply to Zhao Ziyang. In the evening Zhao sent a message back to Li Peng. There was nothing he could do, Zhao's message said, if the Party Center could not admit the mistake.[88]

Perhaps knowing how the course of events would end up, Yan Mingfu, the minister of the United Front and Zhao's ally, came to the square on the evening of May 16, the fourth day of the hunger strike, and spoke with the students. His speech was obviously a farewell, no longer carrying much weight of persuasion:

> My young comrades, the future is yours, and the mission of reform needs you to go on. So you have no right to damage your own health like this, nor can you use life to exchange what you want ... You should cherish yourself and wait for the day when justice arrives.[89]

For someone who had spent eight years in prison, Yan surely knew the meaning of waiting.

At about the same moment, Zhao Ziyang was meeting with Mikhail Gorbachev inside the Great Meeting Hall located on one side of the square. The proceeding was broadcast live on television. Entirely unprompted by his guest and going outside the conventions of diplomacy, Zhao delivered a bombshell. In an elaborate speech, he gave away a known but never-publicized party secret: although Deng had retired from official duties, he was, in effect, in charge. The ultimate decision maker in the party had been Deng all along:

> Since the Third Plenum of the 11th Party Congress in 1978, Comrade Deng Xiaoping has been the party's leader recognized both in the country and abroad ... [After his retirement in 1987,] a decision was made in the first plenum of the 13th party congress that on the matters that are of utmost significance, we still need Comrade Deng Xiaoping to be at the helm ... This is my first time revealing the Party Center's decision.[90]

If the content of Zhao's speech was startling, it is equally stunning that he made it at this particular moment. But why?

### Did Zhao Intend to Betray Deng?

A first explanation, indeed an accusation, is that Zhao abandoned Deng and made him the primary target of the protest. "Although what Zhao revealed was true, his motive makes you ponder why he chose such a moment, when the country was in a life-and-death crisis," wrote Li Peng in his diary. He then bluntly went on, "By doing that, Zhao Ziyang made a declaration to the world: Comrade Xiaoping was responsible for the economic disaster in 1988, and he was also responsible for the current political turmoil."[91] Reportedly, Deng's children and Deng himself also suspected this ill intent. Immediately after the interview, Deng Nan, one of Deng's daughters, was reported to have made a call and sternly asked Zhao, "How dare you reveal Deng's ultimate discretion! You mean to direct society's spearhead toward Deng, don't you? You mean to direct the fire toward Deng, don't you?"[92] In a meeting with the American scientist Tsung-Dao Lee after June 4, Deng expressed his displeasure. He said that Zhao "threw him out during the 'student turmoil.'"[93]

The reactions of the protesters seem to support this explanation. On the evening of May 16, Bao Zunxin, an influential intellectual, was approached by a graduate student: "We think it is now time for us to explicitly raise the banner of 'overthrowing Deng.' We have discussed this among ourselves, and we would like to entrust you to draft a statement."[94] The slogans, statements, and banners in the second day's protest unmistakably showed that Zhao's speech had had that effect. Among the declaratory statements was one signed by a group of intellectuals led by Bao Zunxin and Yan Jiaqi:

> The Qing Dynasty has been gone for 76 long years. But there is still an emperor without a title, a dictator who is old and already boneheaded. Yesterday afternoon, General Secretary Zhao Ziyang told us that every major decision in China has to go through this old and boneheaded dictator ... Down with the personal dictatorship! Dictators will meet no kind end! Overthrow the April 26 editorial! The politics of old men must end![95]

### An Honest Mistake?

But Zhao Ziyang and his supporters vehemently denied any ulterior motive; there had been an honest mistake, they insisted. They offered some good reasons for Zhao's remarks, though they conceded that it had not been a prudent decision. Zhao reported that as early as May 13, two days before his revelation to Gorbachev, in a citizen–government dialogue event, a worker representative had asked why Deng was still in charge after his retirement. In the meeting, Zhao had already talked about the Party Center's decision made in the first plenum of the 13th Party Congress in 1987. The dialogue was not widely covered by the media. "Therefore that [question] made me think: if we report and explain this [decision to keep Deng in charge], it will help protect Deng's image; because it is not that Deng grabbed power, but that it was a solemn decision made by the party congress."[96]

So why choose that particular occasion to explain the decision? Zhao offered an additional reason. It was to clarify what the summit meant:

> The so-called Sino-Soviet summit must be one between Gorbachev and Deng. While Gorbachev was the general secretary, Deng was not. Nor was he [Deng] the president of the state, but merely the CMC chair. So in my mind we should make an explicit

statement that the summit was precisely meant to be between Gorbachev and no one else rather than [Deng].

Zhao went on,

> My speech kills two birds with one stone: to clarify why the Deng–Gorbachev interview was already the summit itself, and to reveal the Party plenum's decision on Deng as the highest leader . . . I heard the initial reactions were all positive. Only later would I learn that both Deng's family and he himself were unhappy about my speech.[97]

Zhao's aide Wu Wei provided an elaborate account in support of Zhao's defense. Echoing Zhao's reasons, he further attested that a speech had been in the works, prompted by the worker representative's question on May 13, and a draft was completed by the evening of May 15. Wu included the draft speech as an appendix to a memoir he wrote many years later, showing that it covered the same points about Deng's role which Zhao had made to Gorbachev. The draft speech, however, was meant for a later occasion addressing party officials.[98] In any event, both Zhao and Wu argued that the speech was meant to clarify and protect Deng's image, not besmirch it. That is a point also backed by the other aides, Chen Yizi and Bao Tong, in their respective reflections.[99]

### A Third Explanation: A Farewell

There is a third explanation that I believe is more convincing. Ever since I was a student protester in 1989, I have struggled with this puzzle. When I interviewed a Tiananmen dissident, he told me that in Zhao's mind it was his last public speech, and under the circumstances he could only make it in that moment with Gorbachev. Without the live television broadcast, his speech would not have been able to reach the audience he wanted. Remember that, on the next day (the evening of May 17), the martial law decision was made and he dissented. Although Zhao was able to make another speech on the square to the occupying students in the early morning of May 19, he would not have known that on May 16. Before entering the meeting hall that evening, as Chen Xiaoya and Su Xiaokang both observe, Zhao Ziyang asked his staff, "Is it live?"[100]

By the evening of May 16, it must have been clear to Zhao that he was reaching the end of his own political career. He had not had a chance to see Deng personally since his return on April 30. He made a request yet one more time on the morning of May 13, but he was seen along with Yang Shangkun. The most ominous of all was the conversation between Deng and Yang Shangkun on May 11 – while it was confidential, it would not be surprising if its content were leaked to the general secretary. It should not have escaped Zhao's awareness that in their meeting on May 13, Yang Shangkun was already obviously leaning against him. On top of these undercurrents, the hunger strike had now created a perfect storm. There was no better cause for his ousting. He could now do nothing more to save his job or avoid an onerous outcome.

In that context, Zhao's revelation was not so much an effort to alter ongoing events as to offer a statement in anticipation of his historical legacy. He was telling the protesters, his allies, his family, and the world that his power had limits and that he had done his best. Additionally, as the dissident speculated, it was also a signal to his supporters that the game was now over and further sacrifice was no longer advisable. Between the lines, it was a message: preserve yourself for another day if you can.

As history often defies one's expectations, that was not Zhao's last speech. He appeared in public for the last time in the early morning at 4:00 a.m. of May 19, in the square. It was vividly captured by the television cameras, with the party secretary looking exhausted and defeated. With tears and in a coarse voice, he pleaded with the students to end the hunger strike and preserve themselves for a future day: "My young comrades, we have come too late, and we are so sorry to you. We are already old, so it matters less to us. But you are young and there are many years ahead of you. So you should live in good health."[101]

### Discussion and Conclusion

Zhao's two weeks trying a "new take" never had a chance to succeed for many reasons. First, he would never have been able to convince Li Peng and Deng Xiaoping to retract the editorial. With it in place, the policy of leniency was devoid of its most critical component. Second, the window would have been closed by Deng Xiaoping regardless of whether or not the new policy succeeded. Sadly, Deng offered the window not for Zhao to succeed but for him to stumble.[102] Third, the dynamics of the student movement followed its own logic, and they reduced the opportunity for Zhao's approach to work.

The political nature was evident in both Li Peng's and Zhao Ziyang's actions. Li Peng had the lion's share of responsibility as an unlikely enabler. Before Zhao's return, he was in charge of the entire leadership, but he did nothing before or during the April 27 demonstration. Then he started the dialogue, de facto recognition of the legality of the protest organizations. Neither of these two major policies were consistent with the April 26 editorial he had championed. He was in a way "lenient," but not because he genuinely thought his measures would be helpful to end the protest. Indeed, he must have been aware of the possibility of backlash. He just did not care enough, for he was focused on the negative labeling which would spell trouble for Zhao Ziyang.

Zhao Ziyang was perhaps correct in his judgment that the protest could have been handled if his advocacy of moderation was heeded. Large-scale mobilization is extremely difficult to wage and much more difficult to maintain. Without the government's provocation, protest may just come and go. If the party had been able to withstand it, the 1989 student protest could have ended without much damage. But Zhao's measures were also political in that, on his watch, the government did not just sit on its hands.[103] Zhao was engaged in a public campaign in this second period that, to a large degree, sided with the protest, hence a "bureaucratic insurgency."

Just as Li Peng vigorously defended the negative labeling of the protest, Zhao's interest lay in removing it. So he continued the dialogue, in which student leaders of supposedly "illegal" organizations, the same leaders who would be on the government's most-wanted list after June 4, played a key role. Under his leadership, he also reversed the long-standing party policy on controlling the media, allowing them to freely cover the ongoing protest. To say that his campaign sided with the students is not to say that he became part of the movement. When the time came, as martial law was announced, the movement did not have a "Boris Yeltsin on the tank" in Zhao. He in fact remained a Leninist party leader until late in his house arrest.[104]

Zhao's brief experiment with moderation led to two immediate results, both of which would significantly contribute to the martial law policy decision to come. One is that the protest escalated rather than subsiding. The hunger strike created a crisis that was enormous and lasting; nevertheless, could that have been ended only through escalated repression from the government side? My research concludes that the crisis did not warrant a military solution, for the simple reason that, if left alone, the student protest could not have sustained further mobilization. The excitement caused by the hunger strike would have subsided too. The protest should have died of natural causes. The next chapter will elaborate these points.

The other is the final split between Zhao Ziyang and Deng. As Chapter 8 will discuss, the split completed the need to "change horse," and it would represent an enormous challenge for Deng to remove an incumbent general secretary in the middle of a national protest movement.

*Part III*

# The Decision for Military Intervention

It is not in dispute that the military operation of June 4 successfully removed the student occupation of the square and ended the Tiananmen Square movement. What this book sets out to challenge is the rationale behind the decision. If, for example, the student protest was not that great a threat to the government, can such a forceful intervention be justified? Even if the protest had to be stopped, did that task require such a large-scale military operation? If the decision was in effect built on a different logic than ending the protest, then what were the other political considerations in the mind of the decision makers?

Part III will devote three chapters to answering these questions.

- Chapter 7, "Was It a Revolution?", assesses the claim that the student protest of 1989 constituted a revolution, one that could have overthrown the government. The question is explored from three angles: the goal of the alleged "revolutionaries," the strength of their movement, and finally whether the state was vulnerable to regime change.

- Chapter 8, "The Martial Law Decision," explores the true challenges faced by Deng Xiaoping in 1989, hence the real logic behind the military decision. I argue that the decision taken in the name of ending the protest was a political play whose aims pointed elsewhere. In the end, he seemed to satisfy many demands with one stroke: with enhanced power, he ended the protest, removed Zhao Ziyang as general secretary, and prevailed in forming a new leadership to carry on his reform mantle.

- Chapter 9, "Military Operation as Symbolic Display of Power," challenges the notion that the military operation was the right response to the protest. I will do so by describing the *manner* in which it was carried out on June 3–4. The tasks of "clearing the square" and securing the city would have required much less. It was "using an ox cleaver to kill a chicken."

# 7    Was It a Revolution?

## April 15–June 3, 1989

The decision to use the military was built on claims of a potential revolution. That is, the student protest would have overthrown the government had it not been stopped. Such alleged danger has been the official justification for its tragic ending. It also serves, academically, as a building block in repression models of state action.[1] It is commonly believed that the student protest had amounted to a "revolutionary situation" that was just short of a regime change outcome.[2] The regime was considered to have had "its closest brush with death," according to one scholar, and "the party was saved only with the help of the PLA, whose tanks crushed the peaceful protesters."[3]

In this chapter I shall pause my narrative of elite politics and devote some space to the movement itself. Let us take a closer look at claims about its revolutionary potential. This will be the only chapter of this book that focuses on the movement itself, and I do not attempt a detailed account. As I stated earlier, the movement side of the story has been diligently written, and some texts are already classics.[4] Many important features of the movement that are germane to my argument have been well researched and are noncontroversial. My attention is therefore on those features of the movement that are indicative of its attempt on political power, and features of the state that are indicative of its vulnerability.

Does a large-scale mobilization such as the Tiananmen Square movement in 1989, left unchecked, lead to a revolution? Those who say yes can cite the examples of the French Revolution of 1789, the Iranian Revolution of 1978–1979, and the Yellow Revolution of the Philippines in 1986, not to mention the global wave of anticommunist success that started in 1989 itself. Famous events aside, those who say no, however, would point to the fact that collective action is commonplace while regime change by popular power is extremely rare:

> Armed insurrection in some form or other is the classic method of making a revolution, and . . . it is bound to imply a clash with professionally trained troops equipped with all the gear of scientific warfare. History shows that, in the last resort, success or failure hinges on the attitude which those armed forces of the status quo government will take toward an insurrection. . . Whatever government or party has

the full allegiance of a country's armed forces is to all intents and purposes politically impregnable.[5]

After citing the above memorable passage by Chorley, Tullock adds, "If it is rare in the study of actual overthrows of dictatorship, it is very common in the romantic literature. The Bastille was actually taken by a regiment of regular infantry, but it is still the legend that it was a Paris mob."[6]

Events of collective contentions are probabilistic and emergent, hence difficult to predict with certainty. Short of making clear-cut assertions, what a scholar can do is identify a series of relevant factors that might increase or decrease the chances of such an outcome. For example, a reformist movement might be less likely to overthrow a regime than a revolutionary one. A weak state mired in financial problems might be particularly vulnerable. In this chapter, we will revisit three grounds on which previous assertions of Tiananmen's revolutionary danger have been built.

The first ground pertains to the intent of the protesters. For a long time Tiananmen protesters have been believed to have held revolutionary intent. That is, they meant their movement to change the regime.[7] However, such claims are not built on what they said or what they did. Close analysis would find the movement to be reformist rather than revolutionary. Throughout the Tiananmen protest, no organizer made any regime change claims; their central demand quickly evolved into a plea to reverse the government's negative framing of their actions. These claims were further supported by their actions – demonstrations, at least up to May 17, were exclusively peaceful and nonviolent. What about the alleged masterminds? At almost every turn, the prominent "black hands" counseled restraint and compromise.

The second ground concerns the strength of the movement. Its size and theatrics notwithstanding, was it potent enough to overthrow the regime? As scholars such as Dingxin Zhao and Xueguang Zhou have convincingly argued, the "large-number phenomenon" that rose out of Tiananmen was more due to ecological and institutional infrastructure than to organizing or mobilizing efforts.[8] As discussed in previous chapters, the highest turnouts took place because a hostile government announcement backfired. These conclusions are backed by the data on the temporal patterns of protest participation. Also, as another indicator of its limited revolutionary potential, the movement was narrowly based among students, intellectuals, and urban residents, while the country's peasants and workers remained on the sidelines.

The third and final ground concerns the nature of the state. After reviewing past major revolutions, we identify four typical pathways for protests to seize political power. But none of them seem to have applied to China in 1989. The country at that historical moment was financially sound, had strong and coherent army and security forces, and was internationally independent. None of its elites, then, would champion revolt.

## A Reformist Movement

### Reformist Claims

Anonymous wall posters often carry colorful language. Demonstrations sometimes involved shouting slogans that might be considered out of line. Even formal statements by student organizations could seem diverse, constantly evolving. Despite all this, however, the overall nature of the protest's claim is not difficult to establish. Take one of the most well-known documents, "the seven-point demand," as an example:

1  Affirm as correct Hu Yaobang's views on democracy and freedom.
2  Admit that the campaigns against spiritual pollution and bourgeois liberalization were wrong.
3  Publish information on the income of state leaders and their family members.
4  End the ban on privately run newspapers and stop press censorship.
5  Increase funding for education and raise intellectuals' pay.
6  End restrictions on demonstrations in Beijing.
7  Provide objective coverage of students in official media.[9]

These were as close to a policy proposal as one can get. Nowhere in these words can one find calls for a transformation in how state power was managed. How did the government make a case that these demands amounted to an anti-system conspiracy? In his post-June 4 report, Beijing mayor Chen Xitong singled out two points as the most important: the demands to re-evaluate Hu Yaobang and to end the campaigns against spiritual pollution and bourgeois liberalization. Then he moved to this conclusion: "The essence of these two points is to obtain absolute freedom of a capitalist nature in China, discarding the Four Cardinal Principles."[10] In other words, it is not what one said or what one did that counted, it was the "essence" that the government imputed that counted. This reasoning is maddening. Such mischaracterization might evoke adverse reactions in open societies, but they were never questioned under the hegemony of party-speak.[11] Using any common sense, one could put no weight on the government's analysis.

If those earliest demands seemed to carry some edge, the overall claims of the movement became softer from there. Given the later escalations of the protest in size and intensity, this observation seems to be counterintuitive. But it is very easy to clarify and explain: while students escalated in their passion and righteousness, their intensity in participation, and their tactics and theatrical effects; they did not escalate their demands. After the

April 26 editorial, their requests were pared down to a simple plea to permit their right to protest in a public place. If the editorial stood in place, student leaders and ordinary participants would be subject to persecution in the aftermath, a danger known in Chinese as "settling accounts after the autumn harvest."

This plea had taken many specific forms over the course of the protests. For example, in the large protest on the day following the editorial's publication, banners and slogans made an ardent effort to declare protesters' fealty to the party. Hence "Long live Reform! Long live the CCP!" "Firmly uphold the Four Cardinal Principles," and so on. In order to reject the notion of "turmoil," protesters put on a show that was pristinely peaceful, disciplined, and well mannered. That was true even during the chaotic days of hunger striking on the square. The ambulances were coming in and out and a sense of crisis was in the air, but the square was in perfect order, maintained by an army of self-organized student marshals. They wore armbands, checking the IDs of individuals coming in to visit the hunger strikers.[12] At the high noon of the hunger strike, the students dropped all other demands except for two: retract the editorial and broadcast the dialogue between the students and the government.[13]

It is conceivable that the students would have asked for more, had the government made concessions. Many would have argued that the government could not afford to make concessions. Would the government have to change the way it responded to future unrest, if it granted some level of legitimacy to the protest? Would China have to undergo recurrent waves of protest if the independent organizations were allowed to stay? These are all good questions. A reasonable answer would be that the government would have to worry about future incidents of protest if it were not firm on the current one. But applying the logic backward – projecting a bigger or even a revolutionary nature for the protest because of what the government did in response – is not persuasive. It would be similar to the previous example of party-speak or, more specifically, the "essence" argument above. That is, it is deploying a *possibility* argument and using what might have happened to characterize what actually happened. Instead, what transpired was actually a student movement that lacked revolutionary claims.

Reading through the slogans, pamphlets, and news releases of the movement, the major claims can be summarized as in Table 7.1. Reformist in nature, they made suggestions for policy changes without threatening the system as a whole, including "the right to express dissent," "mourning," "anticorruption," and "objective journalism." The most prominent was "the right to express dissent," covering such demands as "the release of former activists," "reassessment of post-protest movements," and defending the protest as legitimate and rational. There were also indeed claims that targeted the political system and its

Table 7.1 *Mobilization frames in the Tiananmen Square movement in 1989*

| Frame | Content | Time appearing | Time prominent |
|---|---|---|---|
| Right to express dissent | Release of former activists; reassessment of past protest movements; the legitimacy of the protest; protesters are rational, orderly, and peaceful | January 6 | April 15–June 4 |
| Mourning | Hu Yaobang a great leader | | |
| Anticorruption | A source of social ills, revelation of corrupt officials, demands for officials to declare income | April 15 | April 27 demonstration |
| Political reform | Natural extension of economic reform, incremental social change | April 15 | Never |
| Democracy | Change the system to cure social ills | April 15 | Never |
| Overthrow the government | Past evil deeds by the regime, violent uprising, radical slogans in the otherwise moderate demonstrations | April 19 | Never |
| Objective journalism | Burning newspapers, the famous "News Must Tell the Truth" banner | April 20 | April 20–May 19 |
| Nonviolence | "The army is the people's army," student protesters are nonviolent | May 19 | May 19–June 4 |

political power, such as "political reform," "democracy," and "overthrow the government," but these never advanced to a prominent position and never went beyond being abstract slogans. It is equally telling that, at the height of the tension after the military deployment in the city on May 19, nonviolence was the most prominent frame. The citizens of Beijing proclaimed that "the army is the people's army."[14]

*Nonviolent Tactics*

What about the actions of the protesters? Was there turmoil?[15] Authoritative studies of the Tiananmen Square movement have been abundantly clear in emphasizing the peaceful manner of the protesters, which persisted up until military advance on the night of what would become the well-known massacre.[16]

Here let us use facts cited by the government's own reports to illustrate this point further. On April 24, Li Peng convened an extended Politburo Standing Committee meeting featuring a report by Li's allies in Beijing, Chen Xitong and Li Ximing, and another report by He Dongchang, the head of the state educational committee who was also Li's ally. The premise of these reports and the facts they gathered were used in Li's personal interview with Deng

Xiaoping on the next day, and subsequently served as the basis for the April 26 editorial.[17] They summarized the situation in Beijing and in the nation. The main substantive focus was on how many universities were involved in the protest movement and which universities' students had called for cancelation of classes. Besides a barrage of verbal attacks supposedly recorded at the protest, these reports had almost nothing on violence around the "turmoil." Two instances were mentioned – one in Changsha, one in Xi'an – but none in Beijing. The most severe incident in Beijing was the Xinhua Gate incident, a sit-in previously discussed in Chapter 4.

Even for the sit-in, there was not much of violence to speak of. Zhao Ziyang gave these observations:

> On April 18 and 19, a few hundred people gathered in front of Xinhua Gate. I ordered the video recordings from the Public Security Ministry to review this so-called Students Rushing Xinhua Gate incident. What really happened was like this. The students in front shouted constantly, "Follow the rules, and do not make any mistakes!" In the front, the students were making requests and asking for interviews. The rushing forward was due to pressure coming from behind from onlookers. It was at first a bit chaotic because the people in the rear pushed forward. At the end students set up their own group of marshals, who separated the students and the onlookers.[18]

As discussed previously, there was some confrontation in the early morning of April 20 between students and police. Pictures of an injured student emerged later in the protest movement, as evidence of police violence.[19] The protesters would not see blood again for the entire course of the movement. This only changed on May 19, the day the government implemented martial law.

### "Black Hands" Counseled Restraint and Moderation

Topping the government's list of "black hands" were four intellectuals.[20] Chen Ziming and Wang Juntao earned the longest jail sentences for their involvement in the movement, each of thirteen years. Fang Lizhi's stay in the US embassy and his subsequent exit from China almost caused a diplomatic crisis. Liu Xiaobo, a would-be Nobel Peace Prize laureate, stayed with the students on the square until the last night, and played a role in negotiating a peaceful withdrawal of the students in the early morning of June 4. It is revealing to take a closer look at these four intellectuals' attitudes and actions before and during 1989.

I met Wang Juntao first in 1988 when I was a graduate student at Beijing University. He came to our dormitory for a visit, enlisting some of us for a book project. We were to identify writings of a few Western thinkers and translate them from English into Chinese. I saw him again in 1994, in Washington, DC, right after he had been released on medical parole from a Chinese prison. His colleague, Chen Ziming, the alleged coconspirator of Tiananmen, was still serving his sentence back in China. This time, I paid Wang Juntao a visit, partly to show my respect, but mainly to interview him. I was then a PhD student interested in social-movement research.

Before I talked to him one-on-one, he brought me to a meeting with a score of others, who were mostly his former associates, friends, and admirers dating back to his time in China. When he introduced me, however, he described me as someone who studied movements, "hence someone *who believes in movements.*" Contextually, this appeared to imply that he and the others were, in contrast, those who *did not believe in movements.* People in the room nodded and smiled. I was bewildered by this remark. Wang had been credited by the whole world with helping to lead one of the most extraordinary social movements in history. Yet he all but declared that he did not believe in them. In subsequent interviews, I learned in more detail about his objection to social movements. He told me that he and Chen Ziming had not expected a social movement in 1989, nor had they welcomed it. Their organization had envisioned a reform trajectory for China, including economic and political steps, only to be interrupted by the protest.

Chen Ziming and Wang Juntao first appeared in the public domain in their participation in the 1976 Tiananmen incident in the year of Mao's death, as detailed in Chapter 2. Both were wanted by the police; both briefly served time. When Deng came to power, the historic "verdict" of the government was overturned. Chen and Wang became the April 5 movement heroes of 1976 and enjoyed considerable celebrity. Wang was even elected to the national congress of the Communist Youth League, where he got to meet future party secretary Hu Yaobang. Their celebrity brought them other important connections. In years of social activity leading up to 1989, they were able to have their policy proposals heard by Deng Pufang (Deng Xiaoping's son) and Hu Deping (Hu Yaobang's son). Such access to high officials strengthened their reformist outlook, as they saw the possibility of making social change by feeding new ideas into the state machine.[21]

Other reasons may include the fact that both of them were trained as natural scientists. Wang was a nuclear physics major at Beida for his undergraduate work, while Chen studied chemistry and had a master's degree from another prestigious institute in Beijing. In our conversations, Wang Juntao presented a way of thinking that may be characteristic of "science" – packed with data, concepts, and models. Yet it was science as he understood it: his models were inflexible, resistant to variables that he deemed unimportant. "But everything was interrupted by *xuechao* [the student movement of 1989]," he said ruefully.

"Wait. Student movements had taken place a few times already," I reminded him. For example, the protests in 1986 that contributed to Hu Yaobang's downfall. "We are aware of them," he replied, "that is why we conducted surveys on university students to predict the likelihood of them happening again."

"Did you ever imagine that you guys would be part of it?"

"No. Because we do not believe that is a way to accomplish anything."[22]

This attitude was apparently shared by his partner Chen Ziming. It is worth citing Chen's statement from his post-Tiananmen trial at length:

> Wang Juntao and I believed in political order and stability. We opposed chaos and rebellion ... [We opposed] the prattling about "without destruction there can be no construction" ... Instead we promoted these ideas: "Do not destroy things before you have exploited their full potential; do not start building something new until you have tested your ingenuity." I will regret for the rest of my life that we were not able to exert sufficient influence over the impetuous, emotional students in time.[23]

While they remained on the moderate side of the students' methods of protest, they were supportive of the students' cause and expressed their endorsement in words as well as in actions. They made public statements calling the student movement patriotic, and they took part in the movement by setting up a liaison organization to connect students, intellectuals, and government officials. And most directly, on at least two occasions, Chen wrote a very large check to Liu Gang, who in turn passed along the much-needed funds to the student movements.[24]

However, Chen and Wang did not have enough authority to influence the decision-making of the student leaders, and their counsel against radical methods, such as the hunger strike, was not heeded by the students. This state of affairs was partly rooted in their reluctance to be directly involved in the movement. One can imagine, for example, that had one of their disciples, someone like Liu Gang, a new graduate from Beida, got involved in the forefront of the movement and become an important student leader, with power similar to that of Chai Ling or Wuer Kaixi, the course of the movement could have been different.

The distinction between endorsement of the students' cause and rejection of the students' methods also applied to another "black hand," Fang Lizhi, one of China's most prominent human rights advocates. He was the leading voice for greater democracy in China's political and educational systems, an alleged adult "mastermind" behind the student movement that caused Hu Yaobang's unseating in 1987.[25] But in 1989 he had no involvement in terms of the protest's organization, and from mid-May he began to ask the students to stop protesting altogether. "I didn't take part in any of the students' organized activities in the spring of 1989. But the government seem to feel that my ideas had been a factor stimulating the movement."[26]

According to Brook's interview with him, not only had Fang remained out of the Tiananmen student movement, but also he had criticized his students for going too far, particularly with the hunger strike:

> Once the hunger strike started, the movement went out of control, and I suspected that the government would use military means to end it. These students just did not understand. They grew up in the generation after the Cultural Revolution and had never seen the Party kill people on a large scale. The students loved that line in *The Internationale* about this being the final struggle, but I told those who came to my home that this was most definitely not the final struggle ... They felt that if they just carried this struggle through, they would be victorious. I didn't think so.[27]

Another alleged "black hand," Liu Xiaobo, was in the United States until his return to Beijing in April 1989. He was not involved in any organizing efforts until, just days before June 4, he felt he needed to be part of the Tiananmen occupation in order to have influence over the student movement. He led the "Hunger Strike of Four Gentlemen" to join student occupiers in the square on June 2. His instinct to gain trust and influence by first joining the action proved to be prescient. In a famous scene recorded on camera, he counseled students in nonviolence by smashing a gun obtained by a student activist. He also played a key role in brokering the student withdrawal from the square in the early hours of June 4. Without that negotiation between representatives of the occupiers and the military, the action of "clearing the square" could have turned into a bloodbath.[28]

### Patterns of Mobilization

#### Convergence out of Floodgate

That the 1989 student movement lacked leadership was evident in the patterns of protest mobilization, a far cry from a common charge that the protest was the result of central planning by a group of conspirators, or, as the party terminology puts it, "a handful people with ulterior motives."

Dingxin Zhao has provided an insightful account of the lack of central leadership and the ecological dynamics of mobilization.[29] In a different vein, Xueguang Zhou has suggested that street demonstrations in communist China, at times seemingly co-ordinated, were in fact "unorganized" responses to new policy change.[30] Taken together, two lessons emerged. Large-scale actions are not the result of any central leadership on the part of student protesters. Instead, it is a result of social dynamics triggered by a powerful organization of a different kind – the government.

Figure 7.1 documents the ups and downs of protest participation between April 15 and June 9. Among the three highest points, two bear the direct impact

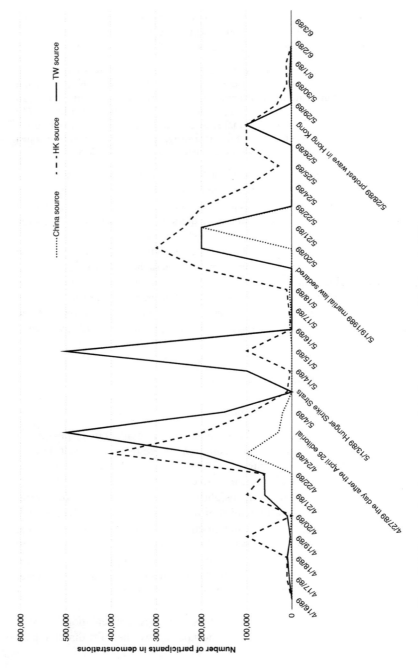

Figure 7.1 Volume of student protest participation over time, April 16–June 3, 1989

of a new and hostile government policy: a high volume appeared on April 27, the day following the publication of the April 26 editorial; another was on May 20, the day after the declaration of the marital law.[31] (The third high volume coincided with the start of the hunger strike on May 13).

### A Narrow Social Base

As mentioned above, the movement was confined within a narrow base. Its cadres and potential rank-and-file participants were drawn from the reform-minded urban intellectuals and their followers on university campuses. For people in factories and those who lived in the countryside, the significance of Hu Yaobang's death or his alleged mistreatment by his conservative detractors were arcane knowledge of high politics. Nor was the urgency of freedom of speech was as widely felt as were pocketbook concerns.

An acute observation by leftist scholar Wang Hui put this point succinctly. To the extent the movement engaged some working-class members, he saw it as a convergence of two opposite grievances. For students, the reform was not fast enough, or, worse, in danger of stagnation without further measures in the political realm. By contrast, for the working class, their protest was precisely against the reform, or in Wang Hui's words, against "the reality of unemployment, the disappearance of social security, the increase in the number of the poor, and other such features of social division behind the myth of 'transition.'"[32]

This disconnect between the intellectual class and the working class has also been noted by other analysts of 1989. Some have copiously documented the elite mentality of the university students and, out of this mentality, how they behaved as they staged their demonstrations.[33] At the end of a study on organizing efforts by the workers and the difficulties this group encountered, the authors concluded, "How shall movements for democracy mobilize ordinary citizens, and how shall workers be incorporated into such a movement and into the new order they seek? There is a strong strain of elitism in Chinese 'democratic' thought that questions the desirability of including ordinary people in the political process."[34] Indeed, the 1989 student movement was never a people's movement.

To be sure, Beijing residents turned out to show their support. At a few critical junctures, the numbers were in the hundreds of thousands. It is also true that many in the ranks of the movement were members of the working class. But most of them did so as a supporting cast unhappy with the government's treatment of the students. For the most part, they made no independent claims through their identity as a political class.[35] When group identities other than "students" and "intellectuals" did appear, it was a result of the political space created by the protest. As Walder and Gong wrote of a worker's organization they studied, it "was more a result of the upheaval than a cause, a movement that took advantage of the political space created by a much larger student movement, the disunity of the government, and the resulting paralysis of the regime's political apparatus."[36]

As a brief account will show, non-students' mobilization was limited to a small portion of self-appointed individuals who did not have real reach into the mass base. As early as the evening of April 15, 1989, the day of Hu Yaobang's death, a group of non-student citizens began to gather around the Monument of the People's Martyrs in the center of Tiananmen Square. From a few dozen gathering there during the first few hours, the crowd had grown to well over a hundred by midnight. For the next several evenings, ten to twenty young workers met after work at the monument to discuss the situation and decide what to do. By April 17, as university students began their marches in the streets of Beijing, these workers discovered that the students were denouncing officials' speculation and corruption – the same kind of thing they had been griping about. By April 18, as more joined their discussions, they began to talk of forming their own organization, and some advocated going back to their work units and carrying out the movement there. After rumors spread about the "bloody incident of 20 April," the group issued two handbills challenging the party's leadership, their economic policies, and their personal corruption and that of their families. This was the founding of the Beijing Workers' Autonomous Federation (BWAF).[37]

The hunger strikes starting on May 13 brought out large numbers of workers from factories and other work units who, for the first time, demonstrated their vocal support for the emerging democracy movement. BWAF marched prominently in each of these demonstrations, displaying their banner alongside those of delegations from the many state-owned work units in the city. BWAF members decided to obtain legal status and went through a series of petitions to government offices, including the All China Federation of Trade Unions, the municipal government headquarters, and the Beijing Bureau of Public Security. All rejected them. Undaunted, the group nonetheless formally declared itself established.[38]

Beginning with the successful blockade of army units by unarmed citizens throughout the city in the early morning hours of May 20 and afterward, mass resistance to the government was suddenly a reality. By daylight on the 20th, BWAF had issued its call for a general strike (excluding essential services, communications, and transportation), to stay in force until the troops withdrew. The militant positions that the workers' organization had articulated and the organization it had developed on the square in the preceding week pushed it to the center of events that were unfolding on the streets. Meanwhile, popular outrage over martial law drove many new recruits into the freshly declared workers' organization, swelling its ranks. On May 20, BWAF began a public registration drive on the square. Blank identity cards were purchased from stationery stores, and membership cards were issued to those who showed both work unit and Beijing resident identity cards. Despite the clear danger that such membership records might present, BWAF claimed to have registered almost 20,000 members by June 3. That was a small fraction of some 3 million workers in Beijing at the time. At its height, in the week before June 4, the union had mobilized some 150 activists working continuously in the square. But since the union had no organized branches in specific workplaces, their calls for strike went largely unheeded. Its membership was decimated in the bloodletting and arrests of June 4.[39]

The government's discourse insisted that students were not able to act on their own accord; instead, they were being used by "a handful people with evil purposes." If this rhetorical strategy counterproductively enraged students into more action, it succeeded in keeping the student movement clean of outside influences. Even student activists voluntarily worked to maintain a student-only image of the protest. They arranged for the marches to be guarded by student marshals to keep away non-student participants. An exception was a motorcycle gang known as the Flying Tigers Motorcycle Brigade. It comprised a hundred or so ge-ti-hu, street venders and small-business owners who were among the well-off class thanks to the reform decade. So-called "problem youths" in the command-economy era without a job in the state sector, some might even have had an unfavorable record with the law. Politically, they were enthusiastic supporters of the reform policy. Thus it was small wonder that they would find solidarity with the students in the movement.

Unlike other groups on foot, the gang was met with cheers and applause. They were fixtures in protests starting with the hunger strike, particularly in the period when troops were prevented from entering the city after May 20. "Even late after midnight," one of the former riders recalled fondly, "our motor brigade commanded a great deal of attention. Wherever we went, we were treated like Li Zicheng's army at the city gate.[40] Tidal waves of the masses came to us with drinking water and boiled eggs. What a moving scene!"[41] Their participation was treated differently from other non-student groups, perhaps partly for the coolness of their style, but more importantly for their usefulness. They quickly served as a communication squad, relaying news about troop movement during the standoff between the military and Beijing residents. They also transported food and water to places where they were needed.[42]

In the meantime, it was a group that government security marked early and worked to disband. Soon the squad was infiltrated by security agents.[43] Part of the intelligence work was reported by the Beijing Daily on May 30 to discredit the brigade. It pointed out that as many as 34 percent of members were "individuals who have been arrested, detained, or imprisoned for crimes of hooliganism, conspiracy, or theft." It also reported that by then the squad's operation was put to an end by "education" and "detentions."[44]

That the student movement caused little disturbance among the workers and peasants was acknowledged by Deng Xiaoping himself on May 16, which was the height of the student movement. In a private conversation with Yang Shangkun, Deng Xiaoping said,

> For the last few years, our economy has undergone a great change. Ordinary folk now have food to eat and clothes to put on. This has happened for all to see. A good economy sets a foundation. Without it, given the student protest like this, we may not be able to last for ten days, let alone a month. Even the peasants could have risen up. Now [with this foundation], *there is no unrest among the peasants across the nation, nor among the workers, by and large.*[45]

Deng's assertion was no exaggeration about the peasants, who made up more than 80 percent of the nation's then population. During the Tiananmen protest, the only instance when they made the news was their one-day demonstrations on May 31 in Beijing's suburbs organized by the city government *against* the student movement. Under the banner "The Masses Resolutely Rally against the Turmoil," the gathering supposedly generated letters to be sent to the Beijing municipal government. "We hope [the government] restores order in the capital as soon as possible, ending the turmoil without hesitation," one published letter read. An official report later claimed that each of the three rallies that occurred that day was attended by more than 10,000 people.

That evening, May 31, the major media outlets of the city (including radio, television, and print) all reported the news.[46] The Xinhua News Agency also carried a report for nationwide distribution.[47] A journalist from Tongxian county reported some interesting details. Peasants were bused from their villages to the county seat, and collected again and sent back after the rally and a march. Their attendance was paid for as two or three days' work. For the local cadres on the state payroll, a bonus was given of between five and thirty yuan. Some work units awarded attendants with a towel or a straw hat.[48]

### Protest Leadership in Disarray in the Last Waning Days

By the end of May, about one week after the excitement of blocking the troops, the occupation of the square, the nerve center of the entire movement, had reached its low point. Here is an excerpt from a Public Security Ministry report dated May 29 and 30:

> [May] 29. A number of brand-new camping tents, coming as a donation from Hong Kong, appear in Tiananmen Square. That is a further indication that the sit-in students have no immediate plan to leave. No longer visited by supporting demonstrators, the crowd is a lonesome sight, despite 300 or so flags planted all over the square. During the daytime, they are casual and relaxed, engaged in activities including sleeping, card games, reading, chatting, and dancing. Some are exploring

their next plans, mentioning topics such as "nonviolent disobedience," "emptying the campus," and so on. Debates broke out at times. Weariness and exhaustion from the movement are becoming the dominant mood, taking over the entire group.[49]

The students were under the spell of weariness and exhaustion, as captured in the above excerpt. A student letter published by *People's Daily* would give a less flattering impression of the scene:

> Now the large square has become a giant garbage dump. I ran into many students who said they had not washed and brushed up for more than 10 days ... Some Beijing students come to display their flags and then disappear. On a hot day they go back to school or home to nap, and only return [to the square] when it gets cooler.[50]

While the letter was obviously a planted work of propaganda, the description of the square was quite accurate based on my own visits. It is also consistent with surviving photographs.

Not a day went by without people debating whether they should withdraw or remain. Leaders from different factions could not agree with one another. One of the most serious decisions was made and announced on May 27, with a plan to withdraw on May 30. The procedure seemed to carry weight, because the meeting was convened in the name of the Joint Federation of All Sides of the Capital, a coalition of at least five student organizations. The news even made it to a Hong Kong newspaper. Hours later, however, the chief commander of Tiananmen Occupation relented.[51]

The student leadership was in disarray. In his study of these organizations, Dingxin Zhao concludes,

> The movement saw the emergence of many organizations and leaders. None of its organizations had a prehistory, however, and none of its leaders were elected by a reasonable number of movement participants via a recognized procedure. Therefore the leaders of the organizations did not really respect each other, or even the organizations they supposedly led; the movement participants did not respect the organizations and the leaders; and organization leadership changed very frequently during the course of the movement.[52]

This analysis is confirmed by a commander of one of the five major student organizations in his memoir.[53]

The occupation was dwindling, as the total number of students who stayed overnight dropped from between 100,000 and 200,000 during mid-May to around 10,000. Among those who stayed, over 90 percent of the students were from outside Beijing. According to Zhao's interviewees, at the occupation's peak over a thousand students from the University of Political Science and Law typically camped at the square. By late May, the number had dropped to about ten. Similarly, from Beijing University, there were only about a few dozen students who still stayed overnight by the end of May.[54]

Since the hunger strike, students from all over the country had begun arriving in Beijing in large numbers. Based on government statistics, in a period of about ten days around 172,000 students from elsewhere arrived in Beijing by train. Considering that many more came by other transportation means, the actual number should be greater than that. So, after May 20, as more and more Beijing students wore out their enthusiasm and left the square, they were gradually replaced by fresh new arrivals from outside the capital. The arrival of these large numbers of students made voluntary withdrawal from Tiananmen very difficult.[55]

That was why the May 27 decision to withdrawal was nullified. Given that the majority of those at the square were students from outside Beijing, any decision to withdraw might not have been successfully implemented at all. Zhao quoted student leader Wuer Kaixi as saying,

> We have thought about leaving the Square many times, but each time we changed our mind. For example, on May 27 we wanted to announce that we should leave the Square on May 30, but our decision was repudiated. Here the most important reason was that the students, especially the outside students, were not willing to leave. Anyone in charge had to support the Tiananmen Square occupation. Were you to ask students to leave, they would certainly try to get rid of you.[56]

The movement needed money. Donations were pouring in, which provided resources to sustain the occupation and made its appearance dignified. But it also exacerbated the leadership's infighting, with rumors flying around about misuse or even theft. At about 4:00 a.m. on June 1, four masked men sneaked in the tent that was privately used by the chief commander of the Tiananmen occupation and her husband, also a vice commander. Apparently a kidnapping was being attempted. Woken up, the couple found their hands tied from behind and their mouths stuffed with towels. After some struggle, the husband was able to remove the towel from his mouth and shouted for help. A crowd arrived and the four men were appre-hended. It turned out that these four men were just disgruntled student leaders who were suspicious of the couple's handling of the large sum of donated funds.[57]

Its leadership thus paralyzed, the continued occupation was not an indication of the movement's strength, but of its weakness. One can imagine what could have been: if the students had indeed withdrawn by May 30, could the June 4 tragedy have been avoided? Or, if the government had waited longer, say for a few more days, weeks, or months, would the occupation have died out, therefore making the "clearing the square" unnecessary? As one tries to answer these questions, one thing becomes quite clear: by the end of May the protest movement was small and in decline.

After the installation of new tents on May 29, the occupation tidied up and presented a new look. In the days that followed, a few more events would take place that drew large crowds to the square, including the unveiling of a large statue known as the Goddess of Democracy. It was made as part of the May 27 decision to withdraw, supposedly to be used to mark the end of the occupation. Now, on May 30, its unveiling became a new event for the occupation itself. Another large event was the hunger strike by the "Four Gentlemen" led by Liu Xiaobo on June 2. But the new festiveness on the square would not sustain the movement much longer.

In one of his diary entries, written on May 31, the student leader who was the subject of the attempted kidnapping complained about his lack of authority: "The morning plan to tidy up the monument area did not get carried out. At 6:30 a.m. when I arrived at the Student Movement Broadcast station, most students on the square were still asleep. I waited for the arrival of the ID cards, nylon ropes, and marshal guards." The previous day, he had ordered 200 marshal guards to partition the area using new ID cards. But he was sent only twenty guards, who arrived half an hour late. "I felt attacked by a sense of helplessness. My mind and energy were exhausted; I had nothing left to carry on the previous plan. No one seemed to understand my intention."[58]

### Was the Regime Vulnerable?

For popular mobilization to affect regime change and hence result in a revolution, there are four typical pathways, including fiscal crisis (e.g., France in 1789; East Germany in 1989), military defection (Romania in 1989; Egypt in 2011), international pressure (Iran in 1979; the Philippines in 1986), and war (America in the 1770s; China in the 1910s–1940s). China did not appear to be predisposed to embark on any of them.

### *China in 1989 Was in Good Financial Shape*

Among the most famous causes of revolution, shortage of government revenue has been one of the key culprits. The English Revolution was triggered by a fiscal crisis that led to a civil war. The French Revolution started similarly, and failure to contain the unrest was partly due to a small and poorly paid army.[59]

Examples that are more relevant to the recent era include China's counterparts in Eastern Europe. Among the root causes of the 1989 revolutions, the failure of the socialist economy is in the foreground of most analyses. Those economies had suffered stagnation for multiple decades. The unsightly scene of bread lines was common, from Moscow to Leipzig to Budapest. The revolutions were, in a sense, the reckoning of this problem.[60]

For example, East Germany's hard-currency debt with the West was as high as 2.2 billion marks in 1970, which increased to 11 billion in 1975 and was at 30 billion in 1985. By the time the Berlin Wall came down, the debt was over 46 billion marks.[61] The debt crisis peaked in 1989. On the domestic front, the entire nation was agitated by the skyrocketing rise of the price of consumer goods; on the

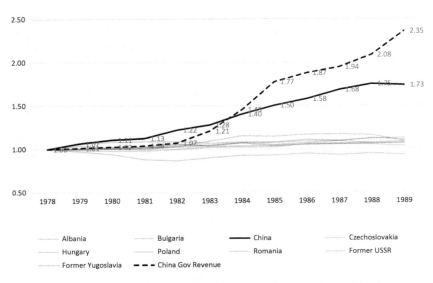

Figure 7.2  China's economic achievements in comparison with other communist countries, 1978–1989

international front, the regime had to give in to a series of concessions, which opened the floodgates for a citizen exodus. The regime collapsed.[62]

But China stood out as an exception because Chinese reforms had brought rapid economic growth for more than ten years. If a planned economy was the curse of socialist countries, Deng's reforms had begun to bid it farewell and lead China into a market economy. They did so with extraordinary results. China's rising economic fortune, in comparison with other socialist nations in Europe, can be illustrated in Figure 7.2. The contrast is stunning.

Crowded at the bottom of the chart are eight lines, respectively representing the GDPs of Albania, Bulgaria, Czechoslovakia, Hungary, Poland, Romania, Yugoslavia, and the USSR. They are all almost flat, in some cases going downward. By comparison, China's GDP steadily and rapidly grew between 1978 and 1989 by 1.73 Times. Along the way, government revenue also grew steadily, the number in 1989 being 2.35 times that in 1978.

Much has been made of economic anxiety and discontent on the eve of Tiananmen in 1989, with the inflation caused by Zhao Ziyang's price reform and the widespread perception of official corruption cited as evidence. But the truth of the matter is that the majority of the population, especially those who lived in the countryside and constituted the vast majority of the nation's population, had for the first time come out of poverty. Their general mood was one of contentment and optimism.[63] Some political polemics might portray the country's overall economic situation as problematic, but a neutral observer would find that the fundamentals were strong. Indeed, if you extend the chart beyond 1989 to cover later decades, the economic trouble in 1988–1989 was barely a blip. China's economy continued to grow unabated for another three decades after 1989.[64]

### Internationally Independent

Popular unrest might paralyze a regime or even cause it to collapse by generating pressure from the international community regarding its violation of the human rights of protesters. That is especially true if the legitimacy of the regime is partially built on the patronage of another, often more influential, country. However, during or after the Tiananmen protest, there were no meaningful international dynamics at work.

In his masterful book *The Enigma of 1989*, Levesque documents the evolution of Gorbachev's international policy and its impact on eventual revolutions in the USSR's satellite countries. In these countries, communist rule had been propped up by the Soviets and, in past years, the USSR had even sent troops to help quell opposition efforts. Yet a changed USSR in the late 1980s took a critical pillar away from each of those regimes. The communist regimes fell one by one as the USSR stood by and, arguably in some cases, even gave the political shifts a nudge.[65]

The Iranian revolution of 1978–1979 and the Philippines Yellow Revolution in 1986 also attest to the critical influence of international dynamics. In these two cases, the patron country was the United States. The US abandoned the shah in Iran and Marcos in the Philippines after a period of protest in which a significant number of civilians were killed by government troops. The abandonment sealed the fate of the regime and ensured the subsequent changes. In a similar situation but with a different outcome, the South Korean dictatorship under Chun Doo-hwan was kept in place by US support after it perpetrated a massacre of civilians in the city of Gwangju in 1980.[66]

By comparison, China under Deng was no one's satellite country. During the Tiananmen Square movement, Deng famously urged his colleagues to ignore "what foreigners will have to say."[67] Note that the concern here was not what foreign countries could *do* to China, but what foreigners will have to *say*.[68] That is, it was only a matter of image. During an earlier occasion in 1987, Deng spoke of his jailing of a prominent dissident: "Look at Wei Jingsheng. We put him behind bars and the democracy movement died. We haven't released him, but that did not raise much of an international uproar."[69]

To be sure, the international community did a marvelous job in the realm of verbal discourse, putting the spotlight on the 1989 movement almost from beginning to end and ferociously condemning repression and brutality. It boosted the drama and might even have pushed popular action. But as far as regime change is concerned, the verbal campaign had its limits. Talk is cheap.

The United States was the country that might have been the most effective at potentially exerting influence on China's policy. But its decree and rhetoric notwithstanding, the US government did not seem to be ready at any point to fight for other people's freedom or democracy unless it served its national interest. In the case of China, the American national interest clearly lay in close co-operation as the Cold War came to an end. According to John Pomfret,

> Beijing became an essential stop for every CIA director, starting with Stansfield Turner, who arrived there on December 27, 1980, disguised with a mustache, to negotiate the particulars of Operation Chestnut, the establishment of a listening post near the China–USSR border. It was a bizarre experience for intelligence officials from two countries that had effectively been at war since 1949. "We had to pinch ourselves to make sure it wasn't all a dream," recalled Robert Gates, then the US national intelligence officer for the USSR, who in the mid-1980s briefed the Chinese on Soviet military developments.[70]

Rejoicing over some important events that involved both China and the US, a Pentagon official wrote in 1989 that China and this Western power "would build on this foundation of trust and therefore become true allies forever."[71]

After the Cold War, in addition to working together on national security issues, the two countries commenced a long and mutually beneficial relationship of economic co-operation. The new wave of globalization was just underway and both sides stood to benefit most from it. And the year 1989 was a critical point of this new beginning.

Not surprisingly, the United States' sanction of China was minimal, and even that was couched by assurances. On June 20, Secretary of State James Baker announced that the United States was suspending high-level contacts with the Chinese. But as early as June 5, the day after the Tiananmen massacre, President Bush, after some gestures of sanctions, had this to say: "It is the time to look beyond the moment to important and enduring aspects of this vital relationship for the United States." On June 30, national security adviser Brent Scowcroft and deputy secretary of state Lawrence S. Eagleburger embarked on a secret mission to Beijing "to keep open the lines of communication." Bush wrote Deng three private letters, one of which complained to Deng about the US Congress trying to cut off trade. During a second trip to Beijing in December, Scowcroft grasped Deng's hand and declared, "My president wants you to know he is your friend forever." He also explained to Qian Qichen, China's foreign minister, that the sanctions were done solely to satisfy the demands of the American people.[72]

### No Elite Would Champion a Revolt

A third plausible pathway from protest to regime change is through internal elite conflict. A reformer could decide to champion the people's movement and declare the start of a new era. More often, a protest may help supply the pretext for a military coup.

In December 1989, Romania first experienced a period of citizen protest. The defense minister, Milea, hesitated to follow Ceausescu's order to fire on demonstrators and reportedly committed suicide. Milea's successor continued to disobey Ceausescu's order and secretly sent the troops back to their quarters. He also sent the dictator to a helicopter and arranged pursuit that captured him as an enemy of the revolution. Ceausescu was executed along with his wife the next day. The dictatorship was overthrown.[73]

In January 2011, a protest in Tahrir Square lasted for eighteen days. The Egyptian military intervened under the Supreme Council of the Armed Forces. It ordered President Mubarak to leave the capital. Hence he officially stepped down from office and effectively ended his rule in Egypt. That the military would move against the commander in chief in this political conflict had its roots in Egypt's recent history since the 1950s. Mubarak had long alienated the military because he relied heavily on a parallel system of armed forces – the security apparatus.[74]

In sharp contrast, and as will be discussed further in the next two chapters, Deng and his regime held a firm grip over the military. Indeed, Deng had been successfully cultivating his power base in the military and derived a great deal of authority from his credentials as a revolutionary commander.

Zhao Ziyang, the most prominent leader whose ideology and power base were close to the goals of the student protest, had neither the political will nor the capacity to even contemplate a military option for his political survival. As discussed in Chapter 3, nominally a vice chair of the CMC, he had never been able to establish a stronghold within the military, partly because he did not show great interest in doing so and partly, as some reports have it, because Yang Shangkun, the man second to Deng in the military, made sure that was the case. Also worth noting is the fact that Zhao, up to the year 1989, was still very much a loyal soldier of the communist system.[75]

### *No Professional Revolutionary Aspired to Take Arms*

A fourth pathway for a revolutionary outcome is civil war. Examples include the American Revolution in the 1770s, the Russian Revolution in the 1910s, and the Chinese Revolution in the 1940s. There are two key related elements in this pathway. One is a group of professional revolutionaries. George Washington and his American revolutionaries come to mind. So do Lenin, Mao, and Deng Xiaoping himself. Their program was not a reformist road to be marched on through protests and appeals, but a declared revolutionary vision to overthrow the old regime with commitment to devote their lives to such cause. The other element is a situation of "dual sovereignty." The regime loses some part of its territory when an alternative state power is proclaimed. But in the case of 1989 in Beijing, as recounted in an earlier section, there was no such leadership. The "adults in the room" – the "black hands" such as Wang Juntao and Chen Zimin – were reformist individuals with no appetite for revolution. If anything, they came out to counsel restraint and moderation.

## Discussion and Conclusion

The 1989 Beijing protest took place amid a wave of revolutions in Eastern Europe that brought down other communist regimes. There seems to be little doubt that China's events of 1989 could also have been a revolution, albeit one that did not succeed.[76] This assessment is exactly in line with the government's justification for bringing in troops to end it.[77]

But was it a revolution? Serious analysis should pierce through the self-serving rhetoric of the perpetrator, the wishful dreams of the sympathizer, and the unsuspecting bandwagons of the media. The question should be answered on four levels: the intent, the show, the impact, and the perception. The show was spectacular, but the other three are in question. As Elisabeth Perry put it, "if the theatrics were first-rate, the politics were less impressive."[78] The government's case mainly concerned the intent – accusing some conspirators who had every wish to see the end of the communist regime. It did not bother much to make a case about the impact – whether the mobilization indeed had the strength and power to do so.

It is tempting to consider China part of the 1989 wave of anticommunist revolutions. Yet what happened in China was far from what happened in Romania, East Germany, Hungary, or Poland. Whereas communism was imposed on the people of these and other Eastern European countries, in China it was an organic outgrowth of the nationalistic struggle for independence. It is not at all an overstatement to say that the Chinese people chose communism. Nor was the China of 1989 in dire economic straits as its Eastern European counterparts were. For ten years, reforms had put the economy in good shape, and people enjoyed unprecedented living standards. China's central government had no revenue trouble, unlike its socialist contemporaries – or, for that matter, the English government in 1642 or the French government in 1789.

Indeed, by historical comparison, the Chinese regime had a firm grip on power. China had just enjoyed a period of peaceful economic growth that had lasted over a decade. The majority of the population, especially the peasants who accounted for about 80 percent of the population, had just been lifted out of poverty. As Deng put it at a different point in time, "reform has saved China from revolution." Nor was China a small country in which signs of disorder would invite outside intervention.

Partly due to these factors, the Tiananmen protest, as spectacular as it looked, was reformist in nature. The movement was spectacular in its size, its dramatic turns, and hence its newsworthiness. But it was a contained affair. It comprised mainly college students and urban intellectuals. There was no significant involvement of people from the working class. Until the troops opened fire, the demonstrators were peaceful and orderly, almost pristinely so. They asked for little more than the ability to publicly demonstrate and to push back a policy that could prosecute them. The regime-changing threat did not exist in the students' demands, nor in the organizers' statements. The elite figures supposedly behind the scenes – such as Wang Juntao, Chen Ziming, and Fang Lizhi – were reformist activists who strenuously counseled restraint and moderation during the actual movement.

Also, the spectacular size and drama of the protest were not a result of the mobilizing strength possessed by any leaders, were they good guys or a "handful of people with ulterior motives." Ironically, it was the government's reactions that created each of the surges, as demonstrated by previous chapters. If left to its own devices, the movement would have naturally subsided and faded away. For example, at the very moment when martial law was chosen by political elites, the students' organization was in disarray and their enthusiasm had already waned.

Neither did government leaders subjectively fear a revolutionary danger. Deng stated as much in a less guarded moment: "As for the student protest, it won't be a big deal at the end."[79] A sense of calm was also evident in Zhao Ziyang, as shown in his demeanor on April 22. Hundreds of thousands of students swamped the square in mourning and protest, while he leisurely arrived at the rooftop and inspected the crowds through a telescope. On the way down his smiling face was caught by a camera. The next day, he embarked on a trip to North Korea, leaving party business behind. He surely did not seem worried about any likelihood of regime change.[80]

# 8  The Martial Law Decision
## May 13–May 19, 1989

After meeting Gorbachev earlier at 10:00 p.m. on May 16, Zhao Ziyang convened an emergency meeting of the Standing Committee. The discussion was "unusually heated," according to Li Peng's diary.[1] It was clear that most participants by that time already had a clear sense of Deng's intention. The Deng–Yang conversation on May 11 must have been leaked.[2] The appearance of Jiang Zemin's name in Deng's remarks conveyed a strong message. Neither did Zhao's own interview with Deng earlier on May 13 go well. All signs pointed in one direction: a hard-line approach against the protest and the end of Zhao's political career.

In this late-night meeting on May 16, the usual veneer of party collegiality was lifted and the comrades took their gloves off. Zhao vigorously defended his viewpoints and reasoning. He did so perhaps for historical records rather than still try to stop the inevitable. His opponents, including Li Peng and Yao Yilin, attacked him, most likely knowing that Deng was on their side.[3]

On the next day, May 17, Zhao wanted to make his last appeal to Deng Xiaoping. Again, this action might have been for closure rather than in any genuine hope. He phoned Deng's office and requested a personal interview. The request was denied, and he was informed only of an official meeting in the afternoon. "I wanted a personal conversation, but Deng decided to hold an official meeting in his residence. That did not bode well at all."[4] Then the important May 17 meeting at Deng's residence took place. There, the decision for martial law was made. Zhao dissented.[5]

On May 18, Jiang Zemin was fetched via a secret flight from Shanghai to Beijing. After arriving at the Nanyuan military airport, he was quickly dressed like an artist, apparently to conceal his true identity. Once in the car, Jiang was told that Deng Xiaoping would see him at the latter's Xishan residence.[6] This would be just hours before Zhao Ziyang gave his tearful farewell address to the students at the square, advising them to stop the occupation and preserve themselves because "you are young," "unlike us who are already old."[7]

On May 19, Deng announced Jiang Zemin as the new general secretary in another meeting at his residence. Given the fact that Zhao was still officially the party secretary, this announcement was extraordinary in revealing how major decisions got made. In his remarks, Deng confessed his "mistake" of having chosen Hu Yaobang and Zhao Ziyang as two previous leaders. "I chose two individuals, and neither of them was a right choice."[8]

Despite being framed as a response to the protest, Deng's decision on the military endgame needs to be understood in the context of these two momentous decisions: removing Zhao Ziyang and elevating Jiang Zemin. It was in essence a three-in-one decision. When he was facing daunting challenges, the supreme leader enjoyed no free rein. As will be detailed below, he had to anticipate opposition, form alliances, and count "votes." In the end, he succeeded by packaging the military solution together with the dismissal of Zhao as a way to gain both the support of the conservatives, who had been keen to unseat Zhao, and the promotion of Jiang, who was acceptable to the conservative elders.

In this chapter I will chronicle the main interactions between Deng and other key figures in the short few days during which the fatal martial law decision was formalized. Here, I use the word "formalized" rather than "made" because, as I stated above, this decision had perhaps been "made" already in Deng's mind and possibly as early as the protest's beginning in April. During the period leading to the formal announcement, Deng had accomplished a flurry of imperative tasks: building an alliance with the conservatives; winning over others (including Zhao's own supporters); and holding two meetings that decided on martial law, dismissed Zhao, and promoted Jiang Zemin.

Before I discuss these events in more details, however, I need to set the stage and present the broader historical context, which is important for understanding why Deng would and could do what he did – that is, using the military to solve problems of domestic politics. In the first section, I explain Deng's firm grip on military power, and in the section that follows I discuss military–civilian relations in communist China.

## Deng the Military Commander

As I have stated several times above, Deng enjoyed unparalleled power over the military because of his position as well as his personal networks. As important, his prestige and authority were also grounded in the fact that, for a decade or so, he had revamped this branch of state power and appointed many of his men to leadership positions.

Like power in other domains, but especially within the military, institutional power without the support of personal networks would not count for much. Hua Guofeng, Mao's successor, who was in short order unseated by Deng, did not have any meaningful influence over the military despite his title as CMC chair in 1977–1978. He was often overruled by Deng's allies such as Marshall Ye Jianying, who quickly pivoted to align with Deng after Mao's death.[9] Similarly, on the eve of 1989, Zhao Ziyang, nominally second in command in the organizational chart of the military, was hamstrung by Yang Shangkun, officially the number three man in the CMC but who was Deng's real right-hand man in the military.[10] By comparison, Deng's roots in the military ran deep. An accomplished commander in the revolutionary wars, Deng was second to only a few as far as relationships and credentials were concerned.[11]

Deng's authority also resulted from his decades of sowing and nurturing his men in the military. Thanks to his past credentials, the military was put under his control as early as the later years of the Cultural Revolution, when he was groomed by Mao as one of two potential successors. When he was called back to Beijing from his political exile in 1973, his new titles included vice chair of the CMC and joint chief of the staff of the PLA. He wasted no time making personnel arrangements with high-ranking officers through waging a rectification campaign (*zhengdun*) in the military. This reorganization was disrupted by his 1976 downfall, but picked up again a year later after he resumed those military posts.[12]

### Climbing to the Top in the Post-Mao Years

As we recall, Deng was officially in political exile at the time of the October arrest of the Gang of Four in 1976. Marshall Ye Jianying reportedly sent his children for Deng "immediately" and personally briefed Deng on the arrest.[13] This was extraordinary because not only was Deng out of power, but at the time Ye, a Mao loyalist all his life, had no immediate plan to nullify Mao's will and unseat Mao's successor Hua Guofeng.

Deng, on the other hand, wasted no time winning over Ye. His efforts included a daring appearance to crash Ye's eightieth birthday party in 1977, as narrated earlier in Chapter 2. The act not only succeeded in endearing him further to Ye, but also impressed other military luminaries attending the party. The generals walked away with the distinct impression that Deng and Ye, the highest-ranking member in the military after Mao's death, were in the "same boat."[14]

Also reported in Chapter 2 earlier, there were a few other occasions when Deng wrested power over the military from the Ye–Hua alliance, such the contests to appoint the most important military posts in the land: the PLA's chief of staff (Yang Dezhi), the CMC's secretary general (Luo Ruiqing), the director of the Political Department (Wei Guoqing), and the director of the Logistics Department (Hong Xuezhi). All were Deng loyalists; as a result, Marshall Ye virtually became a figurehead in the CMC.[15]

Once he had secured control of the PLA's headquarters in late 1977, Deng resumed the rectification campaign that had been disrupted in 1976. In a speech given at a CMC conference, he emphasized that the goal was to "solve leadership problems" at each level of the command system. He demanded that every officer be evaluated for his behavior during the Cultural Revolution. He accused many of "engaging in factional activities," hence subject to expulsion. Conveniently, though, as Jing Huang has pointed out, most of those so accused did not belong to Deng's own "mountaintop."[16] With Deng's top-ranking officers in the headquarters efficient at work, by April 1978 all commander and commissar positions at multiple strata within the army were settled. In some key regional military commands, the rearrangements were made even down to the division level.[17]

### Replacing Hua Guofeng as CMC Chair

While all the reshuffling was happening, Hua Guofeng, as the party chairman, was officially the commander in chief. But this institutional designation gave him little real military authority. Any attempt to tarnish Deng's prestige or influence was duly resisted or even undermined by Deng's newly appointed commanders, as illustrated clearly by the instance in which Hua's request for a military inspection in April 1978 was unceremoniously snubbed. Deng ordered the cancelation behind the scenes.[18]

Deng's power base in the military also helped advance his agenda in ideological debates on general political matters, especially the "truth standard" dispute. Within the same week as the aforementioned snub of Hua, Hu Yaobang organized the publication of an article in the *Guangming Daily* entitled "Practice Is the Only Standard of Truth." Still occupied by Hua's supporters, the party's propaganda system waged a campaign and pushed back at the article. Hua specifically ordered other official media not to "engage in the debate."[19] But with his increasing influence in the military's propaganda machine, Deng successfully ran the "truth standard" debate within the military first, and then decisively won the entire political battle. His point men, including the chief of staff of the CMC, arranged an all-army conference where Deng gave a keynote speech. There, Deng cleared the theoretical obstacle of Mao's doctrine by stressing that the essence of Mao Zedong thought was not what Mao had said literally, but a spirit of "seeking truth from facts." Soon after, the *People's Liberation Army Daily* published a new article elevating such a spirit as "a most basic principle of Marxism."[20]

In the following years, Deng would wage a major war against Vietnam in 1979 and restructure the military in the name of modernization and professionalization. Through the process, he appointed more of his supporters as top generals. After Hua's resignation, the nominal title of commander in chief went to Hu Yaobang, the general secretary, for two years before 1983, when the Central Military Committee was re-established, and Deng served as the chair. By the thirty-fifth National Day military parade in 1984, he was already at the pinnacle of his military power.[21]

## Military–Civilian Relations in Communist China

It is a widely acknowledged norm among modern nations that some level of separation between the military and domestic politics is desired. Indeed, it is practiced as well, although to different degrees. The relationship has been closely studied since Huntington's and Janowitz's classic works.[22] The rationale for this separation is stated nicely by Peter Feaver: "Because we fear others we create an institution of violence to protect us, but then we fear the very institution we created for protection."[23] That is, the military as a force is created to deal with external threats, not for domestic politics. The fact that it is powerful makes it all the more important to keep it at arm's length. If it is used at all in the domestic realm, it should be used like an "airbag," only for emergencies.[24]

### Separation in China: A Case of "High Political Culture"

In real life, the separation between the military and domestic politics is only a matter of degree. Even in Western democracies like the United States, there are still ways to make a political move by bringing in the military as a strategic weapon. For example, an incumbent president can wage a war to enhance his re-election prospects because a wartime president is typically more popular among voters. At the other end of the spectrum, such a separation is virtually nonexistent in many countries.[25] For example, Thailand's military junta had been blatantly running the country in place of a civilian government.

S. E. Finer conceptualizes four levels of military intervention in domestic politics: *influence* – "the effort to convince the civil authorities by appealing to their reason or their emotions"; *pressure or blackmail* – "the military seek to convince the civil power by the threat of some sanction"; *displacement* – "the removal of one cabinet or ruler for another cabinet or ruler"; and *supplantment* – the highest level, which "sweeps away the civilian regime and establishes the military in its place."[26]

Finer further theorizes that the likelihood of military intervention is the function of a country's "political culture," measured by three indicators – whether the country has public recognition of the civilian government's authority as legitimate, well-developed civil institutions, and fixed and orderly procedures for power succession. The better these conditions, the less likely the intervention (or the less severe if it does occur). Communist China seems to fit nicely into his category of countries with a "developed political culture."[27] The political culture is considered "developed" because two of the indicators are present – with public recognition of the civilian government's authority as legitimate and well-developed civil institutions, but without fixed and orderly procedures for power succession. Among these countries, a *coup d'état* is unlikely to occur or to succeed. Yet the chaotic and improvisational nature of power succession often invites some degree of army intervention – more often in the form of influence, pressure, or blackmail than an outright *coup d'état*.[28]

In China, as in Finer's use of the Soviet Union as an example, the legitimacy of the civilian government was quite high among the populace. Whether the feelings were genuine or manufactured, any number of public opinion polls would attest that the ruling party had a firm "public recognition." In the meantime, civic organizations, such as the party itself and its related "transmission belts" to the masses (i.e., the unions, women's organizations, and youth leagues), were also strong. In this context, the military, as one of the key pillars of the regime, did not enjoy a paramount position over other institutions, such as the party and the government. It was one of their equals. It had the power to shape events, but it could not rule by its own strength. Therefore it is categorized under the party's leadership, as a famous CCP slogan goes: "It is the party that rules the gun, not the gun that rules the party."[29] Such arrangements were stable, that is, as long as the governing authorities were stable in their positions of leadership, such as the periods when Stalin or Mao were at the peak of their powers as supreme leaders.

### The Shadow of Military Intervention in Times of Power Transition

In societies like China and the Soviet Union, when it came time for the succession of power at the highest levels, however, the military often became involved in the power struggle. Repeatedly, it played a significant, if not decisive, role. The first time such a moment occurred was before and after Lenin's death in 1923 and 1924. Trotsky was in name the head of the Red Army, and party cells within it tended to support him over Stalin, Zinoviev, and Kamenev, the so-called triumvirate. The whole Moscow garrison was reported also to be on Trotsky's side. The triumvirate, however, was able to exploit a division within the army, pitting the lower-ranking commanders against the ex-imperial officers whom Trotsky relied on. The "emergent command group" tipped the balance in the 1924 Party Congress by placing control of the political command in the hands of Trotsky's enemies. Stalin and his allies won the first round in the power struggle.[30]

If the role of the army in 1923–1924 was political in nature, without an outright deployment of force, the 1953 Beria affair was of an entirely different kind. After Stalin's death, Beria was appointed first deputy premier. His close ally Malenkov was the new prime minister and initially the most powerful man in the post-Stalin leadership. Khrushchev, the party secretary, opposed the alliance between Beria and Malenkov, but he was initially unable to challenge them. His opportunity came in June 1953 when an uprising broke out in East Berlin. Using the uprising, Khrushchev persuaded Molotov and Nikolai Bulganin that Beria's policies were dangerous to Soviet power. Beria's principal ally Malenkov then joined others and abandoned him. Army units entered Moscow from outside to arrest Beria. It is reported that Marshals Zhukov and Koniev carried out the arrest themselves.[31]

Military intervention occurred again a few years later. The Soviet power successions came to no resolution after 1953 with a new fault line drawn between the party apparatus led by Khrushchev and that led by Molotov. In 1956, Khrushchev enlisted Marshal Zhukov and subsequently included the military in the game. He promoted Zhukov to candidate membership of the Praesidium. From there Zhukov worked to crack down on dissent for Khrushchev with a decree that "criticism of the orders and the decision of commanders will not be permitted at [military] party meetings."[32] In June, Zhukov helped Khrushchev in decisively fending off the concerted opposition of Molotov, Kaganovich, Malenkov, and Shepilov. Zhukov was given full membership of the Praesidium.[33]

In China, outright intervention was rare when Mao was still alive, when politics operated under the shadow of his military power. Mao did not need to call in the troops to win power struggles at the highest level. His threat was enough to do the trick. At a Beidaihe meeting in 1959, pre-emptively attacking critics of his disastrous economic policies, Mao famously said,

> if we do ten things and nine are bad, and they are all published in the press, then we will certainly perish, and will deserve to perish. In that case, I will go to the countryside to lead the peasants to overthrow the government. If those of you in the Liberation Army won't follow me, then I will go and find a Red Army, organize another Liberation Army. But I think the Liberation Army will follow me.

In meetings that lasted for many days, Mao purged the then Defense Secretary, Marshal Peng Dehuai, whose crime was that he criticized Mao's disastrous economic policies. Note his bullying tone in the above passage. To silence any possible sympathizers with Peng Dehuai, Mao threatened to dismantle the army and split the party. He clearly abused his power, but none of the senior leaders, including Liu Shaoqi and Zhou Enlai, dared to object.[34]

Nor did Mao need to deploy the military to purge his two heirs apparent. Liu Shaoqi was expunged at the height of the Cultural Revolution, and he died two years later anonymously in a prison cell. In the case of Lin Biao, the perception of a purge was so urgently felt that Lin and his family fled the country only to die in a plane crash. Mao and the party then packaged the incident as a failed coup attempt against Mao's own life.[35]

As I discussed previously in Chapter 2, the military played an explicit and prominent role, however, in the power struggle that followed immediately after Mao's 1976 death. Hua Guofeng was the new party chairman, handpicked by Mao on his deathbed. His power was threatened by a clique of party leaders headed by Mao's wife Jiang Qing, known as the "Gang of Four." Hua and a few prominent military generals formed a temporary alliance. A secret plan was made, in consultation with other key figures (such as Deng Xiaoping, who was previously banished from the leadership by Mao). Marshal Ye Jianying, then the Defense Secretary, led a military operation on October 16, about a month after Mao's death. The members of Gang of Four were all arrested and later sent to jail after a nationally broadcast show trial.[36]

Hua Guofeng's reign did not last long, however. As the commander in chief in name, he did not have any real roots in the army. Generals like Ye Jianying reinstated Deng from his political exile and he became the new paramount leader in just two years. There was no *coup d'état*. But Deng did not need one. The influence of the military on his behalf, or its ability to "blackmail," was unmistakable. Gradually, Deng instituted the new system of "collective leadership," and Hua at the end found himself surrounded by a Politburo Standing Committee consisting entirely of Deng's men. Hua resigned voluntarily.[37]

Such is the communist regime's military–civilian relationship. During normal times of governance, the party rules the army; in the time of leadership succession, the army comes in to make the king. The party governs with supreme power, but in the shadow of the military.

In other words, it was the party-state's tradition to evoke military power in a power struggle, though an outright deployment of force was rare. Deng could use the military as an implicit or explicit threat, if he was so inclined, or if he needed to.

### *The Use of Military Force for Domestic Peacekeeping*

When it comes to domestic affairs, the official line is that the army can serve but it should only be used under extraordinary circumstances. This message has been nowhere better articulated than in the *People's Daily* shortly after the Tiananmen events of 1989:

> Under general conditions, public security cadres and policemen and the Armed Police Forces undertake the task of maintaining stability and normal social order. There is no need for us to use the Army. However, once serious turmoil occurs, and especially when counter-revolutionary rebellion happens, the social order is undermined, and our state power is seriously threatened. When this problem cannot be solved by simply relying on public security forces and legal and administrative means, the Army must be directly used.[38]

This is a "revolution suppression model" in the form of party-speak. The existence of a situation that is out of "general conditions" is the prerequisite for triggering the use of the military, which explains the reasons behind the hardliners' efforts to label the student protest, as discussed in previous chapters. In other words, to justify the use of military force, the party would first pronounce that a "counterrevolutionary rebellion" had happened.

In communist China's history, while the PLA was in reality frequently deployed on domestic fronts, albeit in a limited capacity in most cases,[39] official declarations of martial law were rare. The only known precursor to the Beijing situation may have been the martial law implemented in Lhasa, Tibet, three months earlier in 1989. To quell a wave of ethnic riots, thousands of PLA troops were sent in, which resulted in 387 civilian deaths. The involvement of the PLA troops seemed to be limited, however, as it was reported that most of the killings were in fact committed by the People's Armed Police (PAP).[40]

"When Deng Xiaoping decided to impose – and Li Peng officially announced – martial law in Beijing in May 1989, they were not doing something new," Brown observes in his fine book on Tiananmen history. The Lhasa martial law decision established a legal precedent and added a new item to the party's policy repertoire. That decision was also announced by Li Peng, the premier. "They were drawing on what they thought had been a successful attempt to combat 'turmoil' in Lhasa two months earlier. This precedent surely informed Deng's preference for, and Li's strong support of, a forceful crackdown against protesters in Beijing."[41]

Yet the differences are as important. The first concerns the size and magnitude of military force involved. The Tiananmen crackdown deployed over 180,000 troops mobilized from all over the country, while the Tibet action was a limited deployment of a few "thousands" of troops. The other difference is level of publicity: while martial law in Beijing would unfold with great fanfare for the entire nation, and indeed the whole world, to see, the Lhasa events barely registered among the population outside Tibet. These differences underscore the political character of the Beijing decision: while the military deployment to Lhasa might have been genuinely used to quell the riots, that in Beijing, on the other hand, was aimed at something much bigger than the student protest itself.

### Making a Temporary Alliance with the Conservatives

Ever an "organization man,"[42] in 1989 Deng did meticulous work winning supporters in the time leading up to a formal meeting on military intervention. He called the meeting only when he already had the "votes." And he continued to "lobby" to neutralize possible resistance. Here the words "vote" and "lobby" are used in a more figurative sense than a formal vote or lobbying action in a democratic system. But the idea is similar, in that Deng needed support from others.

*Consulting Chen Yun and Other Elders*

When he was making the martial law decision, Deng's most important support came from Chen Yun and people in Chen's camp, colloquially known as the "conservative faction." It was the same coalition that had worked against Deng's reformist agenda, unseated Hu Yaobang, and now aimed to sack Zhao Ziyang. They included the other five elders – Li Xiannian, Wang Zhen, Peng Zhen, Bo Yibo, Deng Yingchao – and two current members in the Standing Committee, Li Peng and Yao Yilin.

The elders often checked in with one another on a regular basis, either by phone or in person, including when Deng "disappeared" from public view. In his conversation with Yang Shangkun on May 11, Deng revealed that right after Zhao had given his speeches on May 3 and 4, "Comrade Xiannian made a phone call to me" and "Comrade Chen Yun passed on messages." Both of them responded negatively toward Zhao's speeches and advocated a hard-line approach toward the protest.

Among the elders, Li Xiannian was among the earliest besides Deng to know about the May 17 meeting on martial law. Perhaps he was even present at the meeting, as a non-SC member attendant like Yang Shangkun.[43] According to Li's chronology (*nianpu*), Deng dispatched him on May 19, accompanied by Yang Shangkun, to visit Chen Yun to personally brief him on the decision. On the same day, the eighty-year-old Yang paid another visit to Xu Xiangqian, a retired general who no longer held any official title, to "inform him of the current situation."[44]

Upon receiving the visit from Li Xiannian and Yang Shangkun, Chen Yun immediately expressed his full support. He was so firm in his endorsement that he used very poetic phrasing: "Security in Beijing, peace in the Nation" (*Beijing ding, tianxia ding*).[45] It is also clear that Chen Yun was pleased with the procedures through which the decision was made. The wording in his own chronology characterizes it as a decision by the "majority" in two meetings:

> May 16. Evening. The Politburo of the CCP's Central Committee held an emergency meeting. The majority viewed the situation as very urgent, and there should not be any more concessions. But Zhao Ziyang disagreed with the majority and insisted on making concessions.

> May 17. The SC held an expanded meeting. The majority was against Zhao Ziyang's desire to make concessions. It was decided to implement martial law in the Beijing region. Zhao Ziyang made a request to resign, meeting with vigorous criticism. Deng Xiaoping supported the decision of the majority.[46]

Chen Yun's office compiled these records, most likely as a reflection of Chen's personal interpretation of history. It is noteworthy, however, in the above passages, that Chen provided the martial law decision with much-needed legitimacy, and, just as important, he seemed to be content with the level of consultation he received, portraying Deng merely as one of the supporters of a "majority decision."[47]

### Enlisting Conservative SC Members Li Peng and Yao Yilin in the First Line

In the first-line leadership, Li Peng and Yao Yilin were two solid "votes" for Deng's decision. Both took a hard-line stand from the very beginning. Li Peng's diary records numerous conversations between the two, and Yao's position was almost indistinguishable from Li Peng's.[48] Speaking of his failed proposal in early May to retract the April 26 editorial, Zhao Ziyang lamented, "if Deng does not give in an inch, I can do much worse with Li Peng and Yao Yilin, two rigid-minded hardliners."[49]

During the meeting that occurred late at night on May 16, Yao Yilin, "normally quite vague on most occasions," joined Li Peng in their ferocious attack on Zhao Ziyang.[50] In the May 17 meeting, Yao Yilin again accused Zhao of going against Deng Xiaoping in handling the protest and turning Deng into a target of the protest. "This speech [by Zhao on May 4] in effect thoroughly exposed the internal disagreements within the Standing Committee and revealed the opinions of Comrade Deng, both to the students and those with ulterior motives. That in turn escalated the student protest to the point of being out of control." He also cited Zhao's May 16 speech in the meeting with Gorbachev as something sinister harmful to Deng:

> There is another matter that puzzles me greatly. Why did Comrade Ziyang put forward the name of Comrade Xiaoping yesterday in the meeting with Gorbachev? To push Comrade Xiaoping forward under this circumstance is to lay the entire blame on Comrade Xiaoping. That is a call for the protest to target Comrade Xiaoping, adding fuel to the flame.[51]

Li Peng was summoned by Deng privately, hours before Jiang Zemin was announced as the new leader on May 19. Deng gave Li a chance to pledge his support. Obviously, he also wanted Li to shelve his own ambition. After assuring Li that he would continue to be the premier, Deng asked, "What do you think of Comrade Jiang Zemin being the general secretary?" Li immediately expressed support and added, "Comrade Jiang Zemin was seasoned and tested in the 1987 student protest and during this current turmoil. He took firm and clear-cut stands. He is an appropriate choice as he possesses work experience at both local levels and central ministerial levels."[52]

Hence the 1989 student protest produced this extraordinarily odd coalition between Deng Xiaoping the reformer and Chen Yun and his conservative followers. Their common ground was to accomplish the twin task of removing

Zhao Ziyang and ending the protest. For the conservatives, that seemed to be good enough, even sweet in seeing Zhao's downfall. Added to this victory was the fact that the new party secretary general was someone recommended by none other than Chen Yun and Li Xiannian.

"It is perhaps more appropriate to describe Deng's role as a patriarch, not unlike a Mafia godfather ruling from behind the scenes through a network of loyal lieutenants," David Shambaugh once wrote.[53] The story I am reporting here suggests that he did not rule alone like a Mafia boss; he needed others to support him. At the same time, his rule was quite "lonesome" at the time when he decided to discard his closest lieutenant. Ever a strategic master, however, Deng made himself even stronger by building a brand new, if only temporary, alliance with the conservatives.

## Winning the Swing "Votes"

### An Ally of Zhao Ziyang in Standing Committee

According to Zhao Ziyang, among SC members Qiao Shi was said to have cast a vote of abstention in the May 17 meeting.[54] While there have not been other accounts to confirm this point,[55] it is safe to infer that Qiao was at most a reluctant supporter of the military resolution. In his speech during the meeting, which was required as *biaotai*, or "stating your position," he strove to walk the middle ground. On the one hand, he reiterated the official language of "a handful people with ulterior motives" and the like. On the other hand, he emphasized the "patriotic passions" of the students and the general public and urged that their out-of-line words and deeds not be prosecuted in the aftermath. Unlike Li Peng and Yao Yilin, he refrained from attacking Zhao, either for his policies or for his speech that defended those policies.

Indeed, Qiao Shi had long been part of Zhao Ziyang's camp in dealing with the protest. As a senior leader in charge of legal and security systems, he was instrumental in steering clear of violent clashes between law enforcement and student protesters. That was a policy very much in line with Zhao's instruction to "not intervene unless there is beating, smashing, or looting." Which was also consistent with his general political outlook as Zhao's reform ally within the Standing Committee.

But pre-existing factional identities could only go so far. A veteran party organizational and personnel chief, Qiao Shi was more capable than anyone else of discerning the direction of the political winds and reading the writing on the wall. He knew that it was futile to side with Zhao Ziyang on May 17. Hence, regardless of how he felt about Zhao, his later actions suggest that he fell in line quickly. According to Li Peng, Qiao Shi was one of the three top party leaders monitoring the June 3–4 operation. Their group, Li Peng, Yang Shangkun, and Qiao Shi, stayed overnight in a building next to a swimming pool inside Zhongnanhai. In the early morning of June 4, Qiao was also present, again along with Yang and Li, approving the peaceful withdrawal of the students from the square.[56]

### General Yang Shangkun, Another Ally of Zhao's

In his positions as the president of the state and permanent secretary of the CMC, in party policies Yang Shangkun was a default participant at all Standing Committee meetings. It is not clear how his vote was counted when major decisions were made. As we have seen above, when Chen Yun referred to "the majority," he seems to have meant the majority of all of those in attendance, rather than the majority of the five-member Standing Committee. In any case, Yang was among the very key people whose support Deng needed, whether or not he literally voted at the meeting.

Fortunately for Deng, Yang provided support that was the firmest possible. Along with Li Peng, Yang was one of the two most familiar faces of the party leaders who have been associated with the Tiananmen crackdown. He was the very first person to broach the idea of martial law in the meeting on May 17, he gave a high-profile speech on May 20 when martial law was announced to the nation, and he served as the actual commander in chief of the military in the subsequent implementation of martial law, including the June 3–4 operation.

His support for Deng's decision comes as no surprise if one understands the nature of their relationship. Deng and Yang were both Sichuan natives and had been bridge partners for many years. One report suggests that one of Deng's daughters married one Yang's sons. They first met in 1932, when they were in their early twenties, in Ruijin, the capital of the Jiangxi soviet. Their careers closely paralleled one another from then on. Both studied in Moscow, both served as political commissars in the Red Army during the Long March, both worked together in the Central Committee Secretariat during the 1950s, both were purged in the early stages of the Cultural Revolution. Deng was exiled to Jiangxi, and Yang was imprisoned. In 1979, Deng was responsible for Yang's rehabilitation and reinstatement to leadership positions. They served as the two senior ranking members on the CMC and together oversaw the restructuring of the PLA during the decade.[57] If Deng cultivated someone like Hu Yaobang or Zhao Ziyang as his chief lieutenant in the party, he cultivated Yang Shangkun in the 1980s as his chief lieutenant in the armed forces.[58]

In reviewing the Deng–Yang relationship, Zhang Liang notes, "Among the elders in the same generation, if people like Chen Yun, Li Xiannian, and Peng Zhen were Deng's comrades, Yang Shangkun was his friend." Zhang also notes that Deng's trust in Yang exceeded that of "Deng Xiaoping's three point men of the 1980s" – Hu Yaobang, Zhao Ziyang, and Wan Li, for those relationships had more master–apprentice formality, whereas Deng found closeness in Yang as an equal.[59]

Both Yang and Zhao were entrusted by Deng and worked together for Deng's reform endeavor. It was only natural for Yang to work closely with Zhao Ziyang. Yang was widely speculated to have harbored ambition to become the supreme leader after Deng. His plan seemed to be one of continuing to support Zhao as just the party head – that is, as long as he was able to keep Zhao from gaining any significant power over the military. Understandably, Yang did not sign up for a hardline approach to the protest for a while. He managed to give the impression to all three parties – Zhao, Li, and Deng – that he was on their sides. He seems to have been open-minded in his many conversations with Zhao Ziyang. Particularly notable was that he seemed to show genuine sympathy with Zhao's approach in early May, including the idea of retracting the editorial. On May 3, he advised Zhao "to go slow in making the turn." He reported that both Wang Ruilin, Deng's chief secretary-cum-aide, and Deng's children advised Zhao not to rush to engage Deng about retracting the editorial. It was better to "let it fade; no more mention of it."[60]

When Yang was summoned to Deng's house for a lengthy conversation on May 11, he initially seemed to be ready to go either way. He mixed both praise and criticism when speaking of Zhao Ziyang's leadership in handling the protest. Then he seemed to quickly grasp Deng's direction after Deng suggested names such as Jiang Zemin and Li Ruihuan, a strong signal that Deng had decided to change the party leadership. In all likelihood, though, both of them were engaged in a performance. Using opening sentences such as "what do you think of this ... " and "what do you think of that ...," Deng was feigning deference to Yang's opinion, while in effect outlining his own views and plans. If Yang had had to guess these views and plans up to this point, the conversation made them official between the two. Deng must have been certain that by doing this in a private setting, he had already shown enough deference and Yang would go along 100 percent. On Yang's part, while he enjoyed the trust and deference, he at first pretended that he did not know which way Deng might go. He feigned openness, as if to say, "I can be a loyal friend of Zhao's, but if you ask me to do otherwise my choice is also clear to you." Indeed, the conversation ended with Deng's brief reference to the military. The two men were on the same page. Everything was good, Yang assured Deng.[61]

As such, Yang's attitude and behavior in 1989 defies binary characterizations of "reformer" or "conservative." His split with Zhao and support for martial law did not come until the last minute. No wonder Zhao Ziyang wrote of his performance at the meeting of May 17 in his memoir: "Shangkun had been against the idea of martial law all along ... he just changed his mind."[62]

*Statements by Three Revolutionary Veterans*

According to Li Peng's diary, three retired generals were singled out by the official media to signify their support for the martial law decision. Given their health and age, these old guards might have followed the party line less closely than others, so they might have expressed concerns with the decision initially. The propaganda wave might have been using their seniority to stage public stunts. In any case, each retired revolutionary veteran went out of their way to make a public statement.

One of the thee was Nie Rongzhen, aged ninety, one of the two surviving marshals. He received a visit by eleven student protesters at his residence on May 21. He assured the students that the army was only there for "peace and stability." He deemed it rumor that the soldiers would kill any students. Similarly, on the same day, Xu Xiangqian, eighty-seven, the other surviving marshal, received seven students at his residence. He also urged them not to fall for "rumors" and to end the Tiananmen sit-in occupation.[63]

Also featured in the news media was Deng Yingchao, eighty-five, late Premier Zhou Enlai's widow. The couple happened to be the adoptive parents of Premier Li Peng, who was the orphan of a revolutionary martyr. A secretary of Deng Yingchao's appeared in Li Peng's office on May 22, 1989. "I debriefed her in great detail on the turmoil and the party's decision," wrote Li Peng, "the very same day Comrade Deng Yingchao issued a public letter to the citizens of Beijing City, filled with affection and clarity." In the letter, she assured Beijing citizens that the army had entered the city only for peace and urged everyone to support the operation.[64]

## The Fallout of Zhao Ziyang's Dismissal

Zhao Ziyang was effectively dismissed at the May 17 meeting, after which the party's policy decisions were made without him. He was no longer invited to attend any meetings.[65] Indeed, as I noted earlier, Jiang Zemin was fetched to Beijing on May 18 to meet Deng, and his elevation was announced on May 19.

The highest leader in the party-state's organizational chart had been dismissed, and it was done not by a formal procedure but by some party fiat, taking place at the high point of a stormy popular protest. Together, these facts would suggest, by the logic of typical political analysis, that he would be at risk of becoming an opposition leader, if not an outright revolutionary hero. That possibility must have been on Deng's mind.

*Popular Outcry against the Dismissal*

The reaction from society at large to Zhao's dismissal was swift and strong, calling up memories of the dismissal of Hu Yaobang. It upset many that the protest did the opposite of shoring up Zhao's position.

Months before the protest's outbreak, political scientist Yan Jiaqi had already warned his fellow intellectuals to be "on the lookout for an irregular personnel change," in the manner in which Khrushchev lost his job in 1957.[66] Such an "irregularity" was seen as frequent and was bemoaned by other prominent intellectuals. On April 18, three days after Hu Yaobang's death, Dai Qing summarized the dismal CCP history of seventy years in which not a single general secretary kept his position without irregular dismissal.[67] Now, a month later, Zhao Ziyang's name was added to the list. Journalist Chen Xiaoya, a Zhao sympathizer during 1989, simply used the term *coup d'état* for a section about the May 17 meeting in her book on the history of Tiananmen.[68]

The news of Zhao's downfall preceded the May 17 meeting itself. The intellectuals on the lookout had already seen the rising smoke days before. Another prominent public intellectual told me that he detected the winds from the live broadcast of Zhao's interview with Gorbachev on the evening of May 16. Years later I asked him why Zhao Ziyang would say those things about Deng. "Because he knew by then it was over. In the meantime, he wanted to signal to people like me, using live TV, perhaps the only way in which he could reach the intended audience, to say, 'it is over and you should find a way to ensure your own safety.'"[69]

This dissident was not alone in predicting Zhao's dismissal. In the early morning of May 17, hours before the Deng residence meeting had even taken place, Bao Zunxin received a phone call from Yan Jiaqi. He was asked to come to the Institute of Political Science of the China Academy of Social Sciences by 9:00 a.m. for a meeting. There, Yan showed Bao a draft of the "May 17 Manifesto," an essay repudiating the dismissal, which Yan had drafted the night before.[70]

Starting from the morning, the day of May 17 marked one of the largest street demonstrations in the events of 1989 at Tiananmen. By one estimate, the number of protesters reached more than 1.2 million that day.[71] In addition to expressing sympathy for and solidarity with the hunger strikers, the marches that day featured a new theme: attacking Deng. The protest banners read, "We do not need an emperor!" "Deng Xiaoping should step down!"

For the less informed public, the impetus must have been Zhao's remarks the previous evening. For public intellectuals such as Su Xiaokang, Yan Jiaqi, and Bao Zunxin, the underlying cause was a possible wave of repression to come and the pending dismissal of Zhao. "Seventy-six years after the demise of the Qing Dynasty, China is still ruled by an emperor, albeit without a crown, one who is already too old and muddy-minded," declared Yan's "May 17

Manifesto." "Overthrow the April 26 editorial! End the politics of the old man! The dictator must abdicate!" Four professors from Beijing University posted a new big-character post on campus and called on "CCP party members" to "rise to resist the dictatorship!"[72]

The outburst also played out among critical government agencies. "Within the newsroom the collective passions also ran high," wrote Lu Chaoqi, vice chief editor of the *People's Daily*, in his diary entry for May 17. "Those getting excited were not only young people, but also some older comrades whose revolutionary career dated as far back as the Yanan years and the Liberation War."[73] In his entry for May 18, he noted,

> Passions continued to rise within and without the [*People's Daily*] agency. Outside the building in the nation's capital, the turnout at demonstrations to support the students reached more than one million. Many were industrial workers and government officials. Their banners focused their message on demanding Comrade Deng's retirement and Li Peng's resignation. Within the agency, the crowd swarmed the offices on the first and third floors, spilling into the hallways. The boisterous chatter conjured up a sense of crisis, as well as an illusion that political democracy would arrive any minute now.[74]

A similar account at Xinhua News Agency is vividly available from the hand of the agency's newsroom director, Zhang Wanshu. As early as May 15, some of the editorial staff and reporters walked out of the agency to join the demonstrations. They conspicuously displayed a banner announcing they were from "Xinhua News Agency." The chief editor, Mu Qing, tried to stop them at the gate but to no avail.[75] During the evening shift of May 16, Zhang had a lively exchange with two other colleagues. The conversation was apparently prompted by Zhao's remarks about Deng as the ultimate decision maker that had been broadcast earlier in the evening. Some speculated that Zhao's remarks could be seen as clarification with good intentions, while others already worried that they could also be construed as setting up Deng as a target for protesters, and hence would spell the end of Zhao.[76]

### *No Significant Reverberation within Institutional Channels*

Yet the fact that Deng's decisions were unpopular in the street did not translate into any significant traction in elite politics. The popular outcry remained what it was – a popular outcry. There were some attempts to channel the dissent into the political process, but they failed. A petition was signed by fifty-seven members of the Standing Committee of the National People's Congress (NPC), prominent economists, legal scholars, and a leader of the government-sponsored student union. It proposed to immediately hold an emergency NPC meeting to "discuss the urgent situation of the moment," and to explore a way to "legally and correctly resolve the current crisis." However, the petition did not gain any meaningful response within the government, and the organizers – a public intellectual and two graduate students – were later arrested.[77] Significantly, the fact that the NPC president Wan Li was Zhao Ziyang's ally did not make any difference, for he had fallen into line with Deng already.[78]

### Zhao Did Not Put Up a Fight within the Party

On May 20, in another meeting at Deng's residence, Deng "made the call" (*paiban*) to dismiss Zhao Ziyang from the position of general secretary, pending formal procedures and to be announced at a later date. Zhao was not informed. "That meeting cannot be counted as a Standing Committee meeting," Zhao contended in his memoir, "because only three of the five members were present. Hu Qili had not yet been dismissed, nor had I before the meeting. Two of the five members were not even notified to attend the meeting, and the decision was made that way. I do not think that was legitimate."[79]

Alas, formal procedures were not the CCP's strong suit. Was Hu Yaobang not dismissed in the same way three years previously? Plus, as Zhao himself confided to the world when he met with Gorbachev on the evening of May 16, there had been a stated, although unwritten, understanding that Deng was the top decision maker of the party. Therefore the accusation of illegitimacy in Zhao's later writing was more an argument rather than it was any real-time analysis to guide his action at the time. In the days following the May 17 meeting, Zhao behaved every bit like an obedient soldier, if one who felt wronged and mistreated.

Hours after the May 17 meeting, Zhao summoned his chief of staff, Bao Tong, to his home at around dinnertime. "A Standing Committee meeting was held this afternoon at Comrade Xiaoping's residence. The decision was made. I cannot tell you the content of the decision, for it is top secret," Zhao was quoted as saying. "But I want you to draft a letter of resignation for me."[80] The content of the letter was as follows:

The Standing Committee and Comrade Xiaoping:

Given my mental state and my policy skill at this time, I do not think it is still appropriate for me to continue to be in charge of the work of the Standing Committee and implement the decisions of the Center. Therefore I would like to resign from the positions of general secretary of the Central Committee and the vice chairman of the CMC.

Zhao Ziyang
May 17, 1989[81]

While this letter accurately conveyed Zhao's attitude, it was not officially submitted. Bao Tong was told by Zhao that the letter was shelved because "Comrade Shangkun was critical of such an action." "What would the consequence be if the students escalated their action using his resignation as a new pretext?" Zhao cited Yang as saying.[82]

In the early morning of the third day, May 19, Zhao paid a visit to the students in the square. He was instantly welcomed by them, with some even asking for his autograph. A student passed him a microphone and he gave the last public speech of his life.[83] The news media snapped the image that would be forever imprinted in the public mind. In anticipation of a tragic suppression yet to unfold, here was the highest leader of the land who had only compassion and tears to offer. "My student comrades, we have come late! We have come too late! We are sorry!" Zhao choked his words before continuing. He pleaded for an end to the occupation for the sake of the students' lives.

About the pending danger of military suppression, he could not be more explicit than to saying this: "Many issues need time to resolve ... You are young and there is ample time ahead of you. So you should live, and live in good health, until the day China realizes its Four Modernizations." Knowing the long history of how the CCP had treated its dissenters in the past, Zhao's last words seemed to address both the young listeners and himself as well: "You are [young], unlike us. For those of us already old, *wu suo wei le* [it matters much less]."[84]

### *Zhao Had Neither the Will nor the Means to Champion a Popular Revolt*

Thus with this moment Zhao was ending not only his official duties as general secretary, but also his sense of efficacy as his own person. As important, politically he remained a loyal member of the Leninist party, with no plan to do more than step aside after his dismissal. To do otherwise – such as joining the ranks of the rebellion – must have been entirely out of question. Upon much reflection in his last years of life under house arrest, Zhao would become a believer in Western electoral democracy. But that would come later. In 1989 he was at best half an ally of the student protest and would even prove to be an antagonist to those who wished for a different system.[85]

As important, the political means at his disposal were meager. Most of his allies in the party leadership would never break ranks with Deng Xiaoping for his sake. Nor did he have much support in the military. The only traction he could have had might have been to publicly align himself with the ongoing protest, which he did not want to do.

**Discussion and Conclusion**

The political nature of the martial law troops was vividly evident in an episode recorded in Li Peng's diary. After the afternoon meeting on May 17, Li phoned Wang Ruilin, Deng's chief aide and suggested holding an expanded Politburo meeting in the next few days. Among the issues on the agenda was "an organizational settlement" of Zhao Ziyang, hinting at a possible dismissal. But Deng's reply was not forthcoming until later in the evening: "That meeting has to wait until the 'Grand Army' (*dajun*) has entered the city of Beijing. That way, distraction and disturbance can be avoided. The meeting will go more smoothly."[86]

By "smoothly" Deng evidently meant to pre-empt any possible fallout of firing Zhao. First as the premier and then as the general secretary, Zhao had been a leader with significant following and influence. In a sense, turning against Zhao was akin to turning against the entire party-state. Military power became one of Deng's assurances of its going "smoothly."

By taking a hard line against the protest and removing Zhao – two policies favored by the conservatives – Deng built an alliance with his conservative rivals. Indeed, Chen Yun, Li Peng, and their supporters moved quickly to go along with Deng on all the important elements of his other policy changes, including picking Jiang Zemin as the new general secretary. The martial law decision served multiple purposes at the same time.

In sum, as the pages up to this point have attempted to demonstrate, it is political expediency that was behind Deng's military decision, the gravity of which would be measured by a human tragedy of historical proportion. In closing this chapter, we may wonder, were there countervailing forces, such as moral constraint, that worked against making such a decision?

Deng, albeit a communist, was known to be more capable of human compassion than his comrades, such as Mao. He was reportedly an endearing husband, a loving father, and a doting grandfather.[87] He took care of one of his father's wives, not his biological mother, into her old age. She was made part of his household during his good times in the capital as well as during his downtime in Jiangxi during the Cultural Revolution in the 1960s.[88] After a day's labor at a Jiangxi factory when he was exiled, he washed his disabled son Pufang's back every evening, when he himself was already in his sixties.[89] His fondness for his grandchildren was well known, documented in moving detail. There are many photographs showing it.[90] Nor would any fair-minded observer miss his commitment to people's livelihood in his reform policies, which benefited the nation's poor and rich alike, and his refraining from Maoist cruelty in his treatment of his political opponents such as Hua Guofeng, Hu Yaobang, and Zhao Ziyang.[91]

Moral consideration only goes so far for a politician, or Deng has his own way to negotiate moral issues with himself. Historically speaking, as a politician and a communist apparatchik, Deng had been more than capable of ruthlessness when he found it justified. For example, he colluded with Mao in persecuting the Gao–Rao group. He played a leading role in the anti-rightist campaign.[92] He decided in 1979 to launch the so-called Self-Defensive Counterattack War against Vietnam, a war the justification of which was elusive and dubious at best, but which cost the lives of at least 6,954 Chinese soldiers and more than 80,000 Vietnamese.[93]

Conveniently for Deng, institutional restrictions were also thin. There was no strong mantra in the political culture against using the military as a response to political trouble. A successful push to define the protest as turmoil and as an anti-party conspiracy seemed sufficient. There was no armed insurrection, but it was not difficult to proclaim that one existed. There was no revolution, but the army was to be brought in to crush one. Also in Deng's favor was the personal loyalty of the army. He had worked long and hard to cultivate it. In moments like this, his reward from that labor was forthcoming.

9    Military Operation as Symbolic Display
     of Power
June 3–June 4, 1989

The military operation that Beijing carried out in 1989 to end the Tiananmen movement was grand in scale. Mobilized to enter Beijing City were more than 180,000 troops from fifteen of China's twenty-four group armies, plus untold numbers of armed police forces. They arrived from all over the country, including faraway places like Xuzhou in Jiangsu and Xiaogan in Hubei. After a failed attempt to take over the city and a two-week hiatus, the June 3–4 action was forceful, swift, and spectacular. Thousands of civilians were killed.[1]

The most authoritative estimate of deaths, to date, is in the deeply researched chapter "Counting Bodies" in Timothy Brook's *Quelling the People*. He reports the government's admitted number of close to 300 and a Chinese Red Cross estimate as close to 3,000, and also comments on counts by journalists, ranging from thousands to more than 10,000. Based on interviews with doctors who performed rescues on the night of June 3–4, Brook was able to construct a table of casualty statistics from the hospitals located on the major avenues that were involved. Although the numbers are not complete, they form a reasonable empirical base, from which he concludes, "Until information less ambiguous comes along, my fragmentary findings lead me to think that the Red Cross figure of twenty-six hundred that Sunday morning comes closer than any other estimate to the number that died."[2]

The staggering human loss did not go unnoticed. Despite their public justifications, in private, guilt must weigh heavily on those involved. Yang Jisheng reported that in the days following June 4, Deng Xiaoping often sank into long periods of silence, got exasperated for no reason, and returned to his old habit of chain-smoking.[3] Yang Shangkun and Yang Baibing, two top-ranking officers in the army also known as "The Yang Brothers," were reported to have confided their misgivings to a doctor while in their sickbeds.[4] It was revealed in the post-Tiananmen partisan discourse that Chen Yun in fact was against using force.[5] Li Peng penned a memoir widely seen as motivated by his desire to avoid being blamed for the massacre.[6] In another extraordinary note of history, the command of the 27th Group Army garrisoned in Shijiazhuang, Hebei, sent a letter to the province's government in the wake of Tiananmen. It pleaded with them to convey to the civilian public that its units "did not open fire on the people and students in the capital" in their June 4 mission after recurrent incidents in which local residents yelled taunts of "Butchers!" in the face of uniformed soldiers.[7]

The military crackdown proves to be more puzzling than it at first appears. The evil nature of the system? The thirst for blood of its actors? Did Deng not foresee the magnitude of human casualties? These are tempting propositions, but they do not lead us far. If the above misgivings are to be believed, the military action was an extraordinary experience even for the suppressors themselves – the decision makers as well as the military personnel – and this extraordinariness demands explanation.

Nor is it a satisfactory answer to attribute this violent endgame to the danger that the protest was supposedly posing to the regime. Such a model of state reaction, which I call the revolution–counterrevolution model or the revolution suppression model in this book, is flawed on many counts, as I have demonstrated in my previous chapters. I argue that the leaders had other agendas in mind, that they did not seem too concerned with the threat, that the risk of a revolution was not high, and that the movement could have died out by itself through fatigue.[8]

In this chapter, I take up my debate with the revolution suppression model on another empirical ground – the military operation itself. By documenting the process and manners of the military actions, we are able to see to what extent their true purpose was to end the protest. Since we know that the operation did indeed end the protest, a further question is this: were the grandiosity and the potency, and the staggering numbers of human lives they caused, really necessary? If not, why? As a well-known Chinese saying puts it, "Why use an ox cleaver to kill a chicken?"

There are two parts of the puzzle to be solved: the scale of the operation and the severity of its implementation. The first part of the puzzle concerns the large numbers and the wide variety of troops brought in from across the country. Scholars such as Timothy Brook and Wu Renhua offer a number of speculations as to why that was so.

The first speculation is that the troops in the Beijing area might not have been sufficiently reliable to act against the protesters because, by virtue of knowing more about the truth of the political debates and the events of the protest, they might have been sympathetic rather than antagonistic. There is some supporting evidence for this. As I will discuss more below, the commander of the 38th Group Army refused to follow the order supposedly because, as a patient recovering from a leg injury in a hospital in Beijing in the weeks leading up to the implementation of martial law, he became very knowledgeable about the protest's developments. The political commissar and the commander of the 28th Group Army were also reported to have passively disobeyed the order to advance. The group army was also under the Beijing Military Region, though its headquarters were in Datong in Shanxi, some 200 miles from Beijing.

Another speculation is that gathering more troops from the outside was a way to increase the number of units under Yang Shangkun and Yang Baibing, who were military leaders loyal to Deng Xiaoping. This analysis confirms the above thesis about the troops in the Beijing area. There are no definitive data to show that those called up were indeed close to Deng or the two Yangs, although Wu Renhua noted in his analysis that a few group armies were among the most loyal to the two Yangs.[9]

A third speculation is that assembling multiple units with a diverse mix was a way to create a dynamic in which units could police one another and guard against possible mutiny. This also explains the fact that the units brought so many weapons, tanks, and machinery along; they were not for fighting students, but for possible engagement between army units. Wu Renhua notes that on the night of June 3, one group army was often followed by another, with the latter acting in a supervisory capacity over the former. The pairs he cites include the 38th in the front followed by the 188th Division of the 63rd Garrison Army in the rear.[10]

Finally, it is possible that a nationwide mobilization across many group armies was undertaken in order to spread responsibility for the mission, a mission that would likely be recorded in history as highly problematic.

None of the above speculations is backed by meaningful proof. But, taken together, they signify the unwieldy nature of a military solution to a domestic problem. The solution itself not only entails loss of civilian lives, but also is full of peril for the leaders themselves. In order to guard against these perils, such as potential military infighting or mutiny, the only solution is to bring in even more troops so that one unit can police the other. These observations, to some degree, lend support to the revolution–counterrevolution argument in laying out the necessity of the number of troops, once it was decided that they were to be used. But they lend no support to the decision to use the troops in the first place. What, then, explains the troops and their number in the first place?

The second part of the puzzle of the military actions of 1989 concerns the June 3–4 operation – forcefully deploying troops from the outskirts of Beijing to retake the square. It was a deadly undertaking. Almost all the killings – though often called the Tiananmen Square massacre – took place on the routes of the advancing troops, so not in the square proper. Civilian–military confrontations did not happen when the troops arrived in the square; a peaceful student withdrawal was negotiated and successfully carried out. Putting aside the question of the necessity of "clearing the square," a simple question is this: was the mission so difficult that it required all the troops to be there at once?

This chapter will explore these questions through the lens of the thesis of the "symbolic power display." As noted by scholars of social movements, protesters strive to show they are "worthy, united, numerous and committed" through instrumental means (dressing up well, holding hands, turning out in large numbers, and acting bravely, for example) which have symbolic effects.[11] Similarly, state actions in response to protests also have symbolic purposes. These actions may include verbal forms of discourse that are both symbolic and instrumental – such as deploying police and mobilizing countermovements. Government reactions can show that the state is strong, coherent, resolute (or ready to kill if necessary), and benign. Departing from the past instrumentalist view of state action on Tiananmen, I will explore the symbolic meanings of the military deployments and the ultimate purpose of violence in the spring of 1989 in Beijing.

I will do so in five empirical sections. In the first, I report Wu Renhua's estimates and use his data to document and describe the national scope of the mobilization. To appreciate the scale, I will compare the numbers of troops with a few historic military campaigns. In the next section, I will describe the advance of troops to the center of Beijing starting in the afternoon of June 3. This description will lay the groundwork for a later discussion on the necessity of such maneuvers. In the third section, I study the effectiveness of the Chinese military as symbolic instrument. Using post-event reflections written by military men themselves, I will illustrate the morale and cohesion of the troops and explore the sources of this morale and cohesion. In the fourth section, I explore the factor of civilian resistance. There I present evidence against the argument that military violence was caused by civilian violence. Civilian resistance existed but, on the whole, it was not the cause of the operation and was the result of it. The other goal of this section is to understand why many in the crowd underestimated how deadly the engagement of military forces would be and why they resisted with tragic consequences. In the last and fifth section, I compare the mission of 1989 to a similar mission in 1976. I attempt to estimate a minimum number needed to clear the square, using the 1976 operation as a guide. With that estimate in place, I conclude that the troops already deployed to surround the square could have accomplished the job. In other words, the dramatic advance from all directions toward Beijing was not instrumentally necessary at all for the task of seizing control of the occupied square.

## A Mobilization on a Grand Scale

*Compatible in Size with Historical Military Campaigns*

Based on his years of research, Wu Renhua suggests that the number of military personnel was between 180,000 and 250,000. The lower number of the two was reportedly first mentioned by Yang Shangkun in a conversation with Deng Xiaoping.[12]

To illustrate the colossal size of the military force that Beijing mobilized to end the 1989 Tiananmen protest, here are a few historical examples, which all involve armed conflicts between hostile parties.

It was about fourteen times larger than the one the British used in the Philadelphia campaign in 1777, a British initiative in the American Revolutionary War to capture Philadelphia. General William Howe landed 15,000 troops in late August at the northern end of the Chesapeake Bay, about fifty-five miles southwest of Philadelphia. On the American side, General Washington positioned 11,000 men between Howe and Philadelphia but was outflanked and driven back. The American side suffered over 1,000 casualties, while the British lost about half that number. Howe's campaign successfully captured the American capital.[13]

It was also about fourteen times the number of British troops used in the Saratoga campaign in 1777, an attempt by the British high command to gain military control of the strategically important Hudson river valley. It ended with the surrender of the British army, which a historian calls "a great turning point" in the American Revolutionary War. The British army under General Burgoyne numbered about 7,000 regulars and over 130 artillery pieces, organized into two divisions. In addition, Major General William Phillips led the 3,900 British regulars on the right, while Baron Riedesel's 3,100 men held the left. In short, the total number of troops was no more than 15,000. The British were outnumbered by the Americans by about two to one, with 10,000 men under General Horatio Gates, 2,000 under General Benjamin Lincoln, and 15,000 or so in the militias.[14]

A comparable number of forces was used between the Nationalist and Communist armies over the capital, Peking (Beijing), in 1949. At the time, on the defensive side was the Nationalist army under the command of Genera Fu Zuoyi, who had 250,000 troops in twenty-five divisions and two other special units. Besieged by an even larger number of Communist troops, the Nationalist army surrendered the city without a fight.[15]

Another comparable force was used by China in its 1979 war against Vietnam, the second-largest military mobilization in the history of communist China (second to China's involvement in the Korean War in 1950).

Officially known as the "Self-Defensive Counterattack against Vietnam" in 1979, the month-long military campaign deployed 200,000 to 300,000 troops. The casualties of that war, according to one Chinese source, include 6,954 dead and 14,800 wounded Chinese, and 80,000 Vietnamese deaths.[16]

Finally, before its invasion of Ukraine in February 2022, Russian troops deploy around Ukraine's borders are estimated to have been around 190,000.[17]

### *Mobilization from across the Country*

In 1989, China's military consisted of twenty-four group armies under the command of seven military regions. Among them, fifteen group armies were mobilized from four military regions. The Beijing Military Region commanded the armed forces of Beijing, Hebei, Shanxi, and Inner Mongolia; the Shenyang Military Region covered Liaoning, Jilin, Heilongjiang, and part of Inner Mongolia; the Jinan Military Region covered Shandong and Henan; the Nanjing Military Region covered Jiangsu, Zhejiang, Anhui, Fujian, Jiangxi, and Shanghai.

Specifically, the following fifteen group armies ("martial law troops") were called in from these places, according to Wu Renhua:

- the 38th Group Army Infantry from Baoding, Hebei (Beijing MR);
- the 15th Group Army Airborne from Xiaogan, Hubei;
- the 27th Group Army Infantry from Shijiazhuang, Hebei (Beijing MR);
- the 63th Group Army, infantry from Taiyuan, Shanxi;
- the 40th Group Army Infantry from Jingzhou, Liaoning;
- the 54th Group Army Infantry from Xinxiang, Henan;
- the 39th Group Army Infantry from Yingkou, Liaoning;
- the 65th Group Army Infantry from Zhangjiakou, Hebei;
- the 24th Group Army Infantry from Chengde, Hebei;
- the 28th Group Army Infantry from Datong, Shanxi;
- the 12th Group Army Infantry from Xuzhou, Jiangsu (Nanjing MR);
- the 20th Group Army Infantry from Kaifeng, Henan (Jinan MR);
- the 26th Group Army Infantry from Laiyang, Shandong (Jinan MR);
- the 64th Group Army Infantry from Dalian, Liaoning (Shenyang MR);
- the 67th Group Army Infantry from Zibo, Shandong (Jinan MR);
- the Beijing MR Artillery 14th division from Huailai, Hebei;
- the Bejing Garrison from Beijing;
- the Tianjin Garrison Tank 1st Division from Jixian, Tianjin;
- the Beijing PAP Unit from Beijing.[18]

Going through this list, you will not miss the diverse sources of troops mobilized, which underscores the extensiveness of the mobilization. They not only included infantry divisions, but also tank units, artillery units, and airborne divisions. These special forces were deployed with their weapons and machinery in tow.[19]

We also need to note the presence of military force already in Beijing. Naturally, as the capital of the nation, the area in and around Beijing contained a large number of armed units either directly or indirectly under the control of the party leadership. The total number was estimated to be more than 90,000.[20] The Beijing Military Region commanded the Beijing Garrison and the Hebei, Shanxi, and Inner Mongolia Military Districts. It was also the most important and powerful of China's seven military regions. It consisted of six group armies (the most of any military region), including some of the best-equipped and most highly trained ground forces in China. Most were located within 200 miles of Beijing. In addition, within the city of Beijing there were three smaller and less well-armed groups of forces: the Beijing Garrison Command (formally charged with maintaining security within the capital), the Beijing PAP General Unit and Second General Unit under the PAP General Headquarters (GHQ) (largely responsible for protecting buildings and structures politically and strategically important to the leadership and for suppressing public protest), and the Central Guard Unit (responsible for the security of the top party leadership).[21]

## To Seize a City Unarmed

### Troops Were First Blocked and Then Stationed Outside Beijing

The first co-ordinated action of the troops took place on the evening of May 19. The objective seemed to be to enter the city. They were all ordered to enter all at once; it is not clear whether the action was intended to besiege the square or rather to station troops at multiple strategic points. In any case, the operation appears to have been aborted, as Beijing citizens blocked their path. They retreated and settled on the city's outskirts.[22]

It is unclear whether the retreating action was a genuine failure. It could have just been a tentative move to test the water or a grand performance to make a political point.[23] Timothy Brook noted that the night of May 19 had a full moon and speculated that advantage was taken of the higher visibility to aid the operation.[24] The moonlight could also have been part of the stagecraft if performance was indeed the main purpose. The show of citizen resistance seemed to make the case for the martial law troops. In a subtly twisted logic, the spectacular reaction to the act seemed to make it self-evident that it had been necessary in the first place. Moreover, by showing an extraordinary degree of restraint, the operation scored other political points: that the government was benevolent and patient, and that the army was here for peace. That would only be Act I, however. If there was a danger of appearing weak in showing restraint and retreating, later acts by the military would rectify that. Rectify it they did, in monumental fashion.

### A City on Edge but Unarmed

In the days leading to June 3, Beijing was a city on edge. When the full moon had given way to the new moon, the citizen–military standoff had already lasted for two weeks. Yet the suspense did not come from any escalation on the civilian side. Public interest had waned, and the organizations were in tatters. The occupation of the square was on life support, with occasional energy-boosting events to make it seem worthwhile. Nor was there any attempt to arm the protesters. The city was utterly unarmed as far as the civilian side was concerned. There were instances in which protesters found themselves in possession of guns and ammunition, usually after blocking an army truck in disguise. Without fail, the protest leaders advised immediately sending the weapons back to the authorities, or just smashing them to show their resolve to remain nonviolent.[25]

If the city was in no mood for conspiracy, it was not in a state of fear either. Rumors flew aplenty, yet most of them seemed to be rosy. One suggested infighting between two units of the army; another was about possible parliamentary maneuvers to null martial law. And there was occasional real news that was more or less substantiated. Four retired marshals urged the troops not to open fire at the people? Confirmed. A military commander refused to take orders? Confirmed. With the troops still stationed outside the city, order was maintained by the residents. Peace ruled. The protest and the arrival of the troops brought many new things to city dwellers. With their curiosity aroused, they participated in one act after another to satisfy it. Unable to fathom the real danger afoot, they blissfully turned politics, military affairs, and protest into a steady stream of entertainment. It was carnival-like fun.

In the afternoon of June 3, two graduate students from Beijing University decided to pay the square a visit. They had previously participated in all the major events since the outbreak of the protest in April, but had not been in the square recently. During this lower point in the protest and the military–civilian standoff, they had spent their days in the library to finish their master's theses, but decided to take a break that afternoon. It took more than an hour to bike from Beida to the square, weaving through the protesting crowds at major intersections. As they neared the square in Xidan, they smelled tear gas. The agitated crowd relayed that the smell was the remaining trace of a confrontation between PAP troops and the crowd. The square itself was a pitiful sight. Under the searing afternoon sun of June, most of the tents seemed to be sparsely occupied. Some were unattended. The two Beida students walked around the square and checked out the Beida tents. They hoped to find people they knew with whom they could chat and catch up. They found none, so they mounted their bikes and headed back to the campus.

No sooner had they settled back down in their respective dormitories at about 6:00 p.m. than the public speaker on campus set up by the protesters urged students to go out. It was announced that the troops were advancing from the northwest, near the North Palace Gate of the Summer Palace, a few miles from Beida. The male student mounted his bike once again, joining a very large contingent of students heading to the North Palace Gate. The students' mood was urgent yet triumphantly fearless. Some students carried a beer bottle in one hand, raising it above their head, with the other hand holding their bike handlebar. One student was holding an umbrella rod, its length adjustable, shining like a sword. They arrived at the city's edge only to find the scene already quiet, with pushed-over buses lying in the intersection and the remaining crowds regaling them with a tale of another victory beating back the troops. The student contingent turned back toward the campus, supposedly to regroup and plan for another "mission." By the time the students on their bicycles arrived back at the side of their campus, night had long since fallen. It was around 10:00 p.m. Someone uttered a cry of surprise: to their southwest, in the sky above the nearby neighborhood of Muxidi, there were sparks like fireworks or lightning. As the group suddenly quietened themselves, they could hear the muffled sounds of gunshots.[26]

## The Decision to "Clear the Square"

The date and manner of "clearing the square" must have been decided days before the Politburo meeting on the morning of June 2. The meeting – attended by remaining SC members (Li Peng, Qiao Shi, and Yao Yilin) and the active elders Deng Xiaoping, Li Xiannian, Peng Zhen, Yang Shangkun, Bo Yibo, and Wang Zhen – was more or less a process of recasting the behind-the-scenes deliberation into an official occasion.[27] In Zhao Ziyang's absence, Li Peng was the highest-ranking first-line leader. In his diary, he gives a full account of the decision. He starts by defining the square as the political center of the rebellion:

> An important plot of the masterminds and the organizers of the unrest was to continue the occupation of the square. They turned it into the headquarters in their final confrontation with the party and the government, and into the nerve center for the student movement as well as the entire nation. Whatever the government decides to do, there will be a strong reaction from the square."[28]

He then attributed the occupation with inspiring violence, which he saw as a growing threat:

All planned and commanded at Tiananmen Square, there were dare-to-die groups assembled to block the troops, hooligans organized to attack the Beijing Public Security Bureau, news conferences staged, and "Flying Tigers" recruited ... They plot to instigate bloodshed in the square.[29]

Like other speakers to follow, Li Peng concluded his remarks by situating the occupation in the larger national and international context. He cited the hostile news media of the West, Taiwan, and Hong Kong; anti-China groups active in New York; and spies freshly sent from abroad. Together, the party line represented by Li Peng painted the occupation as the central piece of a counterrevolutionary conspiracy.[30]

As party norm requires, all in attendance took turns and voiced their support by repeating the same justification. In characteristic fashion, General Wang Zhen used colorful language to call the square occupiers names and urged "Comrade Xiaoping, send the army to arrest them immediately!" Others gave lengthy reiterations about the connection between the square and the wider conspiracy. Li Xiannian lamented that after two weeks of martial law in Beijing, the square was still like "a cancer of unrest in the body." "A decent square has been ruined, made into something half-human and half-ghost. How can we answer to the people for that?" The meeting was closed with everyone present urging clearing the square "the earlier the better." The voices sounded in perfect accord, including that of Qiao Shi, who as a Zhao Ziyang ally had survived the reshuffling and remained in the SC. He was resigned to concluding that "it looks like it is not possible to expect the students to withdraw voluntarily. Clearing the Square is the only choice."[31]

In the afternoon of the same day, June 2, Yang Shangkun convened a meeting attended by CMC members and the commanders of the martial law troops. The meeting reviewed the speeches given by Deng and others in the morning and made a further decision: "[The CMC] ordered the martial law troops remaining in the suburbs to begin to enter Beijing city starting at 12:00 a.m., June 3 (or midnight of June 2), and to continue onto the patrol destinations."[32]

If not careful, one may mistakenly construe that the order covers the entire military deployment for clearing the square. This part of the operation – coordinated troop advancement *above ground* on June 3–4 – was responsible for all killings and casualties that ensued during those nights, which have been researched and covered in great depth and detail by both scholars and the public. As I will discuss in detail in a later section in this chapter, the June 3–4 operation had another major component – the deployment of troops by other means prior to June 3, including sneaking in troops who passed as civilians, transporting troops by rail through underground tunnels, and deploying those already in the city. In his speech at the June 2 Politburo meeting, Yang Shangkun reported that "martial law troops have already been sent to locations including the Great Hall of the People, Zhongshan Park, the Cultural Palace of the Working People, and the Headquarters of the People's Security Bureau."[33] In his diary entry for June 2, Li Peng confirms this fact with specific numbers. By 3:00 a.m. on June 2 – that is, hours before the Politburo meeting – 25,000 troops were placed in the locations mentioned by Yang in ways "that were incognito." He adds another 3,000 stationed at Beijing East Railway Station, which was also close to the square. He seems to suggest that those troops belonged to the Beijing Military Region.[34] In a later section, I will return to discussing the crucial role played by this part of the deployment, which was *incognito*, in the efforts to clear the square. For now, let us continue to discuss the *above-ground* deployment covered by the CMC order issued in the afternoon of June 2, which played a part in making the tragedy that shocked the world.

### Entering Beijing and Deadly Confrontations

At 4:00 p.m. on June 3, 1989, acting commander Zhang Meiyuan of the 38th Group Army was called to the headquarters of the Beijing Military Region. There he received the order and relayed it back to his unit right away. His partner, the political commissar of the Group Army, Wang Fuyi, received a call from him at 5:00 p.m. The content of the order was as follows: the entire group army was to advance from west to east toward the square; it must arrive on time and must remove any obstacles by all possible means. The first destination was to be the Military Museum. They were required to arrive at the edge of the square at 1:30 a.m. on June 4. The required time for starting the move was 10:00 p.m. The order also revealed that another Group Army, the 63rd, would follow immediately behind the 38th.[35] Also ordered to enter from west to east were two divisions of the 28th Group Army.[36]

In a similar fashion, troops were ordered to enter Beijing, aiming at the square from other directions:

- From east to west, two divisions of the 39th Group Army, starting from Tongxian, reaching Beijing's Bawangfen and Jianguo Gate by 8:00 p.m. on June 3.

- From south to north, the 138th Division of the 26th Group Army, starting at 5:00 p.m. from Nanyuan Airport in the south suburb, advancing along Nanyuan Road, passing Muxiyuan, Yongding Gate, Zhushikou, and Qianmen. Also advancing in this direction are the 58th Division and the 128th Division of the 20th Group Army, from suburban Daxing County to Dahong Gate, Muxiyuan, and Yongding Gate.

- From north to south: the two brigades of 15th Group Army paratroopers, also the 64th Group Army – the 190th infantry division.

- From northeast to southwest, the 118th Division of the 40th Group Army.

- From southwest to northeast, the 127th Infantry Division of the 54th Group Army starting at 9:50 p.m. from Fengtai District, through Liuli Bridge and Guangan Gate toward Zhengyang Gate, and the 162nd Division, advancing through Muxiyuan, Majiabu toward the square.[37]

Just imagine for a minute: as many as about 200,000 troops, fully armed or equipped, were being deployed to capture a square that was utterly unarmed.

As the troops entered the city, restraint was initially exercised in their confrontations with civilians. This passage from Timothy Brook is a typical scene in the major avenues of the night:

> At 9:20 p.m., the force at the Military Museum began to push its way further east. Thousands of workers and students formed a slowly retreating human wall fifteen rows deep across Changan Avenue. Opposite them, across a hundred-meter no-man's -land littered with stones and broken bottles, stood at least five thousand soldiers, helmeted but unarmed. "We will put an end to the turmoil," they chanted. "Soldiers don't stop till the turmoil stops!" A few wielded billy clubs and leather belts, and the rest threw back the stones that demonstrators had thrown at them or stacked along the side of the road. The PAP escorts lining each side of the column's flanks carried AK-47s.[38]

According to Wu Renhua, the first victim of the June 3–4 massacre was thirty-two-year-old Song Xiaoming, a skilled worker of the 283rd factory of the Ministry of Aeronautics and Astronautics. At about 10:00 p.m. on June 3, he was hit in his leg by a bullet from a military truck. At the Wukesong intersection in the path of the 38th Group Army's advance, he was in the middle of a protesting crowd yelling at the soldiers. He was sent to the 301st Hospital but died of blood loss within the hour.[39]

Many more died in more aggressive struggles. Here is another scene, which happened two hours later and was recorded by a journalist. In an intersection where the army's path was blocked by trolleybuses, dump trucks, and several minibuses,

> In front of the flaming barricade, alone, facing the soldiers, four students, their feet planted wide, crack the heavy air with the sound of their waving scarlet banners ... The silk of their university banners gleams in the fire's light, and behind them, the crowd, waiting for the worst, applauded them ... In front of the burning truck, the four banners collapse. Behind, a dozen fleeing students are struck by bullets in the back. Right near me at the end of the canal, a young boy, maybe fifteen, picks up

one more stone to throw one more time. In a fraction of a second, his white T-shirt is stained with red in the middle of his chest.[40]

Was there an order to open fire on civilians, and where did it come from? To date, there is still no definite answer. Wu Renhua conducted extensive research on the question, and found the following. First, in every account printed in *A Day on Martial Law Duty*, the authors only admit to firing in the air and allude to having permission to do so. But this, of course, does not account for the deaths and is therefore a fabrication. Second, the orders seem to have come down at about the same time, around 10:00 p.m. Up to that point, the advancing troops did not take the liberty of interpreting "advance forward by all means" as permission to open fire. This finding was consistent with Timothy Brook's account of various locations in which the confrontations did not yield killings until 10:00 p.m.[41] Third, not every unit received the same order. Wu found that those units who received the order did open fire and kill, including the 20th, 38th, 39th, 40th and 15th Group Armies. The exception was the 54th Group Army, which did not receive the order and locked its ammunition away from advancing soldiers. Wu further speculates that the order came down from the level of the military region command to group army levels and below. The fact that several military region commands made the order simultaneously points to the upper level of the CMC and above as the culprit.[42]

It was a military assault on a city defended only by civilian bodies and blood. About 3,000 civilians were killed in a single night. In sharp contrast, a total of thirteen soldiers, including PLA and PAP personnel, were killed in the June 3–4 operation. They include Yu Ronglu, who was in plain clothes and hit by friendly fire; Wang Qifu, who along with five of his fellow soldiers died in a military truck that was trapped; Liu Guogen, who was brutally murdered by a civilian mob; and Cui Guozheng, who was murdered by another civilian mob. None of them were killed before 12:00 a.m. on June 4. In other words, their killings were not the cause of the military operation, but the result of it.[43]

### Military Morale and the Issue of Disobedience

If the mission is against peaceful civilians, how do military men justify their actions? If the civilian leaders are using the military to display political power, why would they go along, much less kill peaceful protesters? In other words, in order to understand the military mission as political method, we need to understand the nature of this tool. How did the military become a tool ready for use? Elsewhere and in history, soldierly morale is by no means a guarentee for a regime in need.

"For most of the line soldiers their primary contribution to the events of 14 July [1789] was the lack of confidence which they inspired in their officers," writes historian Samuel Scott in an extraordinary passage in his book *The Response of the Royal Army to the French Revolution*. He continues,

> Theirs was a completely passive role, but no less important for that. On 15 July Marshal de Broglie . . . felt forced to admit that the soldiers could not be used against civilians. During the morning of 16 July Louis XVI held a council of war and Broglie repeated that the attitude of the troops precluded any hope of military operations against Paris. When a suggestion was made that the King depart to some provincial fortress, Broglie ". . . declared that he could not guarantee the safe passage of the royal family through a country the whole of which was in a state of insurgency, escorted by troops that were ready to side with the rioters." Resignedly, the King then ordered the line regiments to return to their garrisons.[44]

If the soldiers' passivity cost the French Old Regime in 1789, then in Russia in 1917, discontent with the government among military generals made it possible for the Bolsheviks to take power.[45] In 1986 in the Philippines, a series of military defections helped the People's Power Revolution to succeed.[46] In 2011, the Egyptian president Mubarak lost his grip on the military amid the Tahrir Square protest and fled the country.[47]

### High Soldierly Morale in 1989 and Its Sources

By comparison, remarkably on display in Beijing in 1989 were the loyalty, discipline, and coherence of China's army.[48] The army appears to have been highly effective to serve the leaders as a political tool. There was only one celebrated case of disobedience worthy of history books, but it was singular. Nor did this resistance amount to anything meaningful that could have significantly altered the course of military action.[49]

Chinese soldiers, from generals down to privates, are raised to be political. Experts do not agree on the exact nature of the civilian–military relation in communist China, but few would entertain the notion of military insulation from politics.[50] The interlocking is amply documented. So is the function of the political commissar system.[51]

Yet China's political soldier is not so much an ideological believer as an organizational actor. An organizational actor will follow orders even if he has to discard some previously instilled principles. He is not a mindless robot, however, thanks to the cognitive tools bestowed by his political education. Not only will he follow, but he also "knows" why. The genius of China's organizational control is therefore aided by, or can be transformed into, political control. In a fascinating work, Scobell's case study of China's decision to send troops to Korea in the 1950s nicely illustrates this point. The military men, such as Peng Dehua and Lin Biao, were in fact less supportive of the war than the civilian leader. They held such views due to their anticipation of loss and possible defeat. Yet they quickly got on board with Mao. Their change of heart was made possible by the political work which had already been done on their minds.[52]

The Chinese soldier is trained to see unity, not contradiction, between following the party and defending the people, for in their ingrained "political consciousness" the party knows best what is good for the people. In 1989, the soldiers yelled, "Resolutely follow the Party Center, the State Council, and the Central Military Committee!" That is, the CMC was the party, hence the people. To follow its order was to be "politically reliable."

> I told myself: an army is trained for a thousand days to use for one moment. In this critical situation we face a task that is both challenging and complicated. We must keep a cool head, we must be able to discern right from wrong, and we must be firm in taking a political stand. We must walk the walk in defending the Party Center, the State Council, and the Central Military Committee, and in defending the great capital, Beijing. (Zuo Yingsheng, senior colonel, vice commander of group army)[53]

### Emotion Work and Rationalization: In Their Own Words

From the essays published in *A Day on Martial Law Duty*,[54] we can examine the rationalization process in the soldiers' thinking. While the writings were officially organized to serve a political purpose in a post-event environment, it is worth quoting some at length, if only to understand what the military men were told to think before and during the mission. Reading these essays, we may characterize the thinking process as four steps.

The first is how these military men submerged the events of the day as they echoed the proclaimed mission. It is not odd that their utterances sound uncannily similar to the speeches given by the top party leaders in the Politburo. That is exactly the point, as their reading of the events of the day was filtered by their political education:

> Up to this point, our troops have been subdued by the residents and citizens, which must be unheard of throughout the world. Now the Party Center, the State Council and the Central Military Committee resolve to solve this problem in Beijing. Any hesitation or imprudence on our part will not be acceptable at this critical juncture for the party and the country. (Wang Fuyi, major general, political commissar of the 38th Group Army)[55]

This is General Wang, who saw the restraint of the military as a virtue but something that needed to be ended. In his reasoning, the June 3 order from "the Party Center, the State Council and the CMC" was to resolve a problem, an act that was justified and urgent. It is interesting to note that Wang's partner, Xu Qinxian, the commander of his group army, was dismissed for disobeying the same order. In his essay, General Wang proceeds to specify the square as the strategic target and what his troops were supposed to do. In two passages he completes a stream of logical analysis linking the grand political talking point to a military act at hand:

> It becomes clear that the cancer on Tiananmen Square has to be removed in order to stop the entire unrest. It is unrealistic to hope for an easy solution without paying a considerable price ... We are ordered to press forward to the Square from west to east, removing them by force when encountering obstacles. It is imperative to arrive at the destination on time. (Major General Wang Fuyi)[56]

A second step of rationalization was to situate the task in a mental space, a military setting, with which the military men in Beijing in 1989 were familiar. One way to do so was to juxtapose the current situation with their unit's history, evoking past exploits and glories. This is how General Wang reminiscences:

> I was mighty proud as I witnessed the bravery and gallantry of my troops. Our group army has been following Marshal Peng Dehuai starting from way back in the Pingjiang uprising in 1928. The same bravery and gallantry marked the unit in so many difficult battles: defending Jinggang Mountain, twice seizing Zunyi City, taking Zhiluo Township, fighting in the Pingxing campaign and the Liaoxi campaign, and seizing Tianjin. (Major General Wang Fuyi)[57]

Another way to help was to use a military ploy that had been used before. For example, two infantry divisions of the 38th Group Army were ordered to press forward from west to east along Changan Avenue. The commander deliberately put the two divisions in competition with each other: the divisions were not only ordered to arrive at their destination on time, but also to arrive earlier than the other. The commander used this motivating technique in apparent awareness of past experiences:

> Our group army has a long tradition, with the utmost sense of revolutionary heroism and honor. Internal competition is fierce. We used these two divisions to attack Tianjin during the Liberation War. They raced with each other and the forces gained entry to the city quickly. (Major General Wang Fuyi)[58]

A third step of the rationalization was to formulate a conception of the enemy. The conception would have been straightforward, had they been on a battlefield. But Beijing streets were, obviously, no battlefield.

The military started with the political talking points issued from the central authorities. They urged soldiers to love the people but warned that in many places mixed among the people were "a handful" of "manipulators," "hooligans," and "violent elements." How would the soldiers tell the bad from the good? The logic would be to look at their actions. If they contributed to the disorder or still acted against the people's army, then they must belong to the "handful." Using this formula, soldiers would not have trouble knowing where to aim their rifles:

There were those who cursed, those who made up rumors; worse still, those who beat, smashed, looted, and burned! Oh, people, where is your conscience? Your merciful heart? Are these soldiers not the embodiment of hope and future, just like students? Beijing! Beijing! Oh, people, don't you know how much we soldiers love her [Beijing], embrace her with our heart, just like embracing the sun and our mother? (Senior Colonel Zhang Zuoli, division commander)[59]

Bear in mind that the two-week standoff produced a great deal of pain and suffering among the soldiers. Many were humiliated, and some were injured. This process helped to deepen the "enemy" conceptualization of the protestors, which also took on emotional dimensions:

Accusations and cursing, we tolerated; bricks and pieces of tile, we tolerated; all sorts of insults, we tolerated, and just adjusted our military caps; we tolerated what cannot be tolerated. My heart was drummed with repeated attacks of pain as I saw my soldiers [being insulted]. For the flesh-and-blood young soldiers, their heart beats like everyone else. How extraordinary and praiseworthy is their forbearance!" (First Lieutenant Li Shengshun, company commander)[60]

The last step of the rationalization was forming a sense of honor and glory. The impetus behind the soldiers' action was more than analytical purposiveness, mental familiarity, and repulsion toward the enemy. It was more that it must inspire honor and glory in the soldiers. This colonel's perception of exhortation straddled poetry and delirium:

To this date I vividly remember the scene, or the perception of it. The red color and light seemed to be everywhere. There were red lights along the railway here; there were fires there. The reflections glittered on the faces of our soldiers who seemed to have become thinner overnight ... As we were standing right in the center of the night, I inspected each of my soldier's faces. Our gazes were burning, making sparkles, touching every nerve of mine ... We seemed to forget everything including ourselves, and only one thought was left: Forward! Forward! Forward! ... We linked ourselves arm in arm and attempted to pass the human wall which was blocking us. (Senior Colonel Ai Husheng, regiment commander)[61]

We might imagine that it must have been an excruciating dilemma to perform a military duty against ununiformed "people" and that, once it wass over, one would choose to forget it. But that was not how Major General Fu Bingyao felt:

How much do I long for a day when we could march forward along the same route, so I could relive once more that burning night, so the blood in my whole body could boil up all over again! (Major General Fu Bingyao, commander of the 39th Group Army)[62]

This political mindset was no doubt the fruit of long-term indoctrination. A habit of the heart was instilled in the military men to see things as the party wanted them to see them. Apparently they were able to adjust as the party took a new position and do so quickly enough.

Informational control was also crucial. The martial law troops, those from faraway provinces, reportedly possessed little inkling as to what exactly had been going on in Beijing. Many caught up with current events only when the civilians volunteered to give them an earful.[63] An expert speculated that the very reason the outside troops were called in was not because those stationed in the Beijing area were not numerous enough, but because they knew too much to be relied on.[64] When the May 19 advance stopped, the central command quickly issued an order to retreat. A speedy separation was important in order to prevent information from reaching civilians. Once the troops had resettled in their respective barracks, a political education campaign was set in full swing. The study materials used by the 38th Group Army were typical, including the April 26 editorial and the speeches from the May 18 Beijing rally. Current events were strictly filtered through the party line: the existence of turmoil, the conspiratorial forces behind it, the failure of peaceful measures taken by the government, and so on.[65]

### Exceptional Disobedience

Being better informed than other officers was likely a factor in Major General Xu Qinxian's decision to disobey orders. He was the commander of the 38th Group Army on the eve of the mission, and he refused to take part. In his absence, his army was led by other commanders, subsequently playing a major role. He was later stripped of his ranks, court-martialed, and sentenced to jail for five years.

That spring, General Xu witnessed political events in Beijing from an unusually candid angle. From March until he was summoned, he was there to recuperate from a bone injury in his leg. From the PLA General Hospital in western Beijing, he observed the student protest, from its onset in mid-April to the end. What he learned from his own experience was drastically different from what was relayed by his army command in Baoding, Hebei.[66] This account is bolstered by another piece of information, which came from a very official source, though it cannot be independently confirmed. In a high-profile speech in the wake of Tiananmen, Lieutenant General Liu Yazhou, one of the top military leaders at that time, suggested that Xu's two sons were participants in the student movement and were perhaps in the square at the very moment when he refused to obey orders.[67]

It appears that General Xu's defiance was well thought through. He had returned to Baoding from the hospital, on crutches, to answer the summons. He proceeded to announce the order to his officers, who in turn started to prepare the troops. Then he made a phone call to the Beijing Military Region headquarters and stated that, on account of his injury, he was unfit to lead the mission. The political commissar, Zhou Yibing, warned him that this could be seen as an act of disobedience. Xu was unmoved. This news infuriated Yang Shangkun, who lost sleep for a few nights. Yang signed a CMC order to strip Xu of all ranks and to send him to the military court. Xu went back to the hospital to wait for the military police. "Do you have any objection?" asked the MPs. "No, I have thought this through," Xu replied. "I am mentally prepared. I disobeyed as a soldier, so I deserve this treatment. You may go ahead with your work. As far as the student movement is concerned, I do have my own views, but now is not the time for that."[68]

General Xu's case is confirmed by multiple official sources, including a published history of the 38th Group Army and the speech by General Liu Yazhou mentioned above.[69] Author and journalist Yang Jisheng interviewed Xu several years after he was released from prison. The hero now lives his elder years as an ordinary citizen in Shijiazhuang City, Hebei. Yang Jisheng reports that Jiang Zemin allowed him a pension package commensurate with that of someone with the rank of vice commander of a group army.[70] In his speech, Liu Yazhou recounted the story of Xu Qinxian as a morality tale. He praised Xu for his "inborn talent as a commander" (*jiangcai*), who was "matched by one or two in the Chinese military." Alas, Liu concluded, Xu was not "politically reliable."

In the same speech, Liu offered another case of two "politically unreliable" generals during the Tiananmen mission.[71] On the night of June 3–4, the 28th Group Army were blocked on their way to the square, as were many other units. But unlike most of the other units, they did not manage to press forward "at all costs" and missed the early morning deadline to arrive in the designated location.[72] Liu reported in his speech that the CMC even sent a helicopter to urge the group army commander, Major General He Yuanran, and the political commissar, Zhang Mingchun: "Forward! Forward! And forward at all cost!" That was to no avail.[73] Historian Wu Renhua believed that the two commanders were appalled by the killings going on and committed an act of passive disobedience. Their troops were stalled in Muxidi intersection as late as 7:00 a.m. on June 4. There, many soldiers were unnerved by the civilians parading bodies and bloodied garments in front of them and abandoned their vehicles and equipment rather than forcing their way forward. Their unit suffered the loss of thirty-one armored cars and seventy-four military personnel carriers. After all was settled, Zhang Mingchun was demoted after a six-month investigation, and died at the age of fifty-three in 1990. He Yuanran was also demoted.[74]

A third case of high-level disobedience involved Senior Colonel Xu Feng, the commander of the 116th Division of the 39th Group Army. Colonel Xu led a reconnaissance mission early in the evening of June 3 and learned the scale of killings occurring. Then he got in a division command vehicle and led a contingent circling the city for the entire evening, but without a trace. The

CMC issued numerous radio messages trying to locate them but did not succeed. He was punished and discharged after Tiananmen.[75]

June Dryer has cited a report that, all told, about 400 officers and 1,600 soldiers were discharged for failing to carry out the order.[76] But these numbers seem trivial compared to the total number of military personnel moved to Beijing for the mission, estimated between 180,000 and 250,000. As important, these cases of disobediences did not seem to dampen the high morale of the troops or change in any meaningful way the course of events. The Chinese army as a political instrument was strong and effective in 1989. And those "politically reliable" men were generously rewarded with medals and promotions.[77]

### The Factor of Civilian Resistance

The night would have been less eventful if the crowd had stayed away for fear of the armed forces. Or, if the square's student occupiers had withdrawn early, there would have been no significant confrontation with the soldiers. But, as a whole, the crowd on those Beijing avenues simply failed to imagine, or fear, the horror of a military operation. While we ask why the soldiers opened fire, it is as important to explain the fearlessness of the civilians. The crowds' not retreating in the face of the military marching in unavoidably led to the catastrophic clashes of the night. But let me be clear here, civilian resistance was by no means the cause of the grand military operation.[78]

#### In Normal Times: The Fish–Water Relationship

A typical protester in his twenties in 1989 had perhaps never seen a real uniformed soldier in action for his entire life, much less a column on a mission.[79] The last time the army had a significant encounter with domestic civilians was toward the end of the Cultural Revolution in the 1970s. Mao sent troops to all levels of government "to support the left,"[80] and they were withdrawn after social order was restored. Deng's ascent in the late 1970s terminated such practices entirely. By 1989, the segregation between the army and civilians had been in place for more than a decade. Military bases were normally in suburban areas or provincial regions, often in mountainous terrain, far from big cities where colleges and universities are located.

The army among the people is like a fish in water. However, gone were the wartime years in which guerrilla soldiers and civilians lived and worked side by side toward the same great goal. While this analogy no longer had a physical equivalent, its vivid imagery persisted in people's and soldiers' mutual imaginations and was, as in all things in communist China, portrayed through propaganda. The soldiers' devotion was ubiquitously featured in newsreels, books, movies, songs, and stage performances. To whom were they devoted? The audience often heard three things interchangeably: the country, the people, and the party. Few worried about any possible conflict between or among the three. The propaganda machine was whipped into a frenzy to glorify the 1979 war against Vietnam, which lasted for many years. A soldier named Xu Liang who lost both legs in a skirmish on the Sino-Vietnamese border was hailed a hero. He was paraded on speech tours around the country, and his fame climaxed with him singing on the stage of the 1987 Chinese New Year Gala, which was China's biggest show, televised to the entire population. The song was called "Blood-Crimsoned Glory." In part it runs,

> Oh should I be slain
> Not to see you again
> Will that then extend
> Your wait to no end?
>
> But if that is to be so
> Mourn me not as I go
> For the nation's flag shall flow
> In the color of my blood, glow[81]
> . . .

This song was further popularized by the famous singer Dong Wenhua for the next two years, and by 1989 it must have been familiar to most people in China. It was so popular that even the protesters in 1989 sang it to the soldiers.[82] The song, characteristically, depicts the ultimate devotion of Chinese soldiers. Devotion to whom? Again, to the ears of the civilians, it was unmistakable. Who could better represent the country than "the people"?

### Romantic Imagination: What Might Soldiers Do When in Conflict with "the People"?

Despite their segregation, there was no lack of fascination with the military on the part of civilians. For the seriously minded, this fascination had gone beyond feel-good clichés. In the event of a protest, some political dissidents did wonder how the army would behave. A famous student leader, Shen Tong, in his memoir on his campus life at Beijing University, recalled an encounter in 1988. A man from Anhui Province somehow sneaked into Shen's dormitory and received a warm reception from the students. The man gave a talk about why it was time for them to mount a protest movement. Among his major points was one about potential sympathy from the army:

The Chinese military had changed in recent years because of the changing economic conditions in the countryside. Now that they [soldiers] could take advantage of increased free enterprise, most planned to return to civilian life after a few years of service. These recruits were less likely to blindly follow orders than the traditional recruits had been.[83]

About the army officers, the mysterious guest went on,

Also, China had reduced its military by one-fourth in 1985, and the middle- and lower-ranked officers who remained were educated and would probably sympathize with a student reform movement. High-ranking officers – about four hundred members of the Old Guard – had mixed feelings about Deng Xiaoping and Yang Shangkun ... If a student movement were to arise, the military would not necessarily follow Yang's orders."[84]

Thus did civilians imagine the military. It was a perception fraught with well-meaning misconceptions. First, while the men in uniform may hold dear the principle of "protecting the people," the power of defining who was a friend or foe was held by the politics of the time. That is, to be "politically reliable" was to tread the party line. As discussed above, the party's political work provided the frame, which often was capable of excluding segments of the population from the realm of "the people." Second, this imagination overstated the role of individual agency, as though soldiers or army officials could act out of their personal convictions. The principle at work is always the duty to follow, before personal views.

### Early Encounters in the Days before June 3–4

In due course, the civilians' romantic imagination would meet a rude awakening. But, ironically, the early experiences from the first two weeks following the implementation of martial law seemed to validate it. After they successfully blocked the troops on the morning of May 20, the mood among Beijing citizens was triumphant. Timothy Brook observes,

People drew blithe assurance from the belief that right was on their side ... Nothing indicated that the people were wrong to assume that they were stronger than the Army. Nor did appearances suggest that the government was already set on a course that might lead eventually to soldiers opening fire on unarmed civilians. The first truck of soldiers stopped by the first citizen on Friday night had not pressed forward, and an entire army had been paralyzed. That remained to be the greatest visible truth, and the great false hope. People might believe, with Lao Zi, that "that which is not the Way must come to an early end."[85]

Even for the most sophisticated, the worst-case scenario could not be accepted until the last minute. By then many were dead. Lu Chaoqi, deputy editor in chief of the *People's Daily*, worked a night shift on June 3. He could not sleep in any case, for early signs that evening were ominous. A colleague called around 9:00 p.m. and informed him that the troops had opened fire. Many of his young reporters rushed out to the street to observe and report. Left in the office alone, according to Lu's diary, he thought to himself,

> Confrontation may be inevitable. But in the final analysis the party is a communist party, one that is guided by Marxism–Leninism and Mao Zedong thought, so the army is the people's army. Even if the army really opened fire, their guns must just point to the sky to frighten people. There is no way they would really shoot at the people! To kill unarmed civilians was something even the Beiyang warlords or the reactionary forces of the Kuomintang hesitated to do.[86]

Alas, as his younger colleagues started to return after 1:00 a.m., he realized that an immense tragedy had been taking place. Among the first to report to him was Zhang Baolin, his trousers and shoes soaked in blood. On his way back to the office he had trodden through blood on the streets in the Muxidi area.[87]

### Rude Awakening and Naive Bravado

On the street outside, in the evening of June 3, Shen Tong could not believe that tanks would be used:

> "The tanks are coming!" someone shouted. *It can't be*, I thought. *How can they drive tanks into the downtown area?* A crowd had gathered at the corner of Xidan, and when I got there a seemingly endless line of headlights stretched as far as I could see down Changan Avenue to the west. I couldn't believe my eyes. It was so bright I almost couldn't see. There were maybe twenty army tanks, but it seemed like many more, and they were headed right for us. The people around me were throwing stones at soldiers walking beside them, and in response the soldiers started to spray gunfire at our feet.[88]

A moment later, the protesters did not believe the bullets were real:

> "Rubber bullets!" I shouted as people began to scream with fear. "Stop throwing things – there is no way to stop them!" I found my way through the crowd, trying to get onto the avenue, but I stopped when one of the soldiers fired rapidly at my feet. I wasn't hurt, so I tried to look for shells, to see whether the bullets were real. Hundreds of people rushed into the avenue to put up barricades, but as soon as they reached the middle of the street, a spray of machine-gun fire scattered them. People who had been hit fell to the ground and lay still. *Those people are dead*, I thought to myself. *The bullets are real.*[89]

During the evening of June 3, the students continued their occupation of the square, which was the symbolic center for both sides. Earlier in these pages, I have tried to understand and explain the thinking of the student leaders. I suggest that the shadow of post-Tiananmen persecution figured heavily in their calculus. The April 26 editorial had labeled the activism a crime. The government had stayed firm rather than softening its tone, and that resolve was confirmed by the declaration of martial law. The student leaders faced two tough choices – to end the occupation was to face the certainty of arrest and prosecution; to continue was to face the risk of bloodshed. Perhaps to them the latter seemed a less certain and hence a less horrifying choice. Perhaps, they were just too naive and romantic. Either way, they chose to continue until the very last minute – even when the killings were already happening, they framed their actions as honoring the dead. Their decision to continue the occupation had tragic consequences. Thousands died on the routes leading to the square, all in the name of defending the sit-in students on the square.

For signs of naive bravado, one need to look no further than the name of the occupation organization: Defend Tiananmen Square Headquarters. Chai Ling's title as its head? "Commander in Chief." At one point, Chai Ling considered how her role had changed significantly, taking on a military tone: "I had gone from graduate student to student leader; from student leader to 'mayor' of a small city, worrying about how to supply food, shelter, water, sanitation, and medical care to a growing population on the square; *from mayor to semi-military general, preparing to defend against martial law.*"[90] This mentality persisted in a city besieged by more than 200,000 troops, complete with machine guns and tanks.

In the meantime, there were relentless efforts by intellectuals and dissenting student leaders to end the occupation. But Chai Ling, along with Li Lu and Feng Congde, stood their ground. Their power came from the direct votes of those in the square. They made up their mind to stay, and then asked for a vote. They got the result they wanted every time, from the occupiers – a fact that they later cited as their justification. But most likely they would have been able to persuade the students to vote for leaving if they had so decided. In one of those critical moments, Chai Ling had already agreed to a resolution made by another organization of all-city alliances to end the occupation, days before June 3. Then she relented after a conversation with the deputy commander, Li Lu. She later wrote about her reasoning:

> I was led to believe that some people were selling out the movement by trying to move the students out of the square so the crackdown could happen under cover of darkness ... If that happened with our movement, no one would know about it, and the government could imprison or kill all the key leaders, making it hard or impossible to start another successful movement. So, for me, it was important for the true face of our government to be known to the Chinese people and shown to the world.

Even in my worst nightmares, however, I was not prepared for the extent of the crackdown. I didn't know that words like "blood running like a river" could become so close to reality.[91]

To be sure, such audacity in imagination could be justified as long as the army was kept outside the city. But its persistence was extraordinary even after the first shot was fired in Changan Avenue and the first death was reported back to the square. In the critical moments of the early morning of June 4, also present among the occupiers were four intellectuals – including Liu Xiaobo and Hou Dejian, who joined the occupation in a high-profile ceremony on June 2. The Four Gentlemen, as they would later be called, urged students to negotiate with the troops and secure a safe path to withdraw, but Chai Ling and other student leaders refused. Here is another passage from Chai's account:

> Some students used the loudspeakers to encourage people to stay on the square. "Citizens have risked their lives to block the tanks and troops so we can stay on the square," one student said. "To leave now would render those sacrifices meaningless." Another said, "If we hold out until sunrise, two million Beijing citizens will come to our support. If we leave now, we'll never get back onto the square." Hou Dejian came to me. "What do you think, Chai Ling?" I told him we had received information that if we held out, Zhao Ziyang's army would come to our side. "Is that so?" Hou said.[92]

For Chai Ling, dead-set determination was taking the form of a yearning for martyrdom. And from martyrdom, a romantic call for "a new China." This was her last speech of the night to the remaining students:

> "A colony of ants lived on a tall mountain," I began. "One day, the mountain caught fire. The ants in the colony realized their only recourse was to roll downhill. All the ants formed a large ant ball and rolled down the mountainside. The ants on the outside burned to death, but the ones inside survived. Tonight," I declared, "we are the outside ants. Out of our sacrifice a new China will be born."[93]

## The Possibility of a Low-Key Operation

As the events unfolded, the square was at the very heart. It was the geographical center toward which the troops from all directions advanced. It was the symbolic center for the civilians as well; many bravely risked their lives in the name of defending it. The whole planning and later discourse of the government centered on the key word *qingchang*, "clearing the square." The mass media in the West also called the killings the "Tiananmen Square massacre."

The military action of taking over the square from the occupying students was carried out in one fell swoop, as though overwhelming force was necessary and elaborated co-ordination was required. It was a military strategy of shock and awe, or, in the words of General Yang Dezhi, in another context during

China's 1979 war against Vietnam, "using an ox cleaver to kill a chicken." But did it have to be this way?

### How Clearing the Square Was Done in 1976

A similar situation in the spring of 1976 was handled differently. Recall that that was the protest in the square initiated by mourning for Zhou Enlai. The operation of taking over, clearing up, and cordoning off was carried out in a low-key manner. No one died. Protesters that spring did not camp out in the square, but it was a symbolic center of defiance for quite some time (two weeks). On the morning of April 5, the agitated crowds swelled the square in numbers estimated to be more than 10,000. This was two days after April 3, when the number of people in the square had reached 200,000. They were angered by the removal of the wreaths from the square and by the fact that no explanation was given. According to firsthand testimony, cited by Teiwes and Sun, the police and militia were very restrained, and no arrests were made in the daytime. As night fell and lights were lit, the crowd became smaller and smaller. Starting at 6:30 p.m., the Beijing mayor, Wu De, declared through a loudspeaker system on the square that a handful of bad elements had used the Qingming festival to deceive people, calling on those remaining to leave. Wu's speech played again and again until 11:00 p.m. Then militiamen and plain-clothes police suddenly sprang into action. A spasm of beatings, draggings, and arrests ensued. Order returned in a matter of minutes, because, indeed, the government's force was overwhelming compared to the crowds. While remaining protesters in the square might have numbered fewer than 1,000 by then, the government force consisted of 3,000 militia and 3,000 police. There were another five battalions of Beijing Garrison troops in the background, assumed to have been hidden in adjacent buildings. The square was cordoned off quickly by the armed forces. Then it was taken and cleared.[94]

In the Politburo meetings leading up to the final operation, a military solution was mentioned only once by Jiang Qing and rejected by the others. In an earlier meeting, Mayor Wu even suggested the very sensible solution of waiting it out – let the matter rest a few more days and see what happens. This was angrily rebuffed by Jiang Qing, who accused Wu of "having been poisoned by Deng Xiaoping's thoughts." Wu was even made to self-criticize. On the question of what forces should be mobilized to clear the square and make arrests, however, the moderate voices prevailed. Jiang Qing, backed by the ranking military man present, Chen Xilian, called for the dispatch of regular troops, but her partners, Wang Hongwen and Zhang Chunqiao, supported by the meeting chair Hua Guofeng, insisted that any force should be limited to public security forces and particularly the militia. Jiang was overruled.[95] Understandably there was a deeper reason for the decision. The prevailing faction of Jiang, Wang, and

Zhang would not be about to reap any political benefit if the military was staged front and center, for the army was in the hands of the generals who were allies of Deng Xiaoping.

At the time, mayor Wu De and the Beijing Garrison commander Wu Zhong were jointly in charge of the implementation of the April 5, 1976 operation. In his memoir written years later, Wu De recorded the play-by-play action in detail. Going into the command posts, he shared Wu Zhong's apprehension that confrontation would cause bloodshed, but asked, "who is able to take responsibility for the bloodshed?" By 8:00 p.m., Hua Guofeng and Chen Xilian phoned the headquarters and demanded, "Why has there been no action?" Under pressure, Wu De consulted Wu Zhong, who said, "Now we still have a few tens of thousands of people on the square. We should wait."[96] By 11:00 p.m., most of the people had left, with only about 1,000 remaining in the square. The crowd in the center of the square, at the base of the Monument of the People's Martyrs, also thinned to about 200. Wu De and Wu Zhong then issued the order to send the soldiers in "empty-handed" to close off the perimeter, and dispatched the militia into the square as well. They arrested about 100 protesters and transported them away, expelling the rest. "In the course of the clearing, we could not avoid using violent means," concludes Wu De in his memoir, "but there was no single person killed, I assure you."[97] Another source confirms that there were no deaths. The clearing process led to thirty-eight arrests.[98]

### A Force of between 3,000 and 30,000 Could Have Done the Job

In many ways, to be sure, the 1989 situation was very different. For one thing, at first glance, the square seemed to be much more difficult to clear in 1989 than in 1976. After the declaration of martial law on May 19, the students ended their hunger strike and announced an occupation. A student commander was elected. Student marshals wore armbands to patrol the perimeter of the square. Besides core activists who camped in the center of the square, there were protesters, sometimes thousands strong, who stayed and functioned as a protective belt that needed to be penetrated.

But the obstacles were by no means insurmountable. While it was definitely impractical to clear a square filled with tens of thousands, the number of people in the square fluctuated during the twenty-four-hour cycle of the day. In the small hours of the early morning, the square would be quiet. Many protesters had left and returned home, leaving only the most determined members sleeping. How many of them? Were they too many to be managed – to be arrested or dispersed – by a force that could be deployed to the square?

The best estimate of the number of people occupying the square at night should be around 3,000. As I detailed earlier, the long occupation had worn the protesters down. A week or so into it, the square was littered with piles of trash. Most people slept on the ground with neither mattress nor shelter. On May 31, a Wednesday morning, the public broadcast from "Defending the Square Headquarters" said that the existing tents, which were dilapidated in most cases, would be removed and replaced with the brand-new tents sent by Hong Kong students to form eight blocks on the south side of the monument and two blocks on the north side. The total capacity would be 3,500.[99] On the afternoon of June 3, when I stopped by, the replacement was apparently completed, with only new tents neatly aligned with one another on the square.

There is another way to reach the above estimate. Days into the standoff between the protesters and the army, most students from Beijing's universities had been in the movement for more than a month. They started to leave. Only the students from outside Beijing remained. By May 30, many students from outside Beijing had also begun to pack and leave. A report by the Railway Ministry suggests that, on average, 20,000 students left Beijing by train each day, while only 188 entered Beijing on May 29 and 160 on May 30. Rumors aside, the government troops did not seem to be taking any rapid action and therefore the resident sympathizers also dwindled. As a result, even during the daytime, the overall number of people on the square was a small fraction of that on previous peak days. "May 23, Tuesday. The people of the square during the day were much fewer than other days, about 10,000 only," records one chronology compiled by a researcher.[100] "May 27, Saturday. There are still about 10,000 sit-in students in the square today," he writes in another entry.[101] On May 30, the statue known as the Goddess of Democracy was unveiled. The event boosted the number of people in the square. But the chronicler still only put down the number as "a few tens of thousands."[102] In sum, during the two weeks between May 19 and June 3, there were multiple days in which the size of the crowd on the square was around 10,000 at its highest. They included both those coming to visit during the day and those remaining in tents overnight. These numbers help us to arrive at the estimate that the number who remained overnight should be around 3,000 or fewer.

A third source for such an estimate comes from Chai Ling's memoir. As commander in chief of the Defending Tiananmen Square Headquarters, she described the scene of the last hour of the crackdown:

> Three or four thousand students were seated on all four sides of the monument. They looked calm, yet helpless. Obviously tired, their faces showed the same emotions of loss and defiance that I was struggling with. Girls and boys leaned against each other for support and warmth, like lambs awaiting the chopping block.[103]

Finally, this estimate is consistent with the number of students on the square in the early morning of June 4. By 4:30 a.m., these students were surrounded by troops in all directions of the square. Negotiations between the troops and two protest leaders resulted in the orderly withdrawal of the remaining students. Li Peng cited a report by Luo Gan, and put the number as "2,000 and a bit more."[104] The number was recorded as "a few thousand." Here is a passage provided by an official source:

> Upon hearing the announcement of the notice, the remaining students in the square, numbering a few thousand, formed a marching column, guarded by a circle of [student] marshals linked with each other hand in hand. They left the square in orderly fashion under their respective banners. The martial law troops allowed a generous passage, ensuring that the student withdrawal was swift, glitch-free, and peaceful. But at the end there were still 200 or so students who refused to leave; they were manhandled and pushed out by the PAP soldiers.[105]

There is no question that even on a quiet morning on a day of low protest turnout, the crowd of demonstrators to be cleared from the square in 1989 was much larger than that in 1976. But if estimates of around 3,000 are correct, that was by no means a formidable number to overcome. They were unarmed college students who hadn't even encountered a fist fight their whole lives, much less a firearm. The marshals were also empty-handed, wearing nothing more than a cloth armband. If the government had deployed ten times as many troops as there were protesters, say 30,000, and conducted a swift operation at midnight, the square could have changed hands within half an hour. In the long stretch of two weeks, there had been many such opportunities around midnight or early in the morning. It was entirely feasible for a different operation to be designed than the one actually carried out on June 3; that is, there could have been swift action at first limited to the square itself, during the midnight hours of a low-turnout day, when the surrounding crowds of demonstrators were thin or nonexistent. It could have been done without causing any deaths, just like in 1976.

For this conclusion to be convincing, we also need to address the issue of the crowds surrounding the square. Did the troops need to overcome the other supporting demonstrators around the square in order to get in? The answer is a straightforward no. The square was far away from major residential areas and university campuses. There was no chance that additional demonstrators from outside the square could have got there before swift action had long been completed.

The swarming crowds of June 3, reported to be more than a million, were generated by news of troop advances in the long hours between 8:00 p.m. on June 3 and the early morning of June 4. By then, a swift operation would have been out of the question if the troops had had to be moved from the outskirts of the city. So the second question is this: could the government have stationed enough troops, say 30,000 or more, right next to the square to accomplish the task? At first glance, the answer seemed to be an obvious no. At the outset of martial law, did the civilians not succeed in blocking the army's advances on the night of May 19–20? Did they also put up rigorous resistance against the June 3 evening advances, a resistance so successful that many troops experienced significant delays before reaching their destinations at or close to the square?

### More Than 50,000 Troops Were Already in Place to Be Used

But the sad truth of the matter is that the government had already managed to station large numbers of troops in the locations immediately next to the square before the confrontation between the advancing troops and the resisting citizens on June 3. Those so stationed included regular troops normally stationed there to protect government premises such as the Great Meeting Hall of the People, those transported by underground tunnels, and those who sneaked in wearing civilian clothes in the days between May 20 and June 3. How many of them were there?

On June 1, two parks next to the square – the Zhongshan Park and the Cultural Palace of the People – were closed to the public. They joined other surrounding places, such as the Historical Museum and the Great Meeting Hall, which were all closed to the public earlier for the stationing of troops. According to Li Peng, by 3:00 a.m. on June 2, at least 28,000 troops had formed an encirclement of the square, including 25,000 deployed to the Great Meeting Hall to the east of the square and the Public Security Ministry courtyard to the west, as well as 3,000 in the Beijing East Train Station to the south of the square.[106]

In his book *The Martial Law Troops in the June 4 Affair*, Wu Renhua documented earlier missions prior to or on June 2 by the Beijing Garrison, the 27th, 63rd, 65th, and 24th Group Armies, who transported large numbers of troops from outside. At 5:30 p.m. on May 26, the entire 13th Regiment of the Beijing Garrison set out from their base in Tongxian to enter Beijing. The soldiers and officers were divided into small groups to travel by train or by bus. They were all in disguise, wearing fashionable civilian clothes and resembling city youths or going workers to or from work. At 2:00 p.m. on the following afternoon, the regiment of about 1,500 troops arrived at their assigned destinations, including Zhongnanhai, the Beijing Garrison Headquarters, and the *People's Daily* buildings – all close to the square.[107]

In the same incognito fashion, the 27th Group Army sent multiple units into the city on June 2. These units included one artillery brigade, one logistics regiment, and one communications regiment, in addition to two full infantry divisions. They undoubtedly numbered more than 8,000, given the typical sizes of brigades, regiments, and divisions in the

Chinese army. The incognito operation started at 9:00 p.m. from nearby Daxing County. They took a route along Fengtai Avenue, Lianhuachi in Fengtai District, then Guanganmenwai Avenue, Xuanwu Gate, Heping Gate, Hufang Bridge, Zhushikou in Xuanwu District, and Qianmen Avenue in Chongwen District. The destination was the Great Meeting Hall of the People. Taking an approach of "multiple batches, small sizes, and large intervals," the troops wore plain clothes and moved on foot. Eight stations along the way were set up for co-ordination. Wang Xiaojing, a Beijing native, was put in charge of co-ordination for the 79th Infantry Division. For the machinery and supplies, civilian agencies of the Beijing government were called upon to provide trucks and buses.[108]

Similarly transported to arrive at the Great Meeting Hall before or on June 2 were the 188th Division of the 63rd Group Army and the 193rd and 3rd Divisions of the 65th Group Army. Counting these three divisions, the number of troops was another 10,000 or more. The Great Meeting Hall swarmed with people and living space was extremely tight. Soldiers slept all over the place, including hallways, bathroom floors, and windowsills, and on top of radiators.[109]

Such missions, while successful overall, did not go without glitches. One poorly disguised military truck of the 79th Division was intercepted by protesters on West Changan Avenue in the early morning of June 3. It carried five machine guns, more than 100 rifles, two sets of military radio equipment, and a large amount of ammunition. Thankfully, they were returned to the military after briefly coming under the control of the protesters. At about the same time, part of the 80th Division ran into resistance in Hufang Bridge, Zhushikou, and Taoranting. About 2,000 plainclothes troops were recognized and blocked. During the crash with crowds there, some soldiers and officers were injured, and many more fled the scene and took a detour to reach the Great Meeting Hall individually.[110] Among the least successful earlier attempts to transport troops might have been be the mission from Shunyi and Tongxian, two suburban counties, to the compound of the PSB headquarters next to the square. The 70th and 72nd Divisions, and the 7th Security Brigade of the 24th Group Army, were ordered to advance on the afternoon of June 2. It is curious that they did not disguise the troops in plain clothes, nor did the troops advance in small groups. They took advantage of the darkness of the night and walked on foot. But that proved to be difficult; after more than nineteen hours, only 400 or so had arrived at the PSB headquarters by 6:00 p.m. on June 3.[111]

Another major means for early deployment was through underground tunnels. These included the public subways and a network of secret military tunnels. According to Wu Renhua, by the night of June 2, the 65th Group Army of more than 10,000 troops had arrived in the Great Meeting Hall. They traveled not only above ground, but also through the tunnels. For example, its 3rd Security Division took the subway from Pingguoyuan to Zhongshan Park. Beijing's subway system had been shut down to the public since the declaration of martial law. From Zhongshan Park station they entered Zhongnanhai on foot, then used a secret underground train tunnel to reach the Great Meeting Hall. The double-tracked tunnel was specially designed and constructed for the central leaders to move between Zhongnanhai and the Great Meeting Hall, the so-called Leader Paths.[112]

In addition to the public subway and the Leader Paths, Timothy Brook suggests yet a third system that contributed to the elaborate tunnels underneath Beijing:

> A giant network of tunnels connects the downtown core with the city suburbs. This labyrinth was the result of Maoist guerrilla warfare transplanted to modern urban life. Following the rupture of Sino-Soviet relations in 1960, when China chose to turn its back on its imperious senior partner, the Chinese government invoked the specter of Soviet aerial bombing to revive its sagging popularity after several years of economic mismanagement. The entire population of Beijing was dragooned into volunteering labor to build this network of escape routes underneath their homes and offices. Beijing's subway, which opened in the mid-1970s, is linked to this system. The main tunnel of the underground defense system is wide enough for two trucks to drive abreast. It connects the Great Hall of the People, the center of the state administration on the west side of the Tiananmen Square, with the Beijing Garrison Command in the Fragrant Hills. Further out are located entrances in the countryside at which elderly peasants are posed as watchmen.[113]

It is puzzling why, in 1989, the government did not use the underground method more than it did. The 3rd Division's model of secret deployment seems to have been replicable for other troops: use underground rail to reach Zhongnanhai first, then move to locations next to the square. Yet the above-ground approach seems to have been preferred.

In summary, it is clear that large-scale simultaneous deployment on the ground could have been avoided. So could most of the shooting and killing. As amply documented by historian Wu Renhua and others, and confirmed by Li Peng and official sources, there were enough troops already stationed in Beijing to clear the square, if it was done swiftly and unexpectedly at night. If the advance of other troops from outside the city might still have been needed to control the city beyond the square, the government could have taken the square first before sending more troops into the city. That would have taken the steam out of the citizen resistance, whose goal was to "defend the square."

## Discussion and Conclusion

Why the scale and the manner of a military operation that was massive and spectacularly displayed? Previous scholars of Tiananmen have offered insightful speculations as to why the number of troops was so huge. In this chapter, I have demonstrated that the disproportionate use of military operations to end the Tiananmen movement was for display of power. The show itself was the purpose itself.

Seen from this perspective, we will do well to compare the 1989 military operation with the military parade, a common affair taking place on Changan Avenue and Tiananmen Square every major National Day. Deng had held one, just five years before in 1984; Jiang Zemin would hold another spectacular one five years after 1989 in 1994. The National Day parade as a military operation bears almost all the same key features as the 1989 military operation, and not just its location. In size it is as large as possible to show strength. Weaponry is shown. Troops are diverse. They must show that they are coherent and effective. For effect, their actions must be as conspicuous as possible.

Roger Ebert once wrote,

> The best martial arts movies have nothing to do with fighting and everything to do with personal excellence. Their heroes transcend space, gravity, the limitations of the body, and the fears of the mind. In a fight scene in a Western movie, it is assumed the fighters hate each other. In a martial arts movie, it's more as if the fighters are joining in a celebration of their powers.[114]

The climax of the June 3–4 operation may be best signified by a moment toward the end. "At 4:50 a.m. on June 4 in Tiananmen Square," wrote Wu Renhua, the consummate historian of the events, "Suddenly, from all possible directions, a barrage of flash bombs and tracer bullets were shot into the sky, reminding one of firework displays in a National Day celebration. The entire expanse of the square was at once illuminated with glares and flashes, as bright as the day."[115]

If the military operation was in fact a symbolic display of power, who owned the power? Who was the target audience? Why is such a display of power necessary, at such cost? The most obvious answer is that the government owned the power and the protesters were the target audience. The state not only crushed the protest with its military force but also showed its determination and readiness to use power for deterrence.

But the state that used the power here was not one person or one bloc. The leaders who joined forces in this military action were in conflict with each other, as I have taken pains repeatedly to show in the book. While the military power belonged to the state in name, Deng had the lion's share. Why did he decide to use, or to display, military force? We recall that the semi-retired supreme leader had been struggling with a renewed wave of contention from his rivals and his lieutenants; he tried to dismiss an incumbent general party secretary and appoint a new one of his choice. At his disposal was his grip on military power: he was the chair of the CMC; his right-hand man, Yang Shangkun, was in charge; and he enjoyed personal loyalty among the generals he had personally appointed – which came in handy. By dramatizing his military power through repression of the protest, Deng neutralized possible challenges before they took place.

# Part IV

# The Political Impact

In this last empirical chapter of the book, I will address the political developments that occurred after the 1989 Tiananmen crisis. Subsequent events provide further evidence for me to evaluate the three models. For example, examining what Deng did with his long-term reform plans, such as securing a political leadership loyal to his reforms, is helpful in gauging whether he made the Tiananmen decision to use military action for purposes other than ending the protest. Similarly, post-Tiananmen events are relevant to evaluating the two-way factionalism model. Did Deng's alliance with the conservatives last? If he switched back to rebuild a reformer's coalition, what does that say about the factionalism model?

Deng's leadership succession project was far from complete in 1989. Among other challenges, the new general secretary was still a work in progress. Jiang Zemin, a civilian all his life, needed Deng's support to cultivate a base in military in order to be in command. In the meantime, he was beholden by his other patrons, who were Deng's conservative rivals. Deng needed to help Jiang weather the ideological storms and to woo him to the reform side.

Deng succeeded both in strengthening Jiang and winning him over. To clear Jiang's rivals in the military, Deng removed his friend Yang Shangkun and Yang's brother from the CMC. To bring Jiang into his reform line, he launched a triumphant "Southern Tour" in 1992, an ideological campaign that swept the nation. A Deng–Jiang alliance was forged, and a long cycle of succession politics came to an end.

How Did the Politics of 1989 Contribute to Deng's Post-Tiananmen Success?

First, he succeeded in "changing horse" without incurring great damage. While Jiang's loyalty was dubious at the time, Deng was convinced by his reformer profile and forward-looking temperament. Had the conservatives prevailed in appointing their candidate, reform as Deng envisioned it would not have survived.

Second, Deng installed new reformers to many key positions, which again was made possible by his enhanced power following the Tiananmen decision. Li Ruihuan, then a party chief of Tianjin City and a tested reform leader, would play a critical role in supporting Deng's 1992 Southern Tour campaign and in urging Jiang Zemin to take the reform line.

Third, Deng's control of the military was reinforced further by the events at Tiananmen in 1989. After Tiananmen, he was able to afford to hand Jiang the CMC chairmanship as an important inducement in securing Jiang's loyalty.

# 10 Deng's Long Game
## 1989–1992

At the height of the Tiananmen movement, Deng appointed Jiang Zemin to replace Zhao Ziyang as the new party general secretary. In the months that followed the crackdown, Deng also passed over his chairmanship of the CMC to Jiang. But the political succession was still incomplete. Jiang's power remained nascent and needed to be shored up, especially in the realm of the military. More of a thorny issue is that Jiang's loyalty was split between Deng's reform wing and the conservatives. The situation could be seen through a series of political plays by Deng and his supporters, which culminated in yet another highly visible political contention in 1992 that was known as Deng's "Southern Tour." Jiang fell in with the reform line and became its champion, succumbing to a combination of pressure and enticement. As this chapter will show, Deng's victory over his political rivals in 1989 paved the way for his victory in 1992.

In this final empirical chapter, I will address the political developments that occurred after the events in Beijing in 1989. An account of these events will provide further support for my core argument about the 1989 crackdown. That is, Deng's main concern was not so much about the protest itself as about regaining control over political resistance within the leadership. His main goal was to ensure a new leadership that continued his reform agenda.

Given the fact that Deng repressed a liberal protest movement in collaboration with the conservatives, one would expect a post-Tiananmen China to take a conservative turn, as the two-way factionalism model would predict. Indeed, for a time, as the drumbeat of anticommunist revolutions from elsewhere in the world further alarmed the conservatives, Deng's reform was on trial. The conservatives repudiated it as deviating from socialism and hence as a "peaceful evolution" to capitalism. But once again, Deng proved to be above the two factions. He broke with the conservatives after Tiananmen and insisted that only carrying on further reform and reaping its economic results could prevent the system from falling. In his Southern Tour in 1992, Deng won a decisive victory, one made possible thanks to his earlier work in 1989.

This was Deng's long game: passing his power to a new generation of leaders who would be able to stay on and carry his reform program forward. His longevity obviously was an asset in his rivary with his opponents. Such good fortune had not been at all clear when he was called back to Beijing in 1974. Then aged seventy, Deng was in competition with Wang Hongwen, thirty-nine, to become Mao's successor.[1] At one point, when news of Deng's expanded portfolio reached the domain of Wang and his partners in the Gang of Four, Wang was reportedly exasperated and quipped, "Let us see what things will be like in ten years!"[2] Another matchless asset was his brilliant political mind. His fans included Mao, who said, "Deng Xiaoping is a man who excels in political affairs, and very few people can match him in that respect." On another occasion Mao noted, "Deng is a rare talent. He is known in both military and civilian circles for this. He is like a needle wrapped in cotton. He has ideas. He does not confront problems head-on. He can deal with difficult problems with responsibility. His mind is round and his actions are square."[3]

How does Deng's 1989 decision figure into his long game? To step into his shoes for a minute, we may see the following. Power transition, as a process described above, would not have been possible if he was no longer a supreme leader. More specifically, he needed to be able to choose Zhao Ziyang's replacement to his preference and to shape the composition of the SC to his satisfaction. Neither was possible without co-operation from his conservative rivals. His hold over the military would be a support and also serve as a deterrent against potential challenges – either from supporters of Zhao Ziyang or from those of Chen Yun. Furthermore, after Tiananmen, he needed his power, undiminished, to oversee the succession process in order for Jiang to become a strong leader in his own right. That was what he did. In the three years after Tiananmen, Deng used his expanded power to win over and strengthen the new party secretary, hence defeating his conservative rivals once and for all. In other words, it was Deng's need to maintain and even expand his political power that was the driving force behind his fateful decision to use the military in 1989.[4]

On September 4, 1989, three months after June 4, Deng Xiaoping summoned Jiang Zemin and a few others to his residence. There, Deng announced his "formal retirement." The mood of the day was witnessed as exceedingly cheerful. His daughter noted that on that morning Deng rose early and played with his youngest grandson in good spirits.[5] According to two historians' record, when the guests arrived and the small contingent of black sedans began filling the courtyard, the family's orchard was in full bloom. Colors of the season radiated from walnut, pomegranate, persimmon trees, and grapevines, all in their later stages of fruition.[6] A little later, four grandchildren would collectively present a card to congratulate Deng on his retirement; in a picture of him opening the envelop and perusing the card, the very healthy eighty-five-year-old gentleman wears a broad smile. Those in attendance dutifully feigned their surprise, then regret.[7]

To his audience that day, he cited the party's international image as his reason for retiring. That is, termination of life tenure in the party system would convey a progressive spirit. Besides that, there was another thing that he did not make as explicit: passing his position as CMC chairman on to Jiang Zemin, the newest successor. That was a major step in accepting Jiang into the "core" of the leadership and, just as importantly, turning him entirely to Deng's fold.[8] Deng ended his remarks by solemnly "proposing" Jiang as the new CMC chairman. Two months later a CC plenum was held to officiate both Deng's retirement and Jiang's military appointment.[9]

Yet Deng's withdrawal from the political scene was by no means complete. He seems to have been the first to allude to this at the meeting, noting, "After my retirement from formal duties, so long as I am still around, I could still serve some functions." On another occasion, he told Henry Kissinger, "I am still a citizen of the PRC, and a member of CCP. That means when needed I will render my service as an ordinary citizen and party member." He jocularly added, "Although you have stepped away from your duties as Secretary of State for a while, aren't you still busy with international business?"[10]

Indeed, by that time in 1989, Deng had only carried out the first few steps of his power succession project. Among other challenges, the new successor was still very much a work in progress. Jiang, who had never had any military ties, needed all the support he could harness to become the top leader of the military. Thus Deng had work to do to remove potential obstacles within the military and impart his power and prestige to Jiang. Second, Jiang was in a way still indebted to his conservative patrons, who had been bolstered by the outburst of anticommunist activities from Eastern Europe and the USSR after 1989. Deng needed to help Jiang weather the ideological storms and woo him to the reform side.

Deng succeeded on both counts – strengthening Jiang and winning him over. To make room for Jiang in the military, he removed his longtime loyal friend Yang Shangkun from the CMC, along with Yang's brother, another powerful figure in the military. Most momentously, in the winter of 1992, despite his old age, he embarked on the triumphant Southern Tour, going to cities as far as Shenzhen. He tirelessly held meetings and made speeches, campaigning for his reform agenda. At the same time, he launched ideological counterattacks and pushed back the antireform current from conservative camp. His storm swept the nation. Along the way, the younger conservatives, such as Li Peng and Song Ping, fell in line, their resistance weakened by the declining health or the deaths of their old patrons, such as Chen Yun and Li Xianniang. In the process, a Deng–Jiang alliance was forged, and a long cycle of succession politics came to an end.

## The Selection of Jiang Zemin

### Someone Else Was Favored by the Conservatives

At the time Deng decided to replace Zhao Ziyang, who was, or would become, the ideal candidate? Chen Yun and his conservative colleagues had their eyes set on Deng Liqun, the longtime ideologue. Although already in his seventies at the time, the younger Deng (no relation) had many advantages: his ties to Chen Yun and Li Xiannian, his well-acknowledged talent, and above all his ideological zeal. Deng Liqun was a quintessential defender of the socialist command economy and an ardent doubter of the reform agenda. After Hu Yaobang's dismissal in 1987, he was suggested by Wang Zhen as the replacement.[11] At the height of the student movement in 1989, according to his memoir, Deng Liqun was personally phoned by Chen Yun to hurry back to Beijing.[12]

Like his older patrons, Deng Liqun suffered during the Cultural Revolution. Afterwards he was also an early supporter of Deng Xiaoping's return to power who contributed to the unseating of Maoists. With the rare combination of a college degree and impeccable revolutionary credentials, he was seen as a highly accomplished "theorist" of the party dogma – Marxism–Leninism and Mao Zedong thought. His prestigious credentials included one as an editorial staff member in charge of publishing *Mao Zedong's Selected Works*. He was a strong and longtime advocate of Chen Yun's economic ideas. In 1980, as head of the policy institute of the party's secretariat, he pushed to publish *Selected Works of Comrade Chen Yun*. In 1980 he gave a series of four lectures in the Central Party School focusing on Chen Yun's economic theories, which was an instant sensation and amounted to an act of adulation of Chen Yun.[13]

In 1981 Deng Liqun was promoted to head the Propaganda Department of the CCP, a key position in the party system, and served there until 1987. For years, he guarded the purity of the party, acting as a point man for both Deng Xiaoping and Chen Yun. He fought propaganda battles against those who wanted to extend reform from the economic sector to the political realm, accusing them of "bourgeois liberalization" and "spiritual pollution." His main targets included first Hu Yaobang and then Zhao Ziyang. For Deng Xiaoping, he was useful in fending off too much liberalization in ideology and politics, but the elder Deng was also becoming increasingly weary of his inflexibility in upholding Chen Yun's planned economy. To Chen Yun, he was a valuable warrior in many important political arenas. In earlier chapters I covered his fights with Hu Yaobang and Zhao Ziyang.[14]

If the conservatives were eager for a course correction in Deng's reform agenda, there were no better political opportunities than those provided by the Tiananmen protests and the international anticommunist wave that followed. And there was no one better than Deng Liqun to articulately translate the frustrations and desires of Chen Yun and others of the old guard. While Deng Xiaoping was no fan of the Western political system, he considered the rhetoric of Deng Liqun a hyperbole that was employed to stop his reform efforts. Deng Xiaoping would do all he could to prevent Deng Liqun from becoming his successor.

Little Deng was not able to retain any official title in the party leadership after the 1989 reshuffle, but he did not stop engaging in the ideological debate. Indeed, he went full force to catalog what had gone wrong under Zhao Ziyang in an attempt to invigorate the conservative cause against Deng's reform.[15] For example, in August 1989, during a sojourn in a guesthouse in Shandong, he gave four lengthy lectures, in which he ostensibly repudiated Zhao's policy, but his real target was Deng's reform. Deng Liqun knew too well that his lectures would be recorded and circulated, and hence could go on to serve as the theoretical foundation for future debates to unfold. He meticulously reviewed more than eleven areas of Zhao's behavior and policies. In language reminiscent of that used in the bygone years of Maoist repudiation campaigns, he declared in his lectures that the "essence" of Zhao's policies was to undermine the socialist nature of the system. He also deployed what was often thought of as Maoism's trump card: strong class analysis. He accused Zhao of being a representative of a new social class of Chinese "who eat foreigners' meals, mind foreigners' business, and speak for foreigners' sake:"

> Behind the emergence of a character like Zhao Ziyang exists the foundation of a social class. In the meantime he works to cultivate, support, and develop this class foundation. He then serves as its agent. Comrade [Li] Xiannian once said to me and Comrade Chen Yun: "during the Cultural Revolution Chairman Mao might have been wrong in asserting the existence of capitalist roaders within the party. But given what he has done in these years, does Zhao Ziyang act like a capitalist roader?"[16]

According to Deng Liqun, the primary danger was the end of the socialist system at the hands of enemy forces. He concluded his long lectures by raising the specter of "peaceful evolution":

> The American policy of peaceful evolution, in its original formulation by [Dean] Acheson, places its hope on democratic/individualistic elements in China, who in turn promulgate more like them. On the surface, they seem to be separate individuals or separate groups, but they surely will carry out their ideas to change this world, and

change this country, just as Chairman [Mao] observed. They were the activists of bourgeois liberalization. Once they form a social force, they will wage protests and cause turmoil in all realms, including politics, economy, and ideology, aiming at turning socialism into capitalism.[17]

### Jiang Zemin's Qualities and Connections

If Deng Liqun was judged mostly by what he said, another next-generation leader left much less of a paper trail. Jiang Zemin endeared himself to the old guard mainly by what he did. Rare among his peers, he was seen to have achievements which could appeal to both sides: he had been an effective municipal chief faithful to the reform and opening policies; he had also distinguished himself in his handling of two waves of student protests to the fancy of the conservatives. In other words, he was the embodiment of the essence of Dengism – liberal in the economic realm but conservative in the political domain. Also in his favor was his prime position as the mayor and the party chief of Shanghai, where the elder power holders spent their annual winter vacations. Jiang played host many times and personally charmed the old comrades, remarkably including Deng Xiaoping, Chen Yun, and Li Xiannian.

A grandson of a physician-turned-merchant, Jiang was born in 1926 (hence he was a young sixty-three in 1989) in Yangzhou City, Jiangsu, a trendy region known for its modern contact with Western education and art. He attended a Western-style school from childhood, and was bright enough to do well in the examinations and get into a competitive high school.[18] At age thirteen, he was adopted by the widow of his uncle, who reportedly died for the anti-Japanese resistance cause. Thus, in certain quarters, he would later be counted as a son of revolutionary martyr, a distinction valued greatly by the surviving revolutionary old guard. He himself joined the underground CCP in 1946 as a student activist in Shanghai.

He graduated with a degree in electrical engineering from the renowned Shanghai Jiaotong University. Like Deng Liqun, Jiang was among a rare breed of politicians who had both impeccable revolutionary credentials and a university degree. His English instruction must have started as early as his childhood. As head of state in the 1990s, he carried on conversations in English with Western journalists, such as Mike Wallace of CBS. In the early 1950s, he was sent to study in the USSR for a year, so he spoke Russian too. Legend has it that, in a late 1970s visit to Romania during the Cultural Revolution, he worked very hard to improve his Romanian.[19] On a visit to Chile in 2001, he gave a forty-minute speech in Spanish.[20]

A leading expert observes that Jiang had a typical *haipai* (literally translated as "ocean-style" or figuratively understood as "Shanghai-style") personality. *Haipai* traits include an expansive, outgoing style bordering on the unctuous; an ability to handle oneself to good advantage in public arenas; a soft spot for lavish ceremonies and big feasts; and a concern with public relations rather than substance. A polyglot, Jiang lost no opportunity in demonstrating his skillful use of languages and dialects, including English, Russian, Romanian, Japanese, and Cantonese.[21] His talents and larger-than-life personality were in some ways a reflection of his open-mindedness, a fact that did not escape Deng's notice. Together, they show his intense interest in the world that existed outside China and in modernity and development. Later, under his rule, China was urged to "catch up with the times." He was criticized, and at times mocked, for being overly conscious of his international image.[22]

He was appointed mayor of Shanghai in 1984. Then, he quickly doubled as party chief. Under his stewardship, the largest city in the country did well. He overhauled the unprofitable state-owned enterprises and achieved good results. The living standards of residents improved. The 1986 wave of student protest started from a university in the south and quickly spread to Shanghai. Mayor Jiang personally engaged student protesters and debated with them, but he did not concede an inch of ground to students. His performance was praised highly by the leaders in Beijing, so much so that his exploits of handling student protest was made into a television program, shown to the top leaders in Zhongnanhai. His hard-liner reputation on the issue of student protest was elevated to new heights in the first weeks of the 1989 protest after he fired the editor of a Shanghai newspaper who bypassed censorship and published reports defying the party's control.[23]

### Acceptable to both Camps

This strong record and credentials, however, might not have been the deciding factor. His ambiguous political profile – he seemed to belong to both camps – made him stand out among a half dozen or so leaders who were relatively young, well-educated, and party members since before 1949. None of the remaining four SC members after Zhao Ziyang's dismissal fit the bill, for they were deeply affiliated with one of the two factions. Premier Li Peng (sixty-one) and First Vice Premier Yao Yilin (seventy-two) were Chen Yun's men, while Qiao Shi and Hu Qili were previous allies of Zhao's. Among them, Yao Yilin was once proposed to replace Hu Yaobang, but Deng reportedly rejected the idea outright on account of Yao's age.[24]

Another group of potential contenders included two Politburo members, Chen Xitong (fifty-nine), mayor of Beijing, and Li Ruihuan (fifty-five), mayor of Tianjin. Again, their chances were diminished by their well-known factional affiliations. While as Beijing mayor Chen Xitong might have scored points with Deng with his hard-line "reports" that led to the April 26 editorial, he was also known as deeply connected to Li Peng. Li Ruihuan, on the other hand, was Deng Xiaoping's favorite. He faithfully carried out reform measures in his city and achieved much. He was effective in handling the student protest without showing weakness. It was reported that he was Deng's first choice, yet he had no support from Chen Yun and Li Xiannian. As a compromise, Deng was later able to make Li Ruihuan a new member of the SC.[25]

Chen Yun and Li Xiannian's recommendation of Jiang is well documented. As described earlier, the idea of removing Zhao Ziyang and identifying a replacement came very early. The old men on both sides were deliberating the question even before the student protest reached fever pitch with the hunger strike. The earliest indication on record was an interview between Yang Shangkun and Deng Xiaoping on the afternoon of May 11 at Deng's residence. Deng transitioned their conversation onto this topic delicately and imperceptibly. He first asked Yang's opinions on the mayors of Beijing, Tianjin, and Shanghai on how they managed their cities during the student protest, to which Yang gave a very strong endorsement of Li Ruihuan of Tianjin. He did so perhaps because he knew that Deng was fond of Li. He also praised Jiang Zemin for his firm hand in Shanghai. At this point, Deng said,

> After Jiang Zemin rectified the situation at the *World Economic Herald*, Comrade Chen Yun said to me, "Everyone should learn from Jiang Zemin in handling student protest." [Li] Xiannian also told me, "Jiang Zemin upholds the Four Principles, and at the same time supports Reform and Opening. He is sharp politically, strong in party discipline, and capable of seeing the entire picture."[26]

Li Xiannian apparently took pride in his contribution to Jiang's selection. The compilers of the *Li Xiannian Chronology* make a point to note in the May 20, 1989, entry: "Nominated Jiang Zemin as the party secretary of the Central Committee of the Chinese Communist Party."[27]

### Real Military Power as a Work in Progress

After Deng handed the CMC chairmanship over to Jiang in late 1989, a less formal, yet equally important, process started. That is, Deng would gradually ease out of the position of supreme leadership for Jiang to fill in. As this chapter discusses, the process ran in fits and starts, and clarity emerged only after Deng's Southern Tour in 1992.

One of the challenges facing Jiang as the new CMC chair was how could he command real influence in the military.

### Military Power as an Essential Ingredient in Supreme Leadership

What does it take for one to become a supreme leader? Conventional thinking often points to personal charisma. In the cases of Mao Zedong and Deng Xiaoping and their rise within the communist system, their revolutionary credentials are also cited.[28] By those standards, Jiang Zemin would fall short.

Scholars also recognize the institutional nature of the position. That is, power derives from the unique position of someone who is able to simultaneously control the three major institutions – the party, the state, and the military. They trace the source of the trajectories of Mao and Deng this way. By extension, as I explained earlier, we see the precarious position of Liu Shaoqi, Lin Biao, Hu Yaobang, and Zhao Ziyang, all of whom were entrusted with only one of the three branches of power.[29]

With that insight, the "becoming" part of supreme leadership was a process of obtaining more and more controls that could be managed and engineered. Indeed, both the rise of Mao and the rise of Deng owed more to such processes than to their preordained charisma or credentials. In Mao's case, it was in the early 1940s in Yanan;[30] in Deng's case, it was in the years following Mao's death in the later 1970s.[31]

Deng's plan for Jiang Zemin to become the "core" – his euphemism for supreme leader – focused more on the second understanding of power accumulation. In other words, he needed to help Jiang become the real leader in all three domains. Particularly important was the military, a domain where Jiang was weak. "Institutional authority and personal authority are two preconditions underlying a leader's exercise of power in China's elite politics," wrote a leading expert.[32] According to historian Gao Hua, Mao built his cult of followers not only by changing formal rules – he terminated the three-person committee in the top leadership and replaced it with himself alone, for example – but also by building personal networks with purges and promotions.[33] In Deng's case, according to Yang Jisheng, he wasted no time before appointing his own military generals once he had reached the top in 1978.[34]

The cultivation of the supreme leader's personal power was aided by formal rules and informal conventions governing China's party–military relationship. First, the principle that "the gun is under the party's control" is applied to the utmost advantage of the leader. The "party" in this context is no longer an organization, but the leader himself. According to You Ji, even in the Deng Xiaoping era when collective leadership was hailed as a fundamental principle, major decisions on military matters did not come from the Politburo or the Standing Committee, but from the supreme leader alone; first Deng, then Jiang. For instance, promotions of senior officers above the divisional level are not valid until signed off by the CMC chair. The same goes for the movement of troops, which is strictly controlled by the CMC chair. So while the party's civilian activities are based on collective leadership, the chair of the CMC, in contrast, has unchallenged personal power in appointing the top brass, overseeing troop deployments, and approving budget allocations.[35]

### Jiang Zemin's Resources and Barriers in Amassing Real Military Power

Possessing the CMC chairmanship was a great start for Jiang to become a commander in chief with real power. Although theoretically the CMC was under the Politburo, in reality it operated beyond the Politburo's reach, a convention honed under previous supreme leaders. According to You Ji, the long-established practice can be traced back to Mao, who deliberately separated the state and the military under the formula of *zhengzhiju yi zheng, junwei yi jun* ("the Politburo's realm is state affairs and the CMC's is military affairs"). Deng maintained this division and enjoyed full discretion in military affairs without being beholden to other leaders. Following this convention, as the new CMC chair Jiang would be able to purge or promote senior generals by himself.[36] Furthermore, because of his power in the party-state system, the leader has a unique ability to make bargains in the military's interest. The military could not have found a better advocate in someone who combined powers as party general secretary and state president.[37]

There were hurdles ahead for Jiang, however – for example, from the current powerholders of the military other than Deng himself. Yang Shangkun was the executive chair and permanent secretary of the CMC, overseeing General Political Department (GPD), the General Logistics Department (GLD), General Staff Headquarters (GSH), and other top organs.[38] Later in 1989, after Zhao's downfall, he was made the first vice chair.[39] Over the years, untold numbers of generals were promoted under his wing. A blatant indication of his personal power in the military was the meteoric rise of his brother Yang Baibing.[40]

In 1988, the younger Yang was made director of the GPD and one of the six CMC members, a select echelon which included Deng Xiaoping, Yang

Shangkun, and Zhao Ziyang. During the 1989 Tiananmen affair, Yang Baibing was commander in chief of the martial law troops and reaped accolades. In the reshuffle following Deng's retirement, Yang Baibing was made permanent secretary of the CMC, ranked next to his brother in the committee. The domination of the Yang brothers was so deep that the phrase "Yang Family Army" was widely known both within and outside the military. Before Deng announced his retirement from the CMC, rumors circulated that Yang Shangkun would become the next chair.

Overall, Jiang was slow in gaining traction in the military, at least in the beginning. There were pronouncements emanating from military quarters questioning the legitimacy of his succession. Reports even suggested that Yang Baibing held secret PLA senior staff meetings behind Deng's back and prepared plans to maintain order in the event of Deng's death.[41]

### Jiang Zemin Pulled by Both Sides

Deng's succession project was far from complete with Jiang's appointment in 1989. Given Jiang's conflicting patronage ties to both Deng and Chen Yun, there is little in his background, conviction, or talent to tell which way he would lean and how he would actually manage affairs. Politicians act as the politics of the times dictate; Jiang would not be an exception. Hence, Deng needed to pull Jiang over, which entailed fighting with and fending off antireform currents from conservative rivals.

### *The Post-Tiananmen Assault on Dengist Reform*

Deng's reform faced renewed headwinds in the wake of June 4, 1989. Historical events converged to present unprecedented openings for conservatives waging their assaults. At home, there seemed to be no better exhibit than the Tiananmen movement to show the danger of liberal subversion. By dismissing Zhao Ziyang, Deng seems to have conceded that the overall direction under his lieutenant was not exactly on the right track. Abroad, news from Eastern Europe and Soviet Union was equally troubling. The sequence of government collapses emboldened conservative voices in faraway China. By the time of the failed putsch in the USSR in late 1991, warning against "peaceful evolution" reached a fever pitch.

As international communism descended into turmoil, Chen Yun and his men pushed the debate to new heights. They forced a referendum in the propaganda realm on the nature of the ongoing reform. "Is the reform surnamed Capitalist or Socialist?" they questioned. The philosophical-sounding debate in fact would bear actual policy consequences. For example, should the special economic zone (SEZ), as a cutting-edge reform model, be abolished or continued? If Chen Yun's side prevailed, there would be no official decision to expand the SEZ model to Shanghai, the Chinese stock market, or China's entry into the WTO.

Politically, the debate was relevant, as officials were slated for the upcoming 1992 party congress. If the conservatives won the debate, then Jiang Zemin would be a party chief leading a new crop of cadres who would overall be against reform, which would in turn nudge him away from Deng.

As early as June 1989, prominent party newspapers – such as the *People's Daily* and the *Guangming Daily* – began to publish op-eds criticizing the so-called "cat theory," not so obliquely targeting Deng. Inspired by a new wave of "Mao Zedong fever," these articles held up Mao's socialist ideas as banners and attempted to discredit Deng's reform policy.[42] Deng Liqun delivered his guesthouse lectures in August of the same year, repudiating Zhao Ziyang and warning of "peaceful evolution."[43]

The attack intensified after the abortive Soviet coup in August 1991 and the subsequent disintegration of the Soviet Union. To Chen Yun, "the principal lesson for China was that the CPSU had failed to grasp class struggle." The following month, Chen's son Chen Yuan joined two other authors and published an article in the *China Youth Daily* entitled "China's Realistic Countermeasures and Strategic Choices after the Drastic Changes in the Soviet Union." At the same time, the *People's Daily* printed another article, which suggests a need for a "stimulant to wake people from their dreams in which Westerners are angels who will rescue China."[44]

In December 1991, in the 8th Plenum of the party's 13th Central Committee, the conservatives prevailed on three decisions: initiating a campaign of "learning socialism" in rural areas; confirming the Central Party School's criticism of Li Ruihuan, a reformer ally of Deng; and abolishing the SEZs.[45]

At another meeting in January 1992, a reformer's proposal was attacked by Deng Liqun: "When a communist party's propaganda department does not publicize the basic theory of Marxism–Leninism–Mao Zedong thought, what class does it represent?" Wang Renzhi, another conservative, joined in with the retort: "We should not turn the Propaganda Department into a production and construction propaganda team, and the duty of the Propaganda Department is to publicize the theory and spirit of Marxism–Leninism–Mao Zedong thought."

Amid this rancor, Deng himself, however, remained staunch in defending his reform, and he even suggested removing those who were not, including those who complied with reform in public but boycotted it and acted otherwise in private; those who did not quite understand the party's guideline, which took economic construction as its center, and therefore did not conscientiously implement this principle; and those who were indifferent to the economic development of their own departments or areas and did no practical work.[46]

### Jiang Zemin Seems to Waver

"Under that circumstance, Jiang Zemin was not yet a political strongman," wrote Yang Jisheng in his *Political Struggle in China's Reform Era:*

> Having been put into the position of party general secretary, he had to gingerly perform a balancing act between the two conflicting camps of power. He would tilt to whichever side was stronger at the moment. In the time after June 4, the leftist (conservative) side was not only strong, but also active. Jiang Zemin then said and did a great deal that pleased the leftist side.[47]

He did so by signaling in his speeches. For example, while Deng and the reformers often stressed the need for an open and free space for private enterprise, Jiang took a different stance at the beginning of his tenure, proposing to "ruin them until their house is upside down and their possession is naught" in cases of illegal activity. While Deng and his followers were critics of Stalin, Jiang recycled Mao's admiration for Lenin and Stalin, referring to them, following Mao, as "two indispensable knives." While the hallmark of post-Mao politics was the undoing of Mao's class struggle, Jiang revived the old ghost by saying, "at this time in history, the focus of class struggle is between the Four Fundamental Principles and bourgeois liberalization." Jiang also validated a conservative cry by endorsing the idea of "Anti-Peaceful Evolution" study programs. For another program along the same lines in the countryside, he even proposed using Hunan Province for a pilot run.[48]

### Deng Wages Counterattacks

The assault waged from the leftists (conservatives) did not go unanswered. For an authoritarian regime, the back-and-forth was extraordinarily lively.[49] When Deng spent the 1991 Chinese New Year (January) in Shanghai, through his daughter Deng Lin, he instructed the *Jiefang Daily*, the Shanghai Municipal Party Committee's organ, to publish four serial articles under the penname "Huang Fuping." Based on Deng's remarks, the polemics were designed to urge further reform and opening up the economy.[50] Later writers attribute two memorable passages of Deng's original remarks to a reportedly unpleasant meeting with Chen Yun:

> Some comrades always equate the planned economy with socialism, and the market economy with capitalism ... Remember, planning or market is only a matter of resource allocation, hence by no means the benchmark to distinguish socialism from capitalism. There is planning in capitalism; and market in socialism.

On the matter of opening up, we must have another emancipation of minds. In the 1990s Shanghai needs to take big strides, with innovative ideas, courage to take risks, and do something that has never been done ... For example, we must aim at building [Pudong, Shanghai] into a "socialist Hong Kong," and supply the special policies that befit a free-trade port. They include the establishment of the Pudong Development Zone [a new SEZ], its tax exemption provisions, and free human flow. If we are mired in the debate whether the surname is Capitalism or Socialism, we will surely lose these golden opportunities.[51]

Underscoring the political implication of the ideological debate, Huang Fuping ended the series with the article entitled "Reform and Opening Up Call for a Great Many Cadres with both Talent and Ideas."[52]

### The Conservatives Push Back

The Huang Fuping articles were hailed by many among the intellectuals as the most earthshaking event since June 4 and were branded by overseas media as a "Northern Expedition for Deng's Reform and Opening Up." But they encountered vehement pushback and failed to shake up the political status quo as Deng had intended. Beijing's leftist ideologues launched an attack on them through the *Jiefang Daily* as well. The Central Propaganda Department, headed by conservative director Wang Renzhi and Xu Weicheng, began investigating the origin of the articles, and the *People's Daily* and the *Guangming Daily* were mobilized to refute them. The "Surname Debate" ensued.[53] In an article entitled "Can We Avoid Asking Whether the Surname Is 'Socialism' or 'Capitalism' in Reform and Opening Up?", the author writes,

Under the condition of avoiding asking the question whether it is socialism or capitalism, there indeed exists a group of individuals who attempt to direct Reform and Opening Up in the capitalist direction ... [They] advocate privatization and the market in the economy, the multi-party system and parliamentarism in politics, and pluralism in ideology, sending the cause of socialist Reform and Opening Up to a dead end.[54]

In November 1991, when Li Peng was in Shanghai participating in the opening ceremony for the Nanpu bridge and meeting with senior officials, he criticized the Huang Fuping articles by saying they mistakenly led people to think it was a new message from the (party) center.[55]

### Deng Forces Jiang's Hand: The Southern Tour

Jiang Zemin did not really have a choice but to hold to Deng's side. If he were to continue to oblige his conservative patrons, in the climate of 1990–1992 he would have to do things that Deng did not approve. While he mentioned "class struggle," promoted training programs to "counter peaceful evolution," sanctioned socialist education initiatives, wavered on taking up new reform measures, and so on, all these did not mean he had decided to join Chen Yun's camp. He might just have needed a grace period to find his footing. The last thing he could afford was to betray Deng Xiaoping.

From Deng's perspective, he had given Jiang significant power and ample space to exercise it. He not only transferred official titles to him, but also promoted the idea of having a "core" in the Party Center, and unequivocally named Jiang as that core person. In the meantime, he disappeared from public life and refrained from giving instructions behind the scenes. By his own standard, he had kept his promise that, if he did "something useful" after his retirement, he would do it "as an ordinary citizen and an ordinary party member."[56] Even when he found he had weighty remarks to make – that is, those that would carry monumental historical impact – he strove to say them in private settings, hoping somehow to be heard. For example, his reaction to the aborted Soviet coup in 1991 was made in a conversation with Chen Yun. His reform advocacy in early 1991 was given in closed sessions with local leaders. His ideas found an outlet in the form of articles published in a local newspaper authored by someone with a penname, hence the "Huang Fuping" affair in the *Jiefang Daily*.[57]

### Deng's Southern Tour

That state of affairs lasted until the winter of 1992, when Deng embarked on the historically known "Southern Tour." The narrative is now well known. Accompanied by his daughter Deng Rong, his wife, and other family members, Deng began a southbound journey by train on January 17, 1992. He made a brief stop in Wuhan, and two days later arrived in Shenzhen, in the famed Special Economic Zone. There the new city had been thriving on all things unconventional by the orthodox standard of socialism – foreign investment, private ownership, a stock market, free labor, and so on. Everywhere he went, he praised the economic achievements and not so subtly rebutted the critics of reform. He included Zhuhai, Shunde, and Zhongshan in his destinations, all of which are experimental development zones in the mode of Shenzhen. Everywhere he went, Deng was warmly received and dutifully accompanied by local leaders, normally the first secretary of the local jurisdiction. The local party chiefs were no doubt delighted when their work was praised. Deng ended his trip and was back Beijing on February 20.[58]

In his remarks to the local leaders, Deng's messages were loud and clear: the market reform experiments exemplified by Shenzhen were a huge success for all to see; the country's new era should not reverse such policies and should instead expand them to other regions of the country; the ongoing economic reforms were undoubtedly "socialist" because the means used in capitalist societies could be adopted by socialist China to develop socialist economies, and those who were against such reforms or ineffective in implementing them should be removed from the ranks of the leadership or the bureaucracy. He emphatically warned, "while we should watch out for the danger from the right, at this time the main source of danger comes from the left." These remarks constituted a set of pointed and systematic rejoinders to the leftist assault on reforms that were then prevailing in official media.[59]

Deng's motive was just as loud and clear – to remove obstacles to his reform agenda. His reform program had encountered significant setbacks, which were incited and helped by news from Eastern Europe and the Soviet Union. The leftist theorists in the surname debate had in effect branded his reform capitalist in nature. A proposal to abolish SEZs was made by thirty-five senior leaders in a party plenum, one month before his trip.[60] Pointedly, he suggested that the SEZ reform measure was in fact only in its infancy – he would like to build "hundreds more of Shenzhen," plus a national stock market and the entry of China into the WTO. Before the tour, Deng and his supporters such as "Huang Fuping" had failed to make traction. Deng hoped to give the system a jolt.

Through this unconventional move, Deng's Southern Tour achieved spectacular results. There was an initial embargo on his speeches in the national media. In early March, a few regional papers published photographs of the trip, and China Central TV (CCTV) broadcast a documentary about it. Later in March, the *People's Daily* and the Xinhua News Agency republished a long feature that was previously reported in Shenzhen. It started a media frenzy and the entire political system jumped onto it. The tour would be remembered as one of the most significant moments in the history of the CCP. In the months between the tour and the 14th Party Congress in October of that year, the old guard leftists – such as Chen Yun and Li Xiannian – fell into silence, along with their ideologues, such as Deng Liqun. The leadership structure reconstituted at the 14th Party Congress featured a full cast of reformers. Remaining holdover conservatives, such as Li Peng and Song Ping, had to fall into the new reform line and publicly declare their allegiance. There was even talk about a systematic purge of leftist elements in the system, which was reportedly stopped by Deng.[61]

*Victory Thanks to Jiang and the Post-Tiananmen Standing Committee*

Deng's Southern Tour was not necessarily going to be spectacular. It could have been totally ignored or had very limited impact. The tour could have been reported only locally or by overseas channels. In fact, that was precisely what happened in the first months of Deng's journey, as the propaganda machine was heavily controlled by Chen Yun loyalists at the time. In that case, the tour would not have changed the course of politics. Yet it did. Why?

Most existing accounts take on a celebratory tone and narrate the story as though it was a miracle from the Bible. But if we see Deng for what he was at the time, we see a political player rather than God – he had to try hard to influence other players and make his way. As a former leader with no official title and who had been invisible to the public for over two years, he faced incredible odds. He was still resourceful, but he also had deficits. It is safe to say it was his last "gamble of a lifetime"; he was turning eighty-eight that year.

There were three factors that worked in Deng's favor. In retrospect, these factors ensured Deng's resounding victory, which also helped Deng's effort to bring Jiang Zemin into the fold and once again reaffirm China's political course of reform.

The first factor in Deng's favor was the reform-friendly nature of the Standing Committee, which was newly reconstituted after Tiananmen. This once again underscores the effectiveness of his forceful handling of the Tiananmen affair and subsequent personnel rearrangements. As was argued above, it was critically important for Deng to have Jiang Zemin, rather than someone like Deng Liqun, in charge. Jiang was a reformer in character, if not yet in his new role. Among the five members of the Standing Committee, he managed to appoint two other clear-cut reformers: Qiao Shi – formerly a close ally of Zhao Ziyang's – and Li Ruihuan – Deng's own first choice to replace Zhao Ziyang. The other two members were Li Peng and Song Ping. Hence, the makeup of the SC would be a reformer majority once Jiang had made up his mind.

The Standing Committee led by Jiang Zemin did make positive signs toward the tour early on. In a meeting on February 12, near the end of Deng's tour, an SC meeting passed a resolution to endorse Deng's "important remarks." Four of the five members – including Jiang, Li Peng, Qiao Shi, and Li Ruihuan – went on record expressing their support.

Yet the endorsement from the highest level, by itself, did not become a clear-cut party directive on how to handle the propaganda work of the event, and at work was resistance from the conservative camp at all levels. The content of the SC's resolution was not made public, although its "spirit" was somewhat conveyed through the propaganda system. However, the *People's Daily*, criticized by a Deng Liqun loyalist, resisted openly endorsing even the "spirit," although it was then duly corrected by Li Ruihuan, the SC member in charge of propaganda work. Gradually, the party's leading news outlet published two articles on February 23–24 calling for accelerated reform and opening up. One article asserted that China's past refusal to make use of capitalism's strong points had been the result of leftist errors.[62]

As though to challenge the Standing Committee as the sole power center, thirty-five of the highest-ranking conservative leaders (including Chen Yun, Li Xiannian, Deng Liqun, and Wang Zhen) convened toward the end of February, and signed a letter addressed to Deng. The letter alleged that the party's development had departed from the socialist path, urging Deng to oppose "peaceful evolution" and to ensure the socialist nature of any reform and opening policies. Taking a cue from this pronouncement, a deputy director of the Propaganda Department ordered the *People's Daily* to run a series of articles on the subject of "socialist spiritual civilization." The order was quickly countermanded by Li Ruihuan.[63]

### The Shadow of the Military, Again

The second factor favorable to Deng was a trump card he still held. Who else could help Jiang the most to establish himself? Deng held in his pocket the ultimate prize which Jiang coveted: the number one position in the military, which meant real power. Although Deng had already passed on to Jiang his CMC title more than two years earlier, Jiang would not have full control as long the Yang brothers were still in the CMC. But understandably Deng could only afford to do so if Jiang had proved himself to be reliable as Deng's man.

As a third factor, the military worked as a negative inducement in the meantime: the shadow of another military intervention. Jiang must have known the possibility from knowing the CCP history: the appointment or dismissal of a party chief had ultimately been up to the person who controlled the military. Wang Hongwen was defeated by Deng because of Deng's military credentials. Jiang Qing was arrested after Mao died in the operation led by Marshall Ye Jianying. Hua Guofeng was made a transitional figure, losing to Deng, who commanded loyalty from the generals. More recent cases include the dismissals of Hu Yaobang and Zhao Ziyang.

The former CMC chair's power should not be belied by his avuncular and tourist-like appearances with children and grandchildren in tow. An astute observer discerned an undercurrent beneath the surface:

Although he was no longer the CMC chair, he had the loyal Yang brothers to charge the army for him. During the course of Deng's Southern Tour, Yang Shangkun always appeared by his side, while Yang Baibing was alertly holding the button for military operations for him. When Deng was in Shenzhen, Yang Shangkun and Deng Xiaoping appeared in front of the media many times.

When Deng ended his tour, he made a stop in Shanghai. Yang Shangkun was also there, accompanying Deng among the leaders of Shanghai's party, government, and military on this particular New Year's Eve. To accompany the moment, Yang Baibing made announcements published in the *PLA Daily* that the People's Liberation Army must "safeguard the imperial vessel and protect its journey" for the reform.[64]

The story of Deng's Southern Tour ended with the conclusion of something else: Jiang clarified his political orientation and firmly aligned himself with Deng's reform. In early March, as an indication that Jiang Zemin had made a clean break with the conservatives, the Politburo formally endorsed Deng's remarks and identified leftism as the principal danger. According to Richard Baum, Yang Shangkun and Jiang Zemin led the pro-reform forces in the meeting. Yang claimed to speak on behalf of Deng and, in no subtle way, conveyed his authority as a military leader. He admonished his colleagues to rally around Jiang Zemin as the core of the Central Committee leadership.

For his part, Jiang issued a self-criticism acknowledging that, in recent years, he had not promoted reform and opening up with sufficient rigor. He urged those conservative politicians to embrace Deng's political vision and start self-criticism. The two speeches produced immediate effects. The conservative members of the Politburo began to issue, one by one, their own critiques of themselves. These included Yao Yilin, Song Ping, Li Ximing, Chen Xitong, and Wang Renzhi.[65]

Jiang proceeded to finally establish himself in the military with Deng's full support. After the Southern Tour, Deng wasted no time before changing the military leadership to bolster Jiang. He first secured Yang Shangkun's promise to retire from the CMC on the account of Yang's age of eighty-five. Then, in the days leading up to the 14th Party Congress, scheduled to open in October 1992, Deng sent a letter to recommend that Yang Baibing be dropped from the CMC (compensated by a plum promotion to the Politburo).[66] In their steads, three longtime Deng loyalists were added to the CMC: Liu Huaqing and Zhang Zhen, two aging generals who "had neither ambitions nor any interest in ideological disputes," and Wang Ruilin, Deng's longtime personal aide. These new appointments were made to reinforce Jiang Zemin, who added his own effort to consolidate power, including measures to increase military spending and promoting his own generals.[67]

## Discussion and Conclusion

Deng's victory in 1989 was partial at first. Jiang Zemin's selection owed as much to a few conservative patrons, including Deng's chief policy rivals Chen

Yun and Li Xiannian. Jiang had to serve both Deng and Chen Yun, the "two submits." The conservative push was strong, aided by the unfavorable international environment in 1989 and in the following years. News of communism falling elsewhere revived debates in China on the ideological nature of Deng's reform. The catchword of the time was "peaceful evolution," which warned that China would slowly but surely abandon socialism.

This time, Deng did not contemplate firing Jiang Zemin. He decided to invest more in Jiang, using a combination of sticks and carrots. Deng's point men, who were in charge of the nation's propaganda, waged a pro-reform campaign and promoted Deng's newest assertion that "the real danger does not come from the right [reform] but from the left [the Maoist past]." This campaign was reiterated by various state-run newspapers that were controlled by the army, signaling support from that department. As a carrot, Deng helped Jiang establish and grow his standing within the military, by retiring the Yang brothers – Yang Shangkun, Deng's own right-hand man, and his brother, General Yang Baibing. Jiang fell into the reform line and became its staunchest champion ever after. The "twin summit politics" and the related conservative–reformer division all but ended, with Chen Yun fading from the scene.

How did the politics of 1989 contribute to Deng's post-Tiananmen success?

First, it was critical for Deng's ability to appoint Jiang Zemin as the new general secretary. While Jiang was chosen as a compromise and his loyalty was dubious at the time, Deng was sure of his reformer profile and forward-looking temperament.

Equally important, Jiang's appointment meant that Deng was able to veto candidates favored by the conservatives, such as Deng Liqun. Remember, both previous general secretaries were accused of being soft on political control and too lenient on student protesters. Had Deng not been as strong, he would have been less able to resist a candidate like Deng Liqun.

Second, Deng was able to install Li Ruihuan, a party chief of Tianjin City and an effective reform advocate, in the Standing Committee and put him in charge of ideology and propaganda. Li Ruihuan played a critical role in supporting Deng's 1992 campaign and urging Jiang Zemin to take the reform line.

Third, Deng's continued control of the military proved to be valuable. This control was strengthened by the 1989 Tiananmen events. Not only did he offer institutional power after Tiananmen in the form of the CMC chair, but also he helped Jiang monopolize control in the military by removing the Yang brothers, who had been, up to 1992, controlling the military on behalf of Deng.

In the meantime, Deng began to promote the concept of the "core" at the top level of China's leadership, which signaled open acknowledgment of the limits of "collective leadership." In other words, Deng, the supreme leader, conceded the inevitable emergence of another supreme leader after his retirement. He was resolved to make Jiang one and transferring full control of the military was a critical step.

### The Sorrow and the Flaw of Deng's Long Game

At age eighty-four in 1989, Deng was on the verge of a political crisis. His reform program was at a crossroads, besieged and possibly being undone. The international climate and setbacks in domestic reforms had emboldened his conservative rivals. He urgently needed to settle on a leadership at the top that would continue his policy agenda. Yet his incumbent heir apparent was not effective and was in jeopardy. The Tiananmen protest movement came at a pivotal moment. Ever a master of Chinese politics, he managed to emerge from the political storm stronger than before. By wielding military power, albeit at great human cost, Deng regained his grip. A conservative takeover was avoided. By appointing Jiang Zemin at the top and installing reformers in the Standing Committee, Deng scored a victory.

In this chapter, I have used the word "success" or "victory" to characterize Deng's political project. But success at what cost? In closing, I would like to make this clear: while my analysis shows how Deng's 1989 decisions were connected to his overall succession plan and desire to protect reformist legacies, *I do not claim that he had no other recourse* to achieve the same goal. In this book, I have closely explored the limits of Deng's power, with the goal of demonstrating that even a supreme leader needed to take extraordinary measures to have his way. Nevertheless, it is also important to emphasize the immense power he had in 1989, and he could have afforded to use means that did not involve killing civilian protesters. This is the sorrow of Deng's long game and a stain in the biography of an otherwise great man.

Deng's success was extended into the decades following 1992. Not only did his economic reforms push China into the realm of world superpowers, but his political design also bore fruit. It was an achievement equally unprecedented, although less celebrated. More than three decades after 1989, China has experienced two major power transitions – from Jiang to Hu, and from Hu to Xi – with both transitions orderly and peaceful, hence successful. This is a remarkable feat in a system whose succession politics had been marked by brutal purges and spectacular tumult.

Yet this success has a glaring flaw. Deng's design for political succession can be summed up as "collective leadership" with a "core." The first component, collective leadership, was obviously an attempt to move away from Mao's disastrous personal rule, from which Deng himself had suffered. It was perhaps also inspired by the USSR system practiced after the death of Stalin. The problem lies in the nature of the "core." This "core" could overtake the system and return to dictatorial rule. If a new supreme leader refuses to retire, the system has no means to stop him. Would his formula work in the long run?

# 11 Conclusion

## Tiananmen and China's Communist Authoritarianism

Why the military operation to crack down on the Tiananmen protest in 1989? Over the previous pages I have reconstructed the events leading to the decision in order to explore three lines of argument. The evidence presented has cast doubt on the well-told story of the Chinese government's suppression of a revolution. It has also challenged another conventional narrative of elite factionalism. A third line of argument, the central thesis of this book, seems to have won out.

Remarkably, ending the 1989 Tiananmen Square movement seemed an auxiliary matter to be reckoned with in Beijing's political theater of the time. To the extent that it presented a thorny issue for the government, it was used by the leaders as a tool to resolve the succession struggle. The policy-making process in the name of handling the protest was driven more by the concerns of power distribution within the government compound than by boisterous agitation from outside.[1]

In this closing chapter, I will discuss such evidence and its implications. I conclude that, while the revolution suppression model and the two-way factionalism model fit some parts of the narrative, they differ from the events of 1989 in many fundamental ways. Our three-way succession model, by comparison, fits the key patterns well and is able to reconcile most of the discrepancies.

So what does Tiananmen signify? The movement unfolded in a way that revealed the system's deepest vulnerability. It shows that in an authoritarian regime that is devoid of clear institutional procedures for leadership transition, succession politics can become mingled with mass politics or even with the military and turn dangerous or deadly. To settle such a crisis, the Beijing regime in 1989 killed some 3,000 civilians. Therefore, to argue that Tiananmen was not a revolution is not to argue that the regime was invincible. The danger is constitutional and comes from within.

It was not the first time that communist China was in crisis. Earlier disasters included the Great Famine and the Cultural Revolution, which caused devastating human suffering. This logic will continue to exert its force in the future. It is thus worthwhile to explore the institutional characters of such a system that causes breakdowns, using the event of Tiananmen as a lens. From this perspective, what drove the brutal end to Tiananmen – that is, a moment of "contention triangle," a contention that involves the population, the elite, and the military – was not singular, nor would it be the last. The system will be visited by a "Tiananmen" again as long as the institution of supreme leadership remains a feature of "communist authoritarianism."

## The Inadequacy of the Revolution Suppression Model

As I have narrated in detail throughout this book, elite decisions at Tiananmen, including the final military crackdown, can be examined under different theoretical lenses. The revolution suppression model draws inspiration from classical events such as the French Revolution and the American Revolution, and major historical events in the contemporary era, such as the Hungarian Uprising in 1956 and the Iranian Revolution in 1978–1979. In all those events, the nature of the revolt was unambiguous, as far as the elites are concerned. It is an image of society versus the state, with the elites more or less united. For this model, the military crackdown at Tiananmen is treated as the default position of a repressive political machine. Are the facts surrounding the Tiananmen decisions consistent with this model?

### The Tiananmen Phenomenon against the Revolution Suppression Model: Labeling as Dispute Focus

The first set of predictions from the revolution–suppression model revolves around the substance of elite disputes. In revolution suppression hypotheses, the rebellious nature of an emerging threat is not controversial; if elite disputes exist, they would mostly be about how the state should respond. For example, on the eve of the American Revolution, the nature of the rebellion was commonly understood both by King George III of England and by his government's members. To the extent disagreement existed, it was between those who vouched for a triumphant course of action and those who were cautious. The former side included Lord Sandwich, First Lord of the Admiralty, and the latter included several of the most powerful speakers in Parliament, like the lord mayor of London, John Wilkes, and the leading Whig intellectual Edmund Burke.[2] In reacting to an emerging threat to their rule by a popular mobilization, consensus on the rebellious nature is also common in other historical examples of revolution suppression arguments.[3]

That was not the case for Tiananmen, however. The political nature of the student movement – whether it should be seen as a rebellion or as a patriotic act – was actually the most important part of the elite disputes. In the entire course of the student movement from April 15 to June 4, 1989, the state's major policies in response were the function of a resolution of this debate, and its lack thereof.

Not surprisingly, government response in the initial period was marked by silence and indecision. Protest at this stage was left without being politically labeled, and it kept growing thanks to a reticent Deng at the top, and a pair of the first-line leaders, Li Peng and Zhao Ziyang, in disagreement. That came to a stop with Zhao's diplomatic visit abroad. Zhao's lenient line was set aside, and Li's negative labeling prevailed with the assistance of Deng.

The official denouncement came in the form of the April 26 editorial, although it did not end the labeling issue. Under Li Peng himself, the "anti-party and anti-socialism" label rang shallow without being enforced by any operational actions, and attempts at "dialogue" effectively legitimated the emerging independent student organizations.

Then the negative labeling was contradicted by Zhao Ziyang after his return. In his speech in early May, Zhao praised student protesters as "patriotic." Behind the scenes, he worked to convince Deng to retract the editorial. Where was Deng while all the new debates went on? He was in his second period of silence. Zhao and other state leaders would not be able to see him for more than two weeks.

This is the first clear indication that Tiananmen is in fact of an entirely different nature than those historical revolutionary events on which the revolution suppression model is based. In those events, elites had no quarrel over the nature of the rebellion; they busied themselves in debates on how to end it. In contrast, until very late the Chinese leaders were occupied with debates about the nature of the protest rather than with ways to stop it.

### The Tiananmen Phenomenon against the Revolution Suppression Model: Protest Co-production

The second set of predictions from the revolution suppression model revolves around the notion of ending the protest as a clear goal. Within the logic of the traditional model, to the extent that soft measures or concessions even occur, it is only due to strategic considerations for ultimately achieving that goal.

Evidence to support this characterization is thin in the case of Tiananmen. Government policies made before the military deployment did not objectively slow down, much less end, the protest. More importantly, elites produced these policies with little regard to whether they might backfire. Their main concern was to win the labeling contest among themselves.

*Coproduction of protest*

An alternative reading of the situation is more justified. That is, the spectacular protest was *coproduced* by the elites and the students. Tiananmen as we knew it was *because of* state leaders' action (and inaction), regardless of their intention, not *despite* it. This is supported by three sets of facts.

The first is the level of threat. Contrary to the assumption made by the revolution suppression model that the regime was in existential danger, the communist state in China was, unlike its counterparts elsewhere, quite secure. So, the elites' main concern during the protest lay elsewhere.

The second is the elites' behavior. None of the measures they took was objectively effective in containing the protest. Nor did the intent behind these actions manifest any real intent to end the protest.

Which in turn leads to the third set of facts: vested interests. All of the three key actors, as representatives of their respective factions, had vested interests in letting the protest develop. Deng was playing his long game, waiting for the protest to develop so that he could call in the military; Zhao Ziyang hoped popular sentiments expressed through the protest would strengthen his position as the reformer; and Li Peng wanted the protest to become something consequential, hence a cause to discredit Zhao.

### The Tiananmen Phenomenon against the Revolution Suppression Model: Power Display by Means of the Military

A set of predictions of the revolution suppression model concerns military intervention. It suggests that the protest was too rebellious to be stopped without bringing in the military, that the military was called in for the purpose of ending the protest, and that the size and manner of the operation were necessitated by the challenge.

But none of these are supported by the facts. The protest, if left on its own, could have died down without fanfare. Ostensibly Deng called in the troops to end the protest, but he had two other purposes – to remove the general secretary and to install a new administration of his choice. To showcase his command of the military was his way of enhancing his position of power to accomplish his goal. In terms of the June 3–4 operation, our evidence shows that a low-key operation could have done the job.

### The Inadequacy of the Two-Way Factionalism Model

Another model, the two-way factionalism model, on the other hand, splits elites into two factions, viewing one of them as possible allies of a social movement. As a modified version of the previously conjured image of "society versus the state," the argument suggests that the insurgents may have a potential sympathizer within. A military crackdown is then considered to be a result of elite conflict; that is, the protest's allies, who advocate conciliation and concession, are overpowered by the hard-liners, who promote confrontation and crackdown. This model is one commonly used to understand elite politics in authoritarian systems, and has been applied to autocratic regimes in Riyadh, Cairo, Tehran, and Dakar,[4] as well as in communist states in Moscow, Budapest, Prague, and Beijing.[5]

Two-way factionalism models have four key propositions. First, elites are divided into two camps – the reformers and the conservatives. Second, factional affiliation determines an elite member's position in a policy debate. Third, the progressive faction is supported by popular forces in society; hence this faction acts as an ally. Fourth, suppression of the movement means a win for the hard-liners. As we will see, these propositions match the facts in Beijing in 1989 poorly.

### *The Tiananmen Phenomenon against the Two-Way Factionalism Model: Deng Was His Own Faction*

The first difficulty for arguments from the two-way factionalism model is discerning where Deng fits into the puzzle. It is true that two major factions existed and that their affiliations affected behavior. But Deng was both a reformer and a conservative, depending on the issue. Regarding Tiananmen, it is impossible to classify him under this traditional two-way scheme.

In the years leading to 1989, as described in the narrative on twin-summit politics, Deng was to a large degree a reformer. But, even before Tiananmen, his harsh stand against student protest was well known. His affiliation to either camp all but disappeared during Tiananmen in 1989: he gave private assurances to the reformer Zhao Ziyang before turning against him; he adopted the conservatives' position to suppress the protest but appointed a new leader and a new Standing Committee to steer China in his reformist direction; and three years later, he defeated the conservatives entirely with his 1992 Southern Tour campaign and pushed the country toward full-blown economic reform.

An alternative, better, imagery is one of three camps, with Deng being and operating as a faction of his own. As the supreme leader, he had a distinct set of interests and a distinct set of resources at his disposal to defend them. For the other players known as conservatives or reformers, another layer of identities – whether one was in the heir or counter-heir camp – took on equal, if not even more, saliency.

*The Tiananmen Phenomenon against the Two-Way Factionalism Model: Changing Identities and Factional Realignment*

The two-way factionalism model uses pre-existing affiliations to predict behavior in policy debates. The result is a static picture of factional alignment. But state elites during Tiananmen certainly did not behave this way, as they adjusted their behavior according to political pressure or expediency that was shaped and reshaped by the developing events. Deng's inconsistent loyalty to Zhao Ziyang was a glaring case in point. We can take the number two military leader, Yang Shangkun, as another example. He was an important ally of Zhao Ziyang and had supported Zhao during Tiananmen until very late, only to change his position when he learned of Deng's intentions. Similarly, Qiao Shi, an SC member and Zhao's ally in charge of security, also switched to supporting Deng's crackdown solution. This pattern of alternating sides continued for years after Tiananmen. In 1992, Deng decided to move against Yang Shangkun in order to help the new general secretary consolidate power. Later in the same year and after the conservative defeat by Deng's Southern Tour, Li Peng began to support every new reform policy in order to keep his premiership.

These are less about personal integrity than about political pragmatism. Two factors worked together to reshuffle elite alignments. First, as policy debates shifted from one issue to another – from price reform in late 1988 to handling a student movement in 1989, for example – the stake of the game changed for everyone. Second, politicians in an authoritarian system are motivated more by maintaining trust with the supreme leader more than by serving any interest group. So when the supreme leader switches sides, what can you do?

*The Tiananmen Phenomenon against the Two-Way Factionalism Model: Elite–Protest Disconnect*

Many scholars, particularly those who formerly worked for Zhao Ziyang, tend to make a democracy icon out of the former general secretary. For them, Zhao was an elite supporter of the protest, even potentially an Imre Nagy of Hungary in 1956 or a Boris Yeltsin of the USSR in 1991. A prevailing storyline is that there was mutual support between the student protesters and Zhao, and the military crackdown was a result of Zhao's defeat in the factional politics.[6]

There is some truth to this storyline. The protest was triggered by a reformer's death, featuring conservative figures as targets and advocating further reform. Zhao was lenient toward the protest all along, praised it at times, and worked hard to reverse the party's negative label. And, in an act of heroism, he refused to go along with the military crackdown. But his relationship with the students went only so far. The progressive kindred spirit did not translate into organizational linkage. It was paramount in that system for politicians to keep a healthy distance from popular protest. As party norms and disciplines prohibited it, any attempt at collusion, or even the appearance of it, would be politically fatal.

Nor did the students work to strengthen Zhao's position of power. There was a brief period in early May when the protest subsided, as if Zhao's conciliatory approach had made a difference, but that was quickly ruined by a new wave of escalation via the hunger strike. After that, a new crop of student leaders cared little about whether the movement would help or hurt Zhao.

In retrospect, even if Zhao's conciliatory approach had prevailed and the protest had ended peacefully, would he have been able to champion the students' pro-democracy cause? This is unlikely. The system he led would not allow the independent student organizations to continue to exist, for that would lead student protests to recur at any time. Here, I agree with Dingxin Zhao when he observes that the elites were not divided on the most important issue – the need to defend the system.[7] Indeed, by his own words, Zhao Ziyang remained a steadfast Leninist believer until late into his house arrest, so it was long after Tiananmen, when he was permanently out of power, that he came to support a system of electoral democracy.[8]

### The Tiananmen Phenomenon against the Two-Way Factionalism Model: The Defeat of the Hardliners

Since the two-way factionalism model sees the military crackdown as a win for the conservative faction, a corollary of this explanation would be conservative dominance in post-Tiananmen politics. But that was not at all the case. Not only did Deng appoint a new leadership with more reformers than conservatives, but also he engineered a rout of the conservatives in less than three years. While there were twists and turns, Deng's reformist policy won an overwhelming victory in 1992. That was made possible by steps he took during and immediately following Tiananmen. After dismissing Zhao Ziyang and a few of his allies, the newly appointed leadership was for the most part balanced between the two factions, leaning toward reform. Deng worked on Jiang Zemin, and given time and after some cajoling, Jiang proved able to resist pressure from his conservative patrons and get fully on board with Deng's reform. Deng put another new Standing Committee member, Li Ruihuan, the former mayor of Tianjin, in charge of the nation's ideology and propaganda, a position that helped ensure the success of Deng's Southern Tour. In short, Deng simultaneously ended a progressive social movement while continuing his progressive line of policy.

## My New Explanation: The Three-Way Succession Model

The evidence presented in this book calls for an alternative model, the three-way succession model. It places the supreme leader at the center of elite politics, and the protest on the periphery. The student movement entered the succession equation and changed the means of the power struggle, but it did not replace succession as the top priority. Deng eventually used the protest as justification to demonstrate his military power. Among the other key players under him, the heir hoped to maintain good graces with him, while the heir's rivals used it as a means to undermine such trust.

If the revolution suppression model is built on the assumption of a state that was vulnerable to rebellion, the three-way succession model zeroes in on the supreme leader who was preoccupied by elite politics. His overarching concern was a new party leadership of his choice to carry on his legacy. His task was first complicated by the outbreak of a student movement, but he found a way out by taking advantage of the situation.

Two major resources came to his aid. Contrary to the notion that popular protest represented a threat, in China's communist system supreme leaders such as Mao often thrived in the middle of mass campaigns. Deng does not seem to have been an exception. The key lay in his unmatched power to make pronouncements on a protest's nature, cause, and possible consequence. The political culture was such that he could do so with little regard to facts. This way, a protest became a resource to dismiss or promote leaders and reset political agendas.

As important, the military was at his disposal. When he perceived obstinate resistance within the party, the supreme leader could always threaten a military endgame. In a 1957 party conference, Mao famously threatened to leave his then post to "organize new guerrillas in the mountains." A national mass campaign followed. Similarly, in the Cultural Revolution in the 1960s, Mao first started a national mass campaign, and when the social order was out of control, he called in the military.[9] To use social disorder as a pretext for military intervention was a playbook that Deng adopted in 1989.

If the two-way factionalism model maintains the importance of the ideological divide, the three-way succession model suggests political alliances drawn around political power. As summarized above, the resulting conflict was more complicated than one of two camps, but was a three-way interaction between the supreme leader, his supposed heir, and the "counter heir." Pre-existing factional affiliation would be still significant, but it would not be the major predictor of one's behavior. The military decision, then, was no longer one signaling a victory of the conservatives, but a decision made by someone floating above the two factions. That the conservatives endorsed Deng's decision meant little in terms of setting China's course to their preference, as Deng would deal them a blow in short order in his long game.

How does the three-way succession model account for Tiananmen phenomena that were found to be inconsistent with the other two models? Take protest labeling as an example. When we realize that the elites' main concern was their rivalry, it becomes clear why contesting the protest's political nature was more important than ending it. Similarly, in issuing new policies – Li's permitting dialogues, and Zhao's giving supporting speeches, for example – the actors in fact ended up working to "coproduce" the protest, when they were unconcerned about the actual consequences of their policies. Their focus seems to have been maintaining their own relationship with Deng or undermining that of their rivals.

The new model also explains why military might was deployed so disproportionately to the actual job of dealing with the protest. In the analysis here, the troops were sent more to pre-empt political fallout from dismissing a leader than to end the protest; they were also useful to compel Deng's rivals to accept or compromise on his new slate of leaders after Zhao.

From the lens of the new succession model, we can see why Zhao would choose not to develop a close relationship with the protesters, a relationship that serves as a cornerstone of the two-way factionalism model. Between students' support and Deng's trust Zhao had a clear choice to make: Deng. There were moments when Zhao appeared to side with the movement over Deng, but a more accurate reading should be that Zhao used the movement in hope of lobbying Deng. Deng's trust was the more important between the two in the succession politics.

The new model also resolves the conundrum of Deng's role in the two-way factionalism model. Although Deng had largely been on the reformers' side in previous policy debates, during Tiananmen Deng seems to have formed an alliance with the conservatives in targeting Zhao as well as the student movement. Yet Deng's alliance with the conservatives proved to be only temporary. He installed and cultivated a new crop of reformers and finally defeated the conservatives after Tiananmen. For Deng, succession took precedence over any factional allegiance.

One theoretical intuition behind the three-way succession model is to situate a protest movement in a larger context of political contention. Tiananmen represented a recurrent "contention triangle," mixing elite infighting, popular agitation, and military involvement in China. The features revealed echo those seen through a longer span of history: cycles of protest are regulated by concerns regarding the strength of the supreme leadership; protests are politicized to help or hurt the elites involved; and the power of the military is introduced with serious disputes even among those in positions of authority. Such a contention triangle was not singular; nor would it be the last. The system will be visited by a "Tiananmen" again as long as the institution of supreme leadership remains a feature of "communist authoritarianism."

Seen from the perspective of social-movement research, at the core of the three-way succession model is the theoretical idea on "protest as elite resource." Social protest is known to be a political instrument for the power-less. Less appreciated, however, is the fact that protest can be used by the powerful. Here I am not only referring to state-sponsored popular movements launched by an autocratic leader such as Hitler or Mao,[10] but protest mobilized from below by popular forces in society. Contrary to the unexamined assumption that state elites would always come out to suppress it, we should explore how they may ignore, acquiesce, promote, define, and channel it; in short, turn it to political advantage. They do so for self-protection or political gain at the expense of their opponents. To borrow from Michael Lipsky, who sees protest as a political resource for non-state actors, I suggest that protest can also be an elite resource.[11] It is in the context of a full spectrum of elite choices that we can begin to understand elite behavior, both when elites manage an ongoing protest and when they fashion an endgame.[12]

In their seminal *Dynamics of Contention*, McAdam, Tarrow, and Tilly call for studies that can penetrate the artificial wall between "prescribed politics and politics by other means."[13] The importance is not difficult to see, as they point out, because "virtually all broad social movements, revolutions, and similar phenomena grow from roots that are set in less visible episodes of institutional contention."[14] Many scholars have since heeded the call, including the two original authors' new reflection on "reciprocal relations between electoral polit-ics and social movements," or "ballots and barricades," and those who focus on the various ways political parties interact with social movements.[15] Particularly germane are those who study cleavages that cut through both elite politics and protest campaigns.[16] This book is another effort along these lines, with a case that transcends the boundaries between institutional and extra-institutional politics. It extends the political-process model by exploring protest as a resource of elites and advances our understanding of state repression.

## Institutional Conditions behind the Three-Way Succession Model

Why is Tiananmen better presented through the perspective of the three-way succession model than through the other two alternatives? It is due to historical, as well as institutional, conditions. I have mainly addressed the historical conditions in the narrative. Examples include Deng's age, the heir's precarious position, the unique triggering event for the protest in the death of Hu Yaobang, the country's economic situation and legitimacy, and so on.

In one way or another, I have also touched on three key institutional condi-tions. The first is the supreme leader's role in the occurrence of a national protest. The second is trust as the most important resource for other elites under a supreme leader. The third concerns the relationship between the military and civilian politics. Let me elaborate on these three.

### Supreme Leadership and the Generation of National Protest

Under normal circumstances, elite politics – such as making a policy decision or dismissing or appointing an official – can be considered "contained contention," to use a term of McAdam, Tarrow, and Tilly's. Deliberation is conducted behind closed doors, among familiar figures and heeding a routine script. In contrast, elite politics can be turned into a series of contentions that are "transgressive"; that is, involving "actors with newly constituted identities."[17] Past examples of transgressive elite politics may include Mao's dismissal of Liu Shaoqi in the 1960s during the Cultural Revolution and the removal of Deng Xiaoping by Mao and the Gang of Four in connection with the 1976 Tiananmen incident.

Conceivably, in 1989 Deng's power was strong enough for him to dismiss Zhao in a "contained" episode, in much the same way as he dismissed Hu Yaobang in 1987 and unseated Mao's heir Hua Guofeng earlier. Nonetheless, it was Deng's ability to fire Zhao and to install someone new that was at the heart of policy processes. Although still a supreme leader, his authority was not unlimited. He was constrained by his own commitment to semiretirement, conceding day-to-day operation of the country, as well as by his commitment to his rivals.[18]

The outbreak of the Tiananmen protest presented Deng with two additional challenges.

First, since the protest was based on the very issue of Hu Yaobang's dismissal, it would be extraordinary to dismiss another general secretary for similar reasons and in a similar manner. Second, it would be equally remarkable to appoint a third reformer as the new leader, all the while needing support from the older conservatives and their younger representatives. He found himself besieged by political problems unsolvable through conventional means.

Despite his fading grip on the government, he held the cards that mattered. He could set the tone on a protest, or, just as importantly, choose a silence that could escalate it. The floodgate was opened. Not only did the protest find a political space, but also leaders with differing interests would also start to engage. In this way, two types of contention – elite politics and popular protest – converged into one.

A useful distinction can be made between a time of *stable supreme leadership* and a time of *transitional supreme leadership*. Transition can be a result of the ruler's severe sickness (such as Lenin's strokes) or death, but it can also be a result of a healthy ruler's proactive effort to pass some powers down to others. Either way, the calendar is dictated by the ruler's age.

Leadership succession as arranged by the ruler himself, however, is difficult. Due to the crown prince problem discussed earlier, the ruler's trust in an heir normally cannot last until the end, so that process often starts anew. Within the large cycles of the supreme leader's age, there are smaller cycles. That is, the succession plan starts when an heir is appointed, but soon enough the supreme leader begins to lose faith and trust in him. Until the existing heir is out and the new one is appointed, contentions among elites escalate, at times leading to the inclusion of popular contention, if the supreme leader is so inclined and even if the supreme leader is healthy.

In times of stable supreme leadership, the ruler is the final arbiter of all major political disputes. Elite politics hence follows routines. But "transgressive contention" may arise in times of transitional supreme leadership. The supreme leader may have already delegated a great deal of power away from himself, he may imagine dangers that are nonexistent, and he may just like to give a jolt to the system. In any case, elite politics deviates from the routine, bringing in episodes of public contention.

That, in a nutshell, captures the relationship between the institution of supreme leadership and the generation of large-scale and sustained national protests in communist China. It is the key to understanding why such protests are in fact coproduced by state and society together. While many end in state repression, the state's role as the coproducer is unmistakable, especially if the life course of state action is examined as a whole. Particularly relevant to our Tiananmen case is that the elites helped create a crisis, which in turn allegedly required a military.

### The Centrality of Trust with the Supreme Leader in Elite Politics

Just like politicians in electoral systems, Chinese politicians, like Zhao and Li, also worry about their "votes." The key difference is that, in the latter case, the "votes" are not from citizens outside the governing body but from the supreme leader and other power holders surrounding the supreme leader. Therefore the word "trust" is more apt. Just as an unexpected major event would change the fortune (votes) of politicians elsewhere, the student protest had significant implications for the fortune (trust) of politicians such as Zhao Ziyang and Li Peng. It is an essential point to remember that their political success is decided less by their achievements or popular support and more by their relationship with the supreme leader of the time.

Seen in this light, some seemingly strange behavior during Tiananmen begins to make sense. Take Zhao's visit to North Korea as an example. When he boarded the train on April 23, he was leaving an ever-growing student protest behind and leaving Li Peng in charge. His choice was puzzling. As the number one first-line leader, should he have instead remained on duty in order to make the trouble go away? Or, if he saw the protest as no trouble, but a popular voice in his favor, should he also have stayed to develop some relationship with the protest? Tragically for Zhao, his absence contributed to a turning point in the state response. Li Peng and Deng worked together to issue the damning April 26 editorial.

The best explanation is that, at the time, Zhao felt very secure with Deng. He had private assurances from the supreme leader. Before his departure Deng even promised to make him the leader of the military after his return. That turned out to be a miscalculation.[19]

The importance of trust can also provide a reasonable explanation for another seemingly puzzling action by Zhao. In a live televised interview with the visiting Soviet leader, Gorbachev, on May 16, Zhao told the open secret, unprompted, that Deng was still the one who decided major political issues. That was an extraordinary moment, which triggered anger and resentment from Deng and his children. Why would Zhao seem to deliberately cross Deng in a public fashion? A simple answer is that by then Zhao knew he had lost favor with Deng and how Tiananmen and his fate would end. He said it to make a statement for the historical record.

The issue of trust is also key to understanding the actions taken by Li Peng. As someone in the conversative camp, however, Li did not have much trust with Deng to maintain, so his effort was aimed at sabotaging that between Zhao and Deng. The protest presented an opportunity.

Li was the public face of the repression. His public statements were tough, and his diaries also portray a consistent stand against the student protest. But, at the same time, his actions ran in different directions. From the perspective of the revolution suppression model, it is puzzling why the repressor did not repress. It is equally puzzling from the perspective of the two-way factionalism model why the hard-liner was heavy-handed in words but stayed soft in deeds (until the final extreme measure). But from the perspective of the three-way succession model, these all make sense. A protest, when serious and negative, was always a blow to the record of the incumbent general secretary. If the movement proved to be both negative and serious, Deng would remove Zhao. The task for Li Peng, therefore, was not to end the trouble quickly, but to use it to undermine Deng's trust in Zhao Ziyang.

## The Legitimacy of Military Intervention as a Political Method

In addition to elite politicians and public protesters, the saga was joined by the military. To use "election dispute" as an analogy, for illustration, the Chinese military, then, is used to act as the final arbitrator, like the US Supreme Court. Because arbitration must be symbolic as much as instrumental, Deng did not deploy the army to the capital city merely to use his military power; he showcased it.

The military can be a formidable resource in elite politics. "[T]here is a common assumption, an unreflecting belief, that it is somehow 'natural' for the formed forces to obey the civil power," writes Finer:

> Instead of asking why the military engage in politics, we ought surely to ask why they ever do otherwise. For at first sight the political advantages of the military vis-à-vis other and civilian groupings are overwhelming. The military possess vastly superior organization. And they possess *arms*.[20]

As in cases of other modern states, civilian control of the military is also a norm in communist China, as indicated by the famous dictum "the party commands the gun" – that is, as long as the supreme leader of the system is healthy and fully in charge. The governing is left to civilians, and the military is left room for its autonomy and professionalization.[21] In the meantime, the supreme leader made himself the guardian of the army's interests. The system was stable and suffered few, if any, *coups d'état*, as Andrew Scobell demonstrated.[22] Therefore a separation of the military from domestic politics is a "constitutional reality" in China.[23]

But China's "constitutional reality" is premised on the existence of a supreme leader. Having a supreme leader has two implications. First, he is normally also the most powerful person within the military. He enjoys outsized influence, exponentially above others. For leaders like Mao and Deng, such prestige was partly due the fact that they were seasoned military men and highly decorated in past wars. Second, as a result, the separation of the military from domestic politics is possible only when the supreme leader allows it to be so. He himself can break the norm if he chooses to find a pretext. Then a "constitutional crisis" ensues and the military steps in, as it did in October of 1957 when Zhukov and the military in the USSR helped Khrushchev,[24] and as it did in 1976 when Chinese politicians arrested the Gang of Four.[25]

Military influences succession in the context of a country's institutional framework. Finer classifies the countries of the world into four categories according to their degree of "political culture" and whether they have clear succession rules and procedures. He considers communist states, such the Soviet Union and China, to belong a category high in "political culture" but low in succession rules. In this group,

> civil institutions are highly developed. The public is a proportionately wide one, well organized into powerful associations. Civil procedures and public authorities are well rooted. But unlike the first group, the legitimacy of the procedures for transferring political power and the question of who or what should constitute the sovereign authority are both in dispute.[26]

Finer develops four insights, all of which are applicable to China as a case. First, *coup d'état* is extremely rare. If attempted, it often fails quickly, and the military has to appeal to civilian politicians for help. Second, there is a de facto separation of power between civilian rule and the military in everyday political life. Third, when the time of political transition arrives, however, things can often go awry. Fourth, a military intervention can work through other forms than outright "replacement," much less "supplement." Instead, the military shapes the succession outcome in subtler ways, for example in the form of "influence" or "blackmail." Politicians with military power often can just stage the occasional show of their military power, as if to remind the nation and their elite rivals.[27]

In a one-party system like China's, elite politics indeed operate in the shadow of the military. In most cases, that is sufficient for those who control the military to accomplish what they want. Only in an extraordinary situation would a call be made to involve the army physically. Any possible military intervention should be used only as the last resort, or as an "airbag," as stated by Feaver:

> The military institution is not a political tool of first resort, given the tremendous financial and human costs associated with its use, but different societies will have different propensities for the use of force. Regardless of how cavalierly it is used, however, it is especially kept for emergencies. Like an automobile's airbag, then, the military primarily exists as a guard against disaster.[28]

Tiananmen, with its unprecedented scale of popular mobilization, was used as an emergency to justify military action.

### The Specter of the Next Tiananmen

My core theoretical claim, therefore, is a symbiotic convergence of succession contention and popular contention. Between the two, succession is more likely to be exogeneous as it is dictated by the ruler's age. These ideas can be applied to the post-Tiananmen history of the last three decades, a period of communist history free of a "Tiananmen moment." This relative stability is due to the institutionalization of a clearer succession process after Tiananmen. It cuts the cord off, separating elite conflict from popular contention. These same ideas can also be used to speculate about the future. That is, if succession politics regress, another "Tiananmen moment" could be likely.

In the last three decades, one striking fact stands out: Tiananmen Square has been quiet and clear of protests or movements. It has only been used as a tourist attraction or a stage for statecraft pageantry. Anniversaries of June 4, 1989, are marked by heightened security measures. Gone are the days when it was a symbol attracting occupation by antigovernment protesters. This is so despite citizen mobilizations were not uncommon in locales in China outside the capital city.[29] In short, China has lasted for three decades without another "Tiananmen."[30]

Although still authoritarian and undemocratic, China's political system has undergone a great deal of change, including change in the mode of political succession.[31] Term limits without life tenure were imposed for more than two decades after Tiananmen.[32] Post-Deng leaders do not serve until the end of their life; instead, they pass power down. Such institutionalized succession was practiced successfully in 2002 and 2012.[33]

An elaborate set of rules are devised and agreed upon among the incumbent leaders. These rules include one about age. Any leader, including the party's general secretary, has to retire by the age of seventy, after two five-year terms. Hence no longer can anyone above sixty-seven be eligible to be promoted to the Politburo. A second important rule is about the selection of the new leader. A pattern of "designation two terms ahead" has been practiced: Hu Jintao (in power from 2002 to 2012) was designated by Deng himself, rather than by Hu's immediate predecessor Jiang Zemin (in power from 1989 to 2002), and Xi Jinping (in power from 2012 to the present) was designated by Jiang rather than by Hu. A third set of rules concerns the installation of a new leader. He is put under a process of "succession in training": he is promoted to the Politburo's Standing Committee ten years ahead and then to a vice chair of the Central Military Commission five years ahead.[34]

There is little dispute that the new mode of succession is more institutionalized than those practiced previously.[35] If we refer back to the crown prince problem discussed earlier in this book, we can readily appreciate why that might be the case. For example, the term limits allow power transition to take place periodically without waiting for the frailty or death of the ruler; designation two terms ahead takes the power of designation away from the incumbent ruler, and, by the same token, the power to dispose of a *heir apparent*; lastly, the practice of "succession in training" grows the successor's power many years ahead of time, so his command of power is already quite secure by the time of succession.

However, such reforms – first imagined by Deng and then instituted by his followers – had mixed results. As Deng quickly realized, the institution of supreme leadership cannot be avoided. Hence, in his phrase, "the core of the collective leadership." He therefore permitted leaders who came after himself to also occupy the highest positions in the party, the state, and the military simultaneously. What is unclear is whether this new mode of succession can last.

There are three sets of reasons to be pessimistic. Historically, political changes and successes on the succession front were a result of what I call the

"Deng Xiaoping effects," which might fade over time. In the post-Mao years, Deng capitalized on the ills of Mao's personal rule and vowed to do away with them. He lived long enough to make that happen, albeit with twists and turns that included the 1989 Tiananmen affair. He installed his post-1989 successor Jiang and appointed another heir for Jiang himself. The subsequent successions unfolded very much as Deng had designed. But nothing can guarantee their continuation, and they could well be discarded by a new supreme leader under a new set of historical conditions.

A second set of reasons is theoretical, ingrained in the nature of communist regimes. Based on history of the Soviet Union, Myron Rush formulates a model in which the system swings like a pendulum between "personal rule" and "oligarchy." That is, years of personal rule (such under Stalin) may usher in an age of "collective leadership" (in effect rule by a limited number of oligarchs). Oligarchs rule collectively, but supreme power is developed over time, by occupying an interlocking position across key institutions. When the supreme leader climbs high enough, a new stage of personal rule may begin.[36]

A final set of reasons are empirical. As of this writing, the "Deng Xiaoping effects" seem to be disappearing. History is witnessing the emergence of a new supreme leader in China, who has already amassed in himself an extraordinary bundle of powers, and, in 2017, he rewrote rules regarding term limits for the state president in the state constitution.[37]

Unless a miracle intervenes, China seems to be heading to a repeat of history – one in which a supreme leader rules until his old age and problems surrounding succession emerge anew. Therefore, the specter of the next Tiananmen may well lurk on the horizon.[38]

# Notes

## Preface

1. Timothy Brook, *Quelling the People: The Military Suppression of the Beijing Democracy Movement*, 1st ed. (Stanford University Press, 1998); Wu Renhua 吴仁华, 天安门血腥清场内幕 (The Bloody Clearance of Tiananmen Square) (Zhenxiang Publishing House 真相出版社, 2007); Jeremy Brown, *June Fourth: The Tiananmen Protests and Beijing Massacre of 1989* (Cambridge University Press, 2021).
2. Brook, *Quelling the People*, ix.
3. Jamie Gangel, Jeremy Herb, Marshall Cohen, Elizabeth Stuart, and Barbara Starr, "'They're Not Going to F**king Succeed': Top Generals Feared Trump Would Attempt a Coup after Election, According to New Book," *CNN*, at www.cnn.com /2021/07/14/politics/donald-trump-election-coup-new-book-excerpt/index.html (accessed July 27, 2021). Matt Zapotosky et al., "'Pure Insanity': How Trump and His Allies Pressured the Justice Department to Help Overturn the Election," *Washington Post*, www.washingtonpost.com/politics/interactive/2021/trump-justice-department-2020-election (accessed August 8, 2021).
4. Gangel et al., "'They're Not Going to F**king Succeed.'"
5. Samuel P. Huntington, *The Soldier and the State: The Theory and Politics of Civil–Military Relations* (Harvard University Press, 1981); Peter D. Feaver, "The Civil–Military Problematique: Huntington, Janowitz, and the Question of Civilian Control," *Armed Forces & Society* 23, no. 2 (January 1, 1996): 149–78.
6. Feaver, "The Civil–Military Problematique": 150.
7. Feaver, "The Civil–Military Problematique: 151–152.
8. "Mao's Struggle; He Strings Out the Suspense on Liu Shao-Chi," *New York Times*, July 9, 1967, sec. Archives, at www.nytimes.com/1967/07/09/archives/maos-struggle-he-strings-out-the-suspense-on-liu-shaochi.html.
9. "North Koreans 'Heartbroken' by Kim Jong Un's Weight Loss, Pyongyang Resident Tells State Media," *CNN*, https://www.cnn.com/2021/06/28/asia/kim-jong-un-weig ht-interview-intl-hnk/index.html. (accessed July 23, 2021).

## 1 Introduction: A Decision to Kill

1. Zhang Ganghua 張剛華, 李鵬六四日記真相: 附錄李鵬六四日記原文 (The Truth behind Li Peng's Diary: With the Original Text of Li Peng's Diary) (Aoya Publishing Inc. Limited 澳亞出版有限公司, 2010); Zhao Ziyang 趙紫陽 and Roderick MacFarquhar,

*Prisoner of the State: Secret Recordings of Zhao Ziyang* (國家的囚徒：趙紫陽的秘密錄音) (Shibao Wenhua Publishing Enterprise Company 時報文化出版企業股份有限公司, 2009); Zhang Liang 張良, 中國"六四"真相 (The Truth of June 4 in China), 2 vols. (Mingjing Publishing House 明鏡出版社, 2001), vol. 2. Also see speeches by Li Peng and Hu Quli in Andrew J. Nathan and Wu Yulun 吳與伦, 最後的秘密：中國十三屆四中全會 "六四"結論文檔 (The Last Secret: The Final Documents from the June Fourth Crackdown) (Xinshiji Publishing House 新世紀出版社, 2019), 129–48; 275–81.

2. Wu Renhua 吳仁华, "八九天安门事件逐日大事记" (Chronology of the 1989 Tiananmen Events), at https://blog.boxun.com/hero/201106/wurenhua/10_1.shtml (accessed March 6, 2020), entry of May 17.

3. Zhang Ganghua, *The Truth behind Li Peng's Diary*.

4. For the most authoritative attempt to estimate the number of the dead, see the chapter titled "Counting Bodies" in Timothy Brook, *Quelling the People: The Military Suppression of the Beijing Democracy Movement* (Stanford University Press, 1998), 151–69.

5. The Tiananmen protest has inspired numerous books, including the classic Dingxin Zhao, *The Power of Tiananmen: State–Society Relations and the 1989 Beijing Student Movement* (The University of Chicago Press, 2008); George Black and Robin Munro, *Black Hands of Beijing: Lives of Defiance in China's Democracy Movement* (John Wiley, 1993); Craig Calhoun, *Neither Gods nor Emperors: Students and the Struggle for Democracy in China* (University of California Press, 1997); and Jeremy Brown, *June Fourth: The Tiananmen Protests and Beijing Massacre of 1989* (Cambridge University Press, 2021). Most of these works present the history of the popular mobilization, with only passing mentions od the state response. By comparison, this book will tell the story of the government side. Compared to an excellent account of the government-side story, Brook, *Quelling the People*, this book has a different empirical focus. While Brook documents suppression actions on Beijing streets, I deal with the decision-making process inside the leadership compound.

6. For the pioneering works, see Doug McAdam, *Political Process and the Development of Black Insurgency, 1930–1970* (The University of Chicago Press, 2010); Charles Tilly, *From Mobilization to Revolution*(Addison-Wesley, 1978); Sidney G. Tarrow, *Democracy and Disorder: Protest and Politics in Italy, 1965–1975* (Oxford University Press, 1989). For excellent reviews, see David S. Meyer and Debra C. Minkoff, "Conceptualizing Political Opportunity," *Social Forces* 82, no. 4 (2004): 1457–92; Hanspeter Kriesi, "Political Context and Opportunity," in David A. Snow, Sarah A. Soule, and Hanspeter Kriesi, eds., *The Blackwell Companion to Social Movements* (John Wiley & Sons, Ltd, 2007), 67–90; Doug McAdam and Sidney Tarrow, "Ballots and Barricades: On the Reciprocal Relationship between Elections and Social Movements," *Perspectives on Politics* 8, no. 2 (June 2010): 529–42.

7. Doug McAdam, "Conceptual Origins, Current Problems, Future Direction," Comparative Perspectives on Social Movements: Political Opportunities, Mobilizing Structures, and Cultural Framings, January 1996, at https://doi.org/10.1017/CBO9780511803987.003.

8. This reciprocal effect of protest on elites has gained the renewed interest of theorists. For example, see McAdam and Tarrow, "Ballots and Barricades." Also see Swen Hutter, "Congruence, Counterweight, or Different Logics? Comparing Electoral and Protest Politics," Political Conflict in Western Europe, July 2012, at https://doi.org/10.1017/CBO9781139169219.010.

9. For a general history, I recommend five important books, including Calhoun, *Neither Gods nor Emperors*; Black and Munro, *Black Hands of Beijing*; Zhao, *The Power of Tiananmen*; Brook, *Quelling the People*; Brown, *June Fourth*. Among the important Chinese accounts for the same purpose, Zhang Liang, *The Truth of June 4 in China*; Wu Renhua, "Chronology of the 1989 Tiananmen Events"; Chen Xitong 陈希同, "关于制止动乱平息反革命暴乱的情况报告" (Report on Stopping Turmoil and Suppressing Counterrevolutionary Armed Uprising), *People's Daily* 人民日报, July 18, 1989. National Educational Commission 国家教育委员会, 惊心动魄的56天: 1989年4月15日至6月9日每日纪实 (Fifty-Six Shocking Days: Daily Records from April 15 to June 6, 1989) (National Educational Commission 国家教育委员会, 1990); Yan Xuan 轩彦, 京都血火: 学潮·动乱·暴乱·平暴全过程纪实 (Blood and Fire in the Capital: Student Protest, Turmoil, Armed Uprising and Suppression) (Nongcun Duwu Publishing House 农村读物出版社, 1989).

10. Kurt Schock, *Unarmed Insurrections: People Power Movements in Nondemocracies* (University of Minnesota Press, 2005); Sharon Erickson Nepstad, *Nonviolent Revolutions: Civil Resistance in the Late 20th Century* (Oxford University Press, 2011).

11. Victor Sebestyen, *Revolution 1989: The Fall of the Soviet Empire* (Orion, 2009), 298, 342.

12. Brook, *Quelling the People*.

13. *People's Daily* 人民日报, "邓小平在接见首都戒严部队军以上干部的讲话" (Deng Xiaoping Speech at Meeting with Martial Law Officers above the Rank of Group Army), at http://cpc.people.com.cn/GB/33839/34943/34944/34947/2617562.html (accessed August 3, 2021).

14. *People's Daily*, "Deng Xiaoping Speech at Meeting with Martial Law Officers above the Rank of Group Army."

15. Chen Xitong, "Report on Stopping Turmoil and Suppressing Counterrevolutionary Armed Uprising."

16. Brook, *Quelling the People*; Wu Renhua 吴仁华, 六四事件中的戒严部队 (The Martial Law Troops of the June 4 Affair) (Zhenxiang Publishing House 真相出版社, 2009); Wu Renhua, "Chronology of the 1989 Tiananmen Events."

17. Zhao, *The Power of Tiananmen*, 212.

18. Doug McAdam, Sidney Tarrow, and Charles Tilly, *Dynamics of Contention* (Cambridge University Press, 2001), 207–23.

19. Zhao, *The Power of Tiananmen*, 212.

20. Zhao, *The Power of Tiananmen*, 212.

21. Ezra F. Vogel, *Deng Xiaoping and the Transformation of China* (Harvard University Press, 2011), 595–639; the direct quotes are at 636 and 638.

22. My view presented in this book, that elites during the Tiananmen were busy capitalizing on the political benefits of the protest rather than working to end it, may seem novel among English publications, but it is not so in books published in Chinese. My thinking is greatly shaped by a number of such books, including Yang Jisheng, 中国改革时期的政治斗争 (The Political Struggle during China's Reform Era) (Tequ Wenhua Publishing Company 特区文化图书有限公司, 2004). The same view is also available, albeit implicitly made, in two important books purported to be research materials: Zhang Liang, *The Truth of June 4 in China*, and Chen Xiaoya, 八九民运史 (The History of the Pro-democracy Movement in 1989), 3 vols. (Citizen

Power Initiatives for China, 2019). I have developed this historical insight into an argument of political sociology and presented it with compelling and documentable evidence.

23. Wu Guoguang 吴国光, "政治权力、宪章制度与历史悲剧 —— 《李鹏'六四'日记》导言 (Political Power, Constitutional Institutions and Historical Tragedy: Preface for Li Peng, June 4 Diary)," n.d., at www.hrichina.org/chs/zhong-guo-ren-quan-shuang-zhou-kan/wu-guo-guang-zheng-zhi-quan-li-xian-zhang-zhi-du-yu-li-shi-bei-ju (accessed March 15, 2020); Wu Guoguang 吴国光, "邓小平失踪之谜:有关1989真相的一个推测|动向" (The Myth of the Disappearance of Deng Xiaoping: A Conjecture about a Fact in 1989)," *Huanqiu Shibao* 环球实报 (blog), May 19, 2016.
24. Dai Qing 戴晴, 邓小平在1989 (Deng Xiaoping in 1989) (Xinshiji Publishing House 新世纪出版社, 2019).
25. Li Nanyang 李南央, "鲍彤再看六四 (一):邓小平的一场政变? (Bao Tong Looking Back at June 4: A Coup by Deng Xiaoping?), 纽约时报中文网, January 16, 2019, https://cn.nytimes.com/china/20180523/bao-tong-talks-89-li-nanyang-part1.
26. Andrew G. Walder and Gong Xiaoxia, "Workers in the Tiananmen Protests: The Politics of the Beijing Workers' Autonomous Federation," *Australian Journal of Chinese Affairs* 29 (January 1, 1993): 1–29.
27. If anything, there was an attempt on the government's side to stage a counterprotest against the students, using the peasants from Beijing's suburbs. See Chapter 7 below.
28. *Annual Register 1989*, 3. Cf. Charles Tilly, *Regimes and Repertoires* (University of Chicago Press, 2010), 61.
29. Brown, *June Fourth*, 148–49.
30. Brown, *June Fourth*, 135.
31. Minxin Pei, "The Twilight of Communist Rule in China" (2015), at www.the-american-interest.com/2015/11/12/the-twilight-of-communist-party-rule-in-china.
32. Ted Robert Gurr, "Persisting Patterns of Repression and Rebellion: Foundations for a General Theory of Political Coercion," in Margret P. Kerns, ed., *Persistent Patterns and Emergent Structures in a Waning Century* (Praeger, 1986), 149–68; Mark Irving Lichbach, "Deterrence or Escalation? The Puzzle of Aggregate Studies of Repression and Dissent," *Journal of Conflict Resolution* 31, no. 2 (1987): 266–97; Karen Rasler, "Concessions, Repression, and Political Protest in the Iranian Revolution," *American Sociological Review* 61, no. 1 (1996): 132–52; Ronald A. Francisco, "The Relationship between Coercion and Protest: An Empirical Evaluation in Three Coercive States," *Journal of Conflict Resolution* 39, no. 2 (1995): 263–82; Ronald A. Francisco, "Coercion and Protest: An Empirical Test in Two Democratic States," *American Journal of Political Science* 40, no. 4 (1996): 1179–204; Jenny Irons, "Who Rules the Social Control of Protest? Variability in the State–Countermovement Relationship," *Mobilization: An International Quarterly* 11, no. 2 (June 1, 2006): 165–80; Hank Johnston, *States and Social Movements* (John Wiley & Sons, 2013); Paul Y. Chang, "Unintended Consequences of Repression: Alliance Formation in South Korea's Democracy Movement (1970–1979)," *Social Forces* 87, no. 2 (2008): 651–77; Paul Chang, *Protest Dialectics: State Repression and South Korea's Democracy Movement, 1970–1979* (Stanford University Press, 2015); Dana M. Moss, "Transnational Repression, Diaspora

Mobilization, and the Case of the Arab Spring," *Social Problems* 63, no. 4 (2016): 480–98; Dana Moss, "Repression, Response, and Contained Escalation under 'Liberalized' Authoritarianism in Jordan," *Mobilization: An International Quarterly* 19, no. 3 (September 1, 2014): 261–86. For helpful reviews, see Christian Davenport, "State Repression and Political Order," *Annual Review of Political Science* 10, no. 1 (2007): 1–23. Jennifer Earl, "Introduction: Repression and the Social Control of Protest," *Mobilization: An International Journal* 11, no. 2 (n.d.): 129–43, 15; Jennifer Earl, "Tanks, Tear Gas, and Taxes: Toward a Theory of Movement Repression," *Sociological Theory* 21, no. 1 (2003): 44–68; Xi Chen and Dana M. Moss, "Authoritarian Regimes and Social Movements," in David A. Snow, Sarah A. Soule, Hanspeter Kriesi, and Holly J. McCammon, eds., *The Wiley Blackwell Companion to Social Movements* (John Wiley & Sons, Ltd, 2018), 666–81; Moss, "Repression, Response, and Contained Escalation."

33. Mark Irving Lichbach, "Deterrence or Escalation? The Puzzle of Aggregate Studies of Repression and Dissent," *Journal of Conflict Resolution* 31, no. 2 (1987): 266–97; Ronald A. Francisco, "The Relationship between Coercion and Protest: An Empirical Evaluation in Three Coercive States," *Journal of Conflict Resolution* 39, no. 2 (1995): 263–82; Paul Chang, *Protest Dialectics: State Repression and South Korea's Democracy Movement, 1970–1979* (Stanford University Press, 2015).

34. Donatella Della Porta and Herbert Reiter Reiter, *Policing Protest: The Control of Mass Demonstrations in Western Democracies* (University of Minnesota Press, 1998). David S. Meyer, and Sidney G. Tarrow, *The Social Movement Society: Contentious Politics for a New Century* (Rowman & Littlefield, 1998).

35. Chen and Moss, "Authoritarian Regimes and Social Movements"; Yang Su and Xin He, "Street as Courtroom: State Accommodation of Labor Protest in South China," *Law & Society Review* 44, no. 1 (2010): 157–84; Moss, "Repression, Response, and Contained Escalation."

36. McAdam, "Conceptual Origins, Current Problems, Future Direction"; Kriesi, "Political Context and Opportunity."

37. Earl, "Tanks, Tear Gas, and Taxes," 49; Charles Tilly, *The Politics of Collective Violence* (Cambridge University Press, 2003).

38. Dawn Brancati, *Democracy Protests* (Cambridge University Press, 2016).

39. Nelson A. Pichardo, "The Power Elite and Elite-Driven Countermovements: The Associated Farmers of California during the 1930s," *Sociological Forum* 10, no. 1 (1995): 21–49; Irons, "Who Rules the Social Control of Protest?"

40. Pichardo, "The Power Elite and Elite-Driven Countermovements," 21, emphasis mine.

41. David Cunningham, "State versus Social Movement: FBI Counterintelligence against the New Left," *States, Parties, and Social Movements*, March 2003, at https://doi.org/10.1017/CBO9780511625466.004.

42. J. Luders, "Countermovements, the State, and the Intensity of Racial Contention in the American South," in Jack A. Goldstone, ed., *States, Parties, and Social Movements* (Cambridge University Press, 2003), 25–44.

43. Archie Brown, *The Gorbachev Factor* (Oxford University Press, 1997); Jacques Lévesque, *Enigma of 1989: Fin d'un empire, 1989* (University of California Press, 1997).

44. Mark R. Beissinger, *Nationalist Mobilization and the Collapse of the Soviet State* (Cambridge University Press, 2002).
45. David Harris, *The Crisis: The President, the Prophet, and the Shah – 1979 and the Coming of Militant Islam* (Little, Brown and Company, 2004).
46. Charles Gati, *Failed Illusions: Moscow, Washington, Budapest, and the 1956 Hungarian Revolt* (Woodrow Wilson Center Press, 2006); Victor Sebestyen, *Twelve Days: The Story of the 1956 Hungarian Revolution* (Pantheon Books, 2006); Stanley Karnow, *In Our Image: America's Empire in the Philippines*, reissue ed. (Ballantine Books, 1990).
47. Andrei Codrescu, *The Hole in the Flag: A Romanian Exile's Story of Return and Revolution* (William Morrow, 1991); Peter Siani-Davies, *The Romanian Revolution of December 1989* (Cornell University Press, 2007); Hazem Kandil, *Soldiers, Spies, and Statesmen: Egypt's Road to Revolt* (Verso Books, 2014).
48. McAdam on at least two occasions complains about such a narrow focus. McAdam, Tarrow, and Tilly, *Dynamics of Contention*; Doug McAdam and Hilary Boudet, *Putting Social Movements in Their Place: Explaining Opposition to Energy Projects in the United States, 2000–2005* (Cambridge University Press, 2012).
49. Zhang Liang, *The Truth of June 4 in China*. Andrew J. Nathan, "The Tiananmen Papers," *Foreign Affairs* 80, no. 1 (2001): 2–48; Alfred L. Chan and Andrew J. Nathan, "The Tiananmen Papers Revisited," *China Quarterly*, no. 177 (2004): 190–214.
50. Nathan and Wu, *The Last Secret*.
51. Zhang Ganghua, *The Truth behind Li Peng's Diary*. Yao Jianfu 姚監復, 陳希同親述: 眾口鑠金難鑠真 (Chen Xitong Memoir: Truth Struggles in the Fog of Opinion) (Xinshiji Publishing and Media Company 新世紀出版及傳媒有限公司, 2012); Bao Tong 鮑彤, 中國的憂思 (Perils of China) (Taipingyang Shiji Publishing House 太平洋世紀出版社, 2000); Deng Liqun 邓力群, 邓力群自述: 十二个春秋 1975–1987 (Memoir of Deng Liqun, 1975–1987) (Dafeng Publishing House 大風出版社, 2006).
52. Chen Yizi 陈一谘, 陈一谘回忆录 (Memoir of Chen Yizi) (China Independent Writers Publishing Inc., 2014); Bao Tong, *Perils of China*; Dai Qing 戴晴, "备忘'六四'" (June 4 Memorandum), *New York Times* Chinese website 纽约时报中文网, June 5, 2014, at https://cn.nytimes.com/china/20140604/cc04daiqing; Wu Guoguang 吴国光, "Political Power, Constitutional Institutions and Historical Tragedy: Preface for Li Peng's June 4 Diary; Wu Guoguang, "The Myth of the Disappearance of Deng Xiaoping"; Wu Wei 吳偉, 中國80年代政治改革的台前幕後 (The Front and Back Stages of China's Political Reform in the 1980s) (Xinshiji Publishing House 新世紀出版社, 2013).
53. Zhang Wanshu 張萬舒, 歷史的大爆炸:「六四」事件全景實錄 (A Big Band in History: A Panoromic View of the Events of June 4) (Tiandi Publishing Company 天地圖書有限公司, 2009); Lu Chaoqi 陸超祺, 六四內部日記 (An Insider's Diary of June 4) (Zhuoyue Wenhua Publishing House 卓越文化出版社, 2006); Yang Jisheng 楊繼繩, 中國改革年代的政治鬥爭 (Political Struggle in China's Reform Era) (Tequ Wenhua Publishing Company 特區文化圖書有限公司, 2004).
54. Zhongyang wenxian chubanshe, 邓小平年谱, 1975–1997 (Deng Xiaoping Chronology 1975–1997) (Central Archival Press 中央文献出版社, 2004); Zhongyang wenxian chubanshe, 杨尚昆年谱, 一九〇七—一九九八 (Yang Shangkun Chronology 1907–1998) (CCP Party History Press 中共党史出版社, 2007);

Zhongyang wenxian chubanshe, 李先念年谱 (Li Xiannian Chronology), vol. 6 (Central Archival Press 中央文献出版社, 2011).

55. Jiefangjun wen yi chubanshe 解放军文艺出版社, 戒严一日 (One Day on Martial Law Duties) (Jiefangjun Wenyi Publishing House 解放军文艺出版社, 1989).

56. Wu Renhua, *The Martial Law Troops of the June 4 Affair*; Wu Renhua 吴仁华, 天安门血腥清场内幕 (The Bloody Clearance of Tiananmen Square) (Zhenxiang Publishing House 真相出版社, 2007); Brook, *Quelling the People*.

57. Yang Jisheng, *Political Struggle in China's Reform Era*; Wu Renhua, *The Martial Law Troops of the June 4 Affair*; Wu Renhua, *The Bloody Clearance of Tiananmen Square*; Wu Renhua, "Chronology of the 1989 Tiananmen Events"; Chen Xiaoya, *The History of the Pro-democracy Movement in 1989*, vol. 1; Chen Xiaoya 陈小雅 and Ying-shih Yu 余英時, 沉重的回首: 1989 天安門運動十五週年紀念文集 (A Look Back with a Heavy Heart: Reflection Essays on the 15th Anniversary of the 1989 Tiananmen Square Movement) (Kaifang Magazine Publishing 開放雜誌社, 2004); Dai Qing, "June 4 Memorandum"; Dai Qing 戴晴, "也谈春夏之交" (Also a Reflection on Spring–Summer Time), at www.cnd.org/HXWZ/ZK93/cm9301y1.gb.html (accessed April 4, 2020); Dai Qing, *Deng Xiaoping in 1989*.

58. Addressing state response in a time of popular protest, this book draws inspiration from, and attempts to emulate, a number of books featuring other authoritarian regimes. They include *Failed Illusion* by Charles Gati about elite politics during the 1956 Hungary uprising, *The Prague Spring and Its Aftermath* by Kieran Williams, *The Crisis* by David Harris about political leaders in the Iranian Revolution, *In Our Image* by Stanley Karnow about politicians and the military during the People Power Revolution in the Philippines, *Dissolution* by Charles Maier about the fall of East Germany in 1989, *The Gorbachev Factor* by Archie Brown about the 1989 revolutionary wave, *The Enigma of 1989: The USSR and the Liberation of Eastern Europe* by Jacques Levesque, and finally *The Soldiers, Spies and Statesmen* by Hazem Kandil about elites and protest in Egypt.

59. Zhang Liang, *The Truth of June 4 in China*, vol. 1, 440.

60. Zhang Ganghua, *The Truth behind Li Peng's Diary*, 168.

61. Zhao Ziyang 赵紫阳, 改革歷程 (The Course of Reform) (Xinshiji Publishing House 新世紀出版社, 2009), 47.

62. Nathan and Wu, *The Last Secret*, 137–48.

63. Jeremy Brown, the author of a first-rate account of the general history of Tiananmen, decided not to use the source altogether. See Brown, *June Fourth*. Other experts are less strict, but they also cautioned me to use the conversations carefully or not at all.

64. Chan and Nathan, "The Tiananmen Papers Revisited." The same materials were also published in a Hong Kong press in original Chinese under the title 六四真相 (The Truth of June 4), which is the source I use.

65. Yang Jisheng, *Political Struggle in China's Reform Era*; Zhang Wanshu, *A Big Band in History*; Lu Chaoqi, *An Insider's Diary of June 4*.

66. Zhongyang wenxian chubanshe, *Deng Xiaoping Chronology 1975–1997*.

67. Zhang Liang, The Truth of June 4 in China, vol 1: 522.

68. Theda Skocpol, "Political Response to Capitalist Crisis: Neo-Marxist Theories of the State and the Case of the New Deal," *Politics & Society* 10, no. 2 (March 1, 1980): 155–201.

69. Gordon Tullock, *Autocracy* (Springer Science & Business Media, 2012), 9.

70. Tullock, *Autocracy*, 10, added emphasis.

71. David R. Mayhew, "Congressional Elections: The Case of the Vanishing Marginals," *Polity* 6, no. 3 (March 1, 1974): 295–317.

72. See Myron Rush, *Political Succession in the USSR* (Columbia University Press, 1965), for a discussion of the communist system between personal rule and oligarchy.

73. For an elaborate account to define and discuss the concept of "state-sponsored movements," see Yang Su, "State-Sponsored Social Movements," in *The Wiley-Blackwell Encyclopedia of Social and Political Movements*, at https://doi.org/10 .1002/9780470674871.wbespm395.

74. Josh Blackman, "Opinion: Trump Acts Like a Politician. That's Not an Impeachable Offense," *New York Times*, January 23, 2020, Opinion, at www .nytimes.com/2020/01/23/opinion/trump-impeachment-defense.html.

75. Gati, *Failed Illusions*; Karen Dawisha, *The Kremlin and the Prague Spring* (University of California Press, 1984); Brown, *The Gorbachev Factor*.

76. It dates back to a paper by Andrew J. Nathan : "A Factionalism Model for CCP Politics," *China Quarterly*, no. 53 (1973): 34–66; Andrew J. Nathan and Kellee S. Tsai, "Factionalism: A New Institutionalist Restatement," *China Journal*, no. 34 (1995): 157–92. The debate is nicely presented in volume edited by Jonathan Unger, *The Nature of Chinese Politics: From Mao to Jiang* (Routledge, 2016).

77. Chu-yüan Cheng, *Behind the Tiananmen Massacre: Social, Political, and Economic Ferment in China* (Westview Press, 1990). Richard Baum, "The Road to Tiananmen: Chinese Politics in the 1980s," in Roderick MacFarquhar, ed., *The Politics of China: Sixty Years of The People's Republic of China* (Cambridge University Press, September 2011), 337–467; Lowell Dittmer, "China in 1989: The Crisis of Incomplete Reform," *Asian Survey* 30, no. 1 (1990): 25–41; Lowell Dittmer, "Patterns of Elite Strife and Succession in Chinese Politics," *China Quarterly*, no. 123 (1990): 405–30.

78. For the conceptualization of and empirical research on the crown prince problem, see John H. Herz, "The Problem of Successorship in Dictatorial Regimes: A Study in Comparative Law and Institutions," *Journal of Politics* 14, no. 1 (February 1, 1952): 19–40; Tullock, *Autocracy*; Jason Brownlee, "Hereditary Succession in Modern Autocracies," *World Politics* 59, no. 4 (2007): 595–628; Andrej Kokkonen and Anders Sundell, "Leader Succession and Civil War," *Comparative Political Studies*, June 11, 2019, at https://doi.org/10.1177/0010414019852712. Peter Kurrild-Klitgaard, "The Constitutional Economics of Autocratic Succession," *Public Choice* 103, nos. 1–2 (2000): 63–84.

79. Robert Conquest, *Power and Policy in the U.S.S.R.: The Struggle for Stalin's Succession, 1945–1960* (Harper & Row, 1967); Rush, *Political Succession in the USSR*.

80. Mayhew, "Congressional Elections"; Morris P. Fiorina and Morris P. Fiorina, *Congress: Keystone of the Washington Establishment*(Yale University Press, 1989); Osnat Akirav, "Re-election: Different Skills for Different Roles," *Government and Opposition* 50, no. 1 (January 2015): 90–118.

## Part I  Party-State Leadership in the Deng Era

1. Anthony Giddens, *The Constitution of Society: Outline of the Theory of Structuration*, reprint ed. (University of California Press, 1986). An effective application of this approach is a study by Gao Hua that documents the rise of Mao's power in wartime. See Gao Hua 高華, 紅太陽是怎樣升起的: 延安整風運動的來龍去脈 (How Did the Sun Rise: The Origins and Development of the Yan'an Retification Campaign) (Chinese University of Hong Kong Press 中文大學出版社, 2000).

## 2  The Coming of the Deng Era (1976–1987)

1. Lenin's last testament and Stalin's succession arrangements both aimed at making no one person to stand out; see Myron Rush, *Political Succession in the USSR* (Columbia University Press, 1965).
2. John Dornberg, *Brezhnev: The Masks of Power* (Basic Books, 1974); Bruce Gilley, *Tiger on the Brink: Jiang Zemin and China's New Elite* (University of California Press, 1998); You Ji, "Jiang Zemin's Command of the Military," *China Journal*, no. 45 (2001): 131–38; You Ji, "Jiang Zemin: In Quest of Post-Deng Supremacy," *China Review*, 1996, 1–28; Willy Wo-Lap Lam, *The Era of Jiang Zemin* (Prentice Hall, 1999).
3. They did take some early measures, but they often aborted them. Their last measures were hardly realistic to ensure their legacies. For Mao's case, see Roderick MacFarquhar and Michael Schoenhals, *Mao's Last Revolution* (Harvard University Press, 2009); Frederick C. Teiwes and Warren Sun, *The End of the Maoist Era: Chinese Politics during the Twilight of the Cultural Revolution, 1972–1976* (Routledge, 2014); Yang Jisheng 楊繼繩, 中國改革年代的政治鬥爭 (Political Struggle in China's Reform Era) (Tequ Wenhua Publishing Company 特區文化圖書有限公司, 2004). For Stalin's case, see Rush, *Political Succession in the USSR*; Myron Rush, *How Communist States Change Their Rulers* (Cornell University Press, 1974). Robert Conquest, *Power and Policy in the U.S.S.R.: The Struggle for Stalin's Succession, 1945–1960* (Harper & Row, 1967).
4. Frederick C. Teiwes and Warren Sun, "The First Tiananmen Incident Revisited: Elite Politics and Crisis Management at the End of the Maoist Era," *Pacific Affairs* 77, no. 2 (2004): 211–35; Teiwes and Sun, *The End of the Maoist Era*.
5. See the explanation of "leadership by two lines" in the next chapter.
6. Wang Nianyi 王年一, 大動亂的年代: 『文化大革命』十年史 (The Years of Great Chaos: The Ten-Year History of the Cultural Revolution) (Henan Renmin Publishing House 河南人民出版社, 1988); MacFarquhar and Schoenhals, *Mao's Last Revolution*.
7. Frederick C. Teiwes and Warren Sun, *The Tragedy of Lin Biao: Riding the Tiger during the Cultural Revolution, 1966–1971* (University of Hawaii Press, 1996); Teiwes and Sun, *The End of the Maoist Era*.
8. Based on a detailed account documented in Ezra F. Vogel, *Deng Xiaoping and the Transformation of China* (Harvard University Press, 2011). In a striking parallel to the politics of years later, Mao was not able to trust Deng's politics, while he needed him as a pragmatic leader for economic and other governing matters. This mistrust was similar to Deng's attitude toward his own delegates of governing – Hu Yaobang and Zhao Ziyang.

9. David Shambaugh, "Deng Xiaoping: The Politician," *China Quarterly* 135 (September 1993): 457–90; Lucian W. Pye, "An Introductory Profile: Deng Xiaoping and China's Political Culture," *China Quarterly* 135 (September 1993): 412–43.
10. Vogel, *Deng Xiaoping and the Transformation of China.*
11. Ibid.
12. Teiwes and Sun, *The End of the Maoist Era.*
13. Teiwes and Sun, "The First Tiananmen Incident Revisited."
14. Ibid.
15. Here I lead the reader to speculate without elaboration or proof. Evidence is hard to come by. The closest piece of support was a *Wenhui Daily* article by an anonymous author. It painted Zhou as "the capitalist roader inside the Party [who] wanted to help the unrepentant capitalist roader [Deng] regain his power." This inflamed public opinion in Nanjing, where students posted slogans to "defend Zhou Enlai with our lives" at the Martyrs Cemetery. The *Wenhui Daily* was based in Shanghai, a stronghold of the Gang of Four at that time, so some speculate that the article was a political play. See Teiwes and Sun, "The First Tiananmen Incident Revisited," 214–15.
16. Wu De 吴德 and Zhu Yuanshi 朱元石, 十年风雨纪事：我在北京工作的一些经历 (Tumultuous Events of Ten Years: My Working Experiences in Beijing) (Dangdai Zhongguo Publishing House 当代中国出版社, 2004), 164–65. For estimates of the forces, see Xia Chao 夏潮 and Yang Fengcheng 杨凤城, 龙年之变：中国1976年纪实 (The Change of the Dragon Year: China in 1976) (Hebei Renmin Publishing House 河北人民出版社, 1994), 160.
17. Teiwes and Sun, "The First Tiananmen Incident Revisited."
18. Qing Ya 青野 and Fang Lei 方雷, 邓小平在1976 (Deng Xiaoping in 1976) (Chunfeng Wenyi Publishing House 春风文艺出版社, 1993), at https://book.douban.com/subject/3018087.
19. For illustrations and examples, see Ray Huang, *1587, A Year of No Significance: The Ming Dynasty in Decline* (Yale University Press, 1981).
20. Yang Jisheng, *Political Struggle in China's Reform Era*, 48–70.
21. Yang Jisheng, *Political Struggle in China's Reform Era.*
22. Ibid.
23. Yang Jisheng, *Political Struggle in China's Reform Era*, 50.
24. These remarks were recorded in a letter by Xu's son to his girlfriend. Cf. Yang Jisheng, *Political Struggle in China's Reform Era*, 54.
25. Nie Rongzhen 聂荣臻, 聂荣臻回忆录 (Memoir of Nie Rongzhen) (Publishing House of the People's Liberation Army 解放军出版社), 1986, 867; cf. Yang Jisheng, *Political Struggle in China's Reform Era*, 64.
26. After Mao's reprimand, Ye was released from his day-to-day duties in charge of the CMC. Chen Xilian took his position. See Yang Jisheng, *Political Struggle in China's Reform Era.*
27. Yang Jisheng, *Political Struggle in China's Reform Era.*
28. Yang Jisheng offers a thorough account of research on the event of October 6, 1976. The narrative of that event, including its planning stages, is mainly based on his work. Yang Jisheng, *Political Struggle in China's Reform Era*, 48–70.
29. Yang Jisheng, *Political Struggle in China's Reform Era.*

30. Yang Jisheng, *Political Struggle in China's Reform Era*.
31. Deng Rong, 邓榕, 我的父亲邓小平:文革岁月 (My Father Deng Xiaoping: The Cultural Revolution Years), standard ed. (SDX Joint Publishing Company 生活.读书.新知三联书店, 2013), 523. Cf. Yang Jisheng, *Political Struggle in China's Reform Era*.
32. Yang Jisheng, *Political Struggle in China's Reform Era*, 76.
33. Teiwes and Sun, *The End of the Maoist Era*. Vogel, *Deng Xiaoping and the Transformation of China*.
34. Yang Jisheng, *Political Struggle in China's Reform Era*, 76–77.
35. Yang Jisheng, *Political Struggle in China's Reform Era*, 86–95.
36. Yang Jisheng, *Political Struggle in China's Reform Era*.
37. Jing Huang, *Factionalism in Chinese Communist Politics* (Cambridge University Press, 2006). Also see Shambaugh, "Deng Xiaoping"; Pye, "An Introductory Profile."
38. Vogel, *Deng Xiaoping and the Transformation of China*.
39. Frederick C. Teiwes, "The Paradoxical Post-Mao Transition: From Obeying the Leader to 'Normal Politics'," *China Journal*, no. 34 (1995): 55–94. Here the term "civilian" was more about the nature of Deng's job after 1949 than a characterization of his past military career during the war. Dreyer disputes Deng's military credentials. Part of her argument was based on the fact that Deng was a political commissar rather than the commander most of his time in the revolutionary period, for example, with Liu Bocheng. But in China's revolutionary war, a political commissar was no civilian, a role that was as military as the commander's. As the top two leaders of the unit, they jointly made the military decisions. June Teufel Dreyer, "Deng Xiaoping: The Soldier," *China Quarterly*, no. 135 (1993): 536–50.
40. Shambaugh, "Deng Xiaoping."
41. Teiwes and Sun, *The Tragedy of Lin Biao*; Huang, *Factionalism in Chinese Communist Politics*; Vogel, *Deng Xiaoping and the Transformation of China*.
42. Huang, *Factionalism in Chinese Communist Politics*.
43. Huang, *Factionalism in Chinese Communist Politics*, 353.
44. Huang, *Factionalism in Chinese Communist Politics*, 355.
45. Huang, *Factionalism in Chinese Communist Politics*, 355–56.
46. Huang, *Factionalism in Chinese Communist Politics*, 356.
47. Ibid.
48. Huang, *Factionalism in Chinese Communist Politics*, 356–57. Also see Yang Jisheng, *Political Struggle in China's Reform Era*.
49. Ibid.
50. Ibid.
51. Ibid.
52. Mao Min 茅民, 复兴记 (The Revival of China) (2014), 535–36.
53. Yang Jisheng, *Political Struggle in China's Reform Era*, 6–7.
54. Yang Jisheng 杨继绳, 6; Gao Hua 高華, 红太陽是怎樣升起的: 延安整風運動的來龍去脈 (How Did the Sun Rise: The Origins and Development of the Yan'an Retification Campaign) (Chinese University of Hong Kong Press 中文大學出版社, 2000).
55. He was reportedly opposed to the idea of executing the Gang of Four in 1976. When Hu Yaobang was dismissed in 1987, and Zhao Ziyang in 1989, he did not take pleasure in further inconveniencing them as his political opponents, and suggested

that the party keep their membership. Hu Yaobang even remained a member of the Politburo. In the wake of the June 4, 1989, crackdown, he counseled lenient treatment of four key leaders who were sympathetic to the student movement. There were even some accounts to suggest that he was opposed to the killings, his support of the martial law decision notwithstanding. Yang Jisheng, *Political Struggle in China's Reform Era*, 7; about Chen's attitude toward the June 4 killings, see Richard Baum, *Burying Mao: Chinese Politics in the Age of Deng Xiaoping* (Princeton University Press), 1996.

56. Yang Jisheng, *Political Struggle in China's Reform Era*, 6.
57. Nicholas R. Lardy and Kenneth Lieberthal, *Chen Yun's Strategy for China's Development* (Routledge, 2019), xiv.
58. Lardy and Lieberthal, *Chen Yun's Strategy for China's Development*, xv.
59. Yang Jisheng, *Political Struggle in China's Reform Era*.
60. Pye, "An Introductory Profile." Shambaugh, "Deng Xiaoping."
61. Rush, *Political Succession in the USSR*; Rush, *How Communist States Change Their Rulers*. T. H. Rigby, "The Soviet Leadership: Towards a Self-Stabilizing Oligarchy?", *Soviet Studies* 22, no. 2 (October 1, 1970): 167–91.

## 3 The Fate of Two Successors (1980–April 15, 1989)

1. Deng Liqun 邓力群, 邓力群自述: 十二个春秋 1975–1987 (Memoir of Deng Liqun, 1975–1987) (Dafeng Publishing House 大风出版社, 2006); Yang Jisheng 杨继绳, 中国改革年代的政治門争 (Political Struggle in China's Reform Era) (Tequ Wenhua Publishing Company 特区文化圖書有限公司, 2004); Ezra F. Vogel, *Deng Xiaoping and the Transformation of China* (Harvard University Press, 2011); Jing Huang, *Factionalism in Chinese Communist Politics* (Cambridge University Press, 2006); Chen Xiaoya 陈小雅, 八九民运史 (The History of the Pro-democracy Movement in 1989), 3 vols. (Citizen Power Initiatives for China, 2019), vol. 1; Dongfang Ming 東方明, 鄧小平垂簾聽政 (Deng Xiaoping Rules behind the Curtain) (Tainanmen Publishing House 天安門出版社, 1997).
2. Yang Jisheng, *Political Struggle in China's Reform Era*, 275–76. For an excellent account of how elderly leaders worked to oust Hu, see Yen-Lin Chung, "The Ousting of General Secretary Hu Yaobang: The Roles Played by Peng Zhen and Other Party Elders," *China Review* 19, no. 1 (2019): 89–122.
3. For Zhao, the case is stronger, as Deng on more than one occasion indicated his plan to hand over to him the military chairmanship. Regardless of whether Hu and Zhao were seriously considered as Deng's future successors, the fact remains that they were entrusted to run the country and gradually possessed a great deal of power imparted by Deng. In this sense, the dynamic of the "crown prince problem" still applies.
4. For the conceptualization and empirical research on the crown prince problem, John H. Herz, "The Problem of Successorship in Dictatorial Regimes: A Study in Comparative Law and Institutions," *Journal of Politics* 14, no. 1 (February 1, 1952): 19–40; Gordon Tullock, *Autocracy* (Springer Science & Business Media, 2012), 9; Jason Brownlee, "Hereditary Succession in Modern Autocracies," *World Politics* 59, no. 4 (2007): 595–628; Andrej Kokkonen and Anders Sundell, "Leader Succession and Civil War," *Comparative Political Studies*, June 11, 2019,

at https://doi.org/10.1177/0010414019852712. Peter Kurrild-Klitgaard, "The Constitutional Economics of Autocratic Succession," *Public Choice* 103, nos. 1– 2 (2000): 63–84.

5. Myron Rush, *Political Succession in the USSR* (Columbia University Press, 1965); Robert Conquest, *Power and Policy in the U.S.S.R.: The Struggle for Stalin's Succession, 1945–1960* (Harper & Row, 1967); William Taubman, *Khrushchev: The Man and His Era* (W. W. Norton & Company, 2004).

6. Rush, *Political Succession in the USSR.*; Conquest, *Power and Policy in the U.S.S.R.*; Taubman, *Khrushchev*; Roderick MacFarquhar and Michael Schoenhals, *Mao's Last Revolution* (Harvard University Press, 2009); Frederick C. Teiwes and Warren Sun, *The Tragedy of Lin Biao: Riding the Tiger during the Cultural Revolution, 1966–1971* (University of Hawaii Press, 1996); Frederick C. Teiwes and Warren Sun, *The End of the Maoist Era: Chinese Politics during the Twilight of the Cultural Revolution, 1972–1976* (Routledge, 2014).

7. Ian Wilson and You Ji, "Leadership by Lines: China's Unresolved Succession," *Problems of Communism* 39, no. 1 (1990): 28–44.

8. MacFarquhar and Schoenhals, *Mao's Last Revolution.*

9. MacFarquhar and Schoenhals, *Mao's Last Revolution*, 82.

10. See Chapter 8 below.

11. Lucian W. Pye, "An Introductory Profile: Deng Xiaoping and China's Political Culture," *China Quarterly* 135 (September 1993): 412–43. According Pye, Deng was not even very keen to be on television.

12. His towering legacies include two peaceful power transitions between Jiang Zemin and Hu Jingtao in 2002, and between Hu Jingtao and Xi Jinping in 2012. Both Jiang and Hu retired from the top leadership in their prime. As of this writing, it is every scholar's hope that the legacy will survive.

13. Vogel, *Deng Xiaoping and the Transformation of China.*

14. For Deng's Hakka identity see Vogel, *Deng Xiaoping and the Transformation of China*. For Hu's see Mary S. Albaugh, "The Secret History of the Hakkas: The Chinese Revolution as a Hakka Enterprise," *China Quarterly*, no. 132 (1992): 937– 68. For Hakka cultural and its relationship with rebellions and revolutions, and for the connection between the Hakka population and the communist revolution, see Erbaugh, "The Secret History of the Hakkas"; and Jonathan D. Spence's account of Hong Xiuquan in *God's Chinese Son: The Taiping Heavenly Kingdom of Hong Xiuquan* (W. W. Norton & Company, 1996).

15. Erbaugh, "The Secret History of the Hakkas."

16. Chen Xiaoya, *The History of the Pro-democracy Movement in 1989*, vol. 1, 7–13.

17. Yang Jisheng, *Political Struggle in China's Reform Era*, 116–18.

18. Yang Jisheng, *Political Struggle in China's Reform Era*, 118.

19. See Chapter 2 above.

20. Yang Jisheng, *Political Struggle in China's Reform Era.*

21. Ibid.

22. Yang Jisheng, *Political Struggle in China's Reform Era.*

23. Ibid.

24. The most lucid articulation of this explanation is offered by Yang Jisheng, *Political Struggle in China's Reform Era.*

25. Yang Jisheng, *Political Struggle in China's Reform Era*, 10.

26. Yang Jisheng, *Political Struggle in China's Reform Era*, 11–12.
27. Deng Liqun, *Memoir of Deng Liqun*.
28. Yang Jisheng, *Political Struggle in China's Reform Era*.
29. Yang Jisheng, *Political Struggle in China's Reform Era*, 105.
30. Ibid.
31. Ibid.
32. Ibid.
33. Yang Jisheng, *Political Struggle in China's Reform Era*; Chung, "The Ousting of General Secretary Hu Yaobang."
34. Yang Jisheng, *Political Struggle in China's Reform Era*.
35. Ibid.
36. See Nicholas R. Lardy and Kenneth Lieberthal, *Chen Yun's Strategy for China's Development* (Routledge, 2019), Introduction.
37. See discussion of the odd- and even-year pattern above.
38. Yang Jisheng, *Political Struggle in China's Reform Era*.
39. Deng Liqun, *Memoir of Deng Liqun*.
40. Yang Jisheng, *Political Struggle in China's Reform Era*, 238.
41. Yang Jisheng, *Political Struggle in China's Reform Era*, 241.
42. Yang Jisheng, *Political Struggle in China's Reform Era*, 240.
43. Xiao Donglian 蕭冬連, 中華人民共和國史: 從撥亂反正到改革開放, 1979–1981. 歷史的轉軌 (The History of the PRC: From Rectification and Rehabilitation to Reform and Opening Up, 1979–1981. Turning Point of History) (Chinese Cultural Research Center, the Chinese University of Hong Kong 香港中文大學當代中國文化研究中心, 2008), 403–9.
44. Beijing University 北京大学, "【回眸40年:《人民日报》看北大】1981: '团结起来,振兴中华!'" (A Look Back over 40 Years: Beida in *People's Daily* in 1981: United in Solidarity, Revive the Chinese Nation) at https://pkunews.pku.edu.cn/ztrd/hm40n rmrbkbd/8042e44cefc94bf8890f19b4c2e96a1d.htm (accessed August 5, 2021).
45. *People's Daily* 人民日报, "《小平您好》照片背后的故事" (The Story behind the Picture "Hello, Xiaoping") at http://cpc.people.com.cn/n1/2018/0824/c69113-30247801.html (accessed August 5, 2021).
46. Yang Jisheng, *Political Struggle in China's Reform Era*, 246.
47. Yang Jisheng, *Political Struggle in China's Reform Era*, 248.
48. Yang Jisheng, *Political Struggle in China's Reform Era*, 289.
49. Yang Jisheng, *Political Struggle in China's Reform Era*, 249–50.
50. Yang Jisheng, *Political Struggle in China's Reform Era*, 264–65.
51. Yang Jisheng, *Political Struggle in China's Reform Era*, 266–67.
52. Yang Jisheng, *Political Struggle in China's Reform Era*, 266.
53. See Chapter 6 below.
54. Chen Xiaoya, *The History of the Pro-democracy Movement in 1989*, vol. 1, 164.
55. Yang Jisheng, *Political Struggle in China's Reform Era*, 272.
56. Yang Jisheng, *Political Struggle in China's Reform Era*, 275–76.
57. Yang Jisheng, *Political Struggle in China's Reform Era*, 278.
58. Zhao Ziyang, *Political Struggle in China's Reform Era*; and Zhao Ziyang 趙紫陽 and Roderick MacFarquhar, *Prisoner of the State: Secret Recordings of Zhao Ziyang* (國家的囚徒: 趙紫陽的秘密錄音) (Shibao Wenhua Publishing Enterprise Company 時報文化出版企業股份有限公司, 2009).

59. Yang Jisheng, *Political Struggle in China's Reform Era*, 279.

60. Yang Jisheng, *Political Struggle in China's Reform Era*, 132.

61. Yang Jisheng, *Political Struggle in China's Reform Era*.

62. Wilson and Ji, "Leadership by Lines," 41.

63. Zhang Ganghua 張剛華, 李鵬六四日記真相: 附錄李鵬六四日記原文 (The Truth behind Li Peng's Diary: With the Original Text of Li Peng's Diary) (Aoya Publishing Inc. Limited 澳亞出版有限公司, 2010), 191.

64. Zhao Ziyang 趙紫陽, 改革歷程 (The Course of Reform) (Xinshiji Publishing House 新世紀出版社, 2009), 293.

65. Zhao Ziyang, *The Course of Reform*, 294–95.

66. Zhao Ziyang, *The Course of Reform*, 253.

67. Wu Wei 吳偉, 中國80年代政治改革的台前幕後 (The Front and Back Stages of China's Political Reform in the 1980s) (Xinshiji Publishing House 新世紀出版社, 2013), 118.

68. Wu Wei, *The Front and Back Stages*, 118.

69. Wu Wei, *The Front and Back Stages*, 119.

70. Wu Wei, *The Front and Back Stages*, 120.

71. Zhao Ziyang, *The Course of Reform*, 230–31.

72. Wu Wei, *The Front and Back Stages*, 121–22.

73. Yang Jisheng, *Political Struggle in China's Reform Era*, 287–88.

74. Wilson and Ji, "Leadership by Lines."

75. Ibid.

76. Deng Liqun, *Memoir of Deng Liqun*.

77. See Yang Jisheng, *Political Struggle in China's Reform Era*. In Li Rui's letter, Li reported that Deng Liqun had a long-term affair with Li's then wife, which caused divorce and distress.

78. Around 1986, Deng did mention the possibility of Hu being the state president or CMC chair; however, that was proposed not as an addition to Hu's party duties, but as an inducement for Hu to step down. See Chen Xiaoya, *The History of the Pro-democracy Movement in 1989*.

79. Zhao Ziyang, *The Course of Reform*.

80. Wilson and Ji, "Leadership by Lines."

81. See Chapter 10 below for the "Surname Debate."

82. You Ji, "Zhao Ziyang and the Politics of Inflation," *Australian Journal of Chinese Affairs* 25 (1991): 90–91.

83. See Ji, "Zhao Ziyang and the Politics of Inflation," for a thorough and excellent review on the price reform.

84. Wilson and Ji, "Leadership by Lines."

85. Ibid.

86. Ibid.

87. Ibid.

88. Yang Jisheng, *Political Struggle in China's Reform Era*, 287.

89. Yang Jisheng, *Political Struggle in China's Reform Era*, 288–89.

90. Deng Liqun, *Memoir of Deng Liqun*, 491.

91. Ibid.

92. Wu Wei, *The Front and Back Stages*, 394.

93. Zhao Ziyang, *The Course of Reform*, 259.

94. Yan Jiaqi 严家其, 政治多么简单 (How Simple Is Politics) (Zhengzhong Publishing House 正中书局, 1992).

95. Ibid.

96. Zhao Ziyang, *The Course of Reform*, 260.

97. Zhao Ziyang, *The Course of Reform*, 260. Also see Li Xiannian's speech in Andrew J. Nathan and Wu Yulun 吴與伦, 最後的秘密: 中國十三屆四中全會"六四"結論文檔 (The Last Secret: The Final Documents from the June Fourth Crackdown) (Xinshiji Publishing House 新世紀出版社, 2019), 189–97.

98. Zhao Ziyang, *The Course of Reform*, 265.

99. Ibid.

100. Zhao Ziyang, *The Course of Reform*, 265.

101. Deng Liqun, *Memoir of Deng Liqun*; Dai Qing 戴晴, "备忘'六四'" (June 4 Memorandum), at https://cn.nytimes.com/china/20140604/cc04daiqing (accessed 25 July 2022); Dai Qing 戴晴, "也谈春夏之交" (Also a Reflection on Spring–Summer Time), at www.cnd.org/HXWZ/ZK93/cm9301y1.gb.html (accessed April 4, 2020).

102. Yang Jisheng interview with Zhao Ziyang; cf. Vogel, *Deng Xiaoping and the Transformation of China*. For Zhao's own account see Zhao Ziyang, *The Course of Reform*.

103. Mao Min 茅民, 复兴记 (The Revival of China) (Mao Min, 2014).

104. Yang Jisheng, *Political Struggle in China's Reform Era*, 315.

## 4 Early Response and the Growth of the Protest (April 15– April 26, 1989)

1. Paul Chang, *Protest Dialectics: State Repression and South Korea's Democracy Movement, 1970–1979* (Stanford University Press, 2015); Karen Rasler, "Concessions, Repression, and Political Protest in the Iranian Revolution," *American Sociological Review* 61, no. 1 (1996): 132–52; Ronald A. Francisco, "The Relationship between Coercion and Protest: An Empirical Evaluation in Three Coercive States," *Journal of Conflict Resolution* 39, no. 2 (1995): 263–82.

2. Craig Calhoun, "Revolution and Repression in Tiananmen Square," *Society* 26, no. 6 (September 1989): 21.

3. Zhang Ganghua 張剛華, 李鵬六四日記真相: 附錄李鵬六四日記原文 (The Truth behind Li Peng's Diary: With the Original Text of Li Peng's Diary) (Aoya Publishing Inc. Limited 澳亞出版有限公司, 2010), 66. Also see Li Peng's speech in Andrew J. Nathan and Wu Yulun 吴與伦, 最後的秘密: 中國十三屆四中全會"六四"結論文檔 (The Last Secret: The Final Documents from the June Fourth Crackdown) (Xinshiji Publishing House 新世紀出版社, 2019), 129–48.

4. Zhao Ziyang 趙紫陽, 改革歷程 (The Course of Reform) (Xinshiji Publishing House 新世紀出版社, 2009).

5. Wu Renhua 吳仁華, "八九天安门事件逐日大事记" (Chronology of the 1989 Tiananmen Events), at https://blog.boxun.com/hero/201106/wurenhua/10_1.shtml (accessed March 6, 2020); Chen Xiaoya 陈小雅, 八九民运史 (The History of the Pro-democracy Movement in 1989), 3 vols. (Citizen Power Initiatives for China, 2019), vol. 1.

6. Man Mei 满妹, "追忆父亲胡耀邦最后的时刻" (Remembering My Father Hu Yaobang's Final Moments), at www.chinesepen.org/blog/archives/82236 (accessed March 29, 2020).
7. Wu Renhua, "Chronology of the 1989 Tiananmen Events."
8. Man Mei 满妹, 我的父亲胡耀邦 (My Father Hu Yaobang) (Lianhuanhua Publishing House 连环画出版社, 2005).
9. Man Mei, My Father Hu Yaobang.
10. Zhang Ganghua, *The Truth behind Li Peng's Diary*, 56.
11. Zhang Ganghua, *The Truth behind Li Peng's Diary*.
12. Chen Xiaoya, *The History of the Pro-democracy Movement in 1989*, vol. 1, 20–21.
13. Zhang Liang 张良, 中国"六四"真相 (The Truth of June 4 in China), 2 vols. (Mingjing Publishing House 明镜出版社, 2001), vol. 1, 109.
14. Chen Xiaoya, *The History of the Pro-democracy Movement in 1989*, vol. 1, 21.
15. Zhang Ganghua, *The Truth behind Li Peng's Diary*.
16. Chen Xitong, 陈希同, "关于制止动乱平息反革命暴乱的情况报告" (Report on Stopping Turmoil and Suppressing Counterrevolutionary Armed Uprising), *People's Daily* 人民日报, July 18, 1989; Chen Xiaoya, *The History of the Pro-democracy Movement in 1989*, vol. 1, 45–49.
17. Zhang Liang, *The Truth of June 4 in China*; Chen Xiaoya, *The History of the Pro-democracy Movement in 1989*, vol. 1, 33–35.
18. Chen Xiaoya, *The History of the Pro-democracy Movement in 1989*.
19. Chen Xiaoya, *The History of the Pro-democracy Movement in 1989*, vol. 1, 23.
20. Wu Renhua, "Chronology of the 1989 Tiananmen Events," entry of April 17.
21. Chen Xitong, "Report on Stopping Turmoil and Suppressing Counterrevolutionary Armed Uprising."
22. One would aptly and crudely put it this way: "The law is the whore of politics." See http://blog.sina.com.cn/s/blog_494ab041010007ha.html.
23. I had the opportunities to make firsthand observations as a student between 1981 and 1989, first as an undergraduate student at Tsinghua, then as a master's degree student at Beida.
24. Tong Shen and Marianne Yen, *Almost a Revolution* (University of Michigan Press, 1998).
25. Interviews with former student leaders of the two organizations at Tsinghua and Beida.
26. Ibid.
27. The following events are mainly based on Li Peng's account. The truthfulness of this part of the recording can be ascertained, when comparing his account with others such as Zhao Ziyang's on the same events.
28. Zhang Ganghua, *The Truth behind Li Peng's Diary*, 63. Also see Li Peng's speech in Nathan and Wu, *The Last Secret*, 129–48.
29. Ibid.
30. Ibid.
31. Zhao Ziyang, *The Course of Reform*, 26.
32. Zhang Ganghua, *The Truth behind Li Peng's Diary*, 69. Also see Li Peng's speech in Nathan and Wu, *The Last Secret*, 129–48.
33. Zhao Ziyang, *The Course of Reform*, 25–56.

34. Chen Yizi 陈一谘, 陈一谘回忆录 (Memoir of Chen Yizi) (Hong Kong: 新世纪出版社 New Century Publishing House, 2013.), 567.
35. Calhoun, "Revolution and Repression in Tiananmen Square"; Chen Xiaoya, *The History of the Pro-democracy Movement in 1989*.
36. Dingxin Zhao conducted a thorough investigation of the incident and concluded that the claim was mostly a rumor. See Chen Xiaoya, *The History of the Pro-democracy Movement in 1989*, vol. 1, 50–59; Dingxin Zhao, *The Power of Tiananmen: State–Society Relations and the 1989 Beijing Student Movement* (The University of Chicago Press, 2008), 149–50.
37. Zhang Ganghua, *The Truth behind Li Peng's Diary*, 64–67.
38. Chen Xiaoya, *The History of the Pro-democracy Movement in 1989*, vol. 1, 50–59. See Chen Xiaoya's summary of various witness accounts. Zhao, *The Power of Tiananmen*, 149–50.
39. See Wu Renhua, "Chronology of the 1989 Tiananmen Events."
40. Zhang Liang, *The Truth of June 4 in China*, vol. 1, 157–58.
41. For the interview on April 20 see Zhang Liang, *The Truth of June 4 in China*. For the nomination see Yang Jisheng 杨继绳, 中国改革年代的政治鬥争 (Political Struggle in China's Reform Era) (Tequ Wenhua Publishing Company 特區文化圖書有限公司, 2004); Mao Min 茅民, 复兴记 (The Revival of China) (Mao Min, 2014).
42. Zhang Liang, *The Truth of June 4 in China*.
43. Zhang Ganghua, *The Truth behind Li Peng's Diary*, 75–78.
44. Zhang Ganghua, *The Truth behind Li Peng's Diary*, 74–83.
45. Zhang Ganghua, *The Truth behind Li Peng's Diary*.
46. Zhang Ganghua, *The Truth behind Li Peng's Diary*, 76–80.
47. Ibid.
48. Zhang Ganghua, *The Truth behind Li Peng's Diary*, 80.
49. Mao Min, *The Revival of China*.
50. Mao Min, *The Revival of China*, 562.
51. Ibid.
52. Mao Min, *The Revival of China*. Deng's promise to make Zhao the CMC chair was also reported by Vogel in his biography of Deng. In Vogel's version, Deng would make Zhao the chair right after Zhao was back from North Korea.
53. Mao Min, *The Revival of China*.
54. Chen Xiaoya, *The History of the Pro-democracy Movement in 1989*.
55. Zhang Liang, *The Truth of June 4 in China*, vol. 1, 157.
56. Ibid.
57. Ibid.
58. Zhang Liang, *The Truth of June 4 in China*.
59. Ibid.
60. Ibid.
61. Zhang Liang, *The Truth of June 4 in China*.
62. Zhang Ganghua, *The Truth behind Li Peng's Diary*, 81–84.
63. Ibid.
64. Zhang Ganghua, *The Truth behind Li Peng's Diary*.
65. Deng Xiaoping was not pleased by this. See Zhao Ziyang, *The Course of Reform*.
66. I was one of the students listening with astonishment, and then anger, at Beida that afternoon.

67. Zhang Ganghua, *The Truth behind Li Peng's Diary*.

68. Chai Ling 柴玲, 柴玲回忆录: 一心一意向自由 (Memoir of Chai Ling: Toward Freedom with a Full Heart) (China Independent Writers Publishing Inc., 2014).

69. Chen Xiaoya, *The History of the Pro-democracy Movement in 1989*.

70. Wu Renhua, "Chronology of the 1989 Tiananmen Events"; Chen Xiaoya, *The History of the Pro-democracy Movement in 1989*.

71. Zhao Ziyang, *The Course of Reform*.

72. For examples, see Chen Yizi, *Memoir of Chen Yizi*; Wu Wei 吳偉, 中國80年代政治改革 的台前幕後 (The Front and Back Stages of China's Political Reform in the 1980s) (Xinshiji Publishing House 新世紀出版社, 2013).

73. Bao Tong, a top aide of Zhao Ziyang's, shares this view of a proactive Deng. In his interview with Li Nanyang in 2018, he even suggested that Deng fooled Zhao into complacency when Zhao came to consult him whether to make the trip to North Korea in late April 1989. Deng was reported to assure Zhao that when Zhao came back from his visit, Deng would make him the CMC chair. See Li Nanyang 李南央, "鲍彤再看六四(一):邓小平的一场政变? (Bao Tong Looking Back at June 4: A Coup by Deng Xiaoping?), 纽约时报中文网, January 16, 2019, https://cn.nytimes.com/china/ 20180523/bao-tong-talks-89-li-nanyang-part1. The CMC promise is also reported by Vogel in his biography of Deng.

## 5  Where Was Deng Xiaoping? (April 15–May 11, 1989)

1. Zhongyang wenxian chubanshe, 邓小平年谱, *1975–1997* (*Deng Xiaoping Chronology 1975–1997*) (Central Archival Press 中央文献出版社, 2004).

2. Zhang Liang 张良, 中国"六四"真相 (The Truth of June 4 in China), 2 vols. (Mingjing Publishing House 明镜出版社, 2001), vol. 1.

3. Interview with former participants of the movement 2015.

4. Zhao Ziyang 趙紫陽, 改革歷程 (The Course of Reform) (Xinshiji Publishing House 新 世紀出版社, 2009), 38.

5. Yang Jisheng 杨继绳, 中國改革年代的政治鬥爭 (*Political Struggle in China's Reform Era*) (Tequ Wenhua Publishing Company 特區文化圖書有限公司, 2004), 535.

6. For example, Lowell Dittmer, "China in 1989: The Crisis of Incomplete Reform," *Asian Survey* 30, no. 1 (1990): 25–41; also see Timothy Brook, *Quelling the People: The Military Suppression of the Beijing Democracy Movement* (Stanford, CA: Stanford University Press, 1998), 46.

7. Dingxin Zhao, *The Power of Tiananmen: State–Society Relations and the 1989 Beijing Student Movement* (The University of Chicago Press, 2008); Ezra F. Vogel, *Deng Xiaoping and the Transformation of China* (Harvard University Press, 2011).

8. Minxin Pei, "The Twilight of Communist Party Rule in China," *The American Interest* (blog), November 12, 2015, atwww.the-american-interest.com/2015/11/12/ the-twilight-of-communist-party-rule-in-china.

9. It is the proposition of an "evolving Deng Xiaoping." Endorsed widely by Zhao's colleagues (Qiao Shi), followers (Bao Tong, Chen Yizi, Wu Wei), and former pro-democracy movement participants. Even Chen Xitong went to lengths to deny his role in compiling the Beijing report. This story serves as a morality tale, mostly told from the standpoint of former participants in the movement or sympathetic scholars. It offers

Li Peng and his allies as the story's villains, whose reports are believed to be critical for Deng's assessment.

10. Zhao Ziyang, *The Course of Reform*.
11. Zhao Ziyang, *The Course of Reform*, 51.
12. Interestingly, Zhao did not mean this argument as a criticism of Deng, but as a way to absolve Deng of responsibility for the crackdown.
13. Zhang Liang, *The Truth of June 4 in China*, vol. 1, 109.
14. Chen Xiaoya 陈小雅, 八九民运史 (The History of the Pro-democracy Movement in 1989), 3 vols. (Citizen Power Initiatives for China, 2019), vol. 1.
15. George Black and Robin Munro, *Black Hands of Beijing: Lives of Defiance in China's Democracy Movement* (John Wiley, 1993).
16. The information about Deng's children can be found in Vogel, *Deng Xiaoping and the Transformation of China*. I also use Chinese sources. For example, 高新, at www .rfa.org/mandarin/zhuanlan/yehuazhongnanhai/gx-04262017145212.html; 邓小平家族 简介 (Brief Introduction to the Deng Xiaoping Clan), at http://blog.dwnews.com/pos t-814351.html. Deng Rong's role as her father's personal aide is very clear in published pictures of Deng on the 1992 Southern Tour.
17. Zhao Ziyang, *The Course of Reform*, 34.
18. Zhao Ziyang, *The Course of Reform*, 37.
19. Zhao Ziyang, *The Course of Reform*, 35.
20. Zhao Ziyang, *The Course of Reform*, 67; also see Chen Xiaoya, *The History of the Pro-democracy Movement in 1989*, vol. 1, 435.
21. Lu Chaoqi 陸超祺, 六四內部日記 (An Insider's Diary of June 4) (Zhuoyue Wenhua Publishing House 卓越文化出版社, 2006), 17–18.
22. Yu Guangyuan, note 38, in Chen Xiaoya, *The History of the Pro-democracy Movement in 1989*, vol. 2, 510.
23. Notes 29 and 30 in Chen Xiaoya, *The History of the Pro-democracy Movement in 1989*, vol. 2, 510.
24. Lu Chaoqi, *An Insider's Diary of June 4*, 32–33; Zhang Liang, *The Truth of June 4 in China*, vol. 1, 161–64. Deng might have been candid in his opinion, but in the end he did not appear to be dictatorial on matters like this. Ultimately, in a testimony that he was able to rise above pettiness, the title "a great Marxist" was granted to Hu and added to the official eulogy delivered by Zhao Ziyang on behalf of the Party Center on April 22.
25. Zhang Liang, *The Truth of June 4 in China*, vol. 1, 162–63.
26. Needless to say, it is a maddening exercise.
27. Deng Xiaoping 邓小平1986年12月30日講話, at www.64memo.com/b5/1948.htm.
28. Referring to the state's punishment system. In the systems under Mao, Leninist doctrine characterized the state's violent means against dissent and crime as "proletarian dictatorship."
29. Lu Chaoqi, *An Insider's Diary of June 4*, 17–18.
30. Lu Chaoqi, *An Insider's Diary of June 4*, 32.
31. Wu Renhua 吴仁华, "八九天安门事件逐日大事记." (Chronology of the 1989 Tiananmen Events), at https://blog.boxun.com/hero/201106/wurenhua/10_1.shtml (accessed March 6, 2020). Also see Li Peng 李鹏, 李鹏《六四日记》 (Li Peng's June 4 Diary) (Xidian Publishing House 西点出版社, 2010), electronic version cited by Chen Xiaoya, *The History of the Pro-democracy Movement in 1989*, vol. 1, 139–41.

32. See Deng's speech in Zhang Ganghua 張剛華, 李鵬六四日記真相: 附錄李鵬六四日記原文 (The Truth behind Li Peng's Diary: With the Original Text of Li Peng's Diary) (Aoya Publishing Inc. Limited 澳亞出版有限公司, 2010); see the editorial "必须旗帜鲜明地反对动乱" (We Must Resolutely Oppose the Turmoil), *People's Daily*, 人民日报, April 26, 1989.

33. Zhao Ziyang, *The Course of Reform*, 27.

34. Here Zhao is possibly in denial. Or he mentions his perception of this nonexistent harmony to serve his own logic. Li Peng's assessment on this point is starkly different: that they had many, and huge, disagreements. See Chapter 4 above and Zhang Ganghua, *The Truth behind Li Peng's Diary.*

35. Zhao Ziyang 趙紫陽 and Zong Fengming 宗鳳鳴, 趙紫陽軟禁中的談話 (Zhao Ziyang's Conversations under House Arrest) (Kaifang Publishing House 開放出版社, 2007).

36. Zhao Ziyang and Zong Fengming, *Zhao Ziyang's Conversations under House Arrest*, 51.

37. Ibid.

38. Chen Yizi 陈一谘, 陈一谘回忆录 (Memoir of Chen Yizi) (China Independent Writers Publishing Inc., 2014); Wu Wei 吳偉, 中国80年代政治改革的台前幕後 (The Front and Back Stages of China's Political Reform in the 1980s) (Xinshiji Publishing House 新世紀出版社, 2013); Li Nanyang 李南央, 鮑彤再看六四(一):邓小平的一场政变" (Bao Tong Looking Back at June 4: A Coup by Deng Xiaoping?), 纽约时报中文网, January 16, 2019, at https://cn.nytimes.com/china/20180523/bao-tong-talks-89-li-nanyang-part1/. Chen Yizi, Wu Wei, and Bao Tong. Also interviews with protesters.

39. Zhang Ganghua, *The Truth behind Li Peng's Diary.*

40. Zhang Ganghua, *The Truth behind Li Peng's Diary*, 75, 79.

41. Wu Guoguang 吴国光, "邓小平失踪之谜:有关1989真相的一个推测|动向" (The Myth of the Disappearance of Deng Xiaoping: A Conjecture about a Fact in 1989), *Huanqiu Shibao* 环球实报 (blog), May 19, 2016.

42. "Bumping-head meeting": 碰头会. The term perhaps refers to the ad hoc nature of a meeting that is convened without being previously scheduled, to exchange views on some urgent issues of the day.

43. Zhang Ganghua, *The Truth behind Li Peng's Diary*, 82–83.

44. Zhang Ganghua, *The Truth behind Li Peng's Diary*, 83, emphasis mine.

45. Zhang Ganghua, *The Truth behind Li Peng's Diary*, emphasis mine.

46. Zhang Ganghua, *The Truth behind Li Peng's Diary.*

47. Li Peng, *Li Peng's June 4 Diary.*

48. Deng is recorded to have complained on May 17 that his past instructions to the Standing Committee were leaked, and he warned that his role on that day should not be leaked again. See Zhang Liang, *The Truth of June 4 in China*, vol. 1.

49. Wu Guoguang 吴国光, "政治权力、宪章制度与历史悲剧 —— 《李鹏'六四'日记》导言" (Political Power, Constitutional Institutions and Historical Tragedy: Preface for Li Peng's June 4 Diary) n.d., at www.hrichina.org/chs/zhong-guo-ren-quan-shuang-zhou-kan/wu-guo-guang-zheng-zhi-quan-li-xian-zhang-zhi-du-yu-li-shi-bei-ju (accessed March 15, 2020).

50. Dai Qing 戴晴, 邓小平在1989 (Deng Xiaoping in 1989) (Xinshiji Publishing House 新世紀出版社, 2019), 69.

51. Wu Guoguang, "Political Power, Constitutional Institutions and Historical Tragedy"; Zhang Wanshu 張萬舒, 歷史的大爆炸: 「六四」事件全景實錄 (A Big Band in History:

A Panoromic View of the Events of June 4) (Tiandi Publishing Company 天地圖書有限公司, 2009); Lu Chaoqi, *An Insider's Diary of June 4*.

52. Wu Guoguang, "Political Power, Constitutional Institutions and Historical Tragedy."
53. Zhang Ganghua, *The Truth behind Li Peng's Diary*, 143.
54. Zhao Ziyang, *The Course of Reform*, 37. Zhao also adds that he believed what Wang told him about Deng's health was true.
55. Zhao Ziyang, *The Course of Reform*, 38.
56. Zhao Ziyang, *The Course of Reform*, 40.
57. I draw this point by reading the entire set of multiple volumes of Zhongyang wenxian chubanshe, *Deng Xiaoping Chronology 1975–1997*, as well as the same publication for other former leaders. I also interviewed editorial experts to confirm this point.
58. An extreme example of the censorship is the fact that the second volume of Yang Shangkun's life chronology has yet to be publicly available. Yang died in 1998. The second volume is supposed to cover his life between 1949 and 1998.
59. Yang Jisheng 杨继绳, 中國改革年代的政治鬥爭 (Political Struggle in China's Reform Era) (Tequ Wenhua Publishing Company 特區文化圖書有限公司, 2004), 535.
60. Brook, *Quelling the People*, 46.
61. Vogel, *Deng Xiaoping and the Transformation of China*, 613.
62. See Chapter 3 above.
63. See my earlier discussion on Dingxin Zhao and Ezra Vogel's works on this point.
64. Mao Min 茅民, 复兴记 (The Revival of China) (Mao Min, 2014), 405.
65. Roderick MacFarquhar and Michael Schoenhals, *Mao's Last Revolution* (Harvard University Press, 2009).
66. Zhao Ziyang, *The Course of Reform*.
67. Zhang Liang, *The Truth of June 4 in China*, vol. 1, 365.
68. Zhang Liang, *The Truth of June 4 in China*, vol. 1, 369.
69. Zhang Liang, *The Truth of June 4 in China*, vol. 1, 343–48.
70. See Chapter 7 below.
71. See Chapter 8 below.
72. In Zhao's account, Yang even explicitly rejected the idea of Marshall law proposed by Beijing City leaders at an earlier point. see Zhao Ziyang, *The Course of Reform*, 38.
73. Zhang Liang, *The Truth of June 4 in China*, vol. 1, 343.
74. The above account of the Deng–Yang conversation is based on Zhang Liang, *The Truth of June 4 in China*, vol. 1, 343–49. The fact that this conversation took place is confirmed by Zhang Ganghua, *The Truth behind Li Peng's Diary*; Zhao Ziyang and Zong Fengming, *Zhao Ziyang's Conversations under House Arrest*.
75. Brook, *Quelling the People*.
76. Zhao Ziyang, *The Course of Reform*.
77. Zhao Ziyang, *The Course of Reform*, 40.
78. Zhao Ziyang, *The Course of Reform*, 48.
79. For example, Brook, *Quelling the People*, 46.
80. Wu Guoguang, "Political Power, Constitutional Institutions and Historical Tragedy"; Wu Guoguang, "The Myth of the Disappearance of Deng Xiaoping."

81. See Li Nanyang, "Bao Tong Looks Back at June 4," a four-part series in the *New York Times*, Chinese ed., May 23, May 30, June 4, and June 11, 2018. Like Wu Guoguang, Bao Tong does not have firsthand information about Deng's thinking. His conclusions are based on his reading of the information already publicly available. But both his and Wu's readings are insightful, which I share. Li Nanyang, "Bao Tong Looking back at June 4."

82. Li Nanyang, "Bao Tong Looks Back at June 4."

83. Ibid.

84. See a review of the definition by Andrew Scobell, "Military Coups in the People's Republic of China: Failure, Fabrication, or Fancy?," *Journal of Northeast Asian Studies* 14, no. 1 (March 1, 1995): 25–46.

## 6 How a Moderate Approach Failed (April 26–May 17, 1989)

1. Here I am only pointing out that the political nature of his actions was inconsistent with his claim of intending to calm down the protest. I do not mean to criticize his politics. On the contrary, like many student protesters at the time, I supported his attempt to change the system to become more open.

2. Zhang Ganghua 張剛華, 李鵬六四日記真相：附錄李鵬六四日記原文 (The Truth behind Li Peng's Diary: With the Original Text of Li Peng's Diary) (Aoya Publishing Inc. Limited 澳亞出版有限公司, 2010); Zhao Ziyang 趙紫陽, 改革歷程 (The Course of Reform) (Xinshiji Publishing House 新世紀出版社, 2009); Wu Wei 吳偉, 中國80年代政治改革的台前幕後 (The Front and Back Stages of China's Political Reform in the 1980s) (Xinshiji Publishing House 新世紀出版社, 2013); Chen Yizi 陈一谘, 陈一谘回忆录 (Memoir of Chen Yizi) (China Independent Writers Publishing Inc., 2014).

3. See Chapter 4 above. Also see Zhang Ganghua, *The Truth behind Li Peng's Diary*, 66–70.

4. *People's Daily* 人民日报, "必须旗帜鲜明地反对动乱" (We Must Resolutely Oppose the Turmoil).

5. Dingxin Zhao, *The Power of Tiananmen: State–Society Relations and the 1989 Beijing Student Movement* (The University of Chicago Press, 2008), 212.

6. See Li Peng's daily involvement in his diary, Zhang Ganghua, *The Truth behind Li Peng's Diary*. Also see my analysis of Deng's channels of engagement in Chapter 5.

7. Timothy Brook, *Quelling the People: The Military Suppression of the Beijing Democracy Movement*, 1st ed. (Stanford University Press, 1998), 34.

8. National Educational Commission 国家教育委员会, 驚心動魄的56天：1989年4月15日至6月9日每日紀實 (Fifty-Six Shocking Days: Daily Records from April 15 to June 6, 1989) (National Educational Commission国家教育委员会, 1990).

9. Zhao Ziyang, *The Course of Reform*, 32.

10. Chen Xiaoya 陈小雅, 八九民运史 (The History of the Pro-democracy Movement in 1989), 3 vols. (Citizen Power Initiatives for China, 2019).

11. Zhang Liang 张良, 中国"六四"真相 (The Truth of June 4 in China), 2 vols. (Mingjing Publishing House 明镜出版社, 2001).

12. Chen Xiaoya, *The History of the Pro-democracy Movement in 1989*.

13. Yang Jisheng 杨继绳, 中國改革年代的政治鬥爭 (Political Struggle in China's Reform Era) (Tequ Wenhua Publishing Company 特區文化圖書有限公司, 2004), 267–68.

14. Interviews. I lived on campus at Beida and I knew of such instances myself as well.
15. Wang Chaohua remarks cited by Chen Xiaoya, *The History of the Pro-democracy Movement in 1989*, vol. 2, 176.
16. Zhang Ganghua, *The Truth behind Li Peng's Diary*, 88. Also see Li Peng's speech in Andrew J. Nathan and Wu Yulun 吳與伦, 最後的秘密: 中國十三屆四中全會"六四"結論文檔 (The Last Secret: The Final Documents from the June Fourth Crackdown) (Xinshiji Publishing House 新世紀出版社, 2019), 129–48.
17. Nathan and Wu, *The Last Secret*, 96.
18. Wu Renhua 吴仁华, "八九天安门事件逐日大事记" (Chronology of the 1989 Tiananmen Events), at https://blog.boxun.com/hero/201106/wurenhua/10_1.shtml (accessed March 6, 2020), entry for May 27.
19. Chen Xiaoya, *The History of the Pro-democracy Movement in 1989*, vol. 2, 171–203.
20. Dingxin Zhao, "Ecologies of Social Movements: Student Mobilization during the 1989 Prodemocracy Movement in Beijing," *American Journal of Sociology* 103, no. 6 (1998): 1493–529; Zhao, *The Power of Tiananmen*.
21. Zhao, "Ecologies of Social Movements." Chen Xiaoya, *The History of the Pro-democracy Movement in 1989*, vol. 2, 171–203.
22. Chen Xiaoya, *The History of the Pro-democracy Movement in 1989*, vol. 2, 186.
23. Zhang Ganghua, *The Truth behind Li Peng's Diary*.
24. Zhang Ganghua, *The Truth behind Li Peng's Diary*, 221–23.
25. Zhang Ganghua, *The Truth behind Li Peng's Diary*.
26. Zhang Ganghua, *The Truth behind Li Peng's Diary*, 238.
27. Zhang Ganghua, *The Truth behind Li Peng's Diary*, 228–242.
28. Wu Wei, *The Front and Back Stages of China's Political Reform in the 1980s*, 458.
29. Zhang Liang, *The Truth of June 4 in China*, vol. 1, 244.
30. Zhao, *The Power of Tiananmen*, Chapter 6.
31. William A. Gamson, *The Strategy of Social Protest* (Irwin-Dorsey, 1975).
32. Wu Wei, *The Front and Back Stages of China's Political Reform in the 1980s*, 459.
33. In Chinese characters 邓小平的儿子倒彩票，赵紫阳儿子倒彩电.
34. Ibid.
35. Chen Xiaoya, *The History of the Pro-democracy Movement in 1989*, vol. 2, 254–342.
36. Chen Xiaoya, *The History of the Pro-democracy Movement in 1989*, vol. 2, 254.
37. See an analysis of the United Front among Chinese leaders in Zhao, *The Power of Tiananmen*, Chapter 6.
38. Interviews with former participants of the movement.
39. Zhang Ganghua, *The Truth behind Li Peng's Diary*; Chen Xitong, "关于制止动乱平息反革命暴乱的情况报告" (Report on Stopping Turmoil and Suppressing Counterrevolutionary Armed Uprising), *People's Daily* 人民日报, July 18, 1989.
40. Bao Tong 鲍彤, "鲍彤在學潮和動亂期間言行的交代" (Bao Tong Confession on Behavior during the Student Protest and Turmoil), *Wanwei Forum* 万维论坛, at https://bbs.creaders.net/politics/bbsviewer.php?trd_id=871242&language=big5 (accessed August 5, 2021).
41. Zhang Ganghua, *The Truth behind Li Peng's Diary*, 109.
42. Ibid.

43. Wu Wei, *The Front and Back Stages of China's Political Reform in the 1980s*, 465.

44. Wu Wei, *The Front and Back Stages of China's Political Reform in the 1980s*.

45. Ibid.

46. Xu Jiatun 許家屯, 許家屯香港回憶錄 (Xu Jiatun's Memoir of Hong Kong) (Hong Kong Lianhe Company 香港聯合報有限公司, 1993).

47. Xu Jiatun, *Xu Jiatun's Memoir of Hong Kong*, 373–74.

48. See Chapter 5 above.

49. He could have had a three-to-two majority if he had pushed for a vote, but any major decision resulting from less than a consensus would have been appealed before of Deng and Chen Yun, and Zhao knew that he was unlikely to win such an appeal.

50. As discussed in Chapter 3, Zhao, as the nominal vice chair of the CMC, was never able to plant real roots in the military. Nor could his men develop any tangible penetration into the student movements. Any appearance of collusion with the protest would have been suicidal. See Bao Tong's remarks about how he avoided going out to the sites of the protest in his confession document. Bao Tong, "Bao Tong Confession on Behavior during the Student Protest and Turmoil."

51. Zhang Liang, *The Truth of June 4 in China*, vol. 1, 276–98.

52. Zhang Liang, *The Truth of June 4 in China*, vol. 1, 277.

53. Zhang Liang, *The Truth of June 4 in China*, vol. 1, 295–98.

54. Ibid.

55. Ibid.

56. Mayer N. Zald and Michael A. Berger, "Social Movements in Organizations: Coup d'Etat, Insurgency, and Mass Movements," *American Journal of Sociology* 83, no. 4 (1978): 823–61.

57. Zald and Berger, "Social Movements in Organizations," 838.

58. Chen Xiaoya, *The History of the Pro-democracy Movement in 1989*, vol. 2, 303.

59. Zhao Ziyang, *The Course of Reform*, 42.

60. Chen Xiaoya, *The History of the Pro-democracy Movement in 1989*, vol. 2, 303–13.

61. Zhang Liang, *The Truth of June 4 in China*.

62. Ibid.

63. Zhang Ganghua, *The Truth behind Li Peng's Diary*, 131–13.

64. In Chinese characters 新聞要說真話.

65. See, for example, the *People's Daily*, the *Guangming Daily*, the *Workers' Daily*, and the *China Youth Daily* for those days.

66. Chen Xiaoya, *The History of the Pro-democracy Movement in 1989*, vol. 2, 321.

67. Chen Xiaoya, *The History of the Pro-democracy Movement in 1989*, vol. 2, 322.

68. Zhang Ganghua, *The Truth behind Li Peng's Diary*.

69. Ibid.

70. Li Peng 李鹏, 李鹏《六四日记》 (Li Peng's June 4 Diary) (Xidian Publishing House 西点出版社, 2010); cf. Chen Xiaoya, *The History of the Pro-democracy Movement in 1989*.

71. Zhang Liang, *The Truth of June 4 in China*, vol. 1, 315.

72. See Chapters 5 and 7 of this book.

73. Wu Renhua, "Chronology of the 1989 Tiananmen Events."

74. Doug McAdam, "Tactical Innovation and the Pace of Insurgency," *American Sociological Review* 48, no. 6 (1983): 735–54.

75. Aristide R. Zolberg, "Moments of Madness," *Politics & Society* 2, no. 2 (March 1, 1972): 199, https://doi.org/10.1177/003232927200200203.

76. Zolberg, "Moments of Madness," 199.

77. McAdam, "Tactical Innovation and the Pace of Insurgency."

78. Wu Renhua, "Chronology of the 1989 Tiananmen Events."

79. Zhang Ganghua, *The Truth behind Li Peng's Diary*; Chen Xiaoya, *The History of the Pro-democracy Movement in 1989.*

80. David Garrow, *Bearing the Cross: Martin Luther King, Jr., and the Southern Christian Leadership Conference* (HarperCollins, 2004); Taylor Branch, *Parting the Waters: America in the King Years 1954–63* (Simon and Schuster, 2007).

81. Examples of the former group include Wang Dan and Wang Chaohua; those of the latter include Chai Ling and Li Lu.

82. Zhang Liang, *The Truth of June 4 in China*, vol. 1, 349–51.

83. Zhao Ziyang, *The Course of Reform*, 45.

84. Tao Siliang's father, Tao Zhu, died, like Liu Shaoqi, during the persecution of the Cultural Revolution. He was a high-profile victim, accused of being the number three capitalist roader in the country only after Liu Shaoqi and Deng Xiaoping.

85. Many participants have written accounts of the negotiations, including students and intellectuals. See, for example, Tong Shen and Marianne Yen, *Almost a Revolution* (University of Michigan Press, 1998); Dai Qing "备忘'六四'" (June 4 Memorandum), *New York Times* Chinese website 纽约时报中文网, June 5, 2014, at https://cn.nytimes.com/china/20140604/cc04daiqing; Dai Qing 戴晴, "也谈春夏之交" (Also a Reflection on Spring–Summer Time), at www.cnd.org/HXW Z/ZK93/cm9301y1.gb.html (accessed April 4, 2020). Also see Yan Mingfu's speech in Nathan and Wu, *The Last Secret*, 291–98.

86. Dai Qing, "Also a Reflection on Spring–Summer Time."

87. Bao Zunxing 包遵信, 六四的内情: 未完成的涅槃 (Stories of June 4: Unfinished Odyssey) (Fengyun Shidai Publishing Company 風雲時代出版股份有限公司, 1997), 102; Dai Qing, "June 4 Memorandum"; Dai Qing, "Also a Reflection on Spring–Summer Time," 102.

88. Zhang Ganghua, *The Truth behind Li Peng's Diary*, 156.

89. Zhang Liang, *The Truth of June 4 in China*, vol. 1, 423–24.

90. Zhang Liang, *The Truth of June 4 in China*, vol. 1, 425.

91. Zhang Ganghua, *The Truth behind Li Peng's Diary*, 161.

92. Chen Xiaoya, *The History of the Pro-democracy Movement in 1989*, vol. 2, 435.

93. Zhao Ziyang, *The Course of Reform*, 65.

94. Bao Zunxing, *Stories of June 4*, 132.

95. Bao Zunxing, *Stories of June 4*, 136.

96. Zhao Ziyang, *The Course of Reform*, 75.

97. Ibid.

98. Wu Wei, *The Front and Back Stages of China's Political Reform in the 1980s*, 438–49.

99. Chen Yizi, *Memoir of Chen Yizi*; Bao Tong, "Bao Tong Confession on Behavior during the Student Protest and Turmoil."

100. Chen Xiaoya, *The History of the Pro-democracy Movement in 1989*, vol. 2, 432.

101. Zhang Liang, *The Truth of June 4 in China*, vol. 1, 519–21.
102. As discussed in Chapter 2 above, a student of Chinese communist history cannot help but see a parallel between this and an infamous maneuver by Mao Zedong during the first stage of the Cultural Revolution. Mao seemed to acquiesce to the "first-line" leaders' handling of the student unrest. When he came back to Beijing, he refused to see Liu Shaoqi, a signal that Liu had lost his trust. Then Mao reversed the policy and purged Liu Shaoqi.
103. Zhao Ziyang, *The Course of Reform*, 71–89. I do not mean that there was any collusion. There was no illegal or secret connection between Zhao and the students. In the official meeting that dismissed Zhao on June 23–24, 1989, he was accused of "supporting the turmoil and dividing the party." Afterwards, a three-year investigation was conducted, and no collusion was found. His top aide, Bao Tong, was jailed and was made to write confessions. No collusion on his part could be found either. See Bao Tong, "Bao Tong Confession on Behavior during the Student Protest and Turmoil."
104. On the evolution of his political outlook, see Zhao Ziyang, *The Course of Reform*, 292–300.

## 7 Was It a Revolution? (April 15–June 3, 1989)

1. See Chapter 1 for discussion in detail.
2. Doug McAdam , Sidney Tarrow, and Charles Tilly, *Dynamics of Contention*, 1st ed. (Cambridge University Press, 2001), 193–226.
3. Minxin Pei, "The Twilight of Communist Party Rule in China," *The American Interest* (blog), November 12, 2015, at www.the-american-interest.com/2015/11/12/the-twilight-of-communist-party-rule-in-china.
4. Craig Calhoun, *Neither Gods nor Emperors: Students and the Struggle for Democracy in China* (University of California Press, 1997); Dingxin Zhao, *The Power of Tiananmen: State–Society Relations and the 1989 Beijing Student Movement* (The University of Chicago Press, 2008); Timothy Brook, *Quelling the People: The Military Suppression of the Beijing Democracy Movement*, 1st ed. (Stanford University Press, 1998); George Black and Robin Munro, *Black Hands of Beijing: Lives of Defiance in China's Democracy Movement* (John Wiley, 1993); Jeremy Brown, *June Fourth: The Tiananmen Protests and Beijing Massacre of 1989* (Cambridge University Press, 2021).
5. Katharine Campbell Chorley, *Armies and the Art of Revolution* (Beacon Press, 1973), 11, 16.
6. Gordon Tullock , *Autocracy* (Springer Science & Business Media, 2012), 10.
7. The government dismissed them as disguising their true intent, and sympathetic observers reduced them to a democratic spirit. The assertion of revolution is made by alleging specific actions as part of a larger project.
8. Xueguang Zhou, "Unorganized Interests and Collective Action in Communist China," *American Sociological Review* 58, no. 1 (1993): 54–73; Dingxin Zhao , "Ecologies of Social Movements: Student Mobilization during the 1989 Prodemocracy Movement in Beijing," *American Journal of Sociology* 103, no. 6 (1998): 1493–1529.

9. Wu Renhua, "八九天安门事件逐日大事记" (Chronology of the 1989 Tiananmen Events), at https://blog.boxun.com/hero/201106/wurenhua/10_1.shtml (accessed March 6, 2020).

10. Chen Xitong, 陈希同, "关于制止动乱平息反革命暴乱的情况报告" (Report on Stopping Turmoil and Suppressing Counterrevolutionary Armed Uprising), *People's Daily* 人民日报, July 18, 1989.

11. Many observers in the mass media and many dreamers for democracy in China committed the similar reductionist error of reading a revolution into this and other documents. The logic is this: these demands obviously asked for more freedom, which the authoritarian system was unwilling to give, hence one may have to change the system to achieve these goals.

12. I was a participant in these protests.

13. Chen Xiaoya 陈小雅, 八九民运史 (The History of the Pro-democracy Movement in 1989), 3 vols. (Citizen Power Initiatives for China, 2019).

14. See more discussion on framing and counterframing in Yang Su and Ting Jiang, "Government Counter Framing and Revolutionary No Show in 1989," in Guoguang Wu and Helen Lansdowne, *China's Transition from Communism: New Perspectives* (Routledge, 2016), 80–92.

15. The fabrication of the so-called violent uprising will be addressed in Chapter 9 below.

16. Wu Renhua, "Chronology of the 1989 Tiananmen Events"; Zhao, *The Power of Tiananmen*; Calhoun, *Neither Gods nor Emperors*; Black and Munro, *Black Hands of Beijing*; Brown, *June Fourth*.

17. See Chapter 4 above.

18. Zhao Ziyang 赵紫阳, 改革历程 (The Course of Reform) (Xinshiji Publishing House 新世纪出版社, 2009), 24.

19. Zhao, *The Power of Tiananmen*. See Chapter 4 above.

20. It is not my intention to decide who were the most important "black hands" in 1989. I choose these four for their important role in 1989, but also, just as importantly, because of the research materials available to me about their actions during 1989. A fifth person the government sought to punish severely was Han Dongfang, organizer of a worker's group. The effort to organize workers was not very successful – see below.

21. Black and Munro, *Black Hands of Beijing*.

22. Personal interviews.

23. Black and Munro, *Black Hands of Beijing*, 304.

24. Black and Munro, *Black Hands of Beijing*.

25. Brook, *Quelling the People*, 92–93.

26. Brook, *Quelling the People*, 93.

27. Brook, *Quelling the People*, 92–93.

28. Black and Munro, *Black Hands of Beijing*; Brook, *Quelling the People*.

29. Zhao, "Ecologies of Social Movements."

30. Zhou, "Unorganized Interests and Collective Action in Communist China."

31. The following newspapers were consulted: mainland: *People's Daily* (Chinese); Hong Kong: *Ta Kung Pao* (Chinese), *Wen Hui Po* (Chinese), *Ming Pao Daily News* (Chinese), *Oriental Daily* (Chinese), *Hong Kong Standard* (English), *South China*

*Sunday Morning Post* (English), *Sunday Standard* (English), *Hong Kong Times* (Chinese); Taiwan: *Express* (Chinese).

32. Wang Hui , *China's New Order: Society, Politics, and Economy in Transition*, ed. Theodore Huters, trans. Rebecca E. Karl (Harvard University Press, 2003), 43.

33. Craig Calhoun, "Revolution and Repression at Tiananmen Square," *Society* 26 (September–October 1989): 24. Calhoun, *Neither Gods nor Emperors*. Joseph W. Esherick and Jeffrey N. Wasserstrom, "Acting Out Democracy: Political Theater in Modern China," *Journal of Asian Studies* 49, no. 4 (1990): 835–865.

34. Andrew G. Walder and Gong Xiaoxia, "Workers in the Tiananmen Protests: The Politics of the Beijing Workers' Autonomous Federation," *Australian Journal of Chinese Affairs* 29 (January 1, 1993): 28.

35. This distinction is similar to one made by Roger Gould in his study of the Paris Commune. His research showed that the working-class uprising was mobilized along the lines of human interaction based on community activities as opposed to work by trades. Hence he contends that the "insurgent identities" were not class-based. Roger V. Gould, *Insurgent Identities: Class, Community, and Protest in Paris from 1848 to the Commune* (The University of Chicago Press, 1995).

36. Walder and Gong, "Workers in the Tiananmen Protests," 3.

37. Walder and Gong, "Workers in the Tiananmen Protests."

38. Walder and Gong, "Workers in the Tiananmen Protests."

39. Walder and Gong, "Workers in the Tiananmen Protests."

40. A peasant rebellion army in Ming Dynasty.

41. Song Shuyuan 宋书元, "我的"飞虎队"传奇 (My Tale with "Flying Tiger Squad"), at https://hqsb64.wordpress.com/2016/06/04, 环 64 (accessed August 6, 2021).

42. Song Shuyuan, "My Tale with 'Flying Tiger Squad'."

43. Song Shuyuan, "My Tale with 'Flying Tiger Squad'."

44. Beijing Daily, "短命的'飛虎隊'" (Short-Lived "Flying Tiger Squad"), 隨意窩 Xuite 日誌, June 26, 2012, at https://blog.xuite.net/guominminmin/hkblog/162002736 (accessed August 6, 2021).

45. Zhang Liang 张良, "中国'六四'真相 (*The Truth of June 4 in China*), 2 vols. (Mingjing Publishing House 明镜出版社, 2001) vol. 1 522, emphasis mine.

46. See http://forum.hkej.com/node/50595 (accessed 9 January 2017).

47. Lu Chaoqi 陸超祺, 六四内部日記 (An Insider's Diary of June 4) (Zhuoyue Wenhua Publishing House 卓越文化出版社, 2006), 143.

48. Lu Chaoqi, *An Insider's Diary of June 4.*

49. Zhang Liang, *The Truth of June 4 in China*, vol. 2, 796.

50. Zhang Liang, *The Truth of June 4 in China*, vol. 2, 873.

51. Feng Congde 封从德. 天安门之争: "六四"的關鍵内幕 (Conflict of Tiananmen: An Insider Account of June 4) (Mirror Books, 1998), 348.

52. Zhao, *The Power of Tiananmen*, 146–47.

53. Zhao, *The Power of Tiananmen*, 348.

54. Zhao, *The Power of Tiananmen*, 199.

55. Zhao, *The Power of Tiananmen*, 187.

56. Zhao, *The Power of Tiananmen*, 195.

57. Feng Congde, *Conflict of Tiananmen*, 461–64.

58. Feng Congde, *Conflict of Tiananmen*, 454–55.

59. For the conditions of the royal army see Samuel F. Scott, *The Response of the Royal Army to the French Revolution: The Role and Development of the Line Army 1787–1793* (Oxford University Press, 1978).

60. Charles S. Maier, *Dissolution*, revised ed. (Princeton University Press, 1999); Archie Brown, *The Gorbachev Factor* (Oxford University Press, 1997). Steven Pfaff, *Exit-Voice Dynamics and the Collapse of East Germany: The Crisis of Leninism and the Revolution of 1989* (Duke University Press, 2006); Jeffrey Kopstein, *The Politics of Economic Decline in East Germany, 1945–1989*, new ed. (University of North Carolina Press, 2009); Jacques Lévesque, *Enigma of 1989: The USSR and the Liberation of Eastern Europe* (University of California Press, 1997).

61. Kopstein, *The Politics of Economic Decline in East Germany*, 86–87.

62. Kopstein, *The Politics of Economic Decline in East Germany*. Maier, *Dissolution*; Pfaff, *Exit-Voice Dynamics*; Lévesque, *Enigma of 1989*.

63. I was a graduate student doing fieldwork in Henan Province in 1988. My informants were mostly very happy now that they had had enough to eat for the last few years. They used to consider wheat flour buns and noodles a luxury, so they were celebrating the fact that now those things had become their daily diet. Similar changes and happiness were observed by myself in my own hometown in the countryside in Guangdong and in other research sites such as in Hunan Province in 1986 and Jiangsu Province in 1987. Many of my fellow master's degree sociology students at Beida shared similar assessments from Inner Mongolia and Sichuan.

64. See the chapters by Svejar and Naughton in Loren Brandt and Thomas G. Rawski, eds., *China's Great Economic Transformation* (Cambridge University Press, 2008). The data sources for Figure 7.2 include a) Maddison Project Database 2020, Accessed August 23, 2022. https://www.rug.nl/ggdc/historicaldevelopment/maddison/releases/maddison-project-database-2020; and b) China Statistical Bureau (中国统计局). "China Statistical Yearbook 2021 (中国统计年鉴—2021)." Accessed August 23, 2022. http://www.stats.gov.cn/tjsj/ndsj/2021/indexch.htm.

65. Lévesque, *Enigma of 1989*; Brown, *The Gorbachev Factor*.

66. For the Iranian case, see David Harris, *The Crisis: The President, the Prophet, and the Shah. 1979 and the Coming of Militant Islam* (Little, Brown and Company, 2004). For the Philippines case, Stanley Karnow, *In Our Image: America's Empire in the Philippines*, reissue ed. (Ballantine Books, 1990). For the South Korean case, see Human Rights Documentary Heritage 1980, Archives for the May 18th Democratic Uprising against the Military Regime, in Gwangju, Republic of Korea, United Nations Educational, Scientific and Cultural Organization, at www.unesco.org/new/en/communication-and-information/memory-of-the-world/register/full-list-of-registered-heritage/registered-heritage-page-4/human-rights-documentary-heritage-1980-archives-for-the-may-18th-democratic-uprising-against-military-regime-in-gwangju-republic-of-korea (accessed August 6, 2021).

67. Lu Chaoqi, *An Insider's Diary of June 4*, 17–18.

68. During this period the US provided more than words in some discrete instances, including giving asylum to Fang Lizhi and his wife and evacuating them from China, and helping other dissidents to escape after the June massacre. But despite

these facts, the larger point made here remains intact. That is, the US could not do much to affect the stability of the government.

69. John Pomfret, *The Beautiful Country and the Middle Kingdom: America and China, 1776 to the Present* (Picador, 2017), 506.
70. Pomfret, *The Beautiful Country and the Middle Kingdom*, 501.
71. Pomfret, *The Beautiful Country and the Middle Kingdom*, 502.
72. Pomfret, *The Beautiful Country and the Middle Kingdom*, 515.
73. Andrei Codrescu, *The Hole in the Flag: A Romanian Exile's Story of Return and Revolution* (William Morrow, 1991); Peter Siani-Davies, *The Romanian Revolution of December 1989* (Cornell University Press, 2007).
74. Hazem Kandil, *Soldiers, Spies, and Statesmen: Egypt's Road to Revolt* (Verso Books, 2014).
75. During his house arrest after 1989, his view seemed to evolve away from communist doctrine. He began to explicitly endorse electoral democratic systems in his recorded conversations. But that change took place after 1989. See Zhao Ziyang, *The Course of Reform*.
76. For an influential example, see McAdam, Tarrow, and Tilly, *Dynamics of Contention*.
77. As the next two chapters make clear.
78. Jeffrey N. Wasserstrom and Elizabeth J. Perry, *Popular Protest and Political Culture in Modern China* (Westview Press, 1994), 78.
79. See Chapter 4, "Where Was Deng Xiaoping?".
80. Chen Xiaoya, *The History of the Pro-democracy Movement in 1989*.

## 8  The Martial Law Decision (May 13–May 19, 1989)

1. Zhang Ganghua 張剛華, 李鵬六四日記真相: 附錄李鵬六四日記原文 (The Truth behind Li Peng's Diary: With the Original Text of Li Peng's Diary) (Aoya Publishing Inc. Limited 澳亞出版有限公司, 2010), 128–31.
2. According to Zhang Liang, Zhao knew the tenor of the Deng–Yang conversation. Zhang Liang 張良, 中国"六四"真相 (*The Truth of June 4 in China*), 2 vols. (Mingjing Publishing House 明镜出版社, 2001), vol. 1.
3. Zhao Ziyang 趙紫陽, 改革歷程 (The Course of Reform) (Xinshiji Publishing House 新世紀出版社, 2009); Zhang Ganghua, *The Truth behind Li Peng's Diary*.
4. Here Zhao's narrative, like personal accounts by other leaders, contains a dose of disingenuousness. He sounds poorly informed and politically innocent, more so than he actually was. Zhao Ziyang, *The Course of Reform*, 47.
5. Zhang Liang, *The Truth of June 4 in China*.
6. Chen Xiaoya 陈小雅, 八九民运史 (The History of the Pro-democracy Movement in 1989), 3 vols. (Citizen Power Initiatives for China, 2019), vol. 3, 262–63.
7. Chen Xiaoya, *The History of the Pro-democracy Movement in 1989*, vol. 3, 262–63.
8. Zhang Ganghua, *The Truth behind Li Peng's Diary*, 191.
9. See below.
10. See below.
11. For reviews of Deng's military experience, see June Teufel Dreyer, "Deng Xiaoping: The Soldier," *China Quarterly*, no. 135 (1993): 536–50; Lucian W. Pye, "An Introductory Profile: Deng Xiaoping and China's Political Culture,"

*China Quarterly* 135 (September 1993): 412–43; David Shambaugh , "Deng Xiaoping: The Politician," *China Quarterly* 135 (September 1993): 457–90; Ezra F. Vogel , *Deng Xiaoping and the Transformation of China* (Harvard University Press, 2011); Alexander Pantsov and Steven I. Levine, *Deng Xiaoping: A Revolutionary Life* (Oxford University Press, 2015). For Deng's rise as a "vice commander" of Mao's in the 1950s and 1960s, see Chung Yen-lin 鍾延麟, 文革前的鄧 小平: 毛澤東的「副帥」1956–1966 (*Deng Xiaoping before the Cutural Revolution: Mao's Vice Commander 1956–1966*) (Chinese University of Hong Kong Press 香港 中文大學出版社, 2013); Yen-lin Chung, "The Witch-Hunting Vanguard: The Central Secretariat's Roles and Activities in the Anti-Rightist Campaign," *China Quarterly* 206 (2011): 391–411; Yen-lin Chung, "The CEO of the Utopian Project: Deng Xiaoping's Roles and Activities in the Great Leap Forward," *China Journal* 69 (January 1, 2013): 154–73.

12. Vogel, *Deng Xiaoping and the Transformation of China*, 69–82. Jing Huang, *Factionalism in Chinese Communist Politics* (Cambridge University Press, 2006); Frederick C. Teiwes and Warren Sun, *The End of the Maoist Era: Chinese Politics during the Twilight of the Cultural Revolution, 1972–1976*, 1st ed. (Routledge, 2014).

13. Huang, *Factionalism in Chinese Communist Politics*.

14. Huang, *Factionalism in Chinese Communist Politics*.

15. Huang, *Factionalism in Chinese Communist Politics*, 355–56.

16. Huang, *Factionalism in Chinese Communist Politics*, 356.

17. Huang, *Factionalism in Chinese Communist Politics*, 356.

18. Huang, *Factionalism in Chinese Communist Politics*, 356–57. Also see Yang Jisheng 杨继绳, 中國改革年代的政治鬥爭 (*Political Struggle in China's Reform Era*) (Tequ Wenhua Publishing Company 特區文化圖書有限公司, 2004).

19. Yang Jisheng, *Political Struggle in China's Reform Era*.

20. Yang Jisheng, *Political Struggle in China's Reform Era*.

21. Ian Wilson and You Ji, "Leadership by Lines: China's Unresolved Succession," *Problems of Communism* 39, no. 1 (1990): 28–44.

22. Samuel P. Huntington , *The Soldier and the State: The Theory and Politics of Civil–Military Relations* (Harvard University Press, 1981); Peter D. Feaver , "The Civil–Military Problematique: Huntington, Janowitz, and the Question of Civilian Control," *Armed Forces & Society* 23, no. 2 (January 1, 1996): 149–78.

23. Feaver, "The Civil–Military Problematique," 150.

24. Feaver, "The Civil–Military Problematique," 151–52.

25. Rebecca L. Schiff, *The Military and Domestic Politics: A Concordance Theory of Civil–Military Relations* (Routledge, 2008).

26. Samuel Edward Finer , *The Man on Horseback: The Role of the Military in Politics* (Transaction Publishers, 1988), 77–78.

27. Finer, *The Man on Horseback*, 78–81. For comparison, the other categories include mature political culture at the high end, and low or minimal political culture at the low end.

28. Finer, *The Man on Horseback*, 78–98.

29. Shiping Zheng, *Party vs. State in Post-1949 China: The Institutional Dilemma* (Cambridge University Press, 1997).

30. Finer, *The Man on Horseback*, 96.

31. Finer, *The Man on Horseback*, 96.
32. Conquest, *Power and Policy in the U.S.S.R.*, 338–39; cf. Finer, *The Man on Horseback*, 97.
33. Finer, *The Man on Horseback*, 97.
34. Zheng, *Party vs. State in Post-1949 China*.
35. Frederick C. Teiwes and Warren Sun, *The Tragedy of Lin Biao: Riding the Tiger during the Cultural Revolution, 1966–1971* (University of Hawaii Press, 1996); Andrew Scobell, "Military Coups in the People's Republic of China: Failure, Fabrication, or Fancy?", *Journal of Northeast Asian Studies* 14, no. 1 (March 1, 1995): 25–46.
36. Yang Jisheng, *Political Struggle in China's Reform Era*.
37. Yang Jisheng, *Political Struggle in China's Reform Era*.
38. Andrew Scobell, *China's Use of Military Force: Beyond the Great Wall and the Long March* (Cambridge University Press, 2003), 73.
39. Exceptions include when troops were used to restore order in the wake of the Cultural Revolution mass warfare in the late 1960s. See Scobell, *China's Use of Military Force*.
40. Jeremy Brown, *June Fourth: The Tiananmen Protests and Beijing Massacre of 1989* (Cambridge: Cambridge University Press, 2021), 156–59.
41. Brown, *June Fourth*, 158.
42. For a discussion of Deng's personal style as a party leader, see Pye, "An Introductory Profile."
43. Yang Shangkun had a default right to attend SC meetings as state president. It is possible that Li Xiannian had the same privilege, as he held the official title of the chair of the People's Consulate, the same rank as the state president.
44. Zhongyang wenxian chubanshe, 李先念年谱 (*Li Xiannian Chronology*), vol. 6 (Central Archival Press 中央文献出版社, 2011), 480.
45. Zhu Jiamu 朱佳木 and Liu Shukai 刘书楷, 陈云年谱: 1905–1995 (*Chen Yun Chronology 1905–1995*) (Central Archival Press 中央文献出版社, 2000), 480.
46. Zhu Jiamu and Liu Shukai, *Chen Yun Chronology*, 479.
47. Whether to challenge the procedures is no small matter in a system where there are no clearly written procedures to follow for decision-making. Note that the May 17 meeting took place at Deng's house. In fact, if Deng had not gotten what he wanted, it is likely he would have suggested that a full Politburo meeting be called. Years later, some Zhao Ziyang supporters would call the May 17 meeting a *coup d'état*. See Wu Guoguang 吴国光, "邓小平失踪之谜：有关1989真相的一个推测|动向" (The Myth of the Disappearance of Deng Xiaoping: A Conjecture about a Fact in 1989The Myth of the Disappearance of Deng Xiaoping: A Conjecture about a Fact in 1989), *Huanqiu Shibao* 环球实报 (blog), May 19, 2016.
48. Zhang Ganghua, *The Truth behind Li Peng's Diary*.
49. Zhao Ziyang, *The Course of Reform*.
50. Zhao Ziyang, *The Course of Reform*.
51. Zhang Liang, *The Truth of June 4 in China*.
52. Zhang Ganghua, *The Truth behind Li Peng's Diary*, 192.
53. Shambaugh, "Deng Xiaoping," 460.
54. Zhao Ziyang, *The Course of Reform*.

55. For example, neither Li Peng nor Zhang Liang mentioned any formal vote in the meeting. Chen Yun's *nianpu* does mention support by the "majority." Zhu Jiamu and Liu Shukai, *Chen Yun Chronology*.

56. Zhang Ganghua, *The Truth behind Li Peng's Diary*, 290–99.

57. This summary is closely based on Shambaugh, "Deng Xiaoping," 471.

58. Zhang Liang, *The Truth of June 4 in China*, vol. 1, 343.

59. Zhang Liang, *The Truth of June 4 in China*, vol. 1, 344.

60. Zhao Ziyang, *The Course of Reform*, 37.

61. Zhang Liang, *The Truth of June 4 in China*, vol. 1, 343–49.

62. Zhao Ziyang, *The Course of Reform*, 48.

63. Zhang Ganghua, *The Truth behind Li Peng's Diary*, 215.

64. Zhang Ganghua, *The Truth behind Li Peng's Diary*.

65. Zhao Ziyang, *The Course of Reform*; Andrew J. Nathan and Wu Yulun 吳與伦, 最後的秘密: 中國十三屆四中全會"六四"結論文檔 (The Last Secret: The Final Documents from the June Fourth Crackdown) (Xinshiji Publishing House 新世紀出版社, 2019), 137–38.

66. Chen Xitong, 陈希同, "关于制止动乱平息反革命暴乱的情况报告" (Report on Stopping Turmoil and Suppressing Counterrevolutionary Armed Uprising), *People's Daily* 人民日报, July 18, 1989.

67. Yan Jiaqi 严家其, 政治多么简单 (How Simple Is Politics) (Zhengzhong Publishing House 正中书局, 1992).

68. Chen Xiaoya, *The History of the Pro-democracy Movement in 1989*, vol. 3, 5.

69. Personal conversations, 2013, USA.

70. Bao Zunxing 包遵信, 六四的內情: 未完成的涅槃 (Stories of June 4: Unfinished Odyssey) (Fengyun Shidai Publishing Company 風雲時代出版股份有限公司, 1997); Yan Jiaqi, *How Simple Is Politics*.

71. Wu Renhua 吳仁华, "八九天安门事件逐日大事记" (Chronology of the 1989 Tiananmen Events), at https://blog.boxun.com/hero/201106/wurenhua/10_1.shtml (accessed March 6, 2020).

72. Wu Renhua, "Chronology of the 1989 Tiananmen Events."

73. Lu Chaoqi 陸超祺, 六四內部日記 (*An Insider's Diary of June 4*) (Zhuoyue Wenhua Publishing House 卓越文化出版社, 2006), 79.

74. Lu Chaoqi, *An Insider's Diary of June 4*, 82.

75. Zhang Wanshu 張萬舒, 歷史的大爆炸: 「六四」事件全景實錄 )(*A Big Band in History: A Panoromic View of the Events of June 4*) (Tiandi Publishing Company 天地圖書有限公司, 2009), 176.

76. Zhang Wanshu, *A Big Band in History*, 190–91.

77. Wu Renhua, "Chronology of the 1989 Tiananmen Events."

78. See Wan Li's speech reflecting on his attitude in Nathan and Wu, *The Last Secret*, 243–44.

79. Zhao Ziyang, *The Course of Reform*, 55.

80. Bao Tong 鲍彤, "鲍彤在学潮和动乱期間言行的交代" (Bao Tong Confession on Behavior during the Student Protest and Turmoil), *Wanwei Forum* 万维论坛, at https://bbs.creaders.net/politics/bbsviewer.php?trd_id=871242&language=big5 (accessed August 5, 2021).

81. Wu Wei 吳偉, 中國80年代政治改革的台前幕後 (The Front and Back Stages of China's Political Reform in the 1980s) (Xinshiji Publishing House 新世紀出版社, 2013), 514.

82. Bao Tong, "Bao Tong Confession on Behavior during the Student Protest and Turmoil."
83. Wu Wei, *The Front and Back Stages of China's Political Reform in the 1980s*, 516.
84. Wu Wei, *The Front and Back Stages of China's Political Reform in the 1980s*, 516.
85. For the process of this evolution, see his conversations with journalists published in Du Daozheng 杜導正, 趙紫陽還說過甚麼? 杜導正日記 (*What Else Did Zhao Ziyang Say? Du Daozheng Diary*) (Tiandi Publishing Company 天地圖書有限公司, 2010); Zhao Ziyang 趙紫陽 and Zong Fengming 宗鳳鳴, 趙紫陽軟禁中的談話 (*Zhao Ziyang Conversations under House Arrest*) (Kaifang Publishing House 開放出版社, 2007).
86. Li Peng, electronic version, cited by Chen Xiaoya, The History of the Pro-democracy Movement in 1989, vol. 2, 414.
87. Mao Mao 毛毛, 我的父親: 鄧小平 (My Father Deng Xiaoping) (Diqiu Publishing House 地球出版社, 1993).
88. Pye, "An Introductory Profile."
89. Vogel, *Deng Xiaoping and the Transformation of China*.
90. Mao Mao, *My Father Deng Xiaoping*.
91. Yang Jisheng, *Political Struggle in China's Reform Era*.
92. Chung Yen-lin 鐘延麟, "鄧小平在「高饒事件」中之角色與作為" (Deng Xiaoping's Roles and Activities in the Gao Gang–Rao Shushi Incident), 人文及社會科學集刊 (*General Journal of Humanities and Social Sciences*) 22, no. 1 (n.d.): 521–62. Chung, "The Witch-Hunting Vanguard." Pye, "An Introductory Profile."
93. King C. Chen, *China's War with Vietnam, 1979: Issues, Decisions, and Implications* (Hoover Press, 1987); Xiaoming Zhang, "China's 1979 War with Vietnam: A Reassessment," *China Quarterly*, no. 184 (2005): 851–74.

## 9  Military Operation as Symbolic Display of Power (June 3–June 4, 1989)

1. Wu Renhua 吳仁華, 六四事件中的戒嚴部隊 (The Martial Law Troops of the June 4 Affair) (Zhenxiang Publishing House真相出版社, 2009); Zhang Liang 張良, 中國"六四"真相 (*The Truth of June 4 in China*), 2 vols. (Mingjing Publishing House 明鏡出版社, 2001); Timothy Brook, *Quelling the People: The Military Suppression of the Beijing Democracy Movement*, 1st ed. (Stanford University Press, 1998).
2. Brook, *Quelling the People*, 169.
3. Yang Jisheng 楊繼繩, 中國改革年代的政治鬥爭 (Political Struggle in China's Reform Era) (Tequ Wenhua Publishing Company 特區文化圖書有限公司, 2004), 423.
4. Voice of America, January 17, 2013, at www.voachinese.com/a/yangbaibing-20130117/1585554.html.
5. Richard Baum, *Burying Mao: Chinese Politics in the Age of Deng Xiaoping* (Princeton University Press), 1996.
6. Zhang Ganghua, *The Truth behind Li Peng's Diary*.
7. Wu Renhua, *The Martial Law Troops of the June 4 Affair*, 187; Wu Renhua 吳仁華, 天安門血腥清場內幕 (The Bloody Clearance of Tiananmen Square) (Zhenxiang Publishing House 真相出版社, 2007), 247.
8. See Chapters 7 and 8 above.
9. Wu Renhua, *The Martial Law Troops of the June 4 Affair*.
10. Wu Renhua, *The Martial Law Troops of the June 4 Affair*.

11. Ruud Wouters and Stefaan Walgrave, "What Makes Protest Powerful? Reintroducing and Elaborating Charles Tilly's WUNC Concept," (Social Science Research Network scholarly paper, February 1, 2017), https://papers.ssrn.com/abstract=2909740.

12. Wu Renhua, *The Martial Law Troops of the June 4 Affair*, 23–26.

13. Gregory T. Edgar, *The Philadelphia Campaign, 1777–1778* (Heritage Books, 1998).

14. Dean Snow, *1777: Tipping Point at Saratoga* (Oxford University Press, 2016).

15. He Dong 何东, 北平和平解放始末 *(The Peaceful Liberation of Beiping)* (The People's Liberation Army Press 解放軍出版社, 1985).

16. Kunming Regional Army, "对越自卫反击作战工作总结" (Report on Defensive Counterattacks at Vietnam), at www.mitbbs.com/article_t/LocalInfo/31059433.html (accessed August 6, 2021).

17. "Russia Has Amassed Up to 190,000 Troops on Ukraine Borders, US Warns," *The Guardian*, February 18, 2022, at www.theguardian.com/world/2022/feb/18/russia-has-amassed-up-to-190000-troops-on-ukraine-borders-us-warns.

18. Wu Renhua, *The Martial Law Troops of the June 4 Affair*.

19. Wu Renhua, *The Martial Law Troops of the June 4 Affair*.

20. This is a conservative estimate. Six group armies consisted of about 10,000 men each. According to Swaine, the Central Guard Unit had about 8,000 men, and the PAP General Headquarters had 20,000 men. Therefore, without adding the unknown number for the Beijing Garrison, the total already exceeded 80,000. Michael D. Swaine, "The Military and Political Succession in China: Leadership, Institutions, Beliefs," Product Page, 1992, 84–86, at www.rand.org/pubs/reports/R4254.html.

21. Swaine, "The Military and Political Succession in China," 80.

22. Brook, *Quelling the People*.

23. There is no available historical material to examine the deliberations on the first operation on May 19–20. In October 1989 a major PLA press published the remarkable book *A Day on Martial Law Duties* (戒严一日) (Jiefangjun wen yi chubanshe 解放军文艺出版社) . In two volumes, it is a collection of 180 essays selected from contributions by participants in the mission in Beijing. In an open call for reminiscences, the General Political Department of the PLA encouraged soldiers and generals alike to relate their most memorable moments. Each writing was obviously a political act, and the result would embellish facts and emotions to fit the official line. But the earliest edition is very candid in listing the authors by their real name and rank. This information, when used together with the rosters of army personnel from other sources, allowed historians such as Timothy Brook and Wu Renhua to identify each unit's movements and other major actions during the mission. The book was quickly shortened and altered, and eventually recalled and banned. Nevertheless, the book unfortunately did not document in detail the first wave of action on May 19.

24. Brook, *Quelling the People*, further noted that the June 3 nighttime operation, with bloodshed, was implemented exactly two weeks later, which was a night of total darkness.

25. The scene was recorded by a documentary film directed by Carma Hinton. Richard Gordon and Carma Hinton, *The Gate of Heavenly Peace*, at www.tsquare.tv/film

(accessed August 6, 2021); Wu Renhua 吴仁华, "八九天安门事件逐日大事记" (Chronology of the 1989 Tiananmen Events), at https://blog.boxun.com/hero/201 106/wurenhua/10_1.shtml (accessed March 6, 2020)

26. This account was based on the personal experience of a student.
27. Zhang Liang 张良, 中国"六四"真相 (*The Truth of June 4 in China*), 2 vols. (Mingjing Publishing House 明镜出版社, 2001), vol. 2, 884–91.
28. Ibid.
29. Ibid.
30. Ibid.
31. Ibid.
32. Ibid 892.
33. Ibid 890.
34. Zhang Ganghua 张刚华, 李鹏六四日记真相: 附录李鹏六四日记原文 (The Truth behind Li Peng's Diary: With the Original Text of Li Peng's Diary) (Aoya Publishing Inc. Limited 澳亚出版有限公司, 2010), 288.
35. Wu Renhua, *The Martial Law Troops of the June 4 Affair*, 105.
36. Wu Renhua, *The Martial Law Troops of the June 4 Affair*, 35.
37. Wu Renhua, *The Martial Law Troops of the June 4 Affair*, 36–39.
38. Brook, *Quelling the People*, 121.
39. Wu Renhua 吴仁华, 天安门血腥清场内幕 (The Bloody Clearance of Tiananmen Square) (Zhenxiang Publishing House 真相出版社, 2007), 60; Ding Zilin 丁子霖, 六四受难者寻访实录 (*Recoded Interviews with the June 4 Victims*) (Jiushiniandai Magazine Publishing 九十年代杂志社, 1994), 236.
40. Brook, *Quelling the People*, 122–23.
41. Brook, *Quelling the People*.
42. Wu Renhua, *The Martial Law Troops of the June 4 Affair*, 40–48.
43. Wu listed fifteen deaths in his research. See Wu Renhua, *The Bloody Clearance of Tiananmen Square*, 146–48. I excluded two who were killed outside the time period under discussion, that is, during the June 3–4 operation. For a detailed account of the deaths of Liu Guogen and Cui Guozheng, see Brook, *Quelling the People*, 130–44.
44. Samuel F. Scott, *The Response of the Royal Army to the French Revolution: The Role and Development of the Line Army 1787–1793* (Oxford University Press, 1978), 60.
45. Sean McMeekin, *The Russian Revolution: A New History* (Profile, 2017), 175–212.
46. Stanley Karnow, *In Our Image: America's Empire in the Philippines*, reissue ed. (Ballantine Books, 1990).
47. Hazem Kandil, *Soldiers, Spies, and Statesmen: Egypt's Road to Revolt* (Verso Books, 2014).
48. Here I compare the army in 1989 with those in a few past cases of revolution. But I would like to reiterate a previous argument. The protest in 1989 did not warrant a military intervention in the first place, even if a mutinous or passive army could have led to the government's downfall. See Chapter 8 above.
49. We will further discuss cases of passive resistance later in this section.
50. David Shambaugh, "The Soldier and the State in China: The Political Work System in the People's Liberation Army," *China Quarterly* 127 (1991): 527–68; Andrew Scobell, "Military Coups in the People's Republic of China: Failure,

Fabrication, or Fancy?", *Journal of Northeast Asian Studies* 14, no. 1 (March 1, 1995): 25–46; Andrew Scobell, "Soldiers, Statesmen, Strategic Culture and China's 1950 Intervention in Korea," *Journal of Contemporary China* 8, no. 22 (November 1, 1999): 477–97.

51. Shambaugh, "The Soldier and the State in China."
52. "Soldiers, Statesmen, Strategic Culture and China's 1950 Intervention in Korea."
53. Jiefangjun wen yi chubanshe, *One Day on Martial Law Duties*, vol. 1, 185–90
54. Jiefangjun wen yi chubanshe, *One Day on Martial Law Duties*, vols. 1, 2.
55. Jiefangjun wen yi chubanshe, *One Day on Martial Law Duties*, vol. 1, 85.
56. Jiefangjun wen yi chubanshe, *One Day on Martial Law Duties*, vol. 1, 84.
57. Jiefangjun wen yi chubanshe, *One Day on Martial Law Duties*, vol. 1, 89.
58. Jiefangjun wen yi chubanshe, *One Day on Martial Law Duties*, vol. 1, 85.
59. Jiefangjun wen yi chubanshe, *One Day on Martial Law Duties*, vol. 1, 257.
60. Jiefangjun wen yi chubanshe, *One Day on Martial Law Duties*, vol. 1, 276.
61. Jiefangjun wen yi chubanshe, *One Day on Martial Law Duties*, vol. 1, 163–64.
62. Jiefangjun wen yi chubanshe, *One Day on Martial Law Duties*, vol. 1, 155.
63. Brook, *Quelling the People*.
64. Wu Renhua, *The Martial Law Troops of the June 4 Affair*.
65. Wu Renhua, *The Martial Law Troops of the June 4 Affair*, 89.
66. Wu Renhua, *The Martial Law Troops of the June 4 Affair*, 92; Brook, *Quelling the People*, 79–80.
67. Liu Yazhou 刘亚洲, "信念与道德" (Faith and Ethics), at www.xys.org/forum/db/38/126.html (accessed August 6, 2021).
68. Wu Renhua, *The Martial Law Troops of the June 4 Affair*, 92; Brook, *Quelling the People*, 79–80.
69. Wu Renhua, *The Martial Law Troops of the June 4 Affair*, 89.
70. Yang Jisheng 杨继绳, 中國改革年代的政治鬥爭 (Political Struggle in China's Reform Era) (Tequ Wenhua Publishing Company 特區文化圖書有限公司, 2004).
71. Liu Yazhou, "Faith and Ethics."
72. Wu Renhua, *The Martial Law Troops of the June 4 Affair*, 405.
73. Liu Yazhou, "Faith and Ethics."
74. Wu Renhua 吴仁华, "英年早逝的"六四"抗命將領张明春少將" (Died in Early Age: General Zhang Mingchun Who Disobeyed Orders during June 4), 独立中文笔会 (blog), June 1, 2019, at www.chinesepen.org/blog/archives/82232; Wu Renhua, *The Martial Law Troops of the June 4 Affair*, 405.
75. Wu Renhua, *The Martial Law Troops of the June 4 Affair*, 287–89.
76. June Teufel Dreyer, "Deng Xiaoping: The Soldier," *China Quarterly*, no. 135 (1993): 536–50.
77. Wu Renhua, *The Martial Law Troops of the June 4 Affair*, 72.
78. My analysis of civilian behavior intends no disrespect to those who were killed or injured and those who were later jailed. I admire their courage and their spirit of altruism and human fellowship. I mourn their loss. Their sacrifice – even when merely mentioned or occurring as a quick flash in my mind – has never failed to bring me to tears. Like my fellow protesters at the time, I was among the majority who did not grasp, at least not enough, the monstrous nature of China's military machine if it was allowed to be unleashed on unarmed civilians.

79. After 1989, the government instituted mandatory military training on military bases for all freshman college cohorts.
80. Roderick MacFarquhar and Michael Schoenhals, *Mao's Last Revolution* (Harvard University Press, 2009); Andrew Scobell, *China's Use of Military Force: Beyond the Great Wall and the Long March* (Cambridge University Press, 2003), 94–118.
81. "血染的风采" (Blood-Crimsoned Glory), my translation.
82. In a twist of history, after Tiananmen many supporters of the protest adopted the song to mourn those slain by the martial law troops. The adoption would be odd had one studied the history of China's war against Vietnam. As I mention below in this chapter, Deng's 1979 war cost tens thousands of lives on both sides, yet its justification is dubious at best.
83. Tong Shen and Marianne Yen, *Almost a Revolution* (University of Michigan Press, 1998), 158.
84. Shen and Yen, *Almost a Revolution*, 159.
85. Brook, *Quelling the People*, 76–77.
86. Lu Chaoqi 陸超祺, 六四内部日记 (*An Insider's Diary of June 4*) (Zhuoyue Wenhua Publishing House 卓越文化出版社, 2006), 156.
87. Lu Chaoqi, *An Insider's Diary of June 4*, 156–57.
88. Shen and Yen, *Almost a Revolution*, 322, italics original.
89. Shen and Yen, *Almost a Revolution*, 322, italics original.
90. Chai Ling 柴玲, 柴玲回忆录: 一心一意向自由 (Memoir of Chai Ling: Toward Freedom with a Full Heart) (China Independent Writers Publishing Inc., 2014), 160, original emphasis.
91. Chai Ling, *Memoir of Chai Ling*, 177.
92. Chai Ling, *Memoir of Chai Ling*, 188.
93. Chai Ling, *Memoir of Chai Ling*, 189.
94. For an outline of the events, see Frederick C. Teiwes and Warren Sun, "The First Tiananmen Incident Revisited: Elite Politics and Crisis Management at the End of the Maoist Era," *Pacific Affairs* 77, no. 2 (2004) : 211–35. For the estimates of the militia, police, and the Beijing Garrison troops, see Xia Chao 夏潮 and Yang Fengcheng 杨凤城, 龙年之变: 中国1976年纪实 (The Change of the Dragon Year: China in 1976) (Hebei Renmin Publishing House 河北人民出版社, 1994), 160.
95. Teiwes and Sun, "The First Tiananmen Incident Revisited."
96. Wu De 吴德 and Zhu Yuanshi 朱元石, 十年风雨纪事: 我在北京工作的一些经历 (Tumultuous Events of Ten Years: My Working Experiences in Beijing) (Dangdai Zhongguo Publishing House 當代中國出版社, 2004), 164.
97. Wu De and Zhu Yuanshi, *Tumultuous Events of Ten Years*, 165
98. Wu Renhua, *The Bloody Clearance of Tiananmen Square*, 448.
99. Wu Renhua, "Chronology of the 1989 Tiananmen Events."
100. Wu Renhua, "Chronology of the 1989 Tiananmen Events."
101. Wu Renhua, "Chronology of the 1989 Tiananmen Events."
102. Wu Renhua, "Chronology of the 1989 Tiananmen Events."
103. Chai Ling, *Memoir of Chai Ling*, 188.
104. Zhang Ganghua, *The Truth behind Li Peng's Diary*, 290.

105. National Educational Commission 国家教育委员会, 惊心动魄的56天: 1989年4月15日 至6月9日每日纪实 (Fifty-Six Shocking Days: Daily Records from April 15 to June 6, 1989) (National Educational Commission 国家教育委员会, 1990), 179.

106. Li Peng Diary, electronic ed.; cf. Chen Xiaoya 陈小雅, 八九民运史 (The History of the Pro-democracy Movement in 1989), 3 vols. (Citizen Power Initiatives for China, 2019), vol. 3, 432.

107. Wu Renhua, *The Martial Law Troops of the June 4 Affair*, 432–33.

108. Wu Renhua, *The Martial Law Troops of the June 4 Affair*, 178–80.

109. Wu Renhua, *The Martial Law Troops of the June 4 Affair*, 180.

110. Wu Renhua, *The Martial Law Troops of the June 4 Affair*, 178–80.

111. Wu Renhua, *The Martial Law Troops of the June 4 Affair*, 327–31.

112. Wu Renhua, *The Martial Law Troops of the June 4 Affair*, 304–6.

113. Brook, *Quelling the People*, 57–58.

114. Robert Ebert, "Crouching Tiger, Hidden Dragon Movie Review (2000)," at www .rogerebert.com/reviews/crouching-tiger-hidden-dragon-2000 (accessed August 7, 2021).

115. Wu Renhua, *The Bloody Clearance of Tiananmen Square*, 158.

## 10  Deng's Long Game (1989–1992)

1. Ezra F. Vogel , *Deng Xiaoping and the Transformation of China* (Harvard University Press, 2011).

2. Yu Wei 余玮 and Wu Zhifei 吴志菲, 邓小平的最后二十年 (*Deng Xiaoping's Last Twenty Years*) (Beijing Book Co. Inc. 北京新华出版社, 2013), 136.

3. Both quotes from David Shambaugh , "Deng Xiaoping: The Politician*," *China Quarterly* 135 (September 1993): 457. "Externally round while internally square," meaning a person who is highly principled but flexible in handling affairs, signifies the highest quality for a politician in Chinese culture.

4. Such an analysis is different from the conventional view that subscribes to Deng's personal conviction. Politicians do not always stick to their own political convictions; they can flip based on pragmatic considerations.

5. Mao Mao 毛毛, 我的父亲:邓小平 (*My Father Deng Xiaoping*) (Diqiu Publishing House 地球出版社, 1993).

6. Yu Wei and Wu Zhifei, *Deng Xiaoping's Last Twenty Years*.

7. Ibid.

8. Ibid.

9. Ibid.

10. Yu Wei and Wu Zhifei, *Deng Xiaoping's Last Twenty Years*, 142–43.

11. Zhao Ziyang 赵紫阳, 改革历程 (The Course of Reform) (Xinshiji Publishing House 新世纪出版社, 2009), 224–25.

12. Deng Liqun 邓力群, 邓力群自述: 十二个春秋 1975–1987 (Memoir of Deng Liqun, 1975–1987) (Dafeng Publishing House 大风出版社, 2006), 498–99.

13. Wu Jiang 吴江, 十年的路: 和胡耀邦相处的日子 (*Ten Years on the Road: My Time Spent withHu Yaobang)*) (Jingbao Wenhua Enterprise Company 镜报文化企业有限公司, 1995), 110–13.

14. See Chapters 2 and 3 above.

15. Richard Baum, *Burying Mao: Chinese Politics in the Age of Deng Xiaoping* (Princeton University Press), 1996; Deng Liqun, *Memoir of Deng Liqun*; Zhao Ziyang, *The Course of Reform*.

16. Deng Liqun, *Memoir of Deng Liqun*, 527.

17. Deng Liqun, *Memoir of Deng Liqun*, 528.

18. Chen Xiaoya 陈小雅, 八九民运史 (The History of the Pro-democracy Movement in 1989), 3 vols. (Citizen Power Initiatives for China, 2019), vol. 3, 225.

19. Chen Xiaoya, *The History of the Pro-democracy Movement in 1989*, vol. 3, 257.

20. Jiang Xuan Yantaohui 江选研讨会, "揭秘：江泽民究竟掌握了几门语言？" (The Secret Revealed: How Many Languages Does Jiang Zemin Master?), at https://news.ifeng.com/a/ydzx/20150421/43596515_0.shtml (accessed August 7, 2021).

21. Willy Wo-Lap Lam, *The Era of Jiang Zemin* (Prentice Hall, 1999), 16.

22. Lam, *The Era of Jiang Zemin*.

23. Chen Xiaoya, *The History of the Pro-democracy Movement in 1989*, vol. 3, 258. Also see Jiang Zemin's speech in Andrew J. Nathan and Wu Yulun 吴與伦, 最後的秘密：中國十三屆四中全會"六四"結論文檔 (The Last Secret: The Final Documents from the June Fourth Crackdown) (Xinshiji Publishing House 新世紀出版社, 2019), 251–55.

24. Yang Jisheng 杨继绳, 中国改革年代的政治鬥爭 (*Political Struggle in China's Reform Era*) (Tequ Wenhua Publishing Company 特區文化圖書有限公司, 2004).

25. Zhongyang wenxian chubanshe, 李先念年谱 (*Li Xiannian Chronology*), vol. 6 (Central Archival Press 中央文献出版社, 2011); Zhu Jiamu 朱佳木 and Liu Shukai 刘书楷, 陈云年谱: 1905–1995 (*Chen Yun Chronology 1905–1995*) (Central Archival Press 中央文献出版社, 2000).

26. Zhang Liang 张良, 中国"六四"真相 (*The Truth of June 4 in China*), 2 vols. (Mingjing Publishing House 明镜出版社, 2001), vol. 1, 347–48.

27. Zhongyang wenxian chubanshe, *Li Xiannian Chronology*, vol. 6, 408.

28. Gao Hua 高華, 紅太陽是怎樣升起的: 延安整風運動的來龍去脈 (*How Did the Sun Rise: The Origins and Development of the Yanan Retification Campaign*) (Chinese University of Hong Kong Press 中文大學出版社, 2000). Vogel, *Deng Xiaoping and the Transformation of China*.

29. Jing Huang , *Factionalism in Chinese Communist Politics* (Cambridge University Press, 2006); Shambaugh, "Deng Xiaoping."

30. Gao Hua, *How Did the Sun Rise*.

31. Yang Jisheng, *Political Struggle in China's Reform Era*.

32. You Ji, "Jiang Zemin: In Quest of Post-Deng Supremacy," *China Review*, 1996, 2.

33. Ibid.

34. Ibid.

35. In the case of Deng, although he no longer held an official title as the party secretary, there was a stated rule that he was still the "core" in party matters. His interlocking of party and military authority needs to be understood in this sense. Later, Jiang was made both party leader and CMC chair. You Ji , "Jiang Zemin's Command of the Military," *China Journal* 45 (2001): 131–38.

36. You Ji, "Jiang Zemin's Command of the Military."

37. You Ji , "Jiang Zemin's Command of the Military." Shiping Zheng, *Party vs. State in Post-1949 China: The Institutional Dilemma* (Cambridge University Press, 1997).

38. See Chapter 2 above for an account of how Yang undermined Zhao's attempt to build a footing in the military.
39. Kou Chien-wen 寇健文, "1987年以後解放軍領導人的政治流動: 專業化與制度化的影響" (The Political Mobility of PLA Officers since 1987: Impact of Professionalization and Institutionalization), 中國大陸研究 (*Chinese Mainland Studies*) 54, no. 2 (2011): 11.
40. You Ji, "Jiang Zemin's Command of the Military."
41. Baum, *Burying Mao*.
42. Suisheng Zhao, "Deng Xiaoping's Southern Tour: Elite Politics in Post-Tiananmen China," *Asian Survey* 33, no. 8 (1993): 743.
43. See above in this chapter.
44. Zhao, "Deng Xiaoping's Southern Tour," 744.
45. Zhao, "Deng Xiaoping's Southern Tour," 744–45.
46. Zhao, "Deng Xiaoping's Southern Tour," 747.
47. Yang Jisheng, *Political Struggle in China's Reform Era*.
48. Yang Jisheng, *Political Struggle in China's Reform Era*, 435–36.
49. For an excellent chronological account of the surname debate, see Liu Yong 刘勇 and Gao Huamin 高化民, 大论争: 建国以来重要论争实录 (*The Great Debate: Important Debates since 1949*) (Zhuhai Publishing House 珠海出版社, 2001), 283–311.
50. Zhao, "Deng Xiaoping's Southern Tour"; Yang Jisheng, *Political Struggle in China's Reform Era*, 425.
51. Ibid.
52. Ibid.
53. Zhao, "Deng Xiaoping's Southern Tour," 748–49.
54. Liu Yong and Gao Huamin, *The Great Debate*, 292.
55. Ibid.
56. Zhao, "Deng Xiaoping's Southern Tour."
57. He made only two perfunctory appearances, one in 1990 at the National People's Congress, the other in 1991 in Shanghai to extend New Year's greetings. See Zhao, "Deng Xiaoping's Southern Tour."
58. Chen Xitian 陈锡添, "东方风来满眼春" (The East Wind Brings a Bright Spring), 深圳特区报 (Shenzhen Tequ Daily), March 26, 1992; Yu Wei and Wu Zhifei, *Deng Xiaoping's Last Twenty Years*; Zhao, "Deng Xiaoping's Southern Tour"; Yang Jisheng, *Political Struggle in China's Reform Era*.
59. Chen Xitian, "The East Wind Brings a Bright Spring"; Yu Wei and Wu Zhifei, *Deng Xiaoping's Last Twenty Years*; Zhao, "Deng Xiaoping's Southern Tour"; Yang Jisheng, *Political Struggle in China's Reform Era*.
60. Zhao, "Deng Xiaoping's Southern Tour."
61. Baum, *Burying Mao*.
62. Baum, *Burying Mao*, 345.
63. Baum, *Burying Mao*, 346.
64. Yang Jisheng, *Political Struggle in China's Reform Era*, 439–40.
65. Baum, *Burying Mao*, 347–48.
66. Robert L. Suettinger, *Beyond Tiananmen: The Politics of U.S.–China Relations 1989–2000* (Brookings Institution Press, 2004), 135. Baum, *Burying Mao*.
67. You Ji, "Jiang Zemin's Command of the Military," 136–37.

## 11 Conclusion: Tiananmen and China's Communist Authoritarianism

1. This point about state autonomy is inspired by works on the American New Deal. Skocpol and others argue that the main driving force was not the working-class insurgency of the time. See, for example, Theda Skocpol , "Political Response to Capitalist Crisis: Neo-Marxist Theories of the State and the Case of the New Deal," *Politics & Society* 10, no. 2 (March 1, 1980): 155–201; Karen Orren and Stephen Skowronek, *The Search for American Political Development* (Cambridge University Press, 2004).
2. David McCullough, *Seventeen Seventy-Six* (Simon and Schuster, 2006).
3. Samuel F. Scott, *The Response of the Royal Army to the French Revolution: The Role and Development of the Line Army 1787–1793* (Oxford University Press, 1978). Victor Sebestyen, *Twelve Days: The Story of the 1956 Hungarian Revolution* (Pantheon Books, 2006); Charles Gati, *Failed Illusions: Moscow, Washington, Budapest, and the 1956 Hungarian Revolt* (Woodrow Wilson Center Press, 2006); Gunter Bischof, Stefan Karner, and Peter Ruggenthaler, eds., *The Prague Spring and the Warsaw Pact Invasion of Czechoslovakia in 1968* (Rowman & Littlefield, 2010); David Harris, *The Crisis: The President, the Prophet, and the Shah – 1979 and the Coming of Militant Islam* (Little, Brown and Company, 2004).
4. Masoud Kazemzadeh, "Intra-elite Factionalism and the 2004 Majles Elections in Iran," *Middle Eastern Studies* 44, no. 2 (2008): 189–214; Jonathan S. Barker, "Political Factionalism in Senegal," *Canadian Journal of African Studies/Revue canadienne des études africaines* 7, no. 2 (1973): 287–303.
5. Bischof, Karner, and Ruggenthaler, *The Prague Spring and the Warsaw Pact Invasion of Czechoslovakia in 1968*; Karen Dawisha, *The Kremlin and the Prague Spring* (University of California Press, 1984); Gati, *Failed Illusions*; Sebestyen, *Twelve Days*; Robert Conquest, *Power and Policy in the U.S.S.R.: The Struggle for Stalin's Succession, 1945–1960* (Harper & Row, 1967); John Dornberg, *Brezhnev: The Masks of Power* (Basic Books, 1974); Andrew J. Nathan, "A Factionalism Model for CCP Politics," *China Quarterly* 53 (1973): 34–66; Andrew J. Nathan and Kellee S. Tsai, "Factionalism: A New Institutionalist Restatement," *China Journal* 34 (1995): 157–92; Jonathan Unger, *The Nature of Chinese Politics: From Mao to Jiang* (Routledge, 2016).
6. Wu Wei 吳偉, 中國80年代政治改革的台前幕後 (The Front and Back Stages of China's Political Reform in the 1980s) (Xinshiji Publishing House 新世紀出版社, 2013); Wu Guoguang 吳国光, "政治权力、宪章制度与历史悲剧 — — 《李鹏'六四'日记》导言" (Political Power, Constitutional Institutions and Historical Tragedy: Preface for Li Peng's June 4 Diary) n.d., at www.hrichina.org/chs/zhong-guo-ren-quan-shuang-zhou-kan/wu-guo-guang-zheng-zhi-quan-li-xian-zhang-zhi-du-yu-li-shi-bei-ju (accessed March 15, 2020); Chen Yizi 陈一谘, 陈一谘回忆录 (*Memoir of Chen Yizi*) (China Independent Writers Publishing Inc., 2014).
7. Dingxin Zhao, *The Power of Tiananmen: State–Society Relations and the 1989 Beijing Student Movement* (The University of Chicago Press, 2008).
8. Zhao Ziyang 趙紫陽, 改革歷程 (The Course of Reform) (Xinshiji Publishing House 新世紀出版社, 2009).
9. Shiping Zheng, *Party vs. State in Post-1949 China: The Institutional Dilemma* (Cambridge University Press, 1997); Andrew Scobell, *China's Use of Military*

*Force: Beyond the Great Wall and the Long March* (Cambridge University Press, 2003); Andrew G. Walder, *China under Mao: A Revolution Derailed* (Harvard University Press, 2015).

10. See the conceptualization in Yang Su, "State-Sponsored Social Movements," in *The Wiley-Blackwell Encyclopedia of Social and Political Movements*, at https://doi.org /10.1002/9780470674871.wbespm395. For the Cultural Revolution, see Roderick MacFarquhar and Michael Schoenhals, *Mao's Last Revolution* (Harvard University Press, 2009); for the Nazi movement see Saul Friedlander, *Nazi Germany and the Jews: The Years of Persecution: 1933–1939* (Harper Perennial, 1998); for the Egyptian mass movements, see Hazem Kandil, *Soldiers, Spies, and Statesmen: Egypt's Road to Revolt* (Verso Books, 2014); for the Bolshevik campaigns and the tsar's policies on nationalistic campaigns, see Sean McMeekin, *The Russian Revolution: A New History* (Profile, 2017).

11. For Lipsky's conception, see Michael Lipsky, "Protest as a Political Resource," *American Political Science Review* 62, no. 4 (1968): 1144–58; Michael Lipsky, *Protest in City Politics: Rent Strikes, Housing, and the Power of the Poor* (Rand McNally, 1970).

12. For our concept of elite resources to be clear, we shall add that protest can also be a liability. When elites work to reduce the effect of the liability presented by protest, we may see liability as a negative value of resource.

13. Doug McAdam, Sidney Tarrow, and Charles Tilly, *Dynamics of Contention* (Cambridge University Press, 2001), 6.

14. McAdam, Tarrow, and Tilly, *Dynamics of Contention*, 6–7.

15. Doug McAdam and Sidney Tarrow, "Ballots and Barricades: On the Reciprocal Relationship between Elections and Social Movements," *Perspectives on Politics* 8, no. 2 (June 2010): 529–42; Swen Hutter, Hanspeter Kriesi, and Jasmine Lorenzini, "Social Movements in Interaction with Political Parties," in *The Wiley Blackwell Companion to Social Movements* (John Wiley & Sons, Ltd, 2018), 322–37.

16. Hanspeter Kriesi, Edgar Grande, Martin Dolezal, Marc Helbling, Dominic Höglinger, Swen Hutter, and Bruno Wüest, *Political Conflict in Western Europe* (Cambridge University Press, 2012); Swen Hutter, "Congruence, Counterweight, or Different Logics? Comparing Electoral and Protest Politics," *Political Conflict in Western Europe*, July 2012, at https://doi.org/10.1017/CB O9781139169219.010; Swen Hutter, *Protesting Culture and Economics in Western Europe: New Cleavages in Left and Right Politics"* (University of Minnesota Press, 2014).

17. McAdam, Tarrow, and Tilly, *Dynamics of Contention*, 7–9.

18. Yang Jisheng 杨继绳, 中國改革年代的政治鬥爭 (*Political Struggle in China's Reform Era*) (Tequ Wenhua Publishing Company 特區文化圖書有限公司, 2004).

19. On this and other events described in this section, see previous chapters for detailed accounts and their sources.

20. Samuel Edward Finer, *The Man on Horseback: The Role of the Military in Politics* (Transaction Publishers, 1988), 4, emphasis original.

21. This separation has been true in practice, despite many aspects of civil–military relations that seemingly suggest otherwise. First, civilian leaders, including Mao, Deng, and almost every other civilian leader, were themselves former military men

(Deng was once called "Marshal of the Marshals" by Marshal Ye Jianying); see David Shambaugh , "Deng Xiaoping: The Politician*," *China Quarterly* 135 (September 1993): 457–90. They remained well connected with the army generals. Second, the system of political commissars penetrated the party into the army. Third, Chinese soldiers are not just asked to defend the country, but are also educated to be political. They are encouraged to make political judgments. Fourth, at times, especially under Mao, the military were often used as a model for civilians to emulate, or even used to play a political role in local governments. All these complications may confuse students of Samuel Huntington, whose work on civil–military relations enjoys an enduring following. Samuel P. Huntington, *The Soldier and the State: The Theory and Politics of Civil–Military Relations* (Harvard University Press, 1981). Long debates have been waged among scholars of civil–military relations, generating terminologies such as "the party in uniform," "dual-role elite," and "symbiotic relations." Jeremy T. Paltiel, "PLA Allegiance on Parade: Civil–Military Relations in Transition," *China Quarterly* 143 (September 1995): 784–800; David Shambaugh , "The Soldier and the State in China: The Political Work System in the People's Liberation Army," *China Quarterly* 127 (1991): 527–68.

22. Andrew Scobell, "Military Coups in the People's Republic of China: Failure, Fabrication, or Fancy?," *Journal of Northeast Asian Studies* 14, no. 1 (March 1, 1995): 25–46.

23. China's constitution as written on paper is a complicated matter. It hardly reflects reality in many major areas, including the civil–military relationship. For this reason, I use the word "constitution" in quotation marks. For a summary of the letters in the constitution on such relationships, see Paltiel, "PLA Allegiance on Parade."

24. Conquest, *Power and Policy in the U.S.S.R.*

25. Yang Jisheng, *Political Struggle in China's Reform Era*; Scobell, *China's Use of Military Force.*

26. Finer, *The Man on Horseback*, 79.

27. Finer, *The Man on Horseback*, 77–78.

28. Peter D. Feaver , "The Civil–Military Problematique: Huntington, Janowitz, and the Question of Civilian Control," *Armed Forces & Society* 23, no. 2 (January 1, 1996): 152.

29. I speak of the three decades between 1989 and 2019 as a whole. My characterization fits the reality of the first twenty-five years better than it does the recent years under Xi Jinping's second term since 2017. Direct citizen actions were common under Jiang Zemin and Hu Jingtao in the first two decades after 1989, but they were less frequent in the 2010s under Xi Jinping in his first term (2012–2017) and have become rare since Xi's second term.

30. The Falun Gong religious movement may be the only exception. It had grassroot chapters across the nation and staged a major protest in Beijing at one point. It was quickly and effectively cracked down on.

31. See Wang Feng and Yang Su, "Communist Resilience: Institutional Adaptations in Post-Tiananmen China," in Nina Bandelj and Dorothy J. Solinger, *Socialism Vanquished, Socialism Challenged: Eastern Europe and China, 1989–2009* (OUP USA, 2012), 219–37. Andrew J. Nathan, "China's Changing of the Guard:

Authoritarian Resilience," *Journal of Democracy* 14, no. 1 (February 5, 2003): 6–17; Xi Chen and Dana M. Moss, "Authoritarian Regimes and Social Movements," in *The Wiley Blackwell Companion to Social Movements* (John Wiley & Sons, Ltd, 2018), 666–81.

32. Zhengxu Wang and Anastas Vangeli, "The Rules and Norms of Leadership Succession in China: From Deng Xiaoping to Xi Jinping and Beyond," *China Journal* 76 (July 1, 2016): 24–40.

33. Wang and Vangeli, "The Rules and Norms of Leadership Succession in China."

34. Ibid.

35. Jason Brownlee, "Hereditary Succession in Modern Autocracies," *World Politics* 59, no. 4 (2007): 595–628; Conquest, *Power and Policy in the U.S.S.R.*; Robbins Burling, *The Passage of Power: Studies in Political Succession* (Academic Press, 1974); G. Tullock, *Autocracy* (Springer Science & Business Media, 2012).

36. Myron Rush , *Political Succession in the USSR* (Columbia University Press, 1965); Conquest, *Power and Policy in the U.S.S.R.*

37. Susan Shirk, "Xi Took Charge: Implications of the 19th Party Congress for China's Future," n.d., at https://china.ucsd.edu/_files/2017_xi-briefing-web.pdf.

38. There are those who see any crisis in a bad political system as a welcome opportunity, hoping for a positive change. Others who have looked at history closely, however, would conclude that a crisis in China is more likely to end tragically.

# Index

310    Index

CPSIA information can be obtained
at www.ICGtesting.com
Printed in the USA
LVHW060946030623
748818LV00014B/1295